BENJAMIN HOWARD BAKER
OLYMPIC HIGH JUMPER, ENGLAND GOALKEEPER, CRICKETER,
SWIMMER AND DIVER, TENNIS AND WATER POLO PLAYER
SPORTSMAN SUPREME

Bob Phillips has spent his working lifetime in journalism and press relations and for 17 years was a member of the BBC Radio athletics commentary team, covering all the major events in the World, including the Olympic Games. In recent years he has written a number of books about various aspects of sport, including an account of the 1948 London Olympics which was described by one of Britain's most renowned sports columnists as 'unputdownable'. He is also the author of an acclaimed biography of the multiple Olympic gold-medal distance-runner, Emil Zátopek, and of a history of the progress towards the first sub-four-minute mile. Athletics has always been his major sporting passion, though cycle-racing comes close, and he competed as a runner himself at every distance from the sprints to the marathon, running the London Marathon on two occasions, at what he describes as a consistently modest level. After a dozen marathons, he turned to time-trial cycle racing and his proudest claim is to have once won the Merseyside veterans' 25-mile handicap trophy. In his earlier journalistic career, he worked for newspapers in London, Coventry and Liverpool and now lives with his wife in south-west France, where he cycle-rides six days a week and enthusiastically supports the local wine industry.

BOB PHILLIPS

BENJAMIN HOWARD BAKER
OLYMPIC HIGH JUMPER, ENGLAND GOALKEEPER, CRICKETER,
SWIMMER AND DIVER, TENNIS AND WATER POLO PLAYER
SPORTSMAN SUPREME

To the First XI:
Francesca, Liesel, Ben, Lauren, Loïc, Max and Katie,
Sam, Amy, Jacob, Faith.

First published in Great Britain in 2012 by The Derby Books Publishing Company Limited, 3 The Parker Centre, Derby, DE21 4SZ.

ISBN 978-1-78091-008-6

Printed and bound by CPI Group (UK) Ltd, Croydon, CRO 4YY

CONTENTS

B. Howard Baker stands supreme among Corinthian goalkeepers since the Great War. A great all-round athlete – he still holds the British high-jump record – he was enormously popular with crowds, especially on the Continent. One of the features of his play was his prodigious kicking. At both Hampden Park and Amsterdam he achieved the amazing feat of kicking the ball over the opposing goalline direct from a goal-kick. From 1922 until 1931 he was the Corinthians' regular goalkeeper, and his total number of appearances is the highest reached by any member of the club'.

A History of the Corinthian Football Club, by F.N.S. Creek, published in 1933.

'Benjamin Howard Baker, known as 'HB', who holds the distinction of being the only goalkeeper to score from that position in a competitive match for Chelsea, was a striking figure, renowned for his playfulness. Fans remember with delight HB bouncing the ball round his box, basketball-style, and over opposing forwards' head, while instructions to the players were bellowed from the directors' box through a loud-hailer. Off the field his party piece used to be to kick the light-bulbs from chandeliers eight feet off the ground'.

Chelsea FC The Official Biography, by Rick Glanvill, published in 2005.

'I had always wanted to set a British record in the high jump, and having achieved that I put away my spikes and never jumped again. There were other games I wanted to play. I just loved to play. We thrived on competition, but we gave it a go even if we felt we were going to lose. It wasn't the end of the world, and rivalry was never allowed to get to the point where it interfered with friendships'

B. Howard Baker, interviewed by the *Liverpool Echo* newspaper at the age of 91 in 1983.

INTRODUCTION

No such sporting life as Benjamin Howard Baker's will surely ever be led again
Exactly a century ago the Olympic Games came of age. The Games of 1912 in Stockholm were much the most significant since the modern series had begun in 1896. They were the first to be properly organised and contested. They were also the first in which at least one country, the hosts, prepared its competitors in a highly professional manner, and in which another country, the USA, properly asserted its domination over the inventors of so many of the modern sports, Great Britain.

Even so this was, self-evidently, a very different era. No one then could possibly have imagined that the Olympic Games of London a century later in 2012 would be such a highly commercialised and publicised extravaganza. Within two years of those Stockholm Games the World was plunged into horrific warfare and who could have envisaged that there would ever *be* another Olympic Games? Yet many of the considerations as the Games of 1912 approached remain all too familiar to this day. Will the past excesses of nationalism be quelled? Can the rising costs be curbed? How many gold medals will Britain win? How can the enthusiasm of the British public, described as 'a raucous football-watching flabby mob', be aroused?

This was the age in which Benjamin Howard Baker was to become the outstanding all-round sportsman in Great Britain. He competed as a high jumper at both the Games of 1912 and those of 1920 – without conspicuous success, it has to be said, though deprived of a possible bronze medal by the incompetence of officials – but he was otherwise almost unbeatable in Britain and famously defeated the reigning Olympic champion from the USA. Such was his eminence that he was to remain the country's high-jump record-holder for a quarter-of-a-century, and he also contested seven other athletics events with significant success. Equally renowned as a footballer, he played in goal for both the England professional and amateur XIs during the 1920s. He was close to international honours at water polo, was a tennis champion, a cricketer at the highest club level, and boxed, sailed, rowed, dived and swam with distinction.

For further recreation, as if he needed it, he regularly ran round the roads near his home in an affluent neighbourhood of his native Liverpool more than 60 years before jogging became a universal fad. His sporting life was in no way comparable to that of, say, Usain Bolt and Yelena Isinbayeva, or of Beckham and Ronaldo, or of Federer and Nadal, and anyone with a nostalgic frame of mind might consider that it was the more interesting for that, the more varied, the more enjoyable. Much the salient reason for this was that he remained a dedicated amateur in an era when distinctions were carefully drawn between the 'gentlemen' who played for fun and the 'players' for whom sport was a living and for the most part a very modest one.

In the years before World War One and immediately after, there were few in Britain who took part in sport as a full-time occupation. The regulated wages of League footballers were not much above the national average for clerks and factory workers. Golf and tennis professionals were mainly employed to provide lessons for the affluent members at their clubs and were occasionally granted time off for a lowly rewarded tournament. Moderately paid county cricketers were frequently ousted in August to make way for vacationing undergraduates from Oxford and Cambridge and then laid off throughout the winter. The few athletes who ran for money were those hardy souls (foolhardy, perhaps?) who braved the icy depths of an Edinburgh winter to take part in the handicap races which had been a New Year's Day gambling institution for half-a-century.

Yet sport was on the verge of a radical change. League football was starting to become more materialistic, and critics were bemoaning the over-seriousness of the players and the dullness of the matches. Cricket's hierarchy continued to invariably choose amateurs as captains of England for decades to come, but the County Championship and Test matches against Australia were being played out with ever growing zealousness. Athletics was the major Olympic sport then as now and was to be increasingly used as a political weapon, supposedly demonstrating one nation's physical and moral superiority over others, as was to be exemplified at the disfigured Nazi-organised 1936 Berlin Games. The best tennis players of the day were privileged amateurs of independent financial means, and the first major professional circuit was not set up until the late 1920s.

British international athletes of this era – even those winning Olympic titles – were merely indulging themselves in some enjoyable and beneficial physical exercise before getting on with real life. Though there had been properly organised meetings since the 1860s, athletics was still a makeshift affair existing in the shadow of football during the winter and cricket during the summer. There was no more than a handful of cinder tracks, and competition even for the very best athletes largely consisted of rough-and-tumble handicap events on rutted grassland at village fetes or factory sports meetings. The privileged 'Oxbridge' elite, the Oxford and Cambridge University undergraduates who provided so many members of the British team, regarded the annual March-time Inter-Varsity match as of greater importance than the national championships, perhaps even the Olympics. The vast majority of the working population was denied the time, the opportunity and even the adequate health to take part in such strenuous activities.

So it was an unrecognisable society of athletes compared to that of the 21st century. Among the ranks of those who represented Great Britain either at the Olympic Games or in matches with France or Germany – there were very few other opportunities to compete for their country – in the years between the First and Second World Wars were to be found such diverse achievers for the future as a Nobel Peace Prize winner, a Governor of Bermuda and chairman of the 1948 Olympic Games organising committee, a wine merchant who plotted the World War Two kidnapping of a German general, an aide-de-camp to King George VI, the medical adviser to the 'Save The Children Fund', the father of the editor of *Private Eye*, and an airship captain. Benjamin Howard Baker fitted his sport into his commitments as managing director of a prosperous manufacturing organisation.

Many of Howard Baker's contemporaries, like him, excelled at other sports and were irresistibly interesting characters. On the football pitch, cricket field and tennis court the chums that played alongside him – this dedicated amateur, this dandified socialite, already a millionaire from his business activities – were military officers, stockbrokers, headmasters, company chairmen and landed gentry. Often he was the only non-Oxbridge 'intruder' among the XI playing for the exclusive amateur Corinthian football club. Yet he also lined up in the Football League week after week with the professionals in the Chelsea team who so often relied on their flamboyant goalkeeper colleague to ensure their much needed win bonuses, and who would have been condemned to a life on the factory floor had it not been for their footballing skills.

The captain of the Corinthians was a chartered accountant at the Stock Exchange. Others in the team were a renowned golf-course architect, a future MCC committee-member and chairman of the Football Association, a manager of the England amateur team, and an army officer who rose through the ranks to Lieutenant-Colonel and was awarded the OBE. Some of these bastions of society, these men of power and influence, were among the dwindling band of amateurs who still played in the increasingly competitive world of League football – a very few of them, like Howard Baker, even skilled enough to be selected ahead of the professionals for the full England team.

Yet none of these fellow-sportsmen (and no sportswomen, of which there were very few) could match the remarkable versatility of the subject of this biography. Everybody who met Benjamin Howard Baker during his very long lifetime, which lasted from 1892 to 1987, remembers him as being an elegant and charming companion, and that is hardly surprising. Though an innate modesty was another of his characteristics, he had a great deal of experience to draw on with which to colour his conversation. He built up his multi-million-pound chemical manufacturing enterprise in his native Liverpool and in London. He conversed on intimate terms with the highest and mightiest in sport, in business and in public affairs at official banquets and receptions throughout Western Europe. He was a marvellous acrobatic dancer who cheerfully demonstrated his dexterity at social gatherings with a high kick which set hotel chandeliers jangling. He was of such eminence in his home city that express trains from London would make unscheduled stops in the suburbs to let him off conveniently at the station near his home.

Benjamin Howard Baker...Benjamin Howard-Baker...B. Howard Baker...Ben Howard Baker...B.H. Baker...HB... or just plain Howard Baker. His close friends knew him as 'Howard' or 'Harry'. Call him what you will. The newspapers of the early 1920s were airily inconsistent in the matter, and those are by no means the only variations on his name which appeared in print. His preference was for 'B. Howard Baker' because he felt it distinguished him from others named 'Baker', and as he became life-long friends with one of his Olympic teammates, Philip Baker (later Lord Noel-Baker), the choice made sense.

Foremost among his sporting achievements, B. Howard Baker was by far the best British high jumper to appear in the 40 years or so from before World War One until after World War Two, and he was also a very capable long-jumper and triple-jumper (even English record-holder) and a competent hurdler, pole-vaulter and thrower of the discus, hammer and javelin. He was the Amateur Athletic Association (AAA) high-jump champion on six occasions, in 1910 (still aged only 18), 1912, 1913 and then in 1919, 1920 and 1921. The AAA Championships remained open to the World throughout their existence from 1880 to 2006, and he usually faced strong foreign opposition in search of the title.

He set a British record of 6ft 5in (1.96m) in 1921 which was not beaten until a Scotsman, Alan Paterson, cleared half-an-inch higher a quarter-of-a-century later with the benefit of far more helpful facilities and a superior technique which was largely impractical – and widely regarded as illegal – in Howard Baker's day. His third place in the World rankings for 1921 marginally behind two Americans was the best by a British male high jumper for more than 70 years until Steve Smith – who, like Howard Baker, was Liverpool born and bred – rose to second in the 1992 list. Howard Baker's Olympic Games experiences were of a lesser order than his other high-jump achievements, and were rare deceptions by his own standards.

As a high jumper, he was a member of a very select sub-group of British athletes in the years before and after World War One – the exponents of the field events, those jumps and throws which were then largely disregarded in favour of the more glamorous track races, and even almost a century later it is still the runners who take precedence in any retrospective examination of the sport. When in 2006 one of the foremost British athletics journalists, Mel Watman, with the experience of 50 years of reporting to influence his judgment, came to publish his book of biographies of those he called the 'All-time Greats of British Athletics' only 17 of his 78 chosen subjects were not exclusively from the track or road events. Furthermore, 10 of these 17 were women, though the men in the minority included three Olympic champions – Lynn Davies (long jump), Jonathan Edwards (triple jump) and Daley Thompson (decathlon). Of the 16 athletes chosen from the pre-World War Two years, 11 were also Olympic gold-medallists. Stellar company, indeed!

Howard Baker was never quite in the class of Lynn Davies, Jonathan Edwards or Daley Thompson as an athlete, but none of those select 78 remotely approached his sporting versatility beyond the athletics arena. Had it not been for the war years from 1914 to 1918, when he was aged in his mid-20s and could have been expected to be at his fittest, he would surely have had many more high-jump records and titles to his name. Furthermore, had Great Britain not boycotted the Olympic football tournaments of 1924 and 1928, because of differences of opinion with the sport's international ruling body regarding compensation of players for wages lost while taking leave from their employment, he might well have gained Games selection on two further occasions in a second sport. If he had persevered with water-polo for more than a season or so, that also might have brought him Olympic honours. Fulfilling obligations to all these sporting disciplines in a single Games would have been a tall order, but if anyone could have done it the indefatigable Howard Baker would have been the man.

As if that was not achievement enough, the several other sports of his choice were ones in which he dallied with not only considerable expertise but boundless energy. He would bravely swim five or six miles in the cold and polluted River Mersey with an endurance specialist, J.B. Crossley, who was planning a cross-Channel bid, though there is no record of Crossley ever having succeeded (which is not too surprising as by 1920 only two men had done so: Captain Matthew Webb in 1875 and Thomas Burgess in 1911). Howard Baker also practised impromptu high-diving, which had its own hazards as on one occasion after taking off from a 40ft-high vantage-point he hit his head on a piece of driftwood and suffered concussion. He risked further bodily harm just for the pleasure of the exercise by sparring regularly with the strapping heavyweights at Liverpool Amateur Boxing Club! In his first years of athletics competition, high jumping took second place during the summer to playing cricket every Saturday for Liverpool CC and on occasions for the Lancashire second XI.

Despite his skills, none of these activities were taken too seriously. When he was interviewed on tape in 1982 by the sports historian, John Bromhead, he cheerfully admitted, 'I fooled about at everything. I didn't cultivate the boxing. It's an unpleasant sort of business. It was really a social thing and just something to get up a good sweat. I had just a couple of seasons of water polo with Everton in the Liverpool League and I regarded that as a rather dirty sort of game, with all that underwater fouling. F.A.M. Webster, the leading athletics coach of that era, wrote an article in which he said I was among the six best all-rounders in the World, but I don't know where he got that from'. Actually, the question to be asked is 'Who could the other five possibly be?' Even in the USA, already the dominant Olympic nation, there was no obvious candidate.

At tennis Howard Baker never progressed beyond the qualifying rounds of the All-England Championships at Wimbledon, but he was clearly a player of considerable ability despite not having taken up the game until 1920 at the age of 28. He concentrated on the doubles because a knee injury from his high-jumping days restricted his mobility about the court too much for singles. He was talented enough to share in Welsh covered-courts' doubles titles, where his partner was a prominent player named Billy Radcliffe, who was a near neighbour from Formby, in Lancashire, and clearly was also someone of considerable substance as he would arrive at matches in style, driving his own Rolls-Royce. Radcliffe was skilled enough to reach the third round of the Wimbledon singles, and having previously figured in two other Welsh men's doubles victories he could presumably have afforded to be discriminating in his choice of partners. He later suffered the misfortune of being blinded in one eye when hit by a tennis ball.

In 1983, when Howard Baker was approaching his 92nd birthday, the eminent sports writer, David Miller, went to see him, and the subsequent article in *The Times* was headlined 'A Sportsman As Famous As Douglas Fairbanks'. Miller justified the claim (though perhaps aggravating the *cineastes* in not specifying whether he meant Fairbanks Senior or Junior) by describing the distinguished, upright, sparkling-eyed, silver-haired gentleman he had met as 'the dandy socialite of the Twenties who was as well known to waiters and hall porters as Douglas Fairbanks'.

In League football Howard Baker was on the books of six different clubs at various times while always remaining an amateur: Blackburn Rovers and Preston North End in 1913–14, Preston North End again and Liverpool in 1919–20, Everton in 1920–21 and in 1926–27, Chelsea from 1921–22 to 1925–26, and Oldham Athletic in 1928–29. He made no first-team appearances for the first three of those clubs, and the reason that he was denied his chance to make a mark at Liverpool in particular was that he was still a novice goalkeeper, having only just switched from playing centre-half, and he was understudy to Elisha Scott, the Northern Ireland international who continues to this day to be described on the Liverpool FC website as 'arguably Liverpool's best ever goalkeeper'. After a couple of games for the Merseyside city's other major League club,

Everton, towards the end of the 1920–21 season, Howard Baker then signed for Chelsea and appeared with great distinction in 93 matches – even selected on two occasions for the England *professional* team – over the next five seasons before he finished his League career as an emergency replacement with 11 more games for Everton and one for Oldham.

Between 1922 and 1931 he also made 210 appearances for the London-based Corinthian club (in later years to become Corinthian-Casuals), entitled such in memory of the affluent city-state of Greek antiquity, and he merited special mention when Edward Grayson wrote a history in 1955: 'His black goalkeeping jersey ribbed with white, together with his spectacular and debonair fielding of the ball and his hefty kicking for Everton and Chelsea, made him one of the most colourful as well as popular sights on modern soccer grounds in the 1920s'. The Corinthians, wrote Grayson, 'were exceptional…the last flickers of the glory that was Corinth'. In the 'Encyclopaedia of British Sport', published in the year 2000, it was stated of the Corinthians that they 'espoused amateur values, a sense of sportsmanship, and an unselfish joy of the game at a time when professionalism was much on the increase'.

It's a wonder that Howard Baker's tireless sporting endeavours ever allowed him time for anything else, but they did, or rather he made them do so. Among his other abiding interests was collecting antique furniture, and it's perfectly possible that he opted to play regularly in League football for Chelsea, rather than for the clubs on his doorstep with which he had been connected, Liverpool and Everton, simply because after home matches at Stamford Bridge he could happily stroll along the fashionable King's Road calling in at any antique shop with a window display which took his fancy. There would be a chat with the owner and sometimes a purchase to add to his collection before proceeding on his way to Euston Station to catch the train home.

It must have become a very familiar feeling for him to step out on to Chelsea's Stamford Bridge turf. All his AAA high-jump successes had been achieved each summer on the same ground, as the Championships were held there every year throughout his active career, and in all from 1909 to 1931. Apart from the attraction of the King's Road antique-shops, his involvement with Southern-based football clubs came about because of his business interests. He had joined his father's Liverpool-based company manufacturing paint, soap, disinfectants and chemicals, which had a London office, to where he travelled down twice a month to combine work with sporting pleasure, and it was said that he arranged for the firm's paint supplies to be stored conveniently under the Stamford Bridge grandstand. Clearly there was no obsession with health-and-safety regulations in those days!

Howard Baker was not the product of a public school, nor of Oxbridge, in an age when that counted for a great deal. He was a very singular man, indeed, with his own philosophy throughout his life, and some of that certainly had to do with his formative years at the end of the 19th century and at the beginning of the 20th century in the thriving city of Liverpool. This was a place which in so many ways reflected the economic achievements of the Industrial Revolution that had made Britain the World's premier power. By the time that he achieved the peak of his sporting career Britain had suffered horrendous losses in the war that was supposed to end all wars and was no longer the same political and economic force, but on the playing-fields of the 1920s Britons were still capable of stirring deeds, and he was in the very forefront among them.

What a life was this! Competing twice in the Olympic Games. Keeping goal in front of 60,000 fervent spectators. Standing alone and courageous on the edge of a high-diving board. Swimming manfully between the ferries and the tugboats, buffeted by the swirls and eddies of the muddied Mersey. Scurrying back and forth across the tennis court. The occasional leisurely game of cricket (though still hitting plenty of runs) at the pastoral Aigburth ground which had so delighted Neville Cardus. Showing off his dancing skills, which even enthralled the exquisite Lillie Langtry, actress friend of Oscar Wilde and Sarah Bernhardt and mistress of King Edward VII, on one memorable occasion. Then, as an exceptionally successful businessman and sports administrator, and an honoured guest and confidante, providing his advice and guidance for many more years to come to each of the sports he had graced.

No one in British sport in the future will ever emulate such a life as was led by Benjamin Howard Baker.

ACKNOWLEDGEMENTS

A list of the numerous books, newspapers, magazines and other publications which were consulted in the course of writing this book is to be found elsewhere, but I owe a particular debt of gratitude to the circle of athletics statisticians and historians with whom I am in constant contact and to the numerous football enthusiasts who have responded to my requests. If the terms 'statisticians' and 'historians' suggest fusty academics hunched over their keyboards and manuscripts in monastic book-lined studies, then nothing could be further from the truth. Research into sporting history, and particularly if it is concerned with athletics, by its very nature demands precision – after all, athletics performances can be measured to the nearest hundredths of seconds or centimetres – but the infectious enthusiasm of such as Peter Lovesey, Ian Tempest, Dave Terry and David Thurlow goes far beyond a mere encyclopaedic knowledge of facts and figures. There is, too, a 'premiership' of devoted football historians such as Rick Glanvill and Rob Cavallini who are equally ready to share their knowledge and expertise. I thank them all for their invaluable help and guidance. My thanks, too, to Derby Books for accepting the idea of this biography, and I am also grateful for assistance from the following:

Neil Allen, Eddie Almond, Paula Bailey-Thomas, Ann Baker, the late Philip Baker, A. Ballard Peck, David Barrington, Harold Benson, Bob Birrell, Dick Booth, Ken Box, John Bromhead, Tony Brown, Rob Cavallini, Geoff Clarke, Gill Cussons, Jack Davidson, Frank Davies, Mike Dooling, Robert Engelmann, the Reverend Canon Bob Evans, the Reverend Tom Farrell, Fred Forrest, Cris Freddi, Arild Gjerde, Chris Goodwin, Stan Greenberg, Lee Grooby, Mike Holmes, Manfred Holzhausen, Ben Howard Baker, Richard Hymans, Gordon Innes, Paul Jenes, John W. Keddie, Kevin Kelly, Lynn Kerslake, Gordon Lawton, Bill McEvoy, Tom McNab, Peter Matthews, Keith Morbey, Wilf Morgan, Maurice Morrell, Colm Murphy, Bobby Quinn, Steve Smith, Richard Stanton, Ceri Stennett, Phil Stephenson-Payne, John Sturgeon, John Taylor, Mel ap Ifor Thomas, Martin Thompson, Mel Watman, Alf Wilkins.

Statistical and biographical note

Measurements of high-jump performances are given in the manner in which they were first recorded i.e. for performances in Great Britain and the British Empire/Commonwealth up to the 1960s in feet and inches, with the metric conversion in brackets. For performances in the Olympic Games and other international meetings the original measurements in metres and centimetres are given. Track races in Britain were usually timed only to the nearest one-fifth of a second until post-World War Two. The distances run were almost always in imperial measurement (i.e. 100 yards, 220 yards, 440 yards, 880 yards, one mile etc.) until the end of the 1960s.

Athletes, cricketers and footballers were usually referred to in British newspapers before World War Two by their surnames only or by their initials and surnames only. For this book first names have also been given where known and where appropriate.

'Controlled recklessness, an ignorance of all caution': the essence of the high jump

Many, many intensely pleasurable days of my life have been spent in athletics stadiums in some 30 different countries – attending most notably numerous Olympic Games, World Championships, European Championships and Commonwealth Games, but there were rewards to be found at a host of other meetings much less grand. Whatever the event, whatever the standard, the great beauty of athletics is its variety. Athletes run, athletes jump, athletes throw, and though it's inevitable that the sprinters arouse the greatest passions, every gold medal is equal. A race-walker who earns one can go back to his native land, as Jefferson Perez did to Ecuador after the 1996 Olympics in Atlanta, and be fêted as a national hero, just as the sprinter supreme, Usain Bolt, was in Jamaica after the 2008 Games. Athletics is a three-ring circus, with several events happening – each of them demanding contrasting skills of speed, stamina, strength and suppleness –and great deeds being achieved simultaneously.

Whenever I'm asked to name the outstanding sporting achievement I have ever been present in the stadium to witness, the answer is a simple one: Bob Beamon's astonishing 8 metres 90 long jump at the 1968 Mexico Olympics, though England's World Cup win at Wembley two years before comes close, as does Chris Boardman's track cycling Olympic gold medal of 1992! The occasion of Beamon's massive leap is enhanced by the memory of the late Chris Brasher, himself also an Olympic champion, turning to me in the press-box that afternoon and exclaiming as the measurement, incomprehensibly far beyond the previous World record, had at last come up on the electronic scoreboard, 'Phillips, you'll never see that again in your lifetime!'. Well, as it happens, I did because I was also in the stadium in Tokyo 23 years later when Mike Powell jumped 8 metres 95.

Yet Beamon's giant leap for mankind was not the most dramatic happening at those Mexico Games of more than 40 years ago. Despite all the profusion of this and other World records broken in the explosive events boosted by the thin air of Mexico City's high altitude, the *coup de théâtre* occurred in another of the jumps entirely.

When the qualifying round of the high jump began three days later, there was an audible gasp of delighted disbelief resounding round the terraces as the fifth man in the order of competition in 'Group A' flung himself over the bar. The height was of no consequence 2.03 metres, compared with the existing World record of 2.28 – but for almost all of us, myself included, this was our first sight of Dick Fosbury, the American who had invented a radically new style which involved clearing the bar on his back. It was an intensely dramatic few moments as he sprinted in towards the uprights and twisted in the air to arch himself over. There were many others there that day, I am sure, who like me turned to their neighbours and asked wonderingly, 'Did he really do that?'.

The day following he satisfied our curiosity by repeating the exercise a dozen times, eventually clearing 2.24 at his third attempt to win the gold and then failing three times at a World-record 2.29. Is there any other athlete who has never held a World record but has such a secure place in the history of the sport? Is there any other technical advance so inaptly entitled as the 'Fosbury Flop'? Why not, much more fittingly, 'Fosbury Flight'? In reality, high jumping suffered in the end, though it was no fault of Fosbury's, because everybody began doing it, and there is really rather a repetitiveness to the event now, which causes one to yearn for the glorious elegance of the 'Straddle' style, which involved clearing the bar face down, as exemplified by the lithe and lissome Rosi Ackermann, the East German who held the World record from 1974 to 1978, the first woman to clear two metres. It was another East German, the Olympic decathlon champion of 1988, Christian Schenk, who was the last front-rank athlete to persevere with this technique. There was a touch of the graciousness of Fonteyn and Nureyev about them, whereas the 21st century generation, however superior the heights they clear, impress more with their acrobatics than their aesthetics.

Still, there's one aspect of high jumping which has been shared by every generation from the dilettante Oxford and Cambridge gentlemen amateurs of the 1860s to the slick and sophisticated professionals of 150 years later, and this has been summarised the most succinctly by two renowned coaches, Charlie Rader and Mike Holmes.

Rader, admirably, practised what he preached, representing the USA in veterans' competition and setting a high-jump World record for 45-year-olds in 1993, and he was still active in the event past his 60th birthday. He had much that was instructive to say about all the intricacies of the angle of the approach, the length of it, the speed of it, and the precision of the takeoff, but ultimately, he cheerfully admitted, success depended on nothing more than 'controlled recklessness…an ignorance of all caution…a desperate reckless explosion upward'. Holmes, himself a prolific shot-putter and discus-thrower well into his veteran years and a successor to B. Howard Baker as president of Liverpool Harriers, was coach to the most successful of all British high jumpers, Steve Smith, and suggests that it would take a master's degree thesis to explain all the complexities of high jumping but that it ultimately came down to two fundamental requirements: a takeoff which raises the centre of mass as high as possible and a clearance which allows the centre of mass to pass as close to the bar as possible.

Howard Baker, hampered in his high-jumping career by archaic techniques and primitive facilities, enthused late in life about what he might have achieved with the Fosbury Flop, devised almost half-a-century after he had retired, having been one of the most able exponents of what would now be regarded as an outrageously uneconomic method known as the 'Eastern Cut-Off'. It was one of his few unrealised ambitions, and as you will discover there was rather more to the life of B. Howard Baker than just high jumping.

Aspiring to life on the rising ground where oak trees grow

Benjamin Howard Baker was born at West Derby, in Liverpool, on 15 February 1892. His father, also named Benjamin Howard Baker, had left the family home of Acle Hall, in the village of Acle in Norfolk, to move to a house in Liverpool owned by his wife and to start a business in the city because *his* father, who had led the life of a country gentleman and was an enthusiast for prize-fighting and professional running, had dissipated the family fortune through gambling. The house in Liverpool provided a refuge for Mr and Mrs Baker, but in any case the city was a logical place for a young man to make his way in the latter part of the 19th century as it was a thriving port and commercial centre. The population increased during the 1890s alone by more than 167,000 to almost 685,000. It was a regular feature for transatlantic liners to make their maiden voyage from the city and tens of thousands of emigrants to the USA passed through each year.

Liverpool in the early 1900s was an exultant place in which to live and work. A century later the term 'Merseypride' was coined by John Belchem, professor of history at the University of Liverpool, in a book of essays which he composed about the city, drawing on the mass of literature which had been published on the subject: 'Merseypride was at its height in the Edwardian years, a confidence embodied in the imposing architecture (and attendant public sculpture) of the new Pier Head: the Mersey Dock and Harbour Building (1907), the Royal Liver Building (1911) and the Cunard Building (1913), the photogenic sea-facing skyline by which Liverpool remains instantly recognisable. Immune to the blandishments of Westminster, local 'boss' politicians revelled (American-style) in the bustle and manipulation of the municipal 'machine'. Jealously upholding Liverpool's provincial pre-eminence, they defended its prize status as the 'second city of the Empire' against Glaswegian pretension'.

In 1892 Howard Baker's father is listed in the street directory for Liverpool as being a commercial traveller, but by 1900 his profession is given as that of a 'dry salter' and his address as 48 Tue Brook Crescent, which is a tree-lined enclave of Marlborough Road. The heads of the households in the immediate vicinity included an accountant, a draper, a grocer, a master mariner, a surgeon and a timber merchant; in other words, staunch representatives of the emerging middle class created by the economic transformation of Britain. In the 21st century Marlborough Road is still a quiet and affluent residential area close to the traffic-filled West Derby Road. This part of Liverpool is at the top of a steep climb from the River Mersey and would have been a favoured location in the late 1800s for professional men and merchants and their families to move away from the clamour and pollution of the docks.

Shortly before his death in 2009, one of Howard Baker's sons, Philip Baker, then in his 80s and living in Sussex, vividly recalled what he had been told about those early days of building a thriving business. He related the tale of what started as a 'cottage industry' as follows: 'Because my great-grandfather had left the family in straitened circumstances, my grandparents went away from Acle rather than hang their heads in shame in a village where the locals had been in the habit of tipping their hats to them. My grandmother had inherited a small house in Liverpool, and that is where they went. My grandfather then set up a business in his garden-shed making wood preservatives, disinfectants and other products based on phenol, or carbolic acid as it is better known, using ideas which he had brought with him from Norfolk. During the school holidays my father would take a suitcase full of samples and visit all the woollen mills across the North of England to sell the wares'.

Philip was given his first name by his father in honour of Philip Baker (later Lord Noel-Baker), who had also taken part in the Olympic Games of 1912 in Stockholm and 1920 in Antwerp and was silver-medallist at 1500 metres on the latter occasion. Howard Baker and his middle-distance-running namesake, who was to give a lifetime's service to the cause of peace, established their friendship as two of the few athletes to have achieved Olympic status both before and after World War One. A Cambridge graduate, the future Lord Noel-Baker served on the secretariat at the peace conference of 1919 and at the League of Nations until 1922. He became the first honorary secretary of the Achilles club, formed for Oxford and Cambridge graduate athletes in 1920, and he was a professor of international relations at London University and then a lecturer at Yale University, in the USA. A Labour member of parliament for Coventry from 1929 to 1931 and for Derby from 1936 to 1970, he held several ministerial posts during and after World War Two and was awarded the Nobel Peace Prize in 1959. An interesting and influential friend to have!

Clearly, Benjamin Howard Baker's father made a success of his business because by 1921 his job title was 'wholesale druggist' and he had moved to a house at Mines Avenue, Aigburth (pronounced 'Egg-b'th'). There certainly wasn't a coal-mine, or any other sort of mine, within many miles, and the road had been named after Edward Mines, the architect of the seven select houses in it. The family's neighbours were a corn merchant, a physician, a Unitarian minister and a solicitor. Aigburth has always been one of the most appealing areas of the city and over the years has numbered among its many notable residents J. Bruce Ismay (managing director of the 'White Star' steamship line and a controversial 'Titanic' survivor), Dixie Dean (Everton and England footballer), Ken Cranston (Lancashire and England cricketer), George Melly (singer, art expert and *bon viveur*) and Gloria Grahame (Hollywood film actress). Aigburth's name was derived from the Old Norse and Old English languages and its meaning is 'rising ground where oak trees grow'.

In the mid-19th century Aigburth had been described as 'a wealthy and fashionable district extending along the banks of the Mersey and studded with the noble mansions and splendid villas of the Liverpool bankers and merchants, the salubrity of the air and the delightful scenery inviting their residence here'. Much the same description could have been applied 70 years or so later, when the Baker family were living there, and in the 21st century the district still retains much of its Victorian charm. In 2007 a property correspondent for 'The Guardian' newspaper remarked, perhaps over-imaginatively, that 'Aigburth clings for dear life to the coat-tails of Mossley Hill and Sefton Park, where they drink turtle soup with golden spoons for breakfast. Aigburth hasn't gone quite so hoity-toity yet. It's more your 'boho', villagey kind of place'. Even as the economic recession took hold in 2011 a five-bedroomed detached house in Aigburth was valued at £1.25 million.

Young Benjamin Howard Baker grew up in an enthralling but ruthless era. At the beginning of the 20th century Britain had the World's largest and most powerful navy. The British Empire was the greatest the World had known and was at its pinnacle, containing India, Canada, Australia, New Zealand, the British West Indies and vast areas of Africa, including South Africa, Rhodesia, the Anglo-Egyptian Sudan, Nigeria and Sierra Leone. Britain's population at the time of Queen Victoria's death in 1901 after reigning for almost 64 years was 32.5 million, and 80 per cent of them were housed in cities and towns which had vastly increased in size during the Industrial Revolution. Conditions for this urban population were often appalling, and in 1906 David Lloyd George, the President of the Board of Trade (and a future Prime Minister), put it on record that 10 million workers lived in chronic destitution.

From an early age Benjamin Howard Baker took part in athletics, cricket, football and swimming, and as the son of a successful businessman – in fact, the only son, with three sisters – might have been expected to benefit from some sort of exclusive and expensive education, but he mentioned in passing in his 1982 interview with John Bromhead that

'Father was determined I should not go on to public school', without explaining the reason why, and added that he was educated privately with the help of the Vicar of West Derby. Throughout all his years to the age of 18 the youngster attended Marlborough College, which was a small independent preparatory and secondary school no more than a few minutes' walk away from the family home. The solid but grim college buildings still stand, though now divided into apartments.

Coincidentally, Howard Baker was a contemporary of another outstanding all-round sportsman, Max Woosnam, who was born in Liverpool six months later, and who was to become a football international, captaining England and Manchester City, and a fellow-Olympian as a tennis player, winning the men's doubles at the 1920 Olympic Games and also at Wimbledon the next year. Woosnam was the son of the Reverend Canon Charles M. Woosnam, who was chaplain-superintendent for the Mersey Mission to Seamen in the city centre, and it is unlikely that the two boys met as Woosnam went off to boarding school at the age of seven and then to Winchester College and to Cambridge University from 1912 to 1914. Woosnam was the subject of a biography published in 2006 and entitled *All-Round Genius: The Unknown Story of Britain's Greatest Sportsman*...and precisely the same description could, of course, be given to Howard Baker's life. The two of them were to become great friends in the 1920s.

Howard Baker readily recalled for John Bromhead his introduction to serious athletics at the relatively late age of 18: 'Tommy Blair, who was the president of Liverpool Harriers, enrolled me as a member and persuaded me that I was a potential champion. He was a friend of my father's and was his guest at my school sports of 1910. Seeing me in action in the high jump he insisted that I became a club member and entered me for the Northern Counties' and the AAA Championships the same year. These proved to be a springboard for my subsequent successes'. Some springboard! Within a few weeks of taking high-jumping seriously for the first time the novice had placed second in the Northern event to Clive Taylor, of Polytechnic Harriers, and then beaten Taylor for the AAA title!

Tommy Blair was a highly influential man in Liverpool sporting and business life, as he was also secretary of the Mersey Dock and Harbour Company. He was an extrovert character who liked to cut a dash at athletics meetings, revelling in the duties of 'announcer' at a time when microphones were yet to be invented, and Howard Baker had vivid recollections of him 70 years or so later: 'He liked a couple of pints! He was the acknowledged megaphone man, and he loved announcing that I'd broken a record'.

Public school and then perhaps Oxford or Cambridge University would have provided Benjamin Howard Baker with a privileged upbringing which could have led, had he chose, to a comfortable career in the professions or in the civil service, but his father clearly had other ideas for him. It was the destiny of the son of the house to take over the family business, and from those formative years as a teenager persuading hardened mill-owners to buy his father's products was developed a keen business sense...and a competitive urge which only the demands of the athletics arena, the football stadium, the cricket pitch, the swimming pool and the lawn-tennis court could properly satisfy.

ARE YOU A 'GENTLEMAN' OR A 'PLAYER'? THE BURNING QUESTION OF THE SPORTING AGE

To understand B. Howard Baker's life-long devotion to amateurism in an increasingly professionalised sporting world, it is worth taking a close look at the development of the range of sports invented by the British during the 19th century. Among the principal architects of the laws that governed the two key activities, athletics and football, was Sir Montague Shearman, and he was the very stuff of which the British Empire had been made; a dedicated defender of all the upright principles for which the leaders of society in the realm of Queen Victoria stood. His education had been impeccable: Merchant Taylor's public school and St John's College, Oxford. His address was a discretely fashionable one: Eaton Gate, in South-West London. He belonged to gentlemen's clubs which provided seclusion for the most honoured leaders of society, including the Athenaeum, where Dickens, Thackeray, Conan Doyle, Rhodes and Churchill were also members. He was a Judge of the High Court of Justice. Sport was his abiding passion, but his views on it were surprisingly inconsistent for someone of such an ordered judicial mind.

He wrote the *magnum opus* of 19th century sporting history – the 464-page 'Athletics and Football', first published in 1887 – and in it he enthusiastically supported the legalisation of professionalism in football, which had happened only two years previously. He stated his opinion thus: 'As soon as there was money to be made out of football playing, it became not only natural but inevitable that the mechanic and artisan class of players should desire to share in it, and as undisguised professionalism is honest and sham amateurism dishonest the Association wisely recognised facts'. Yet Sir Montague, who had been one of the co-founders of the Amateur Athletic Association in 1880, was completely averse to the idea of the AAA opening their doors to all as readily as the Football Association had done. Athletics, he strenuously argued, must remain purely amateur.

The 'pedestrians' – as the professional athletes of the time were called – were anathema to him. He bemoaned the fact that 'the state of amateurism has never been so bad as it is in the present day', and he continued: 'Thousands of men of every class of the community but, for obvious reasons, chiefly those of the lower class, found that by taking up amateur athletics there were prizes to be won, which were readily exchangeable for cash, and opportunities also could be provided for making money by betting in those mysterious ways which have long been so familiar upon the turf and with the professional pedestrians…the ranks of so-called amateurs are crowded with athletes who have absolutely no further thought in entering for races than the amount of money they can, by fair means or foul, extract from them'.

There was much in what Sir Montague claimed, and accusations of the 'fixing' of races and prosecutions for it were to be commonplace for years to come. Yet was there really any great difference between working-class athletes earning a pound or two by trading in their un-needed prizes won at local sports meetings and working-class footballers receiving much the same amount for turning out for their clubs? Were there not newly-recognised professional footballers who were also primarily concerned with 'the amount of money they could extract'? If one of the finest legal minds in the land could discern a difference of morality between the two sports where none of significance apparently existed, then it is hardly surprising that lesser intellects should have followed the same train of thought.

Sir Montague found unexpected allies for his cause in the North of England. The Northern Counties' Athletic Association actually pre-dated the AAA by being founded in 1879 and its definition of amateurism was of immense historical significance because it rejected the clause excluding 'mechanics, artisans and labourers' which had been a cornerstone of the rules of the London-based and now practically moribund Amateur Athletic Club. This club had set itself up as the would-be national administrative body 13 years before, and though it was superseded by the AAA its credo was passed on. One of the objectives of the enterprising Northerners was 'to deal repressively with the abuses now prevalent in athletic circles', and this meant to their way of thinking the strict rejection of professionalism in any form, exactly as Sir Montague would argue his case.

Rugby football was to face a similar situation to athletics, socially and geographically, in 1895, when 22 Northern clubs met to form a separate union, but the terms of reference on this latter occasion were very different as the main item of business that day was to recognise the principle of 'broken time' payments – in other words, compensation paid to players for losing wages when taking time off from work for training or matches. Thus what came to be known as the Rugby League was formed. Among those pioneering clubs were Bradford, Huddersfield, Leeds, St Helens and Widnes, and it is intriguing to note that athletics clubs in the very same cities and towns had been represented at the formative Northern Counties' AA meeting of 16 years before. It needs no leap of imagination to appreciate that the respective sets of officials would have come from much the same social background, and some would certainly have been personally acquainted. Yet their separate collective decisions could not have been more different and would define in sharply contrasting ways the nature of their respective sports for the best part of a century to come.

In this 21st century age, in which nine-year-olds are signed to contracts by League football clubs and teenage athletes retire because they say their lottery funding is inadequate, it's difficult to appreciate that it mattered very much whether you were an amateur or a professional not only in the 19th century but throughout B. Howard Baker's sporting career and for several decades beyond. The term 'amateur' now has an entirely different connotation to that of a hundred years or so ago. Maybe it's because there are so few sports in the 21st century where amateurs are still recognised as a separate category that they are now usually thought of as being second-rate. Yet the word 'amateur' in French has a different meaning altogether; an *amateur d'art* is an art-lover, an *amateur du sport* is a sports-lover, and by definition both are very well informed about their interests. Benjamin Howard Baker remained a respected amateur throughout his sporting life, and that was a matter of natural choice. He loved sport for sport's sake.

Even had he been so inclined, there was very little in the way of professional athletics before and after World War One to entice him. There was certainly no income of any consequence to be made from his lawn tennis or water polo, and – as has been already pointed out – the wages of even the best of professional footballers were not much more than they could have earned in a factory. Howard Baker had no need of that – he *owned* factories. It is one of the most interesting aspects of the whole question of the development of sport in the late 19th century and the first half of the 20th century that the attitudes towards professionalism varied so markedly from one sport to another. The administrators of athletics and rugby union football wanted no dealings at all with those who ran or played for money, whereas those for cricket and association football were much more accommodating towards paid participants. The lawn-tennis authorities loftily ignored the issue because their game at both national and international level was exclusively one for players with independent means.

These pioneering rulers of sport were, of course, drawn from the privileged classes of society. They were Victorian men (no women, naturally) of substance and influence, for the very great part educated at the leading public schools and at Oxford and Cambridge Universities, but there was a myopic, even perhaps hypocritical, tendency to their views. For example, so long as a cricketer could be described as a gentleman, and that meant certainly not anyone in 'trade', he could earn money from his sport, and in substantially larger amounts than did the professionals, while remaining an unsullied amateur. The most renowned sportsman of the latter 19th century, Dr W.G. Grace, derived a generous income from his skills on the cricket pitch but retained his amateur status for no better reason than that he did not depend on sport for his living. Even the Modern Olympic Games, when they were begun in 1896, were dedicated to the amateur ideal, though the Games in Ancient Greece had been rabidly professional, and this was at the behest of Baron Pierre de Coubertin, the Frenchman largely responsible for the revival. He was an avid admirer of the concept of chivalrous sport prevalent in the public schools of 19th century England.

In athletics there was no common ground for the amateurs and the professionals. When undergraduates at Oxford and Cambridge had met in the first Inter-Varsity contest in March 1864 the winning performances had mostly been of no consequence – such as 10.5sec for 100 yards, 4min 56sec for the mile, 18ft (5.49m) in the long jump – and for much of the remainder of the century the amateurs were no match for the professionals. In any case, no such 'match' could take place. No amateurs were ever sanctioned to compete against professional 'pedestrians' by the grandees of the AAA after its foundation in 1880 by three Oxford University men: Clement Jackson, who was a tutor; Bernhard Wise, a scholar and president of the university athletics club; and Montague Shearman, then a 33-year-old graduate launched on a distinguished legal career.

To their credit, the AAA followed the lead of the Northern Counties' AA in deleting the clause which barred 'mechanics, artisans and labourers', though their list of rules still began with the categorical statement that 'an amateur is one who has never competed against a professional', and no thought was entertained that the AAA perhaps should have gone further than had the Northern Counties and opened the sport to all, whether paid to compete or not, as had happened in cricket and would do so in association football.

Despite numerous abuses over the years in various countries of the increasingly outdated principles of amateurism, involving the disqualification of such outstanding athletes as Olympic champions and World record-holders, and then from the mid-20th century onwards the advent of state-aided sport on a massive scale in Eastern Europe, it would not be until 1982 that athletics would go 'open'. Even then the World ruling body retained its anachronistic title of 'International Amateur Athletic Federation' for many more years before contriving to retain the initials IAAF by slipping conveniently into the alternative of 'International Association of Athletics Federations' in 2001.

The yawning void in standards between amateur and professional athletes in the latter 19th century was aptly illustrated just a month after that first Oxford v Cambridge match of 1864, which is rightly regarded as the birth of modern organised athletics, when the mile record was reduced to 4min 20½sec by a seasoned professional, Teddy Mills, in a race in Manchester. Mills had been a dyer's assistant by trade but was a proficient runner at every distance from 440 yards to 10 miles, so famous throughout the land that he was known as 'Young England'. He earned enough money from his race wins to own a chain of public houses, and when he died in 1894 he left the enormous sum of £55,000 in his will.

In 1886 the incomparable Walter George, the greatest middle-distance runner of his era, having eventually turned professional in the absence of any further amateur opponents to test him, ran the mile in 4min 12¾sec, and this performance remained unsurpassed by anyone else, amateur or professional, until 1915. George had petitioned the AAA in 1882 to let him race against the leading professional of the day, Will Cummings, with the proceeds going to charity, and there was widespread public support for the idea, but George's request had been refused, and so he turned professional, and it was against Cummings that he eventually set his marvellous record.

A professional of an earlier generation, John Howard, had achieved the astonishing long-jump distance of 29ft 7in (9.01m) in 1854 with the aid of a four-inch high takeoff board and 5lb weights which he threw behind him as he took off to give him extra impetus – perhaps worth five feet or so in the distance he achieved. Over the next half-century the best in conventional circumstances for an amateur was 24ft 11¾in (7.61m) by an Irishman, Peter O'Connor, in 1901, and nine metres still remains the ultimate target for long jumpers of the 21st century with their myriad advantages such as vastly increased international competition, scientific training methods, sophisticated medical support and benevolent all-weather runway surfaces.

Small wonder, then, that the amateurs of the 19th century preferred to keep their distance, but it was at a cost. The AAA introduced a new rule in 1892 to the effect that 'a competitor who asks for and/or receives expenses ceases to be an amateur', and there were transgressors who soon fell foul of the regulations. In 1896 Charles Bradley, Alf Downer, Fred Bacon, George Crossland and Harry Watkins were disqualified for life, and as between them they were the leading runners in Britain at every distance from 100 yards to 20 miles this was a painful body-blow to the sport. The banned athletes had clearly been receiving or demanding generous sums of money to compete, but the rule was promptly changed the next year to allow expenses to be paid. The law, it can be said in the cosy hindsight of more than a century later, was an ass…and would remain so for a very long time to come.

Alf Downer was a sprinter with ideas well before his time, training twice a day and advocating speed-ball punching more than 80 years before it helped a fellow Scot, Allan Wells, to win an Olympic 100 metres title. Downer had set an amateur record of 31⅖ sec for 300 yards in 1895 which would still be regarded with respect to this day, and after he turned professional he published in 1902 his 'Running Recollections' in which he fired off a broadside at his former opponents: 'How many so-called amateurs run for the pure love of the sport? Do not the most – in fact, by far the most – enter and try to win only at those meetings where the best prizes are given, and in many cases where there is the most gambling? I do not blame them – far from it – but I do condemn the smug hypocrisy of the governing body who recognise these things and, knowing them to be contrary to their laws, make no attempt to prevent them, because they know that by doing so they will only bring about their own undoing'.

Sour grapes, perhaps? Or maybe Downer was simply unable to resist the temptation to work up a story in the time-honoured tradition of a sporting celebrity hoping to sell more copies of his book? Still, there was some considerable justification for Downer's complaints, and his fellow sprinter, Charles Bradley, with whom he had equalled the World record of 9 ⅘ sec for 100 yards in 1895, could have been forgiven for feeling equally aggrieved. Bradley, ironically, was a member of the Huddersfield Cricket & Athletic Club which had been among those founders of the Northern Counties' AA to have set their faces firmly against any hint of professionalism, and he had won the AAA 100 yards every year from 1892 to 1895.

An athlete who was much more eminent than Downer, Bradley and their contemporaries soon suffered the same fate of exclusion from amateur competition. Alfred Shrubb – 'The Little Wonder' – was one of the most renowned sportsman of his era, the finest distance-runner in the World in the early years of the 20th century, but maybe too honest for his own good. Called before the AAA committee in London to explain the financial arrangements for meetings in the Midlands and Scotland in which he had competed, he guilelessly produced a telegram which he had received from the organisers of a forthcoming tour of his in Canada, in which the promoters cheerfully informed him that there was a 'fortune here for you'. Shrubb's amateur career was ended there and then.

Within 48 hours of his appeal against suspension being dismissed in January of 1906 Shrubb made his professional debut, and prizes of £100 were immediately being publicised in connection with his forthcoming races. The average weekly wage for a skilled factory worker was £1.75. Among Shrubb's numerous outstanding achievements as an amateur had been times of 9min 9⅗ sec for two miles, 14min 17⅕ sec for three miles and 29min 59⅖ sec for six miles, which all stood as British records for more than 30 years, and his name would have been as well known to youngsters like Benjamin Howard Baker, then aged 13, as those of the renowned cricketers, C.B. Fry and W.G. Grace.

In Howard Baker's era of amateur athletics, immediately before and after World War One, the British Empire and the USA were largely dominant, with the gradual incursion of distance-runners and javelin-throwers from Finland and Sweden, and there seemed not to be too much bother about 'sham amateurism'. Professional athletics still survived, though it was widely discredited because of 'fixed' races, betting coups and unruly crowds, and therefore it was nowhere remotely on the scale of the mid-19th century, and what there was rarely achieved a standard to match the best of the amateurs.

The situation regarding one of B. Howard Baker's other favourite sporting pastimes of the 1920s, association football, was very different, even though the origins of the game were of much the same social standing. The Football Association had been founded in 1863 by public-school old boys' clubs in the London area, and the narrow class structure of this formative era was neatly illustrated by Sir Montague Shearman in his history of the game: 'Before the institution of a London v Sheffield match as an annual fixture in 1871, it may almost be said that football, until that date, was rather a recreation and a means of exercise for a few old public-school boys than a really national sport, and it was not until 'the seventies' that football began to be an attraction to the general sporting and athletic public'. Even this London-Sheffield match to which Shearman refers was no epoch-making breach of geographical and social barriers — the Sheffield club had been founded by former pupils of one of England's most famous public schools, Harrow.

The FA Challenge Cup was instituted in that same year of 1871 and a team which called itself the Wanderers — so named because the players had no fixed home ground — won five of the first seven Finals. The Wanderers were largely Old Etonians and Old Harrovians, and one member of their side on three occasions was the Honourable Arthur Fitzgerald Kinnaird (later Baron Kinnaird), who had been educated at Eton and Cambridge University, and who then went on to gain two further Cup-winners' medals as the captain of his old boys' club. Lord Kinnaird served as FA treasurer and then as president from 1890 until his death in 1923, and it was to be said of him more than a quarter-of-a-century later that 'he did more than any other single individual to fashion the game as we know it today...although a staunch amateur himself, he was able to understand the role that professionalism could have in establishing his sport as the country's national game...he believed in football's ability to bring together on the field men of all classes'.

The winning teams in the first 14 FA Cup Finals through to 1884–85 were all amateurs — in addition to the Wanderers, there were two wins each for Old Etonians and Blackburn Rovers, and one each for Oxford University, the Royal Engineers, Old Carthusians, Clapham Rovers and Blackburn Olympic. The adeptness of the mill-workers and their neighbours from the Lancashire town of Blackburn showed how far the game had already spread to the working class; the Olympic club which beat Old Etonians 2–1 in the 1882–83 Final was made up of three weavers, a spinner, a cotton-machine operator, a dental assistant, a master plumber, an iron-foundry worker, a picture-framer and a clerk, with a public-house landlord as their captain and coach.

However, they were 'sham amateurs'. By the club's own admission, the Olympic players were receiving £1 a game appearance money, which was no doubt a very welcome addition to their occupational wages, though it would have presented no great attraction as a sole source of income, and so they were breaking the rules until the advent of professionalism in 1885. Despite the endorsement of the likes of Lord Kinnaird and Montague Shearman, it was only with some reluctance on the part of the upper-crust administrators that the decision was taken, and it was, in effect, no more than a recognition of a *fait accompli*, in view of the unashamed admissions of payments which had been made by clubs such as Blackburn Olympic and Preston North End. The cryptic wording of the rule change transparently demonstrated the fact that the stable-door was being closed long after the horse had bolted: 'It is in the interests of Association football to legalise the employment of professional players'.

The concession had its immediate effect. When Blackburn Rovers won the FA Cup for the second successive year in 1885–86 all but two of the team were professionals, of which seven had played as amateurs the previous year, and five of those were receiving FA Cup winner's medals for the third successive year. No doubt they all kept their day jobs, as the rewards for the players were still hardly extravagant – the club's total wage bill for the season was £615. Their opponents, West Bromwich Albion, fielded seven professionals and four amateurs.

Richard Holt's 1990 history, *Sport and the British*, has a lucid explanation for the acceptance of professionals in the game. 'The grandees of the Association game were even more privileged than their rugby counterparts, coming as they did from the most ancient of public schools rather than the newer foundations', Professor Holt wrote. 'Perhaps this is the reason for their more paternalistic attitude to the needs of common people who wished to play 'their' game. 'Soccer' players – the term itself is Oxford undergraduate slang – were at first confident enough of their status to share their game with teams of mill-workers. When it became evident several northern teams were paying their players, there was certainly some strong criticism from purists and demands for the expulsion of the culprits. However, more cautious counsels prevailed and professionalism was permitted'.

Cricket's controlling body, the Marylebone Cricket Club (MCC), had found no difficulty in dealing with the issue of professionalism, based on that subjective judgment that if you were a 'gentleman' who did not depend on the game for a living then you were an amateur. The professionals and the amateurs (the latter often earning more from the game) played alongside each other at every level, though some quaint customs from the Victorian era were to be sustained for a very long time to come. England's Test teams of the 20th century were invariably captained by an amateur, almost regardless of whether he was actually worth his place in the team, until 1952, and every year two sides representing the 'Gentlemen' and the 'Players' would troop out of their respective dressing-rooms for their annual class-conscious encounter. This fixture dated back to 1806 and only finally came to an end in 1962 when distinctions between amateurs and professionals were abolished.

One illustration of the attitude regarding cricketing amateurs which still prevailed in the years after World War One is to be found in the journalism of J.A.H. Catton, the editor of the *Athletic News*, which had a circulation of some 200,000 in 1920. Catton has been described as 'a hugely influential figure in the development of British sports reporting from the late-Victorian period through to the inter-war years', and in 1925 he wrote about the England Test captaincy issue and sided very much with the traditionalists: 'The leader, preferably, should be a typical English gentleman who has the education, the natural courtesy, the charm of manner, and perhaps even the wealth to grace any assembly or social event, and to make our Colonies feel that the old country, that 'Home', can still send forth true-born English gentlemen with our love of a game for the sake of a game'.

One of the men who had fitted that bill to perfection was much the most famous of those amateur cricketers to have also played in an FA Cup Final. He was the hero of all England, C.B. Fry, who was a full-back in the losing Southampton side in 1901–02 and was idolised for his various other sporting exploits by every schoolboy throughout the land. In 1903 the young Howard Baker, then aged 10, was taken to Goodison Park to see Fry play for the visiting Portsmouth team against Everton and the memory remained with him until the end of his life.

Charles Burgess Fry was the very picture of the perfect English sporting gentleman. He had played for the full England Football XI against Ireland the season previous to his Cup Final appearance, but his daring deeds on other playing-fields were what had already brought him nationwide fame. In a rather casual manner, as befitted a typically languid Oxford University undergraduate, he had equalled the World record for the long jump at the university sports in 1893 and might well have won the event at the first Modern Olympic Games of 1896, but like so many of his fellow-athletes he was unaware at the time that they were taking place. He graduated with a first-class honours degree in classics and played cricket for Sussex from 1894 onwards, was capped for England for the first time two years later, and had enjoyed an astonishingly successful season in 1901 when he scored 3,147 runs at an average of 78.67, including 13 centuries, of which the last half-dozen were in successive innings. Such was Fry's fame and reputation beyond the boundaries of the cricket-field that he was once invited to become the King of Albania!

Throughout the first 20 years of Benjamin Howard Baker's life Fry would continue to be a pre-eminent figure in British sport and the natural successor to one of the best-known men in all the land, Dr W.G. Grace, who had been an accomplished athlete in his younger and slimmer days, as a hurdler, but by 1901 was aged 53. Though still capable of making 1,000 runs a season, he had played his last Test for England two years before and was naturally in some decline. The gentlemen amateurs, Fry and Grace, provided Howard Baker and hundreds of thousands of other English youngsters with the ideal role model, or perhaps one should rather say 'idealised'. Sporting professionals were for the most part accorded the same status as domestic servants — useful about the house but not to be seen dining at the same table.

The most celebrated of all amateur footballers to have played for the full England team at the turn of the century was Gilbert Smith, familiarly known by his appropriate initials 'G.O.'. Described as the greatest centre-forward of his day, Smith had been educated at Charterhouse public school and Oxford University and was still an undergraduate when he won the first of the 20 international caps which he earned between 1893–94 and 1900–01. The quintessential amateur, he set an England scoring record with five goals in one match against Ireland and was also a fine cricketer, hitting a century against Cambridge in the Inter-Varsity match of 1896 and later playing for Surrey. Smith remained a member of his school old boys' club, Old Carthusians, and of the leading amateur side, Corinthian, throughout his international career, but many other amateurs continued to play regularly alongside the professionals in League football in the years leading up to World War One.

Nine members of the Great Britain team which won the gold medals at the 1908 Olympics were amateurs with League teams at some time during their careers, including Harold Hardman, who is one of only three amateurs in the 20th century to have won FA Cup winner's medals and was a member of the Everton team in 1905–06. He was to become chairman of Manchester United and was in office at the time of the 1958 Munich air disaster. Six of the victorious Great Britain team in the 1912 Olympic Games tournament played for League clubs — Bradford City, Chelsea, Derby County, Hull City, Portsmouth and Reading.

One of the foremost influences for Howard Baker was undoubtedly Vivian Woodward, who was an Olympic gold-medallist in both 1908 and 1912 and had a brilliant playing career as a centre-forward through to the beginning of World War One, winning 44 amateur caps for England and 23 full international caps, while always remaining an amateur. Howard

Baker came to know Woodward well. Born in 1879, and so by 13 years the elder of the two, Woodward had joined Tottenham Hotspur in 1902 when the club was playing in the Southern League, and he was their first goalscorer when they entered Division Two of the Football League in 1908–09. He accumulated 58 goals for England in amateur internationals, including six in one game against Holland, while his 29 goals in full internationals remained an England record until it was beaten by both Tom Finney and Nat Lofthouse in 1958.

Woodward had moved from Tottenham Hotspur to Chelsea in 1909–10 and after his playing career had been brought to a close during World War One when he was wounded in action in 1916 while serving as an officer in the Middlesex Regiment, he became a director of both Tottenham and Chelsea. He had obtained leave of absence from the army to see Chelsea play Sheffield United in the 1914–15 FA Cup Final and was asked by Chelsea to join the side, but he refused to take the place of a professional, Bob Thomson, who had been in the team in the earlier rounds. The football writer and historian, Bernard Joy, who himself was an amateur international in the 1930s (and once for the full England team) while playing League football for Arsenal, wrote in later years, 'The gesture was typical of Woodward. He was as great a sportsman as he was a footballer'. Thomson, incidentally, was to play 95 matches for Chelsea despite the apparently insurmountable handicap of having lost the sight of one eye in childhood.

Even after the war Howard Baker was by no means alone in his decision to remain unpaid while regularly playing League football, and though it was a tradition that was gradually dying out it was doing so in some style. When a persistent injury eventually contributed to costing him his place in the Chelsea team in 1925–26 there were no more than half-a-dozen amateurs still playing regularly in the four divisions of the Football League, but the annual FA Charity Shield match between representative teams of the leading amateurs and professionals was won by the amateurs in the seasons 1925–26 and 1926–27 by scores of 6–1 and then 6–3, with Howard Baker in goal on the first occasion.

Howard Baker's selfless dedication to the spirit of amateurism exactly echoed that of Vivian Woodward's. When the economic depression began to take hold in the latter 1920s Howard Baker tendered his resignation as goalkeeper for Chelsea in the Football League, even though as an amateur among professionals he had made the position very largely his own over the preceding seasons to the extent of being selected for England. His reason for offering to stand down had nothing to do with waning skills, fitness or enthusiasm, or even the demands of his expanding business life. Rather, he sincerely believed that he was depriving a professional of a living at a time when unemployment in all walks of life was soaring, and he wanted to make amends and provide a job for someone who needed it. He was persuaded by his professional teammates to change his mind, and that reaction indicates how highly he was thought of. There may well also, of course, have been an element of self-interest among his paid colleagues. Howard Baker's skilful goalkeeping contributed handsomely to their win bonuses!

His Liverpool-born contemporary, Max Woosnam, also extolled the virtues of amateurism. As a footballer he moved on from Chelsea to Manchester City after accepting a senior management position with the Crossley Brothers engineering firm in Manchester and played 89 matches through to the 1924–25 season, once captaining the full England team against Wales. It was said of Woosnam by his daughter in his biography that 'he had nothing against professionals, and he campaigned very hard for amateurs to play alongside them, but he believed that everyone, regardless of whether they were being paid to play the game or not, had certain standards to uphold and a code of behaviour to follow'. Standards to uphold? Codes of behaviour? These virtues meant rather more in the 1920s than they do 90 years later. Amateur or professional? A gentleman or a player? Those descriptions still carried much social kudos in that era.

B. Howard Baker was one of the last of the line – an amateur who held his own with the best of the professionals. Edward Grayson, the historian of the Corinthian club, wrote in 1955: 'The First World War killed the Golden Age of Corinthian and cricketers. The years between the First and Second World Wars buried it. Nevertheless, for a time during the 1920s the flame of life flickered on through such men as B. Howard Baker'. The metaphors were mixed but the meaning abundantly clear.

FANCIFUL, UNCERTAIN, BUT 'PERHAPS NOTHING IS SO PRETTY AND INTERESTING AS A HIGH JUMP'

The Olympic Games in Ancient Greece, which lasted from at least 776BC to the end of the fourth century AD, laid the foundations for the modern athletics programme. The events contested were four races of various distances from about 190 metres to some 5000 metres, together with long jumping, discus throwing and javelin throwing. Even the pole vault has its origins in the dexterity of Greek cavalrymen in using their lances to leap into their saddles, though they never apparently tried this as a competition.

The Greeks in all probability also knew nothing of high jumping, and the pre-eminent authority on the subject, Professor H.A. Harris, in his book, *Greek Athletes and Athletics* published in 1964, provides a practical explanation: 'So far as we know, the Greeks practised only one jump, the long jump. The Greek countryside is furrowed by so many ravines that the ability to long jump is valuable for moving rapidly across it in war, while there are few natural obstacles which demand high-jumping skill'.

The four jumps and the four throws now contested in athletics, and known as the field events, are the high jump, pole vault, long jump, triple jump, shot put, and throwing the discus, hammer and javelin, and they all evolved in various ways from military or rural needs. Skill in throwing light-weight implements was valuable in battle. Strength in lifting heavier objects was useful in agriculture. Clearing a stream or a ditch on your own two feet, or by using a pole to lever yourself across, was an asset in any form of travel or rural labour.

Of even greater antiquity and longevity than the Ancient Olympics were the Tailteann Games, held in Ireland from 632BC to AD1169, and evidence has been uncovered of Irish tribesmen in the third century AD undertaking some form of high jumping to test their physical fitness for battle, but in conventional athletic terms the high jump has to be regarded as a relatively modern event. One of Britain's foremost historians of the sport, the late Eric Cowe, came across accounts of the high jump being held regularly at Highland Games meetings in Scotland throughout the 19th century, and he was able to compile a progressive list of 27 reasonably authenticated best performances which advanced from 5ft 2in (1.57m) in 1827 to 5ft 10½in (1.79m) in 1869.

More recently, it was reported by a Scottish writer, Jack Davidson, that a great all-rounder, Donald Dinnie, born in 1837, claimed to have high jumped 6ft 1in (1.86m), 'while there appears to be general acceptance of his having achieved 5ft 11in on several occasions'. Dinnie was a stonemason by occupation and of impressive physique, 6ft 1in (1.86m) tall and weighing 15 stone (95kg), who later made a living as a music-hall strong-man in North America, Australia, New Zealand and South Africa. Such was his national fame as a thrower that during World War One Scottish regiments named their 50lb artillery shells 'Donald Dinnies'. There is even an account of Andrew Milne, an army sergeant from Forfar, high-jumping 6ft 4in (1.93m) in 1865, but as this sort of achievement would still have ranked among the dozen best ever in Britain more than 90 years later it is not regarded as credible. Those dedicated to the statistical exactitude of athletics naturally tend to think in such realistic terms, but others of a more romantic streak of nature may prefer to give Sgt Milne the benefit of the doubt.

All of these Scottish athletes were competing as professionals and are not mentioned at all in the various editions of Sir Montague Shearman's comprehensive history of athletics published from 1887 onwards, for the simple reason that he presumably had never heard of them. His earliest references to the high jump are in connection with the first Inter-Varsity match between Oxford and Cambridge in 1864 when the event was won at a respectable height of 5ft 6in (1.68m), and Shearman later noted, wonderingly, in relation to the 1880s that 'even at the present day foreigners hear with incredulity that men can jump more than 6ft in height'. By 'foreigners' Shearman meant continental Europeans; throughout the 19th century the best high jumpers were to be drawn exclusively from England, Scotland and Ireland or from the USA.

The supreme value of Shearman's history is that he gives us some vivid descriptions of the style of high jumpers in the 1870s and 1880s, and it thus becomes clear that there was not all that radical an improvement in techniques between then and the era of Howard Baker and his British contemporaries from 1910 onwards even through to World War Two. 'Perhaps nothing is so pretty and interesting as a high jump', Shearman wrote, 'and a light-weight jumper who leaps straight over his obstacle and alights on the balls of his feet is almost certain to be graceful in his movements. Still, there are a variety of different styles of high-jumping, and some successful performers get over the bar sideways with a crab-like motion which is more effective than beautiful'.

The finest high jumper of this era was – almost inevitably – an Oxbridge product. Marshall Brooks was a youthful phenomenon who had first shown an exceptional aptitude for the event at Rugby School, and then when he went up to Brasenose College, Oxford, he achieved the best authenticated performances ever on four separate occasions. At the Oxford University sports in March of 1876 he cleared 6ft (1.83m) in the most appalling weather conditions of sleet, snow and high winds, and then three weeks later on a warm day at the Inter-Varsity match at the Lillie Bridge ground, in London, near to where the Stamford Bridge stadium now stands, he went over 6ft 2½in (1.89m) with his feet apparently clearing the bar by two or three inches.

At the age of 18 Brooks had played rugby football for England against Scotland and he was still only 20 years old when he achieved his best high jumps, but after winning another competition three days later he never competed again, the reasons for which are unexplained but maybe had something to do with attention to his studies. He graduated from Oxford with an M.A. degree and in later life became a Justice of the Peace for Cheshire and for Lancashire. No English high jumper was to achieve anything better in recognised competition until Howard Baker did so 44 years afterwards, and Brooks's jump remained an Inter-Varsity record until a Danish undergraduate at Cambridge, Ivar Vind, beat it at last 72 years later in 1948! Vind, as it happens, was something of a dilettante throwback to an earlier generation, renowned for nonchalantly smoking a cigarette in a long holder between jumps!

Brooks's father was Thomas Brooks, who had been educated at Eton and then made his fortune as a quarry-owner. He became the High Sheriff of Lancashire and in 1891 was created Baron Crawshaw by Queen Victoria. Marshall Brooks (later, as the son of a baron, to be entitled the Honourable Marshall Brooks) had been born in Tarporley, which is still in the heart of the Cheshire countryside, some dozen miles from Chester, in 1855. He lived to the age of 88, dying at Tarporley on 5 January 1944, by which time the World record for the high jump had risen to 6ft 11in (2.11m), but as this performance – by a Californian, Lester Steers, in 1941 – had been accomplished with all the advantages of the far more efficient 'Straddle' style of clearing the bar face down, and with a much superior and safer take-off and landing area, Brooks could perhaps have been forgiven for thinking in the last years of his life that not too much progress had been made as regards the fleeting pastime of his youth.

Shearman affirms that Brooks was well above average height and delighted the crowd at Lillie Bridge by walking back under the bar after he had made his record-breaking clearance. In a marvellously detailed account of Brooks's appearance and his high-jump technique, Shearman wrote: 'He was a tall, cleanly built, and rather thin man, with a good deal of strength as well as spring, and his manner of jumping was very striking, although not very graceful when he got over great heights. He took very little run, and in fact almost walked up to the bar, springing straight over it with legs tucked up high and well in front of him, and invariably looked, when his legs were once over, as if his body would fall crashing on the bar; but he nearly always managed to jerk his body forward again and to alight upon his toes'.

High-jump competitors of that era, and well into the 20th century, were sometimes provided with a cinder takeoff area, or used the cinder running track, but more usually it was a grass surface on which they competed, with all its attendant problems if conditions were wet, and it was from grass that Brooks set his record. Shearman says that generally in competitions a mattress was provided for jumpers to land on, though it seems to have been a matter of choice as to whether they made use of it, and in any case it was probably no more than a thin covering and went only a little way towards softening their landings. There is an engraving at the British Library showing the 1884 AAA high-jump winner, Tom Ray, clearing the bar and falling towards a type of mat which appears to be no more than some six feet square and a few inches thick. The expression on Ray's face is not clear but may well have been one of apprehension!

It should not be too surprising, therefore, that Shearman remarked of high jumpers that they were often described as 'fanciful and uncertain...one man wants to jump with the sun on his right, another with the sun on his left. One likes to alight upon the mattress which is always kept for the purpose, another is 'put off' if he sees the mattress in front of him. Another sticks a bit of paper into the ground to guide him as to his takeoff. While yet another hangs a blue handkerchief on the bar to show him where he is to jump to'.

Brooks's record was marginally surpassed by an Irishman, Patrick Davin, in 1880, though Shearman was a shade sceptical, commenting, perhaps tongue in cheek, that 'there is indeed not the least reason to doubt the *bona fides* of the performance, but it is perhaps natural that a good many Englishmen should have suspicions that Irish patriotism might manage to elongate a measurement a quarter of an inch when the downfall of Saxon supremacy could be secured thereby'. Davin, who was a solicitor by profession, and therefore presumably a zealot for accuracy, called for a spirit-level on the occasion of his record to ensure that the ground was level, and he surely proved his true worth to any English detractors by winning the 1881 AAA championships event at 6ft 0½in (1.84m), which remained a meeting record for 12 years. Shearman said admiringly of him:

'His appearance was watched with great interest and he certainly showed magnificent power on that day...Davin was a tall strong man of quite 6 feet in height and might almost be described as a young giant, being, although very well-shaped, a strong heavy man. His style of leaping was quite different to that of Brooks, as he trotted up towards the posts and with one prodigious bound in the air went clean over the bar. In one of his leaps, when he was clearing about 5ft 9in in height, we saw him take off six feet before the bar and alight six feet on the other side, and when over the bar his body was almost perpendicular. In fact, he took a downright honest leap at the bar in much the same way as a man would leap over a hedge and ditch from the road'. When Peter Lovesey, the pre-eminent chronicler of Victorian athletics, came to write the history of the AAA in commemoration of its centenary in 1980, he aptly described high jumping of those early years as being 'for a long time regarded as akin to hurdling'. Davin's jumping style was clearly 'akin to hurdling' because the reporter for 'The Irish Sportsman' who witnessed the record jump stated that it was measured at 14ft 4in (4.37m) from take-off to landing.

It is fair to say that at least until the late 1880s high jumpers relied largely on natural ability and simply cleared the bar in whatever manner they thought best without any recourse to a detailed study of technique. The foremost of athletics statisticians and historians, Dr Roberto Quercetani, explained this further in his comprehensive history of the sport, first published in 1964: 'In those days high jumpers apparently showed little or no concern for the position of their centre of gravity *vis-à-vis* the crossbar. They simply drove all parts of the body as high as possible'. The first exception to this generally held belief would seem to be an American, William Byrd Page, who employed what was described as 'a slight backward lay-out' and who remarkably achieved 6ft 4in (1.93m) in 1887, though he was only 5ft 7in (1.70m) tall.

The next high jumper to come close to exploiting his physique to the full was another Irishman, Michael Sweeney, whose style involved clearing the bar one leg at a time, rather than feet first, and came to be known as the 'Eastern Cut-Off'. Born in Ireland, Sweeney had emigrated to the USA, and though his World-record of 6ft 5in (1.97m) in New York in 1895 was not that much superior to the best of his fellow Irishmen who had stayed at home it was nonetheless of great significance for the fact that, like Byrd Page, he cleared nine inches above his own head. Writing more than 60 years later in a comprehensive training manual published by the Achilles Club, Arthur Selwyn, who was himself a Great Britain high-jump international in the 1930s, said of Sweeney's performance that 'this incredible record was the first made with anything like a scientific style'. Sweeney remembered particularly in his autobiography of 1940 that the official who first congratulated him as he was helped out of the landing-pit was no less than a future President of the United States, Teddy Roosevelt, who was at the time the New York Police Commissioner.

During this same decade a namesake of Howard Baker's coincidentally achieved some remarkable high-jump performances, though who can say whether or not they were genuine? Robert H. Baker was an American stage entertainer who performed numerous startling feats of jumping and is said to have cleared 6ft 8¼in (2.04m) in August of 1898, though the exhaustive researches in recent years of the athletics historian, Peter Lovesey, have not uncovered any contemporary reports of the feat and the manner of it. Baker was a member of an act called the Robinson Baker Trio which appeared at music-halls throughout Britain in the last years of the 19th century and he retired in 1900 as self-proclaimed 'Champion Jumper Of The World'.

It may be that he used a raised takeoff, or even a springboard, to achieve such heights, and it could also be that the measurement was inaccurate or deliberately exaggerated for dramatic effect. Yet is it not equally feasible that by dint of constant rehearsal and public performance he had simply perfected a technique which was far superior to that of his contemporaries, whether or not they were competitors or entertainers? If so, he was 35 years ahead of the times because no greater authenticated height was attained until 1933 by a Californian college student, Walter Marty, using the 'Western Roll' style, which involved clearing the bar on his side.

For 40 years, from 1880 to 1920, the British high-jump record was to remain in Irish hands, apart from a brief and unverified intrusion in 1890. The Irish domination is an interesting phenomenon, and no doubt the reluctance with which many Irishmen viewed continued allegiance to Britain helped fuel the ambitions of Irish athletes to beat the English. More prosaically, the Industrial Revolution had some effect because it witnessed a huge shift of population in England from the countryside to the towns, whereas Ireland remained largely rural, and so jumping and throwing events which had traditionally featured in country sports meetings continued to figure much more prominently there. Even so, further explanation is needed and no one is better placed to provide it than the leading 21st-century authority on Irish athletics history, Colm Murphy, who has written several books on the subject:

'There was a division in Ireland in the 19th century between the modernists and the traditionalists. The modernists aped everything that was initiated in London – new trends, new fashions – and in sport this extended to rugby, cricket, football, boxing and athletics. So far as athletics was concerned, the traditionalists viewed the running events as another of those foreign influences and so were inclined, instead, towards the jumping and throwing events in which the English were not very interested. Then there was the fact that the survivors of the Irish famines, of which the worst was in the late 1780s, tended to be those who were stronger and fitter. The population of Ireland was eight million in 1840 and England's was not even double that. By then the food that was available to the rural Irish population meant that on average the people were taller and heavier, more rangey and with more spring, than the English. As an example, at the time of the Boer War at the end of the 19th century four out of every five potential army recruits in London were rejected because of malnutrition, but only one in five in Ireland was rejected'.

A major reason for that English lack of enthusiasm for the technically-demanding jumps and throws was the adverse aspect of the Oxbridge influence, which was that athletic achievements should be seen to be effortlessly attained, and that training and proper preparation were somehow ungentlemanly. Interestingly, Sir Montague Shearman – though a product of that system – did not entirely share the creed. He cautiously advised the prospective high jumper that 'he will do no harm if he indulges in a bit of sprinting and takes exercise canters' but emphasised that 'for his main practice he must jump over a bar daily'. In writing this, Shearman must have known full well that almost the only high jumpers of that era who had the time and opportunity to follow such sound advice were Oxford and Cambridge undergraduates.

The sole English high-jumper of real note over the period of some 35 years which separated the feats of Marshall Brooks in the late 1870s and then the beginning of Howard Baker's career was George Rowdon. A member of the Teignmouth Football Club, in Devon, and a domestic servant by occupation, Rowdon was described as small and lightly built. He won the AAA title in 1886, 1887, 1888 and achieved some remarkable heights in obscure circumstances in the West Country. His best authenticated performance was 6ft 2in (1.91m) at Paignton in 1887, but he had two clearances which were very much higher of 6ft 5⅝in (1.97) and 6ft 5½in (1.97) within a fortnight in August of 1890. The first of these was set during a sports meeting for army volunteers at a camp on Dartmoor and the second in the village of Chudleigh, on the edge of Dartmoor, and both are regarded by researchers as not being achieved under acceptable competitive circumstances. Montague Shearman noted that Rowdon 'afterwards exhibited his wonderful leaping powers at the music halls'.

The first Irishman – and therefore representative of Great Britain – to win an Olympic high-jump medal (silver in 1900) was Pat Leahy, the AAA champion of 1898–99 who probably deserves a very much more prominent place in athletics history than he has been accorded. He cleared the bar on his side, rather than his back, and this method anticipated by a decade or so the Western Roll technique developed in the USA which was to become the habitual manner of World record-breaking for much of the first half of the 20th century. Leahy's best performance of 6ft 4¾in (1.95m) was achieved in 1898, but he is believed to have gone higher after emigrating to the USA and was still capable of 6ft 3in (1.91m) 10 years later. His younger brother, Tim, who was 6ft 1in (1.86m) tall, cleared two inches above his own height in 1910. There were six brothers and three sisters in the family, and one of the latter, Ellen Mary, audaciously gave high-jump displays and claimed that she had cleared 6ft (1.83m) on five occasions! Whatever the truth of that, the most renowned high jumper in the family was yet another brother, Cornelius (known as 'Con'), who never quite held the British record – his best was 6ft 4½in (1.94) – but was AAA champion every year from 1905 to 1908 and was also the gold-medallist at the 10th anniversary Olympic Games in Athens in 1906 and equal second at the London Olympics of 1908.

Yet another Irishman, Tim Carroll, born in 1888, who improved the British record to 6ft 5in (1.95m) in 1913, was to continue competing until his mid-30s, and he became Howard Baker's chief rival in domestic competition and also took part in the Olympic Games of both 1912 and 1920, though never winning an AAA title. Howard Baker usually had the better of their frequent contests, but that is another story to be told in a later chapter. What is worth emphasising at this point is that the strictures placed on high jumpers in Howard Baker's era were very much greater than in subsequent years. Few if any of the much higher jumps to be achieved with the various styles which rendered obsolete the 'Scissors' – so named because of the scissors-like action of the legs in crossing the bar in succession – and the related Eastern Cut-Off would have been acceptable to judges in the years leading up to World War One and immediately afterwards. The regulations set out in the competitors' handbook for the 1912 Olympic Games explain why:

'Neither a 'saltomortal' nor a flying leap over the bar shall be permitted. By a 'saltomortal' is meant a somersault over the bar, and by a flying leap is meant a jump over the bar head and hands first, with the breast toward the bar so that the upper part of the body comes to the ground first'.

Each of the jumping styles in use during the 19th century and beyond the mid-20th century would have been inhibiting simply because of the necessity for the competitors to land on their hands and feet on the sand or grass made available to them if they were determined to avoid risking serious injury. The fist World record using the 'Western Roll', which entailed clearing the bar on one's side, was not set until 1912, at 6ft 7in (2.00m). No World record was set with the 'Straddle', for which the jumper rolled chest down over the bar and landed on his side or back, until 1936, and it was 1973 before any World record was set with the Fosbury Flop, which involved crossing the bar on one's back and head first, and even then not by its inventor, Dick Fosbury. 'Straddling' or 'Flopping' in the 1920s was as unthinkable as walking on the moon, though the term 'flopper' had already been coined by then to describe the bizarre and hazardous style of a pre-war British high-jumper of some modest repute, Alfred Bellerby, who cleared the bar in such a manner that he landed on one shoulder, presumably not without some shock to the system.

The method used by most jumpers, including Howard Baker in the latter part of his career, was described aptly by Guy Butler, the prolific Olympic athlete and coach, as the 'turn-in-the-air' style when he wrote about it in 1929, and the reason for its more formal title of Eastern Cut-Off was one of geographical origin – 'Eastern' as in East Coast of the USA to differentiate from the Californian-inspired Western Roll first demonstrated in 1909. As Butler pointed out, it required 'great flexibility and perfect muscular condition', and in particular the athlete had to ensure that after crossing the bar he was able to twist his hips around in order to land safely on his hands and feet in the unforgiving sand.

Butler's concise descriptions of each of the high-jump actions in his book, *Athletics and Training*, published in 1938, are still relevant more than 70 years on. The Scissors was relatively simple to execute and to explain, but the Eastern Cut-Off and Western Roll were rather more complex. Butler's interpretations were, in summary, as follows:

Scissors. In its most crude form it consists of a run from the side and a take-off from the outside foot, the jumper clearing the bar in a sitting position with the legs passing in succession over the bar rather like that of the two blades of the scissors.

Eastern Cut-Off. Approaching either from the front or at an angle of 45 degrees, the take-off is made from the leg furthest away from the bar and a strong kick is given with the leading leg. The take-off leg assists the upward movement also by means of a strong kick and when that has reached a point several inches higher than the leading foot the body is heeled over to the right. After the legs have passed the bar the hips are turned away from the bar by a backwards kick of the take-off foot. The jumper lands on his right leg facing the bar. *(Readers of this book who are of an active disposition might like to try the exercise themselves in order to understand it better!)*

Western Roll. Approaching usually from about 45 degrees, the take-off is from the inside foot and thus is unlike the other three styles. The outside leg kicks upwards very strongly and the inside arm is also punched upwards. As the body is about to pass the bar the shoulders are straightened by a secondary kick of the leading leg and the jumper lies sideways along the bar. The 'roll' is usually achieved by a downwards and backwards sweep of the right hand, driving the hip away from the bar for a landing on hands and feet.

Before World War One Howard Baker had employed the rudimentary Scissors action, but he was one of the very first British athletes in a technical event to benefit from expert advice as Walter Knox, the Canadian who had been enterprisingly appointed by the AAA as Chief Coach in 1914, persuaded him to change to the more efficient Eastern Cut-Off. Knox was himself an excellent all-round athlete who ran 100 yards in $9\frac{3}{5}$ seconds in 1907, which was equal to the best ever achieved by either a professional (as he then was) or an amateur. Though Knox's appointment was brought to a sudden end by the outbreak of war, Howard Baker remembered the lessons well when peace was restored, as confirmed by Captain F.A.M. Webster, that most perceptive of British coaches between the wars, who later wrote of Howard Baker that in 1910 he was 'entirely without form' but by 1919 he 'showed such an improvement in style'.

As Guy Butler had indicated, it was not a simple process to learn the new technique. A graphic description of the demands which it placed upon the athlete and coach was to be given by Arthur Selwyn, the Achilles club international and coach of the 1930s, who wrote of the Eastern Cut-Off: 'This is a scientific deviation from the scissors which, apart from the extreme difficulty of achieving and timing the theoretically low position of the centre of gravity that it offers, scores heavily for take-off and grace. It is fascinating to attempt and often extremely pretty to watch – indeed, it is a fairly safe bet that the prettier a cut-off is the better it is. Yet it is much harder for the normal man to execute than either form of the Western Roll or the simple form of the scissors'.

Though not obviously as effective as the Western Roll or the Straddle, to say nothing, of course, of the Fosbury Flop, it was possible to achieve very respectable heights with this Cut-Off. As an illustration of this, the Rumanian athletics historian, Leonid Nichitin, who has made a specific study of performances achieved with this technique, contributed some unique data to the February 2005 issue of the journal of athletics history, 'Track Stats', and listed the 'World record' for the Cut-Off as 2.09m by Nagahiko Adachi, of Japan, which was set as late as 1970, while in the 1930s an American, George Spitz, and the 1934 European champion, Kalevi Kotkas, of Finland, had come within two centimetres of the existing World record of 2.06. By 1953 the World record had still only advanced to 6ft $11\frac{5}{8}$ (2.12), using the Western Roll. Eventually, of course, the Cut-off was left much further behind when the first of those Fosbury Flop World records was set at 2.30m in 1973.

How, then, do the various high-jump techniques compare so far as potential performance is concerned? The problem with this sort of evaluation is that they have not developed concurrently. Nobody in the 21st century uses any style other than the Fosbury Flop. The Straddle hasn't been practised for almost 20 years and the last men's World record with it was in 1978. No World record has been set with the Western Roll since 1953 (men) or 1956 (women). The Eastern Cut-Off still produced a women's World record-holder from China in 1957 and the Scissors survived as an anachronism for women through to 1961 because the virtually invincible Iolanda Balas, of Rumania (140 consecutive victories), set 14 World records with it. Asked, specifically for the purposes of this book, to consider the efficiency of the various methods, Mike Holmes, coach to Great Britain's most successful male high jumper, Steve Smith, made the following observations:

'The early techniques were primarily devised on the requirement that the athletes landed on their feet. It was only as landing-areas were built up and had foam chunks strewn around that the straddle could develop, and the Flop thereafter. Clearly, also, training methods and equipment development have led to improved performances which are very difficult to factor into any comparison. It would be a strange sporting World if fashion in technique held sway for very long over effectiveness, and based on the 'law' that the most effective technique will eventually predominate it demonstrates that the Flop beats the Straddle beats the Western Roll beats the Eastern Cut-Off beats the Scissors.

'The main drawback of the Western Roll and the Cut-Off is that at some point the entire body is above the bar, thus failing to follow the basic tenet that the centre of mass of the jumper passes as close to the bar as possible. This has to cost 10 to 12 centimetres. At no point does the entire body of a Flopper or a Straddler appear above the bar. There's always some body part below the bar at any point in these jumps, and definitely more of the body remains below the bar in the Flop than the Straddle, which is why the former will always be the more effective — maybe to the extent of four centimetres at a guess. Because jumpers have cleared 2 metres 18 or so with the Scissors, I suspect that if worked on by the very best modern-day jumpers the Scissors or the Eastern Cut-Off should deliver jumps in the low 2.20s'.

Despite the advocacy of such informed coaches as Captain F.A.M. Webster and Guy Butler, the only notable British high jumper who seems to have taken up the Western Roll in the years before World War Two, and then only briefly, is the aforementioned author, Arthur Selwyn, who was the Inter-Varsity winner for Oxford in 1938. The first to do so with real success at international level was Howard Baker's successor as British record-holder, Alan Paterson, who came to prominence in 1944 as a 16-year-old in Glasgow, coached by his father, having switched from the Scissors two years before, and who then set a British junior record at 17 of 6ft 2½in (1.89) and improved Howard Baker's record in 1946 and again in 1947, eventually becoming European champion in 1950. He had the natural physical advantage of growing to an immense height — he was 6ft 6¾in (2.00m) tall.

Even allowing for inbred British conservatism, it does seem extraordinary that it was not until 34 years after the first World record had been set with the Western Roll that a British record was achieved with the same method. It was largely due, of course, to Howard Baker's exceptional ability that his record lasted so long, but that does not explain why more advanced techniques were not tried. Such exposure as British high jumpers of the 1920s and 1930s had to outside influences should have taught them something. There were nine Britons in the Olympic high jumps of 1924, 1928 and 1936 (no one in Los Angeles in 1932), of which only two qualified for a final, and one of those was born in British Guiana (now Guyana). Of the three competitors in Berlin in the last of those years none ever did better than 6ft 4in (1.93) during their careers, compared with the 6ft 9¾in (2.08) which was the best by the American, Cornelius Johnson, who won the gold medal, using the Western Roll, as had the gold-medallists in 1924 and 1928.

The indefatigable F.A.M. Webster, in one of his unending succession of training manuals, wrote despairingly in 1929: 'I am bold enough to believe we have today in the UK high jumpers, and indeed all classes of field events men, as strong, springy and naturally gifted as any others the world can produce. But our men do not develop into world's record-breakers because they are not given the encouragement of competition and training facilities, and even moderately scientific instruction is extraordinarily hard to come by'. Webster enthusiastically described Howard Baker as 'simply bubbling over with energy' but reckoned that the Western Roll was 'the most perfect form of jumping yet discovered' and that 'Baker did not have the advantages enjoyed by the Americans of learning good style while still a schoolboy'. The Olympic 100 metres champion of 1924, Harold Abrahams, and his brother, Dr Adolphe Abrahams, in a jointly-written book in 1936, sensibly stated of the Western Roll: 'Undoubtedly the fact that the vast majority of high jumpers of first-rate ability employ this Western form argues that it must possess qualities designed for excellence which are in the main lacking in other forms'.

As an aside, it is worth mentioning that the first Olympic women's high-jump title was won by Ethel Catherwood, of Canada, at Amsterdam in 1928 with a World record of 1.595m, the bar having been set at 1.60m and then re-measured. The following year a Dutchwoman, Carolina Gisolf, cleared 1.608m, and it could be said that considering the limited competitive opportunities available to them women high jumpers in that decade – all of them employing the antiquated Scissors – had held their own with the men, as progress in later and more enlightened years was surprisingly slow. In 1929 the men's World record stood at 2.03m; in other words, a fraction over 42cm better than the women's. By 2011, with all the benefits of eight decades of equality, the difference between the men's and women's records – 2.45m and 2.09m – was still 36cm.

Having compared at length the various high-jumping styles, it should be said that rather too much can be made of the matter. In a much later era when the Straddle was almost obligatory for male high jumpers – 14 of the 17 Olympic finalists in 1960 used it – one of Britain's most experienced and articulate coaches, John Le Masurier (not to be confused with the 'Dad's Army' actor, John Le Mesurier!), observed soberly in the pre-Fosbury era: 'Although it is important to realise that at bar level the Straddle is more mechanically sound than the Western Roll and the Eastern Cut-Off, and much more so than the Scissors, too much emphasis on form in the air can be dangerous. It is vitally important to remember that this is HIGH jumping and that at least 90 per cent of the jump is concerned with 'lift' or 'spring' at take-off'.

Howard Baker would have revelled in the technical advances that came too late for him. There was an over-riding regret about his high-jumping career that he was to express in later life. 'I used to enjoy acrobatics as a hobby, somersaults and all that', he was to muse at the age of 80, 'and I would have dearly liked to develop the Fosbury Flop style of jumping. It was not allowed in my day. We had to jump with our head above our buttocks. When the rule was changed it meant that much greater heights were possible'.

He would have been amused to learn that Lester Steers, the American who held the World record from 1941 to 1953 with the Straddle technique and was the first man to clear seven feet, albeit in an 'exhibition', never managed better than six feet with the Eastern Cut-Off style which was predominant in Howard Baker's day.

THE GAMES DRAW NEAR, BUT THE BRITISH MAKE DO WITH A HAPPY-GO-LUCKY APPROACH

The astuteness of the Liverpool Harriers stalwart, Tommy Blair, in espying young Howard Baker's athletic potential was quickly rewarded. With no experience of high-jumping other than in make-do school events, the teenager's debut in serious competition was an astonishing revelation of natural talent. Entered for the Northern Championships as a member of Marlborough Old Boys' Football Club, he and Clive Taylor put on a display of what the *Manchester Guardian* called 'fine jumping'. Taylor eventually won at 5ft 11in (1.80m), but Howard Baker cleared only an inch less to also beat the previous meeting record. A mere dozen or so Englishmen had ever jumped over a bar higher than the raw recruit from Liverpool did that day.

A month later Howard Baker beat Taylor, winning the first of his six AAA titles, though he needed no more than 5ft 9in (1.75m) to do so. Only one other Englishman had won the AAA high jump since 1897, all the other titles going to Ireland or the USA. Taylor, who was actually a member of the London-based club, Polytechnic Harriers, but clearly must have had a Northern birth qualification, was a highly versatile athlete who in 1914 would earn another AAA second place but at 100 yards, finishing less than a yard behind the renowned Olympic bronze-medallist and British record-holder, Willie Applegarth. The conditions at that 1910 meeting were most unhelpful as *The Times* reported that 'the heavy track and the waterlogged turf were against good times in the races and even fair performances in some of the field events'.

There was no reason for Howard Baker's victory to attract attention from the national press, other than perhaps because of his age. The winning height that he achieved was the lowest at the Championships since the year of his birth, 1892, with the exception of 1903 when the World record-holder for the long jump, Peter O'Connor, of Ireland, had been the only competitor. Yet the *Liverpool Daily Post & Mercury* could justifiably have made more of the achievement, especially considering that the only other placing of any consequence whatsoever in any of the events by a local athlete was fifth in the 220 yards. The newspaper's report merely mentioned in passing 'a fine accomplishment for one whose youth gives him ample time to 'train up' to better things'. His primitive 'Scissors' method of clearing the bar would certainly have attracted no comment, adverse or otherwise, as almost everybody jumped that way.

Having won the next year's Northern title at 5ft 7in (1.70m), Howard Baker found the weather to be much better for the AAA Championships, and his opposition was also of a different order, as in clearing 5ft 9in (1.75) again he finished third to Robert Pasemann, of Germany, who won at 6ft 0in (1.83), and one of the Leahy brothers, Tim, at 5ft 11in (1.80). *The Times* provided readers with a delightful description of the German's tireless versatility in simultaneously winning the pole-vault title: 'Pasemann, soaring with most beautiful ease, jumped 12ft and ran off unconcernedly to take his turn at the comparatively insignificant height to which pole-less man is limited'.

Despite his meteoric rise – literally so! – as a high jumper Howard Baker was not at all fully committed to athletics. In fact, it would be more accurate to describe him as a footballer/cricketer first and foremost. He was playing centre-half for the Marlborough Old Boys in one of the numerous League competitions in Liverpool and was already making an impression beyond the city boundaries while still in his teens. Two days before his 19th birthday in 1911 he was one of only three players from Liverpool in the Lancashire FA team of amateurs which played a match against London at Herne Hill. One of the others was the goalkeeper, Ted Taylor, of the Liverpool Balmoral club, who would soon afterwards turn professional with Oldham Athletic – with which club Howard Baker would coincidentally make his farewell League appearance in goal 18 years later – and would also be capped for England after World War One.

The Lancashire players were sent instructions beforehand to meet at Crewe Junction on the Friday evening to catch the 7.32 train for Euston, arriving at 10.45 – 'Dinner will be served in the Dining Car on leaving Crewe'. The kick-off was at 3.30 on the Saturday afternoon. They were told to make their own arrangements for the return journey and that a train would leave Euston at 5.55 that evening for Liverpool and another at 6.05 for Manchester, Bolton and Blackpool. Considering that the match would not have finished until after 5pm, it seemed wildly optimistic that any of the team could get washed and changed and then catch a train from South London across the city to Euston to arrive in time for their connection to the North.

During the summer of 1911 Howard Baker played 16 matches for Liverpool Cricket Club, and on the day that an 'Empire Athletics Festival', in which he would surely have had an interest, was taking place at Stamford Bridge to celebrate the coronation of King George V he was instead content to turn out for Liverpool CC's Second XI against Rock Ferry at Aigburth, and the following Saturday he was top scorer with 47, batting at No.6, in a total of 191 against Rainhill II. He was promoted to the first XI for four matches and merited his place with an innings of 77 on one appearance – and it is even suggested that he made a century on two occasions, though this may have been at a lower level of the game. Thus almost his every Saturday from May to the end of August would have been taken up with cricketing, and so he had no more than a handful of high-jump competitions to hone his skills. The Liverpool Cricket Club, many of whose players were clearly of independent means, ranged far and wide, including a midweek public schools' tour each season which took the players to Eton and Rugby.

Frustratingly, the coverage in the various Liverpool newspapers of the time of Baker's occasional athletics exploits is sparse, but a pattern that does emerge from the bare results which appeared in the columns of the *Daily Post and Mercury*, the *Courier* or the *Echo* is that throughout his high-jumping career he was to almost invariably win his contests in the North of England by very large margins, even when conceding as much as 12 inches (30cm) in handicap events, and that he seems to have regularly stopped jumping once he had cleared a height that satisfied him. It can only be supposed that maybe there were times when he was thinking about saving his energies for a game of cricket that evening or perhaps a swim in the Mersey!

The Olympic Games were not regarded in Britain in 1912 by either the public or the press with anything approaching the fervour which surrounds every form of preparation, however trivial, 100 years later. But that is not to say that journalists disregarded 'a good story' when they sensed one. *The Times*, for all its merited reputation as the 'top people's newspaper', was not averse to taking issue with the establishment when the circumstances were felt to be justified, and the British Olympic Association came under severe attack from the athletics correspondent, who remained anonymous, as was then the custom in the press, but was most probably Henry Perry Robinson, a versatile journalist who would later be knighted for his reporting of World War One. Presumably tipped off by a BOA member who attended the closed-door sessions, and writing in January, Perry Robinson accused the Association of being 'torn by internal dissension', adding scornfully that 'it is difficult to realise how such an unwieldy body can have come into existence'.

Two months later *The Times* enterprisingly sent Perry Robinson off to Stockholm to see how the arrangements for the Games were progressing, and his reports must have aroused mixed feelings among those of the British officials and athletes who read them. All the work was well in hand, which was good news, but the Swedish hosts were by no means confining their planning to the architect's drawing-board. Perry Robinson revealed that a highly qualified coach from the USA had long since been engaged to work with the prospective local competitors. It was, he said, 'in the nature of a revelation in comparison with our gay, happy-go-lucky ways'. The message was clear: anyone who imagined that Britannia still ruled the waves as far as sport was concerned might very soon be disillusioned.

Trials for the athletics events in Stockholm were staged by the AAA at Stamford Bridge on 18 May, which was inordinately early in the season as a true form-guide except for the Oxbridge men, but the deadline set by the Swedish Games organisers for Olympic entries was 6 June. Maybe, too, athletics promoters then as now had a sharp eye for such an attractive-sounding title as 'Olympic Trials' on the posters which would serve to draw the crowds in. In any case, it was a fairly academic matter because in those days up to 12 competitors per event were allowed for each country at the Games, and so the trials would have served no better purpose than to merely prove that all the possible contenders were reasonably fit. What was also demonstrated – if it needed demonstrating at all – was that the jumps and throws were lagging far, far behind the more popular events.

Altogether, 114 selections (some athletes named in two or more events) were announced two days later for the Olympic track races, the marathon, the cross-country and the walk. Yet there were only six men named for the field events: Howard Baker in the high jump, Sidney Abrahams in the hop step and jump (later to be re-titled, less accurately, as the triple jump), and four others for the hammer throw, including – most bizarrely – the Irish-born John Flanagan, who had won gold for the USA at the Games of 1900, 1904 and 1908 and had then returned to his native land but had given no indication of resuming competition on behalf of any country, let alone Great Britain. Howard Baker's high jumping and the discus throwing of an Oxford undergraduate, Walter Henderson, were the only field-events performances 'which would have been considered first class in America', reported *The Times*.

That same weekend the composition of the Great Britain football team for Stockholm was decided. Rather, it would be accurate to say the 'England' team as no Scots, Welsh or Irish players were considered. Amateur international matches between England and Scotland would not begin until 1926, and so direct comparisons could not be made there. Wales had lost all five matches played against England since 1908, but Ireland had won 3–2 in Belfast in 1910 and held England to 2–0 at Huddersfield in November of 1911 despite being reduced to 10 men, and therefore some of the Irish players certainly had a claim. Most notable among them were Belfast Celtic's goalkeeper, F. W. McKee, and their outside-left, Louis Bookman. McKee had been in the winning team against England, while both had played in the latter game. Bookman's father, originally named Buchalter, had been a Rabbi in Lithuania who had brought his family to Ireland in the 1890s to escape persecution, and Louis Bookman is believed to be the first Jewish footballer to gain international honours. He also played for Bradford City as an amateur and then for various other League clubs before and after World War One as well as representing Ireland at cricket on 14 occasions.

The two players in the GB team who had been gold-medallists in 1908 were an Oxford graduate, Arthur Berry, who now played for Oxford City, and the best known amateur footballer of his era, Vivian Woodward. The selectors, in justifying their deliberations, could further reasonably point to the fact that eight of their nominees had been in the England team which had beaten Denmark 3–0 at Park Royal, in West London, the previous October, and then Ireland the next month, and the Danes were reckoned to be potentially the most serious opposition in Stockholm.

Having already proved himself a centre-half of exceptional ability during the 1910–11 season when he was playing for Marlborough Old Boys, Howard Baker had then been the lone Liverpudlian in an England trial for uncapped amateurs in January of 1912 at Oxford which resulted in a 3–0 win for the South over the North, which probably put paid to his chances of Olympic consideration, though he was also the only player in the match ever to eventually progress to post-war international honours. The first-choice centre-half named in the Olympic team was Ted Hanney, of the Southern League club, Reading, who played only briefly in Stockholm, suffering injury in the first game, but turned professional with Manchester City soon afterwards for what was then the princely sum of £1,250 and appeared in 78 matches for the club before and after World War One.

However premature the timing, public interest had certainly been aroused by those 'Olympic Trials' for the athletes at Stamford Bridge because 10,000 spectators had turned up, and they no doubt particularly appreciated the high jump in which both Howard Baker and the Irish-born Tom O'Donahue, of Waterloo Harriers, which was another Liverpool club, cleared 5ft 11in (1.80m). Howard Baker then went over 6ft 0in (1.83m) in an 'exhibition' – which is how any height achieved after the event had been won was described in those days, though O'Donahue presumably also tried 6ft on this occasion. Howard Baker thus became only the fourth Englishman after the Honourable Marshall Brooks, George Rowdon and the Inter-Varsity winner of 1901, 1902 and 1903, Gerald Howard-Smith, to have cleared the 6ft height which still represented an achievement of real note in the event 25 years after Sir Montague Shearman had first written of the 'incredulity of foreigners' that such a thing was possible. The one other achievement to remark upon was by George Hutson, of Surrey AC, who ran 5000 metres in 15min 13⅗sec, which was within a dozen or so seconds of the current World record.

There was another encouragingly large crowd of 15,000 for the AAA Championships at Stamford Bridge on 22 June, and Howard Baker won in excellent weather conditions at 5ft 9in (1.75m) from the same Clive Taylor, of Polytechnic Harriers, who had placed second to him two years before. Howard Baker then had the bar set at 6ft 0in (1.83), which he also cleared. Maybe in doing so he was thinking ahead to the requirements of him in Stockholm so soon afterwards, but just as at the trials in May there had not been many other performances at the Championships to inspire confidence in British hopes for Stockholm. The calibre of the high-jump was, frankly, derisory – the winner, of course, excepted – as there were only four competitors in total. The 100 yards was won by a South African, George Patching, a full 1½ yards ahead of Britain's best sprinter, Willie Applegarth, of Polytechnic Harriers. A German, Hanns Braun, had taken the 880 yards title for the third time in four years. Maybe the win by George Hutson in the then standard event of four miles promised something, but even that was 23 seconds or so slower than the Championship record for this event.

One of the few other home athletes to impress was another of those exponents of a 'Cinderella' field event. A farmer from the West of Scotland, Tom Nicolson, won his sixth hammer-throw title since 1903 – and would be Scottish champion every year from 1902 to 1924, by which time he would be 44 years old. He had also placed fourth at the London Olympics. Another winner with an even more extensive pedigree than Nicolson's was an Irishman, Dennis Horgan, taking his 13th victory in the shot since 1893, but he declined the invitation to go to Stockholm with the British team, which could have been a matter of political conscience or simply the fact that at the age of 41 he did not relish his chances against the best of the Americans. If politics was, indeed, the reason for his decision not to go then it reflected a fairly recent change of heart because he had won the silver medal for Great Britain in 1908.

Further Irish Olympic absentees were another of the Leahy brothers, Tim, who did not present himself for the AAA Championships that year, though he had been second ahead of Howard Baker in 1911, and Percy Kirwan, who had won the AAA long-jump title for the previous three years and at his best would have got close to an Olympic medal. Maybe Kirwan, for one, shared Horgan's aversion to competing under the British flag. There was no triple jump, discus or javelin at the AAA Championships, and so no form at all to go on. The nadir was reached in the pole vault where the only competitor was the ironically named A.E.O. Conquest, of Herne Hill Harriers, who must have been pleasantly surprised to win the one and only title of his career so easily at the age of 36. It was too late in life and too low a height, though, for Arthur Conquest to aspire to Olympian standards.

Despite the May trials the British preparations for those Games seem to have been characteristically perfunctory, if the comments of the correspondent for *The Times* are to be believed once more – 'gay, happy-go-lucky', to recall the terms used forebodingly in the columns of the same newspaper earlier in the year. Adopting a sartorial theme, the writer darkly remarked: 'Many of the British team have had no more vital communication with the advisory board than is necessary to provide a suitable costume in which to run at Stockholm. Clothes may make the man, but they do not make the athlete. Might not some of the scanty funds that have been spent on the making of the clothes have been properly diverted to the making of the athletes?'

The criticism was almost certainly fully justified. It's a fact that the sporting bodies involved had given some attention to ensuring that their Olympic competitors would be better prepared than they had been in London in 1908, but it is questionable as to whether their initiatives were in any way effective. As Peter Lovesey was to point out in his centenary history of the AAA, published in 1979, 'strenuous efforts were made to rehabilitate British athletics before the next Olympics' in response to the disconcerting superiority of the USA on that previous occasion, but 'unhappily for British hopes other nations had learned the lessons of the London Olympics and trained assiduously for Stockholm'. In theory the appointment of a 'Chief Athletics Adviser' to the AAA had seemed like a good idea, but the timing was naive. This had happened only six months before the Olympic athletics began, and it was completely unrealistic for the authorities to believe that the man in question, Fred Parker, from London Athletic Club, could achieve much of value in the short time remaining.

Making the best of it, Parker put forward the idea – revolutionary for that era – that the Government should come forward with some funding for the Olympic team, but he must have been well aware that even that would not have an effect on the level of performances until the Games planned for 1916. He probably realised that there was no chance of his proposal being accepted, but he was of an independent frame of mind which stemmed from the fact that he was by no means obliged to the AAA for a living. Aged 48, he was the Lambeth-born son of a banker and the brother of a stockbroker. When the Stamford Bridge ground had been rebuilt in 1905 as a sports stadium for the masses he had been described 'as the driving force behind this visionary scheme', and it was to become the home of Chelsea Football Club and of British athletics from 1909 onwards as the venue for the AAA Championships and numerous other meetings. It was said admiringly of Parker that 'his head was in the commercial World'. He knew, far better than the AAA hierarchy, that only a significant financial input would bring Olympic success, and even that had to be regarded as a long-term investment. He would have been equally at home a century later advising the masters of UK Athletics, the eventual successor to the AAA as ruling body, to the same effect.

The priorities which prevailed in British athletics in 1912 were confirmed by the fact that only eight of the 67 athletes who were finally selected for Stockholm were jumpers or throwers. The demographic spread of the team-members makes interesting reading: 27 of them (40 per cent of the total) came from clubs in and around London, headed by nine from Herne Hill Harriers and eight from Polytechnic Harriers; 13 came from the North of England, of which all but three were distance-runners or walkers (the exceptions being Alan Patterson, of Salford Harriers, at 400 and 800 metres and Howard Baker and Tom O'Donahue in the high jump); 11 were from Oxford or Cambridge Universities; Ireland and Scotland each provided three; and there was just one each from the Southern counties of England and from the Midlands. Thus the contribution by Oxbridge to the British team represented just over 16 per cent of the total.

The Scottish hammer-man, Tom Nicolson, was not available for the team because he had farming duties which needed his attention, and that was a pity because he, too, could have been a medallist. His winning performance at the AAA Championships would have been comfortably good enough for second place in Stockholm. W.E.B. Henderson, whose discus throw at the May trials had been remarked upon by *The Times* had no chance to prove himself again as his event would not even be recognised by the AAA for another two years, but he was selected for Stockholm nonetheless. Familiarly known at Oxford as 'Herkers' because of an apparent resemblance to the Greek god, Hercules, Walter Henderson was to have a long and fruitful athletics career, competing at the AAA Championships from 1900 to 1923, with high placings in four different events. There were not, of course, any Olympic athletics events for women in 1912, and they would have to wait another 16 years for recognition (though even then Great Britain did not join in), but there would be competition in Stockholm for women in swimming (27 entries for the 100 metres freestyle) and in diving and tennis.

Neither Tom O'Donahue nor Tim Carroll had been among the paltry entry of four competitors who had turned up for the AAA Championships. Carroll was a member of the Royal Irish Constabulary, which was Ireland's main police force, and maybe his duties had kept him away from the AAA meeting, but he was also affiliated to one of the pre-eminent London clubs, Polytechnic Harriers, and apparently had no qualms about representing Britain. O'Donahue's selection had no real justification other than that he was one of the few field-events athletes to have achieved anything of note at the trials back in May. At the Northern Championships on 1 June, which were held across the Mersey from Liverpool at the Tower Athletic Grounds, New Brighton, Howard Baker beat O'Donahue very easily with a record 5ft 11½in (1.81) to the Irishman's moderate 5ft 6in (1.68).

Presumably Howard Baker would have known little about who exactly he would face in competition in Stockholm, but he would remember well enough his versatile German conqueror for the AAA title the previous year, Robert Pasemann, and could reasonably have anticipated that the USA would be strongly represented, having won the Olympic title in 1896, 1900, 1904 and 1908. Even with so many places available, the USA's Amateur Athletic Union had still held three regional trials for the team, and the high-jump results would have made daunting reading for Howard Baker, had he been aware of them:

Western trials – 1 George Horine 6ft 7in (2.01), 2 Edward Beeson 6ft 4½in (1.94). Horine's jump beat the World record of 6ft 6⅛ (1.98) which he himself had set two months before.

Central trials – 1 Alma Richards 6ft 1in (1.85), 2 Earl Palmer 5ft 11in (1.80).

Eastern trials – 1 Egon Erickson 6ft 2⅝in (1.89), 2 Harold Enright, John Johnstone 6ft 1½in (1.87).

Thus six Americans had jumped higher – and three of them very much higher – than Howard Baker had done at the AAA Championships, and the World record of Horine's would assuredly have seemed totally out of reach. Anyone outside the USA who had seen these results might reasonably have concluded that all the medals in Stockholm were already accounted for. As it happens, a future World record-holder, Ed Beeson, did not go to Stockholm and four others who missed the US trials were added to the team, but as these recruits included the superlative all-rounder, Jim Thorpe, who had high-jumped 6ft 5in (1.96) in June, the US contingent was if anything strengthened, not weakened.

The entire US team would, of course, be well prepared and highly competitive, as they had already demonstrated to the discomfiture of their British hosts at the London Games of 1908, and it would have been chastening for Willie Applegarth and his fellow British sprinters, for example, when they learned that Fred Ramsdell, the American who had beaten them all for the AAA 100 yards and 220 yards titles in both 1910 and 1911 had not even qualified for his country's team. Even more surprising to those Great Britain athletes who were regular readers of *The Times* would have been the discovery that the Swedish competitors chosen for the Games had been assembled in Stockholm ever since April. A highly experienced American coach, Ernest Hjertberg, had been appointed as early as 1910 to advise the athletes, and Fred Parker, the AAA appointee so late in the day, could have rightly mused that he had long since been left at the starting-line.

And so the British contingent – the athletes, the footballers and the champions of a dozen other sporting disciplines – set off for Stockholm. Notably absent from his figurative position at the helm was the formidable Lord Desborough, who had delegated the on-board duties to other officers of his much disparaged British Olympic Association. Baron Desborough was otherwise engaged at the Henley Royal Regatta and would not arrive in Stockholm until four days after the Olympic athletics had begun!

As to the manner born, educated at Harrow and Oxford, where he had been a fine miler, his Lordship relished a challenge. He had rowed in an eight-oared boat across the English Channel, had twice swum the waters at the foot of Niagara Falls, had shot big game in Africa and India, and had climbed five Alpine peaks in eight days. Now, though, national pride was at stake, and this was not an issue which could readily be resolved by sending a gun-boat. Instead, a passenger-steamer sailing serenely into Swedish waters, its decks and saloons crowded with those 'happy-go-lucky' sportsmen and a demure minority of sportswomen, would have to defend the nation's honour.

Chivalrous contests and ludicrous contrasts at a Games to save the Olympic ideal

Baron Pierre de Coubertin, founding father of the modern Olympic movement, had expressed every confidence that the Games of 1912 would be a success, but he could have been excused if a note of desperation had crept into his voice. Stockholm had been chosen as the host city three years before, and that was considered quite enough advance notice in that era to have everything ready in time, but the evidence of history was not on the side of the eager Swedes.

The Olympic Games had been revived in 1896, and there had been four others since, including an interim 10th anniversary edition in Athens which was the only one to have turned out to be the amicably competitive celebration for which Baron de Coubertin had hoped. The Games of 1900 and 1904, in Paris and St Louis respectively, had been disjointed sideshows drawn out over many months. Rome had originally agreed to be hosts in 1908 but had withdrawn late in the day because of economic problems and London had stepped in, only for their Games to be stigmatised by constant squabbles between the British and American athletics officials, culminating in a farcical 400 metres, in which a lone Briton, Wyndham Halswelle, was required to 'walk over' after one of his US opponents had been disqualified in the original race and the two other finalists, also both American, had withdrawn from the re-run in solidarity.

The selection of Stockholm had been made at the International Olympic Committee meeting of 1909, and Baron de Coubertin's speech on that occasion had maybe come across as a shade too dogmatic for some of the delegates. His recommendations must have sounded more like a set of instructions, as he insisted, 'It will be necessary to avoid attempting to copy the Olympic Games of London. The next Olympics must not have such a character. They must not be so competitive. There was altogether too much in London. The Games must be kept more purely athletic. They must be more dignified, more discreet, more in accordance with classic and artistic requirements, more intimate, and above all less expensive'. High hopes, indeed.

To give the Swedish organisers their due, they took the Baron's sentiments to heart, but their proposals fell on deaf ears. Reducing the programme to the four sports of athletics, gymnastics, swimming and wrestling was a drastic measure which was bound to upset those with vested interests in so many other Olympic activities. By the time that the schedule had been debated by the IOC assembly the original eight days of competition suggested by the Swedes had swelled to 78, from 5 May to 22 July, and the number of sports from four to 14. The budget had increased six-fold. Such uncontrolled inflation would, of course, become a familiar experience for Olympic organisers over the next 100 years.

The IOC's 44 members from 31 countries included 11 Counts, five Barons (one of them Britain's Baron Desborough), two Princes and a Marquis, and they all had their varying obligations to those that they represented – though 'represented' is not the appropriate term because they were members by invitation from the existing IOC committee-members without recourse to any form of democratic election by their respective nations. Thus it was that cycling, equestrianism, fencing, football, modern pentathlon (at the recommendation of Baron de Coubertin, so he only had himself to blame), rowing, shooting, tennis (indoors and out), water polo and yachting all found their way on to the schedule. Oh, and by the way, there were also to be demonstrations of baseball, horse-racing, pony-trotting, Icelandic wrestling, caber-tossing and quoit-throwing to fill in the occasional spare hour or so.

King Gustav V formally opened the Games on the morning of Saturday 6 July, although by then a number of gold medals had already been decided, and the British Olympic Council had its part to play in the formalities at the opening because the Reverend Robert de Courcy Laffan, present in his capacity not only as an IOC member but as secretary of the British Olympic Council and manager of his country's team, had composed a prayer specially for the occasion which rather neatly drew sporting allusions into a theological framework:

'Thou hast called Thy children hither from all quarters of the Earth, from the East and from the West, from the North and from the South, to show forth in frank and chivalrous contests Thy sacred gifts of manly prowess, and to teach and learn by turns the secrets of manly strength and manly endurance'.

It was not quite so universal a spread as the Reverend's grandiloquent references to 'East' and 'West' might have suggested. There were 28 countries which had sent teams to Stockholm, which was five more than there had been in London, and these included Australia and New Zealand (combined), Chile, Egypt, Japan and Turkey, but Africa was almost entirely unrepresented, apart from the all-white South African team, and Asia scarcely so. The Stockholm organisers claimed a figure of 3,282 competitors, but this included more than a thousand gymnasts, many of whom were confined to giving displays and did not take part in the official medal-earning events, and the more realistic figure was 2,500 or so, of which no more than 57 were women.

The Olympic Stadium in Stockholm still stands in its original form and has an ambiance all of its own with splendid arches, towers and sculptures, built in the style of a Swedish mediaeval castle, which gives it more of the appearance of a National Trust site of historical value than a sports venue, but it is no mere monument to a bygone age and is still very much in regular use a century later for one of the annual Grand Prix meetings staged by the sport's ruling body, the International Association of Athletics Federations (IAAF). The track for the Games of 1912 had been an odd 383 metres in circumference but has long since been lengthened by that vital 17 metres to conform to international standard and 83 World records have been set there over the years. No one in 1912 could have imagined in their wildest dreams 5000 metres being run in 13min 16.6sec by Ron Clarke, of Australia, as happened in 1966; or a high jump of 2.42m by Patrik Sjöberg, of Sweden, in 1987; or 800 metres in 1min 41.73sec by Wilson Kipketer, a Danish-naturalised Kenyan, in 1997.

Of the respective World records in 1912 for those three athletics events mentioned above two were set at the Olympic Games themselves that year: 5000 metres in 14min 36.8sec by the Finn, Hannes Kolehmainen, and 800 metres in 1min 51.9sec by Ted Meredith, of the USA. The advance of 80 seconds or so at 5000 metres from Kolehmainen to Clarke represents about 1¼ laps of the Stockholm track, as it was in 1912, and the difference of a shade over 10 seconds at 800 metres between Meredith and Kipketer is equivalent to about 70 metres. The height achieved by Sjöberg three-quarters of a century on would be more than 40 centimetres above anything that anyone had been capable of by 1912.

The athletics events began in the afternoon following the opening ceremony. Sessions were to be held morning and afternoon, but it was rather in the nature of a multi-sports carnival because gymnastics and wrestling would be taking place simultaneously at the same venue. On the opening day the one athletics final was the javelin throw in which to the crowd's delight a Swede, Eric Lemming, beat the World record-holder from Finland, Juho Saaristo. This was an entirely predictable result as Lemming had also won the gold in 1906 and 1908 and Scandinavians were totally dominant in the event. Lemming had set 13 successive World records from 1899 onwards until Saaristo had surpassed him the previous May to become the first man to throw more than 60 metres. To set that performance in context, the World record had advanced by 1984 to 104.80 metres, and the nervous authorities then hastened to change the specifications of the implement to reduce the distances thrown and thus avoid the risk of spectators being speared.

None of these performances by Lemming and Saaristo had been officially ratified for the simple reason that the World governing body, under its original title of the International Amateur Athletics Federation, was not to be founded until 1913, and by then Lemming had regained the record. Lemming achieved 62.32m a couple of months after the Games, and such was the unforgiveable lack of interest in the event in Britain that the country's best performance at the time was not much more than half that distance. Nevertheless, the holder of it, Frederick Kitching, could not be faulted for his enthusiasm. Originally from Darlington, in County Durham, he had competed in the standing long jump at the 1908 Olympics and then become one of the very first Britons to attempt to specialise in the javelin, though handicapped by having to throw an unbalanced and over-flexible implement with a heavy metal head and a thin whip-chord binding which cut into his hands.

Then, thanks to the efforts of one of the very few British coaches with any interest in the field events, F.A.M. Webster, who was himself to become a very capable exponent of the event, superior-quality Finnish birch-wood javelins were made available, and Kitching improved modestly to 143ft 3in (43.66m) in 1914, but that was the end of his sporting career as he was killed in action during World War One. Webster, or Captain Webster as he preferred to be known after the war, was to figure very prominently in British athletics for decades to come, and Howard Baker would be one of the athletes to benefit from his advice. Yet not even the visionary Webster could possibly have imagined in his wildest dreams that one day (5 August 1984, if you really want to be precise) a Briton would win the javelin silver medal at the Olympics – he would be David Ottley. Or that on a later date (2 July 1990) another of the World records to be broken in the very same Stockholm stadium where the 1912 Olympics had taken place would be in the javelin by a second Briton, Steve Backley, with a throw of almost 90 metres.

As for a British woman winning an Olympic javelin title, as Tessa Sanderson was to do in 1984, or breaking the World record, as Fatima Whitbread would do two years later…well, that would have been laughed to scorn in 1912 as the fantasy of a feverish mind. Women throwing the javelin? I say, chaps, gels throwing things about! What on earth would our dear Queen Victoria have said about that?

Confusingly for modern followers of the sport who care to look back to the 1912 Stockholm Olympic results, there was another javelin competition at the Games three days later in which the throwers used each arm in turn to propel the implement, and the gold medal was decided on aggregate, won by Saaristo with a better throw than he had managed in the earlier event. There were also to be competitions for the standing high jump and standing long jump and for the shot and discus using each arm in turn – all of which were regarded as conventional events then but were living on borrowed time, as they were never to appear in the Games again.

The qualifying round for the high jump was at 9 o'clock on the following morning, Sunday 7 July, and thus involved a most unaccustomed prompt start for the athletes concerned, though that was nothing compared to what was being demanded of the road-racing cyclists. Their event had begun at 2am and involved the 123 riders going off at two-minute intervals because the police would not allow them for safety reasons to all start together. Not only that, but a distance of 320 kilometres had to be covered round and round the shores of Lake Malar! The winner was a South African, Rudolph Lewis, who pedalled away at 2.02am and reached the finish 10 hours 42 minutes and 38 seconds later – in other words at around 12.45 in the afternoon, long after the high-jump contestants had completed their labours. A valiant Briton, Fred Grubb, whose preference was for mere one-hour track races, took the silver medal some nine minutes behind Lewis.

It was not only the earliness of the hour that would have been a novel experience for many of the high jumpers. Sunday sport was a commonplace happening in continental Europe but virtually unheard of in Britain and the USA, and as a concession to the sensibilities of those countries the Games organisers had arranged the timing of the events so that competitors, officials and spectators could attend church services if they wished. The fact of having to qualify at all would also place demands on athletes such as the British high-jump trio, accustomed as they were to intimate and relatively brief competitions in which only three or four men might be involved. Fortunately, neither the USA nor even the Swedish hosts had exercised their right to have a full complement of 12 contestants, but there were still to be 27 athletes taking part, all of them from Europe or the USA, including an aristocratic duo from Hungary, as follows:

Finland – Arvo Laine.

France – Georges André, André Labat.

Germany – Hans Liesche, Franz Röhr.

Great Britain – Tim Carroll, Benjamin Howard Baker, Tom O'Donahue.

Hungary – Count Lajos Ludinszky, Baron Iván Wardener.

Italy – Alfredo Pagani.

Norway – Olav Aarnes, Otto Monsen.

Sweden – Paulus Af Uhr, Gösta Hallberg, Karl-Axel Küllerstrand, Ragnar Mattson, Richard Sjöberg.

USA – Jervis Burdick, Harold Enright, Egon Erickson, Harry Grumpelt, George Horine, John Johnstone, Wesley Oler, Alma Richards, Jim Thorpe.

Apart from the impressive results in their trials, three of the US squad had won national titles in the past, and Grumpelt and Johnstone had both cleared 6ft 3in (1.91) in doing so, but again this sort of detail would almost certainly have not been known to their opponents. *The New York Times* confidently predicted a sweeping success; their headline to a Games preview reading 'American Jumpers Lead The World', followed by a sub-heading to the effect of 'Uncle Sam's Olympic Candidates All Capable of 6 Feet 2 Inches or Better'. It was further reported that, to a man, their high jumpers employed the lay-out technique, except for Horine, with his innovative Western Roll, and Richards, who cleared the bar 'with his knees drawn up to his chin'.

What Howard Baker would presumably have been aware of regarding the opposition he would face was that the Frenchman, Georges André, had won the silver medal at the 1908 Games and ought therefore to be regarded as a strong challenger. One of the titled Hungarian competitors, Count Ludinszky, had studied at Cambridge and had tied for first place in the Inter-Varsity high jump of 1909. Howard Baker's conqueror in the previous year's AAA Championships, Robert Pasemann, was also in Stockholm with the German team but restricting himself to the pole vault and long jump later in the week.

Grumpelt, aged 27, was by several years the oldest man in the competition. Liesche, Howard Baker, Küllerstrand and Johnstone were all aged 20, and Küllerstrand (born 1 March 1892) was the youngest by a fortnight over Howard Baker. Athletics, in those far-off amateur days, was a leisure-time recreation for young men, many of them at university, to be abandoned as soon as a living had to be earned. Only the craggy weights men – the shot putters and hammer throwers – and the grizzled marathon runners tended to be older.

The Games organisers had thoughtfully provided three separate landing-pits set out alongside each other inside the curve of the track near to the start of the 100 metres, and so the qualifying round was conveniently held in simultaneous groups. The AAA had only recently conceded that 'a pit of sand or soft earth may be dug for competitors to alight in', and so the facilities in Stockholm would have been a pleasant surprise for Howard Baker and his colleagues compared with what they were used to. The target for the competitors was 1.83m, equivalent to 6ft, and everyone clearing that height would go through to the final. The admirably comprehensive English-language official report of the Games contains a wealth of information about the track and field events, and we are told, for instance, of the high-jump qualifications that 'in consequence of the practical way in which the jumping-pits had been arranged the round was soon finished'.

Everything went well for Howard Baker and he was described as 'the best man in the first group, as he managed to clear every height at the first time of asking', thus equalling his personal best. It was also said, somewhat contradictorily, that 'the Americans, of course, proved themselves the best men, but Horine was clearly not in his finest form'. In fact, though Horine managed to clear the required height, three of the US jumpers and the fancied Frenchman, André, failed to do so, as Burdick and Enright could go no higher than 1.80 and Oler and André no better than 1.70, but Howard Baker would surely have noted that in the third qualifying group both Richards and Thorpe were impeccable, 'clearing 1.83m with ease', according to the Games report. The 11 who qualified were Liesche (Germany), Carroll and Howard Baker (GB), Baron Wardener (Hungary), Küllerstrand (Sweden) and Erickson, Grumpelt, Horine, Johnstone, Richards and Thorpe (all USA). The third Briton, O'Donahue, was unable to get over any height and was the first to have been eliminated, though in any case he would have had to have achieved a personal best to have advanced to the final.

Incidentally, also among the non-qualifiers was the Norwegian, Olav Augunsen Aarnes, who nevertheless in the fullness of time set some sort of record by living to the age of 103, dying in 1992. Yet even he was outdone by another Stockholm Olympic competitor. A Finnish gymnast, Viktor Kivenhiemo, who qualified as a doctor of philosophy and had attained the age of 105 before his death in 1995!

The 10,000 metres heats had got under way while the high jumping was in progress, and discouragingly for Britain five of their seven entrants failed to get through to the final. Maybe the thought occurred to the British team management that if so many of the much vaunted distance-men were falling by the wayside what hope did that hold out for mere high jumpers? In the afternoon there was no better news. The USA took the first three places in the 100 metres and not a single Briton reached the final. Nor were there any Britons in the pentathlon, in which the 26 contestants were required to complete the long jump, javelin, 200 metres, discus and 1500 metres in rather less than 4½ hours during the course of the afternoon. The versatile Jim Thorpe, having already qualified for the high-jump final, won every one of the five pentathlon events except the javelin to take the gold medal by an enormous margin, though the tale of his participation at the Games and its repercussions was by no means to end there, as shall be related in due course.

The high-jump final began at 3 o'clock on the afternoon of the following day, Monday, and to further regale the spectators wrestling bouts had already been going on for an hour and would continue until 5pm, while the 800 metres final would be at 3.30 and the tug-of-war, the 4 x 100 metres relay heats and the 10,000 metres final would take place from 4.15 onwards. To complete the varied programme of entertainment the 22 members of the Norwegian men's gymnastics team would perform their exercises for an hour from 3 o'clock, to be immediately followed by the Danish contingent.

The high-jump proceeded smoothly enough through the first three heights, all 11 men clearing 1.60m, 1.70 and 1.75, with only a single failure, and that was by Thorpe, which was hardly surprising as he must still have been feeling the effects of his multiple efforts of the day before. At 1.80 there were first-time failures by Richards, Grumpelt (both somewhat surprisingly), Küllerstrand, Wardener and – most disappointingly – Howard Baker and Carroll. This height was equivalent to 5ft 8¾in and ought to have been well within the grasp of the two Britons. Carroll soon made amends by getting over at the second attempt, as did all of the others…except Howard Baker. A third and final attempt at any height is always a harrowing experience, and even more so when you are the only man in that situation and your 10 rivals are keenly looking on, but really ought not to have presented any major problems. Yet it did. Howard Baker failed again, and his Olympic high-jump competition was over. Even the official report, having singled Howard Baker out for praise in the qualifying round, noted quizzically that he now 'did not seem to be in very good form'.

Of course, these things happen, and particularly so at an Olympic Games where everything is different to the more common-or-garden competitions – packed grandstands of spectators looking on, a weight of expectation on your shoulders, national pride and team obligations at stake, a host of press reporters with pens poised to heap praise or retribution on their subjects. So much can go wrong when you are hundreds of miles away from home in a different country, eating different food, living in close proximity with a couple of thousand or so others equally pent-up. The fact is that even though he had twice been AAA champion, Howard Baker had the experience of no more than half-a-dozen serious high-jump competitions in his young life and it was not enough to cope at this Olympian level.

What a daunting sight the sextet of confident and skilled Americans must have made, all of them well coached and technically proficient, any one of whom was good enough to become the Olympic champion! Howard Baker was still using the primitive Scissors technique of his Marlborough Road schooldays and was accustomed to winning events at the height which he was now attempting only so that he could stay in the competition. In the later years of his life he did not talk publicly of his Olympic experiences, and so we shall never know why he did not do anywhere near as well in Stockholm as he might have hoped for. But then perhaps he could not fathom the reason either.

As the competition continued it rather seemed for a while as if the Americans, for all their strength in numbers, might be beaten. By the time that the bar had reached 1.91m only Richards, Horine and Liesche had survived, and when the Americans had two failures and Liesche sailed over 'with the greatest confidence' it looked as if the German would win, but then at the first try at 1.93m Richards cleared comfortably ('with a couple of inches to spare', according to the reporter for *The New York Times*) and Liesche failed. After a second failure, Liesche apparently waited nine minutes while the military band played victory anthems before making his final jump, and only then did so at the insistence of the officials. By modern rules he might well have been disqualified for exceeding the time limit, but he knocked the bar down anyway and the gold medal went to Richards.

The result of the high-jump final was as follows: 1 Alma Richards (USA) 1.93m, 2 Hans Liesche (Germany) 1.91, 3 George Horine (USA) 1.89, 4 Egon Erickson (USA) 1.87, 5 Jim Thorpe (USA) 1.87, 6 Harry Grumpelt (USA) 1.85, 7 John Johnstone (USA) 1.85, 8 Karl-Axel Küllerstrand (Sweden) 1.83, 9 Tim Carroll (GB), Baron Iván Wardener (Hungary) 1.80, 11 Benjamin Howard Baker (GB) 1.75.

In contrast to the lean and lithe Liesche – 6ft 2in (1.88m) in height and weighing no more than 10st 8lb (67kg), a perfect build for a high jumper – the new champion was not the most appealing looking of athletes, tall but ungainly in build. What was of more importance, though, was that his technique was effective. He was aged 22, a Mormon, and a student at Brigham Young University, in Utah, and his style was vividly described as that of 'one who goes straight for the centre, and using full face at it with knees doubled up and feet close together, flies the bar like a good horse would'. He was a typical product of American inventiveness, having been spotted at university playing basketball by a coach, Eugene L. Roberts, and persuaded to have an attempt at a 6ft bar, which he promptly cleared.

Richards qualified as a lawyer after World War One but chose to teach instead and years later wrote of the closing stages of the Stockholm high jump: 'I was representing our country against a fine athlete from another country. I felt weak and as if the whole world was on my shoulders. As I walked back to make my jump I said a prayer and asked God to give me strength, and if it was alright that I should win that I would do my best to set a good example all the days of my life'. It should be noted that the remainder of his athletics career was not as blameless as he had promised the Almighty in the heat of the Olympic moment because he was to be temporarily suspended by the US authorities in 1915 for claiming excessive expenses – the sum was $20.79.

He died in 1963 and when in 2002 the Winter Olympic Games came to Salt Lake City, in his native state of Utah, a local newspaperman found a lady aged in her 90s who had been a neighbour as a child of Richards and she fondly recalled, 'He was just a lanky farm boy running across the fields and jumping over the fences'. There was an Irish connection for Richards — nicknamed 'Pat' and later to become US national decathlon champion — as a grandmother of his had been born in County Down, and even Jim Thorpe, who was a Sac-and-Fox Indian by birth, had an Irish connection in his mixed heritage through one of his grandfathers.

The fact that George Horine was relatively unsuccessful in Stockholm would surely have caused other jumpers and their coaches to doubt whether his innovative Western Roll method, by which he raised his centre of gravity by a significant margin in clearing the bar on his side, was any real improvement on what they already knew. They were wrong, of course, but only time would tell them that. It was said that Horine had been ill during the transatlantic crossing and had then expended too much energy demonstrating his new technique to intrigued athletes and coaches before the Games began, and it would have been interesting to know what the consensus of opinion was among those seeing the Western Roll for the first time. Horine dropped out of competition after the Olympics, and when he returned four years later there were some misgivings expressed even in his home country, as *The New York Times* reported: 'There are plenty of critics who contend that his system of rolling across the bar after he has raised himself to the stick makes him an acrobat rather than a high jumper. Yet the fact remains that some of the World's best authorities have pronounced Horine's style faultless'.

In British terms at these Olympic Games of 1912, the outcome of the high jump was actually no bad result for Carroll and Howard Baker as the only better field-event placing by a fellow team-member would come from another Irishman, Denis Carey, who was sixth in the hammer. However, Howard Baker was not alone among the British team in suffering disappointment that Monday afternoon in Stockholm because there were no Britons in the 800 metres final, in which the USA again took all three medals, and one of the British pair in the 10,000 metres did not finish and the other did not even start as the first of what would be a legion of 'Flying Finns', Hannes Kolehmainen, who was also to win the 5,000 metres, came home for the gold medal with more than half-a-lap to spare.

The most unexpected result of all was the eclipse of the tug-of-war team of hefty City of London policemen, defending the title they had won in 1908, by an even more powerful phalanx of Stockholm constables, who surely then deserved to be excused crowd-control duties to celebrate their success. The standing long jump had been held in the morning and went to a Greek ahead of two brothers from the USA, with the two Britons in 14th and last places of the 19 competitors. Unnecessarily, there were six heats of the 4 x 100 metres relay, though only two countries needed to be eliminated, and the quartets of Canada, the USA, Great Britain and Sweden each in turn solemnly ran round on their own to qualify.

Not at all surprised by this turn of events was the man from *The Times*. Of the high jump he had said beforehand that 'at present the United States seems certain to win', and on the Tuesday morning he returned to what was by now a familiar theme of his of Anglo-American rivalry: 'The man who is to beat the Americans this year must not only be a great athlete, but he must have undergone a thorough and scientific course of training, and in this the Americans are, of course, pre-eminent. Not even the Swedes (and they have an American trainer) have had anything like the care lavished on them that has been spent on the Americans. Partly it is, of course, a result of the American genius for specialising and concentration on whatever may be the immediate thing in hand, whether in sport or in business. The contrast with our happy-go-lucky ways and the ineffectiveness of our British Olympic Council is almost ludicrous'.

Yet it was not just the Council worthies who came in for criticism. 'One of the 'stars' among the British athletes told me that so far not one word had been said to him by anybody on the subject of training', related the correspondent of *The Times*, only to conclude, 'He added that he would have been extremely annoyed if anybody had spoken to him. Such conditions and such a mental attitude are unthinkable from the American point of view'. So there you have it: apparently no interest by the British management in giving coaching guidance and no interest by the athletes in receiving it. If this was indeed the case, it was no wonder that the medal successes were few and far between.

The representative of *The Times* in Stockholm was certainly Henry Perry Robinson, because his name appears in the list of accredited journalists published in the official Games report. His social background placed him very much among the English establishment, but his media career had been, and would continue to be, an unusually varied one. Born in 1859, he had been educated at Westminster School and Christ Church, Oxford, and had then gone to the USA, where he had stayed for 20 years, working mainly as a magazine editor. He returned to London in 1900 and joined *The Times* as a news correspondent. There was nothing in his past experience to suggest that he would become particularly interested in athletics, but it seems apparent that behind the habitual cloak of anonymity under which he and his colleagues wrote in those days he was also the author of the great majority of the articles which subsequently appeared in his newspaper evaluating the British team's performance, criticising the British Olympic Association and its Council, and proposing reforms for the future.

Perry Robinson was to be one of the five journalists approved by the British government as war correspondents in 1914 for which he received his knighthood and dubbed himself Sir Harry Perry Robinson. He had been the author of a book in 1908 entitled *The Twentieth Century American*, expressing an Englishman's view of the USA, which was very favourably reviewed by *The New York Times*, and he had a clear vision of what he saw as his journalistic role. He once wrote, 'The English newspaper speaks to the educated class, trusting, not always with justification, that opinion once formulated in that class will be communicated downward and accepted by the people'. Perry Robinson contributed to an immensely significant upward turn in the fortunes of *The Times*, the circulation of which had sunk to 38,000 in 1908 but recovered dramatically to 278,000 during the first tenure of office by a renowned editor, Geoffrey Dawson, from 1912 onwards.

There was an altogether different aspect of the high-jump competition, of which there was no mention at the time but which was to surface many, many years later. During his taped interview with the sports historian, John Bromhead, 70 years afterwards, Howard Baker related an intriguing tale about his Stockholm experience: 'I was sitting down waiting to jump and I saw that one of the Americans had extremely nice jumping shoes. I asked him if I could look at them, but he didn't want to show them to me. Well, it turns out that underneath the heel spikes there was a little spring! I've forgotten his name, but he didn't do very well'. As there were nine US competitors in the event it's not worth conjecturing as to who the miscreant might have been and what advantage – if any – he might have gained and Baker did not say how he came to learn about the device.

Unconventional shoes which were deemed to provide some sort of excessive aid to their wearers were to figure more prominently in high-jumping folklore many years later when an athlete from the USSR – not yet in existence as a political entity in 1912 – beat the World record in 1957 with the benefit of a three-centimetre thick extra sole on his takeoff shoe. The rules regarding shoe manufacture were quickly changed to ban the Soviet innovation, though there is no note that the international authorities had ever put their foot down in an earlier era regarding springs.

Dave Terry, one of Britain's leading sports historians, who has made a special study of the evolution of rules in various disciplines, points out that the first set of regulations for international athletics was not formulated until 1914, and neither those nor the revised version of 1921 made any reference to footwear, other than for the tug-of-war, which was then considered part of the athletics programme, and would be so for another 60 or so years at the AAA Championships. He has also noted from the photographs taken of the high-jump competition in Stockholm that the Americans all appeared to have built-up heels to their shoes, with spikes inserted there as well as on the soles, and his belief is that others such as Baker who wore shoes with flat and spike-less heels were the ones with the advantage.

By the time that the Stockholm athletics events were completed on 15 July, the USA had convincingly proved its superiority: their athletes had won 16 gold medals, Finland had won six, Sweden three, Great Britain two, and Canada, Greece and South Africa one each. Of the total medals, gold, silver and bronze, the USA had 41, Finland and Sweden 13 each, and Great Britain eight. The two British gold medals had been won by Arnold Jackson at 1500 metres and by the 4 x 100 metres relay team, and there had been a silver for Ernie Webb in the 10,000 metres walk and five bronzes for Willie Applegarth at 200 metres, George Hutson at 5000 metres, and the teams in the 4 x 400 metres relay, the 3000 metres track race and the 12 kilometres cross-country.

In the overall standings of gold medals for all sports in Stockholm the order of countries was as follows: USA 25, Sweden 24, Great Britain 10, Finland 9, France 7, Germany 5, Norway 4, South Africa 4, Australasia (Australia & New Zealand combined) 3, Canada 3, Hungary 3, Italy 3, Belgium 2, Denmark 1, Greece 1, Switzerland 1. By 21st-century standards, third place in an Olympic medals table would be regarded as a resounding success for Great Britain, ahead of every other European country except the hosts, but it goes without saying that the Games of 1912 were totally dissimilar to what those of, for instance, 2008 would be. Apart from any other consideration, there were 87 countries which were to win medals at the 2008 Games, and almost half of them did not even exist independently in 1912.

The memory of one of those British competitors in Stockholm remained particularly vivid for all time. Lord Noel-Baker never forgot his first Olympic experience – on the contrary he continued to wax lyrical about it. Asked to record his most vivid memories of the Games, he ignored the silver medal which he won in 1920 and instead wrote: 'The Stockholm Games were an enchantment – the word was Coubertin's in the speech with which he brought them to a close. As a competitor, I thought them an enchantment and looking back, six decades, two World Wars and twelve Olympiads later, my memories enchant me still'. His final clarion call was inspirational: 'We went to Stockholm as British athletes. We came home Olympians, disciples of the leader, Coubertin, with a new vision which I never lost'.

In 1912 he was plain Philip Baker, a 20-year-old undergraduate at King's College, Cambridge, who finished an honourable sixth in the 1500 metres won by his compatriot from Oxford, Arnold Jackson. Their experience, unbeknown to either of them or to the 2,500 or so other competitors in Stockholm that year, represented the end of an Olympic era because the Games of 1916, scheduled for Berlin, would, of course, never be held and among the victims of the World War responsible for that cancellation would be 16 British Olympic gold-medallists across the range of sports. Not surprisingly, therefore, it was only some years later that it began to become apparent that the Games of 1912 – well organised and conducted with little or no ill will – had set a standard of excellence for the distant future. It was a standard that was not always to be matched, but it was one which surely helped to preserve the Olympic ideal at least in some form which would win the approval of Baron de Coubertin.

Philip Baker must have been heartened when he read a letter in *The Times* very soon after the Games had finished which rejected wholeheartedly calls that were being made for Britain to withdraw from the Olympic movement because competition was getting altogether far too serious. The writer was one of Baker's teammates in Stockholm, the hurdler, Gerard Anderson, who implored: 'Whether or not we organise our athletics before the next Olympiad, it is inevitable that British competitors will travel to Berlin in 1916. They cannot be expected to stay at home in deference to views with which they may not agree, or to be satisfied with parochial sports when they have the chance of representing their country. Go they will; no argument can make any difference to the fact. It only remains to settle whether the British contingent is to consist of a keen but inglorious mob, or of a properly selected, properly trained team which will, it is hoped, do credit to the country'. Unfortunately, only Philip Baker and a few others would have realised the full significance of the letter. Oddly, Anderson did not identify himself as a competitor in Stockholm. Nor did the Letters Editor of *The Times* apparently realise the fact.

There were certainly British athletes in Stockholm who could justifiably be described as 'inglorious', or worse, but a teammate who sprang to their defence was the one who would most definitely have been placed in the 'glorious' category. Arnold Jackson was a remarkable natural talent who seems to have trained very little, if at all, for his 1,500 metres victory in World-record time, and his own letter to *The Times* contained the admonition: 'Let us not forget that under the circumstances our men for the most part ran above any previous form that they showed in England'. Of Howard Baker, in particular, he said, perhaps over-indulgently, 'Who can grumble at a man who is beaten when he clears 6ft?'

One anticipated victory in Stockholm had been that of the England football team, representing Great Britain, though Denmark had lost only 4–2 in the final despite being reduced to 10 men when one of their players was injured. For Howard Baker, who would naturally have viewed that result with interest, football with the Northern Nomads was to occupy him during the winter of 1912–13, with the welcome interruption of a belated further athletics appearance on 7 December at Cambridge on behalf of an AAA team against the university. The inclement choice of date was to suit the start of the season for the undergraduates, and at least there was the delightful prospect of taking dinner with all the competitors and officials in one of the college halls that evening. Howard Baker duly won his event at 5ft 9in (1.74m) and the AAA honorary secretary, Percy Fisher, sent him a charming letter afterwards: 'On behalf of the Association I desire to thank you for your kindness in competing against the Cambridge University AC on the seventh inst. and to congratulate you on your excellent performance in the High Jump. I trust that your success will in a measure compensate you for any inconvenience caused you by training during the off season and in such wretched weather'.

Fisher, who has his small but significant niche in athletics history as one of the four men who decided the distance of the 1908 Olympic marathon, 26 miles 385 yards, which would become universal from 1924, would have been unaware that Howard Baker probably regarded his exertions each Saturday on the football field, plus his swimming, as quite sufficient to keep him in condition for an unseasonable high-jump outing.

He would have had no idea that in World terms he ranked as the equal 27th high jumper of the year with his best performance of 6ft 0in (1.83) which he had matched in the Stockholm qualifying round. The idea of collating statistics in order to compare athletes from different countries and provide a guide to form in the major championships only began to surface in the 1920s, and it was not until another 40 years or so later that a Czech enthusiast, Vladimir Visek, was the first to undertake the painstaking task of reconstructing from contemporary newspaper reports the rankings for as early as 1912.

Of those high jumpers ahead of Howard Baker, 20 were from the USA, plus two from Ireland (Tim Leahy and Tim Carroll) and one each from Australia (Lester Kelly), Germany (Hans Liesche), Hungary (Baron István Wardener) and Norway (Gerhard Olsen). Carroll, Liesche, Wardener and Olsen had all competed in Stockholm but not Kelly. The leader in the rankings was not the Olympic champion, Richards, but the bronze-medallist, Horine, with his World record of 6ft 7in (2.01) in California in May. Horine had originally been a Scissors jumper with a best of only 5ft 1in (1.55) as a youth, but when his family had moved house the back-yard would only accommodate a practice area for him if he approached the bar from the left-hand direction and so he devised a method of rolling over the bar on his side and still landing on his hands and feet. Seven of the next 10 World record-holders up to 1953 would employ the same Western Roll technique developed so opportunely by Horine, though the credit for first using it, in 1909, ought really to go to another Californian of lesser repute, Dave Martin.

One high jumper whose tenure in the front ranks would barely survive the year's end was Jim Thorpe, who had won both the five-event pentathlon and the 10-event decathlon in Stockholm and had been justifiably told by an admiring King Gustav at the medals presentation that he was the greatest athlete in the World (Thorpe apparently replied, 'Thanks, King'). In January of 1913 it was revealed that Thorpe had earned money playing baseball four years before and he was duly stripped of his Olympic medals. The penalty was harsh, but the rules were crystal clear and Thorpe could hardly claim ignorance of them. The entry form for Stockholm had contained a detailed declaration regarding amateurism to be endorsed by each individual signatory, as follows:

> An amateur is one who has never competed for a money prize or for monetary considerations or in any way drawn pecuniary gain from the exercise of his sport, competed against a professional, taught in any branch of athletics for payment, sold, pawned, hired out or exhibited for payment any prize won in a competition.

Thorpe, who died in 1953, was posthumously reinstated by the ruling body in the USA, the Amateur Athletic Union, 20 years later and was pardoned by the IOC in 1982, but it has to be said that these decisions were founded on sentiment and not on legal reasoning. Thorpe had broken the rules as they stood in his lifetime, and as they had been clearly set out for him and every other Olympic competitor to read so he had to pay the price. Whether Howard Baker made the acquaintance of the luckless Thorpe in Stockholm is not known, but if he had done so he would have found that they had a lot in common, despite their vastly different social and ethnic backgrounds. Not only was Thorpe a great all-round sportsman but also, like Howard Baker, he was a highly accomplished dancer.

Haphazard, untrained, unsophisticated, unreliable. £100,000 will change all that
The 1913 athletics season began in England as it always had done, with hardy athletes at Oxford and Cambridge braving the frosts of January and February. It was scarcely the season for grand endeavours that would promise even grander endeavours to come, but it was of necessity if the various undergraduates were to stake their claim for a place in the coveted Inter-Varsity match in March. This would be a special occasion, the 50th in the series since the era of organised athletics competition had been inaugurated in 1864.

Such were the weather conditions that the final day of the Oxford University sports was in jeopardy until the Iffley Road track had at last thawed out sufficiently by three o'clock in the afternoon to allow a start to be made. Arnold Jackson, the Olympic champion, won the mile in a rather slower time than that to which he was accustomed – 4min 26⅕ sec – but this was still a performance of great merit on the clogged and heavy surface, and the wonderful deer-like stride which had carried him to Stockholm gold remained unimpeded by the clinging cinders. The Inter-Varsity match, happily for all, ended in a draw, as each university won five events. One of Jackson's Stockholm teammates, Henry Ashington, achieved a remarkable treble for Cambridge in the 880 yards, the 120 yards hurdles and the long jump, beating C.B. Fry's meeting record in the last-named event.

Yet the occasion managed to neatly encapsulate all the virtues and failings of English athletics. The report in *The Times* contained the gratuitous and downright ill-mannered comment that 'so long as there are such tiresome things as Weights and Hammers and Rhodes Scholars to heave them, it seems likely that Oxford will begin the Sports – to borrow the language of another game – two up with eight to play'. Both the shot put and the hammer throw had been won by an American undergraduate at Wadham College, Oxford, W.A. Zeigler, and arguments were to rage in the letters columns of *The Times* during the year as to whether it was right and proper to allow Rhodes Scholars to compete at all against younger and less mature undergraduates.

The scholarships had been initiated after the death of the great Empire-builder, Cecil Rhodes, in 1902 to bring outstanding college graduates to Oxford from countries throughout the World, and one of the very first of these from the USA, Wesley Coe, had set a shot-put record at the 1904 Inter-Varsity match which would last for 34 years. Zeigler was probably far too polite to respond to the denigration of his efforts by *The Times* but no doubt he had a few thoughts about the matter. He had studied at Grinnell College in Iowa, which had a strong tradition of social activism, having been founded by an eminent church minister who was a dedicated supporter of the abolition of slavery and to whom had been directed the famous injunction by the journalist, Horace Greeley, 'Go West, young man! Go West!' Zeigler, assuredly, would have favoured such brave American adventurism over such myopic English conservatism.

Additionally, for those who cared to read more into the bare results of that Inter-Varsity meeting, Arnold Jackson's mile triumph, impressive as it was, represented once again the expression of a natural genius which would be limited to all but the very few in future years as other countries appreciated the value of proper training. Henry Ashington, who would also win the high jump in the 1914 fixture, was an exceptional all-rounder who might have become a decathlete of note had he been so inclined in future years and – more to the point – had he not been killed in action in 1917 while serving as a captain with the East Yorkshire Regiment, but such versatile skills as his were to be indirectly called into question later in the year by Sidney Abrahams, one of whose brothers, Harold, would become Olympic 100 metres champion.

Sidney Abrahams, who had finished two places behind the Harrow-educated Ashington in the Olympic long-jump final, deplored the obsession of England's schools with all-round achievements, whereby the major prize at the annual sports would go to the 'Victor Ludorum' who had spent the afternoon in a mad dash, running every track race from 100 yards to the mile and high jumping, long jumping and shot-putting in order to gather together sufficient points for the prize. Abrahams thought this was 'physically mischievous' and he concluded that because of it 'athletics remains as a kind of pariah at the Public Schools, allowed to exist but not given any status or dignity'.

Howard Baker set a personal best of 6ft ½in (1.84m) at the Crewe Alexandra Sports on 14 June and duly won his third Northern Counties' high-jump title at Headingley, Leeds, with a Championship record of 5ft 11¾in (1.82). Previewing the AAA Championships to take place on 5 July *The Times* hailed him as 'possibly the best high jumper England has had for the last 20 years'. Such an assessment was perhaps self-evident, though the supporters of the Devonian, George Rowdon, might have quibbled, and Howard Baker won at 6ft 0in (1.83) again and beat a contingent of five Swedes in the process. Sweden had sent over a large group of athletes to contest nine of the AAA events, and as Britons were also successful against them in the four miles, the 120 yards hurdles and the long jump this might have been seen as a sign of some improvement since Olympic year.

Actually, it was not quite the first time that an English-born high jumper had repulsed Continental opposition in the 33-year history of the AAA meeting because a German, Berti Weinstein, had placed fifth when John Banks, of the Midlands club, Sparkhill Harriers, had won in 1909. It should be further pointed out that neither Weinstein then nor the Swedes four years later were of the highest quality of opposition. Weinstein had not competed in the 1908 Olympic high jump, though he was seventh in the long jump, and none of the Swedes had been in the 1912 Olympic high jump, though one of them, Inge Lindholm, had been 12th in the triple jump and equal eighth in the pentathlon.

It was, in fact, a bizarre sort of high-jump competition at these 1913 AAA Championships. There were 11 men taking part, which was more than twice as many as had turned up for the event at any of the previous meetings since 1880, but any hopes that Howard Baker had of some rivalry to provide inspiration were soon dashed. Eight of the 11 failed at what some of them might have considered to be an ambitious opening height of 5ft 9in (1.74), including three of the Swedes, and among these was Gösta Holmér, later to become one of the World's foremost coaches.

It was a pity that Howard Baker's Irish teammate in Stockholm, Tim Carroll, chose not to make the journey to Stamford Bridge. That year Carroll won the second of what would be his seven Irish titles at a modest height of 5ft 3in (1.60), but less than a month after the AAA Championships he cleared 6ft 5in (1.96) at Kinsale, on the coast of County Cork. This performance was never accepted by the AAA as a British record, for whatever real or imagined defect, but there was every reason to believe that it was perfectly genuine.

The Championships also featured fine performances by two of Britain's Olympic medallists as there was a sprint double by Willie Applegarth, including a British record of 21⅗ sec for 220 yards, and a Championship best by George Hutson at four miles, but otherwise there was not much to show that any lessons had been learned from Stockholm. A Swede, John Zander, who had placed seventh in the Olympic 1500 metres, won the mile in the slowest time since 1900 and there was no sign of Arnold Jackson or Philip Baker. After his Inter-Varsity mile win in March, Jackson had been elected president of Oxford University Athletic Club, and presumably – with no Olympics to arouse his interest in the summer months – he was content to combine these ceremonial and administrative duties with sharpening up his golf handicap. The correspondent of *The Times* took a rather more cynical view, though without pointing the finger at Jackson, Baker or any other individual, remarking of the university athletes: 'Even when an Olympiad comes round, the summer term, with all its exacting duties and delights, is an almost insuperable obstacle to hard training and regular practice'.

The much more significant happening of 1913 so far as the next Olympic Games was concerned was the launch of a £100,000 appeal by the British Olympic Association to finance the team to go to Berlin for the 1916 Games. The Duke of Westminster was supported by the Lords Grey, Harris, Roberts, Rothschild and Strathcona and set the ball rolling with a donation of £1,000, but the target figure was immensely large and the project aroused wildly mixed reactions, with the letters columns of *The Times* again filled with articulate – as one might expect – and often highly entertaining viewpoints.

That prolific letter-writer, Sidney Abrahams, who had won the long jump at the AAA Championships, entered the debate with a plea for better preparation: 'It is no offence to desire to see this country do its best in these contests; to increase the number of athletes all over the country by giving facilities for practice and competition, winter as well as summer; to give such men the experience which sometimes alone stands between them and the abandonment of their sport; to induce the public schools to raise the status of athletics and thereby to gain recruits from the ranks of those sacrificed to the fetish of cricket and football, with which athletics need not interfere. In a word, to popularise a form of sport which indifference to organisation has caused to suffer from diminished interest, and which is open to every class, and particularly to the working classes, is a praiseworthy effort'.

Abrahams's views were heartfelt. Birmingham-born, he was the son of a Jewish refugee from Poland and went to Cambridge University. He became a distinguished lawyer and was knighted in 1936, though it was that younger brother, Harold, who was to achieve lasting fame and dramatised cinema-screen immortality by his victory in the 1924 Olympic 100 metres. Among the support for Sidney Abrahams's stance was a witty contribution from S.P.B. Mais, who had been captain of the Oxford University cross-country team in 1909: 'It matters not intrinsically whether we ever again enter for these Olympic Games. It does not in the least affect our position as a nation, but if we do, there ought to be at least some semblance of a real attempt to get our best men to represent us and not a team chosen as haphazard, untrained, unsophisticated, unreliable'.

Mr Mais passionately supported the fund-raising campaign, saying that it would be worth £100,000 'to see this nation change from a raucous football-watching, latest-cricket-news reading, flabby and morbidly curious mob to a well trained competitive army of would-be athletes – professional or amateur, I really do not think it matters which'. Now, if that sounds like the sort of sentiment which could as easily and as justifiably be expressed a century later, then Mr Mais himself would have perhaps been the last to be surprised.

Stuart Petre Brodie Mais (who preferred to use his middle Christian name, Petre) had also been born in Birmingham, and after graduating from Oxford in English literature he became an astonishingly prolific author, writing more than 200 books concerned with travel, history and literary criticism, among other subjects. During his lifetime he was a teacher, a journalist and most notably of all a BBC radio broadcaster from the 1920s onwards who became so nationally famous that he received as many as 500 letters a day from listeners. He presented programmes dealing with the depression years and unemployment which roused the interest of the Royal family, and he started a 'Letter from America' in 1933, 13 years before Alastair Cooke began his series. Mais's later sporting achievements were modest by any comparison; it was said of him as a village cricketer in Sussex that he 'scored one century, never got put on to bowl, and was noted for dropping catches'.

Howard Baker was meanwhile enjoying a winter of football and swimming. In advance of the Neptune Swimming Club Gala on 31 October at the Guinea Gap Baths, Seacombe, on the Wirral, his name was emblazoned in red letters on the publicity posters, promising an 'exhibition' appearance. Quite what form this took is unclear either in advance or in the subsequent press reports, except that he and C.S. Smith 'gave displays that were much appreciated'. Charlie Smith was the goalkeeper for the Great Britain water-polo team which had won Olympic gold medals in 1908 and 1912, and no doubt he and his Olympic high-jumping colleague were cheered to every echo from the Guinea Gap rafters.

Further excitement was caused by the 'Liverpool Gentlemen' who gave the 'Liverpool Ladies' (including the Olympic relay champion, Annie Speirs) 25 seconds' start in a 4 x 50 yards relay and beat them. There was plenty else to entertain the spectators because Miss Minnie Harrison, of the Liverpool Ladies' SC, surpassed the English 'plunging' record with a performance of 57ft 3in. Six days later Miss Harrison sparklingly celebrated Guy Fawkes Night by plunging more than 60ft for the first time. Plunging was a widely popular sport at the time, with a national-championship event held since 1895, and it required the competitor to make a simple head-first dive into the water and then swim as far under the surface as he or she could. It was to remain a Merseyside speciality until World War Two, as a Liverpool policeman, F.W. Parrington, won the national title 11 times from 1923 onwards and set a British record of 86ft 8in (26.42m) at Bootle in 1933 which still stands to this day – and probably, therefore, for eternity.

It seems likely that it was around then that Howard Baker also formed the notion of taking up diving as yet another strenuous activity. It could conceivably have been the breath-taking feat (literally, of course, *not* breath-taking!) of Miss Harrison that provided the inspiration, or perhaps it was the dexterity of a man named Harry Crank, who was a Lancastrian who had represented the Bolton Swimming Club. He had competed in the 1908 Olympics and now described himself as 'The Acrobatic Professional Diving Champion of the World', making at least one appearance at the Guinea Gap Baths. He was to be another World War One victim, dying on active service in 1917.

In November *The Times* published yet another assessment of the state of British athletics, and this in the form of a long leader article entitled 'The Changed Conditions of Sport' and credited to 'a correspondent'. The terminology was such that readers familiar with the subject would have assumed, perhaps rightly, that the anonymous contributor was the same man who had reported at length on the events leading up to the Stockholm Olympics, the Games themselves, and then their repercussions. He wrote: 'As both American and the Continental nations are bringing to athletics and to preparation for the Olympic Games a strenuousness of effort and concentrated purpose to which we have not yet been able to force ourselves, so in the other fields the former introduced a lavishness, a specialisation, an organisation which is somewhat disconcerting to our established habits'.

The writer's summing-up was a masterly overview of the situation which was Shakespearean in its cadence: 'We are in a sense finding the table turned upon us. Having, not of purpose but by our example, brought the World to a new enthusiasm, the World is applying to it in all departments an earnestness much greater than our own. The problem is how far we should welcome foreign intrusion and innovation and learn to adapt ourselves to new standards which are not of our making'. Howard Baker, the personification of 'new enthusiasm', occupied himself to good effect on the football field that month and was chosen at centre-half for Lancashire amateurs who gave the professional Birmingham side a good match on their own ground before going down 4–2.

Though playing most of his football with the Northern Nomads alongside other amateurs of a similar disposition as regards occupation and social class – businessmen, civil servants, schoolmasters for the most part – Howard Baker had also signed forms for Blackburn Rovers. This was a bold decision on his part because the famous club which had been one of the founders of the Football League in 1888 and winners of the FA Cup five times before the turn of the century was in the midst of yet another highly successful run. The First Division Championship had been won in 1911–12, and after a fifth place the following season the title was to be regained in 1913–14, and by a seven-point margin over Aston Villa. Four of the Blackburn players were in the England side during the season, including the peerless full-back and captain, Bob Crompton, completing his sequence of 41 caps, and forwards Danny Shea, Eddie Latheron and Jock Simpson. It's a nice historical perspective to note that in that 1913–14 season Chelsea finished eighth, Manchester United 14th, Everton 15th and Liverpool 16th. Woolwich Arsenal, as they were then called (at least until the end of the season), were third in Division Two.

In November 1913 Howard Baker was given a run-out at centre-half in a Central League match for the Rovers reserves against Everton reserves at Ewood Park, and the reporter for the local newspaper, the *Northern Daily Telegraph*, writing under the pseudonym of 'Ivor', thought Howard Baker's appearance of sufficient importance to refer to it in the opening lines of his match account. The Rovers won 3–2 and Baker earned a special commendation – 'both defences were being kept constantly on the alert and Baker, the Rovers new man, was doing much good and vigorous work'. Several other players of future note were also involved in the game: for the Rovers Sam Wadsworth, who was to move to Huddersfield Town and win nine England caps at full-back during the 1920s, captaining the side on four occasions; for Everton George ('Jud') Harrison – no Beatle relation! – who had 190 first-team matches between 1913 and 1923 and earned two caps in 1921–22 at outside-left, one of which would be alongside Howard Baker, and Alan Grenyer, a postwar 'victory' international who played 148 times in the Everton first team.

The regular Rovers' centre-half was Percy Smith, who had played 240 times for Preston North End and then joined the Rovers in 1910, staying until after the war and appearing in 172 matches. By the 1913–14 season Smith was approaching his mid-30s and the astute Rovers manager for 22 years, Robert Middleton, may well have seen the gifted amateur, Howard Baker, as his successor, or at least as a very useful replacement from time to time. However, Smith obstinately stayed fit and Howard Baker had to settle for a place in the reserve team, where he developed a penalty-scoring ability which would be put to good use in a spectacularly different context many years later. More of that anon.

Everton's reserves went on to win the Central League title that season. The League had been formed in 1911 principally for the reserve teams of Midlands and Northern clubs in the Football League and the first title-winners had been Lincoln City, to be one of the founders of Division Three North in 1921–22. Manchester United had won the next season. Unfortunately, despite his impressive debut, Howard Baker was not able to force his way into the Rovers team for any First Division matches, and he didn't stay long, though it was probably not through frustrated ambitions that he registered soon afterwards with Preston North End, who were in the throes of getting relegated again from the First Division, having regained a place by winning the Second Division title the previous season.

Ironically, Howard Baker was no better off as regards first-team selection there than he had been as understudy to the ex-Preston man, Percy Smith, at Blackburn. Preston's incumbent at centre-half was Joe McCall, who had been with the club since 1905 and was virtually an ever-present in the side throughout his long career, making 370 first-team appearances up to 1924. McCall was an adept organiser and had been appointed club captain, and though on the small side for his position at 5ft 8in (1.73m) tall he had won the first of five England caps in March of 1913, scoring a goal in the 4–3 win over Wales, and was to be made captain for his final appearance against Ireland in 1920. It can be surmised that Howard Baker was content to play the occasional game for Preston's reserves (though they were no more successful than the first XI, placing 16th of 20 in the Central League), honing his skills as a promising amateur still in his early 20s.

No doubt the management of both Preston North End and Blackburn Rovers saw particular advantage to the agreements they reached with Howard Baker. After all, they knew that they would be able to call on a very capable recruit more or less whenever the emergency arose, and it was not costing them a penny in wages. That would not have mattered one bit to Howard Baker, who had other pressing maters to deal with; the flourishing family business was no doubt demanding more of his attention and the time would not have been right for a permanent obligation to League football. This was a pattern which would repeat itself later in life before he discovered his true destiny in the game, but like so many other aspiring sportsmen he would very soon have to put his ambitions on hold in the intervening years while a rather more serious confrontation took place.

As the year drew to a close the athletics season at the universities was by no means over, or rather it was starting its 1914 campaign a couple of months early, and two new arrivals at Oxford as Rhodes Scholars were already making their mark. Norman Taber, from the USA, won the 440 yards, 880 yards and mile in an afternoon at the inter-college sports, and proved that even American *runners* were better than English weight-men by also placing first in the shot. Bevil Rudd, from South Africa, won races at 100 yards and 440 yards and both he and Taber would go on in later years to benefit from their Oxford experience. Taber was already an Olympic champion for the 3000 metres team race in Stockholm, as well as placing third in the 1500 metres close on Arnold Jackson's heels and would set a World record for the mile of 4min 12⅗sec in 1915. Rudd would return after war service as a Lieutenant with the Argyll and Sutherland Highlanders and then as a Major in the Tank Corps to become Olympic champion at 400 metres and bronze-medallist at 800 metres in 1920.

Before the year was over the British Olympic Council set out its plans for the first £50,000 which they awaited to fill their coffers, promising £16,000 to the AAA, £3,600 to the Irish AAA, £1,000 to the Scottish AAA, £2,730 to the National Cyclists' Union, £1,945 to the Amateur Gymnastics Association £2,050 to the Amateur Wrestling Association and £5,577 to the Amateur Swimming Association, among other beneficiaries. Presumably all these figures were agreed upon as a result of budgets submitted by the various ruling bodies, and it can only be guessed at as to whether the various officials involved were already rubbing their hands in glee at the prospective windfall or whether they might have been confiding to each other in private, 'We'll believe it when it happens'.

ENTER THE 'CRAFTY, CANDID, ROGUISH MAN' WHO HAD BEEN BROUGHT TO ENGLAND'S RESCUE

Walter Knox was the very antithesis of the gentleman amateur. He was a marvellously talented Canadian all-round athlete who would have seriously challenged Jim Thorpe for his gold medals in Stockholm. Unlike Thorpe, whose brief career as a wage-earning baseball-player was no more than a youthful indiscretion, Knox was a self-confessed 'vagabond professional' who toured the World racing against all-comers. He was also not the least averse to masquerading under a pseudonym and placing favourable bets on himself with unsuspecting bookmakers before making his coup…and then his getaway.

Definitely not the sort of chap one would have thought suitable to rub shoulders with the high and mighty of the Amateur Athletic Association – its president since 1891 had been the Right Honourable Viscount Alverstone, GCMG, PC, who had penned the letter which issued the challenge from Cambridge to Oxford which led to the promotion of the World's first organised athletics match of 1864. From 1900 to 1913 he was Lord Chief Justice of England and had been the judge at the much-publicised trial in 1910 who sentenced Dr Crippen to be hanged for the murder of his wife.

Yet Viscount Alverstone and his AAA committee were pragmatists, and they knew that professional coaching could make a difference. Walter George, whose mile time of 4min 12¾sec from 1886 was still unbeaten almost 30 years later, was now a journalist and had published the latest of his influential training manuals in 1913. Jack White, who had set a six miles time of 29min 50sec in 1863 which would remain unsurpassed by any other Briton for 73 years (!), had been coach to London Athletic Club and Cambridge University from the 1880s until he fell ill in 1907. Most notable of all was Mike Murphy, a son of Irish immigrants, who had advised the US Olympic teams of 1900, 1908 and 1912, and of whom it was said had 'the remarkable ability to discern talent and then to train and inspire young men to achieve beyond expectations'.

Murphy had died in June of 1913, and his passing would have been a salutary reminder to Britain's athletics officialdom of the superiority of the American athletes the year before in Stockholm. However dated the attitude might seem a century later, Englishmen believed firmly in the ideal of 'Play up! Play up! And play the game!', as proclaimed by Sir Henry Newbolt in his famed poem of 1892, *Vitae Lampada* (or 'The Torch of Light'), which began

'There's a breathless hush in the Close tonight'. The reality, of course, was that a far more rational approach to training and preparation was needed for the next Olympics scheduled for 1916, whether it was a matter of national pride or simply of the AAA and the British Olympic Association keeping face, and no one had more expertise to offer, especially in the neglected field events, than Walter Knox.

F.A.M. Webster, in his familiar evangelical mode, had published one of his numerous books, *Olympian Field Events* in 1913, for which Sir Arthur Conan Doyle, creator of Sherlock Holmes and an accredited correspondent at the 1908 Olympic Games, provided the introduction, and Webster modestly acknowledged the want of outside help: 'There is also a great need for the professional coach, but until such time as these coaches are obtained it is my hope that the suggestions as to methods of practice set out in this volume may be of assistance to those who practise field events and those who may be induced to take them up'. Webster made another significant observation: 'That it is our methods, and not the men, who are wrong is clearly evidenced by the fact that the greatest exponents of field events in the United States of America are Scotchmen and Irishmen who have emigrated across the Atlantic'.

Walter Knox was a Canadian, born in Listowel, Ontario, in 1878. He had started competing in athletics at the age of 18 – coincidentally, in the year of the first Modern Olympic Games – and from 1900 onwards began to amass victories and records, eventually amounting to a claim of 359 wins during his career. At the 1907 Canadian Championships he had taken five titles in a single afternoon, at 100 yards, the pole vault, long jump, shot and hammer, and he had on another occasion beaten Bobby Kerr, the Olympic 200 metres champion of 1908, at the latter's preferred distance. As a professional Knox had run 100 yards in 9⅗sec and had other performances of 12ft 6in (3.81m) for the pole vault, 24ft 2in (7.36m) for the long jump, 47ft 4in (14.42m) for the hop step and jump, 46ft 5in (14.14m) for the shot and 128ft (39.02m) for the discus, all of which were better than any Englishman had ever achieved.

He had been coach to the Canadian Olympic team in Stockholm, where the Yorkshire-born George Goulding had won the 10,000 metres walk and Calvin Bricker (long jump) and Duncan Gillis (hammer) had taken silver medals. Additional to his official commitments Knox had gone off on his own to tour the Highland Games circuit in Scotland and had notched up 40 wins to supplement his income, returning in 1913 for a similarly successful venture. He was also a mining prospector and shares speculator, from which he was to earn a comfortable living until his death at the age of 73, and when in 1974 the Canadian historians, S.F. Wise and Douglas Fisher, wrote a 338-page volume of biographies of 'Canada's Sporting Heroes' they said of Knox that 'if a magic computer could be programmed to assess all the athletes in Canada's Sports Hall of Fame it is likely the machine would come up with the name of Walter Knox as the best of them all...as crafty, candid and roguish a man ever to capture the imagination of Canadians '.

This unlikely candidate, this 'crafty, candid and roguish man', was appointed as the chief coach to the AAA in February of 1914 for three years at £400 a year, which was the same salary as members of parliament were earning then, and immediately decided that his priorities should be the field events. Accordingly, he set about travelling the country, giving demonstrations of jumping and throwing. Peter Lovesey, in his AAA centenary history, noted that 'one early coaching success by Knox was to persuade the champion high jumper,

Howard Baker, to abandon the schoolboyish scissors style and use a cut-off technique', and Howard Baker himself later paid generous tribute to Knox's expertise. Knox must have worked fast because war broke out only six months after he had arrived in England and he had to go back home. At the AAA general committee meeting in October it was minuted that the Olympic Council 'considered it desirable to terminate Mr Knox's engagement as Chief Coach in view of there being no chance of the Olympic Games being held in 1916'.

Knox sailed away with a £400 pay-off cheque in his pocket, and after the war he coached the Canadian team again at the 1920 Olympics and then worked in Ontario from 1925 onwards. So his talent was lost to English athletics and the subject of coaching did not figure again in the deliberations of the AAA until 1923, when A.B. George, brother of the great miler, Walter George, was appointed both manager and coach to the 1924 Olympic team, which seems on the face of it to have been a bit of a tall order. According to the anonymous and highly-informed athletics columnist who wrote under the name of 'Strephon' – an odd choice as Strephon was a figure in classical poetry conventionalised as 'a rustic lover' – for the widely-read sports newspaper, *The Athletic News*, the AAA missed another chance of making use of Knox's expertise after World War One. 'Strephon' wrote in 1920, 'In all loyalty and good faith Knox offered his services afresh to the authorities on this side, though coming here would have meant loss of money to a man who is nowadays deeply interested in gold exploration, but as coaches are not required by the AAA he was left to accept the invitation of the Canadian authorities'.

In the same column 'Strephon' examined the issue of 'diving' in the high jump, whereby athletes who did not land on their feet were thought to be jumping unfairly, and directed a spirited commendation at Britain's best two exponents: 'Our two great jumpers of the present time, B. Howard Baker and T.J. Carroll, are scrupulously fair leapers; there never was a fairer than the former, who has had very hard luck with his shots at 6ft 5in. As I have often declared, had he been less powerfully built in the shoulders and hips, and kept those parts of his body clear of the cross-bar on the downward journey, he would have been a 6ft 5in man or better all right'.

As Peter Lovesey suggested, 'What transformations Knox might have made in the overall strength of the nation's athletics we can only speculate', and one can't help thinking that, given the renewed opportunity, Knox would have found a way of overcoming the disadvantages of Howard Baker's bulk and put his powerful build to even better use. Eventually there were to be some worthy coaching initiatives in the inter-war years, particularly with the start of the AAA summer schools at Loughborough in 1934, for which F.A.M. Webster was one of the organisers, and among the visiting coaches would be the Frenchman Pierre Lewden, who had been a high-jump rival of Howard Baker's and had beaten his AAA Championships record in 1923, but the impetus had been lost in the 1920s. The standard of field events progressed painfully slowly: the British pole-vault record remained unbeaten from 1891 to 1928, the long-jump record from 1901 to 1962, the shot from 1906 to 1929, the discus from 1912 to 1928 and the hammer from 1923 to 1947!

At least through Knox's temporary presence Howard Baker can claim to have been one of the very few beneficiaries of the Olympic Council's fund-raising scheme. Sadly, a notional 'financial father of the team' for which Sir Arthur Conan Doyle had appealed was not to be found, and neither was the general public to be persuaded to dig into their pockets to finance the preparations for the 1916 Games. In January of 1914, just as Walter Knox was about to arrive, the special committee set up by the Council to administer the fund, which included Sir Arthur among its membership, resigned en bloc, with the chairman, J.E.K. Studd, pointing out that as little more than £11,000 had been subscribed or promised towards the £100,000 target there was no point in continuing. Studd, incidentally, later became Sir John Studd and Lord Mayor of London and president of the MCC. He was one of three Studd brothers who had successively captained Cambridge University at cricket, and all of them were in the side which famously beat the Australian tourists in 1882. Of the fund-raising fiasco he might have mused that he and his colleagues had, figuratively speaking, been skittled out before lunch on the opening day.

A sorrowful leader article in *The Times* heaped blame on the diehards who had opposed the idea of financing the Olympic team as smacking of professionalism and concluded: 'It is right that our men should be amateur. That our methods should also be amateur – to use the word in a different sense – is wrong. For that only means that they will be feeble and haphazard'. The words were surely those of Henry Perry Robinson, or at the very least inspired by him. The irony of the situation was that the Duke of Westminster and his five aristocratic co-supporters of the fund could surely have raised the entire £100,000 between them without delving too deeply into their bank-accounts. Sir Arthur Conan Doyle believed that the target figure was far too high and bemoaned the fact that it had been decided upon at a committee meeting which he had missed because he was on holiday.

As his contribution to helping improve the competitive opportunities for British athletes at the start of the 1914 season, Philip Baker had taken a team at his personal invitation to meet Cambridge University at Fenner's in mid-March and though it was a cold and showery day there were some commendable performances. Howard Baker, responding to his friend's call and fitting in an unexpectedly early start to his athletics season between his various football commitments, won the high jump at 5ft 10¾in (1.80m) and only just failed at 6ft. It was apparently a long-drawn-out affair, though it is not obvious why because one of the Leahy brothers, Tim, competing as a member of Polytechnic Harriers, had got no higher than 5ft 6¾in (1.69), though he had a best of 6ft 5in (1.96) to his credit from the previous year, and the other three competitors – Henry Ashington and Arthur Willis for the university and M.A. Cooper, of South London Harriers, for Philip Baker's team – managed only 5ft 5in (1.65).

Churlishly the correspondent for *The Times* complained that the meeting was 'rather longer than it need or would have been if jumpers and weight throwers had condescended to perform simultaneously instead of occupying the stage one after the other in solitary and tedious splendour'. It required no intimate knowledge of athletics on the part of the reader to comprehend that it was the officials and not the athletes who decided the timetable and this editorial judgment really seemed to smack of pure prejudice against the field events. The deeds of the sprinter, Willie Applegarth, though he was beaten at 100 yards, and of Philip Baker himself, who won the half-mile to lead his team to victory, were clearly more to the reporter's taste.

One of the first of the athletics results to be publicised as summer approached would no doubt have aggrieved Sidney Abrahams when he opened his copy of *The Times* in his barrister's chambers at Inn's Court one morning in the early spring. A boy at the Dulwich College Sports had won seven events in a single afternoon – the 440 yards, 880 yards, one mile, 120 yards hurdles, steeplechase, high jump and long jump, and had also tied for first place at 100 yards. It might have been thought that Mr Abrahams' dire warnings that such over-exertion would be 'physically mischievous' were fulfilled as the precocious youth was not to be heard of when athletics resumed after the war, but in this instance there was a rather good excuse. A.E.R. Gilligan was beginning a first-class cricket career instead in 1919 which would last 13 years, including 11 Test matches for England. The Australian vice-captain M.A. Noble, in a rare display of bonhomie towards the arch-enemy, was to describe Gilligan as typifying 'the Englishman at his best, dignified, discreet, cautious, charming and optimistic in the face of all kind of difficulties'.

Among the numerous other reports of public-school sports days which were a regular feature in *The Times* every April was one concerned with St Paul's, in London, where C.H.L. Skeet was the winner of the 'Victor Ludorum' all-round title which Sidney Abrahams so abhorred, and those who cared to read the small print of the detailed results might have noticed that a boy named H.M. Abrahams confined himself to winning the 100 yards and placing second at 300 yards. No doubt the thought of his elder brother's reaction had he taken on any heavier schedule that day would have concentrated the future Olympic champion's mind wonderfully on his mere two events. As it happens, the New Zealand-born Challen Skeet also preferred a cricketing career, playing for Oxford University and Middlesex after the war, and maybe these two examples served to support the other salient point that Sidney Abrahams had made in past correspondence to *The Times* – that athletic talents were being 'sacrificed to the fetish of cricket'.

In June Howard Baker won his fourth successive Northern high-jump title at Fallowfield, in Manchester, and needed no more than a 5ft 8½in (1.74) clearance to do so, but he fell short of an over-confident prediction by the *Liverpool Daily Post* that his 'appearance in the 120 yards hurdles will be watched with more than passing interest'. He lost most decisively by a reported 14 yards, though maybe some small consolation for him was that the man who beat him was an athlete of genuine class, George Gray, of Salford Harriers, who was AAA champion in that event in 1913 and 1914 and at 440 yards hurdles in 1919. Gray would be one of Baker's Great Britain teammates at the 1920 Olympics and would narrowly miss reaching the high hurdles final.

Presumably still feeling in need of a trifle more exercise, Howard Baker also came second in the hammer throw to England's leading exponent, Alfred Flaxman, and though the distance was unrecorded, and therefore likely to have been of modest proportions, it was a brave enough venture in itself for Howard Baker to pit himself against such a specialist in a complicated art which, if not performed with sufficient care, could have caused the thrower rather than the implement to be flung out of the circle, which would have vastly amused the 2,000 spectators present that afternoon. Flaxman, who was also by contrast to his muscular athletic ability a talented violinist, was an innovator of weight-training for athletes many years – even generations – ahead of his time and was advised by the famed music-hall strong-man, Eugene Sandow, but was to be killed in action with the South Staffordshire Regiment in 1916.

The next weekend Howard Baker was at the Crewe Alexandra FC Sports, which was to become a regular fixture for him, and had another comfortable and highly encouraging win at 6ft 1½in (1.87m), with his nearest 'challenger' managing only 5ft 6in, but the day's activities were rather more notable for Howard Baker's appearance in the pole vault and javelin. The winner of the former event was Joe Birkett, of Waterloo Harriers, at a mere 9ft

(2.74m), and his brother, Fred, was also an accomplished pole vaulter as well as a nationally-ranked high jumper and was to be Howard Baker's coach in the future. All that can be gleaned from the results is that Howard Baker was second, but here was another example of his readiness to take up any event which caught his fancy, however little preparation he had done, or even none at all. In the javelin he produced a performance of real value, even if the distance was ordinary, when he lost to F.A.M. Webster by a few inches, 122ft 9in (37.42m) to 122ft 2in (37.24m). Webster was a pioneer of the event in Britain as both a competitor and a coach, with a best throw to his credit of 176ft 5in (53.78m), and was no doubt impressed by Howard Baker's casual mastery of the basics.

That same month Webster published yet another of his impassioned books, and this one was entitled *The Evolution of the Olympic Games*. It contained some reflections on the state of British society written in an oddly high-flown style which was characteristic of him. Webster declaimed: 'I ask you, ye people of England, what are we doing to keep this glorious heritage? Can ye look back and consider our disgraceful defeat at Stockholm in 1912 and yet say that we stand where our forefathers stood in Nelson's day? But what can one expect of the milk-and-water, cigarette-smoking generation, bedecked in rainbow socks and waisted coats'.

Rainbow socks, indeed! Whatever next! It is easy enough almost a hundred years later to scoff at such apoplexy, and Webster's sentiments were really not much different to what is often voiced by one generation about the next. Whether such expressions of feeling contributed anything worthwhile to the continuing debate on that Olympic 'defeat' is another matter entirely, and *The Times* certainly didn't think so, deciding in its review of Webster's book that 'so much unfortunately of what he has written is calculated to provoke irritation and hostility'. The remark has the ring of Henry Perry Robinson again.

Howard Baker had another 6ft (1.83m) clearance at the Huddersfield Cricket & Athletic Club sports on 27 June, and there's a photograph in existence of him apparently attempting a record 6ft 5in in that competition, and there is certainly evidence that on occasions after winning his event he would have had the bar put straight up 12 inches or so to give the crowds a treat. At the AAA Championships on 3-4 July, which were to be, unbeknown to the competitors and spectators, of course, the last to be held before the outbreak of war, he again met up with formidable American opposition, as he had at the Olympics, though his Irish teammate from Stockholm, Tim Carroll, once more did not appear. Howard Baker got over 6ft 2in (1.88), easily exceeding his heights at the four previous AAA meetings which he had contested, and still lost by half-an-inch to one of the Americans, Wesley Oler, but was ahead of the other, John Simons. Oler and Baker had both failed at 6ft 3in (1.91) and Oler won at the jump-off height, and then maybe he and Simons hit the town to celebrate American Independence Day. This meeting was attended by a crowd of 15,000 and the highlight for them must have been Willie Applegarth's World record of 21⅕ sec for 220 yards, achieved despite a cold drizzle during the day which rendered the track heavy.

Even so, *The Times* had much to say about the Anglo-American high-jump contest, describing it as 'the most interesting of the field events'. Commending the sportsmanlike attitude of the spectators, the reporter, presumably Perry Robinson, noted: 'And so with the stern contest in the high jump, which was being fought out at the other end of the greensward by B.H. Baker, the holder, and two American specialists – you could tell by listening to the sudden outcries whether the jumper had safely crossed the bar or not. What you could not tell was whether it was the Englishman or an American'. The competition stayed vividly in Baker's mind over the years and he remembered almost 70 years later that 'we jumped for nearly an hour'. Note: a lengthy event by domestic standards but not at Olympic level.

Applegarth also won the 100 yards again at those Championships, and on the Friday evening George Hutson had taken the four miles for the third successive year and the following afternoon won the mile. Sadly, Hutson was dead within 10 weeks of this fine double at the age of 24, killed in action serving with the Royal Sussex Regiment. Though no one among the throng of spectators, athletes and officials at Stamford Bridge that afternoon was yet to know it, even if some of those who were better informed might have suspected so, the war which would claim the lives of Hutson and so many millions of others had already been set in motion. Archduke Franz Ferdinand of Austria had been assassinated six days before.

A novel feature of the Championships, and maybe providing further evidence of the influence of Walter Knox, if only temporary, was that at long last the 440 yards hurdles, the hop step and jump, the discus and the javelin were added to the programme. As Denmark, Finland, Hungary and Sweden took eight of the nine top-three placings in the three new field events – the lone intruder being Patrick Quinn, of Ireland, second in the discus – Knox was given a forcible reminder of how much work needed to be done in these disciplines.

It would seem, too, from this final sporting fling before those hostilities of a much more serious nature began that Knox's coaching expertise had not yet borne full fruit so far as Howard Baker was concerned, even though he was jumping higher than ever before. 'Oler's method was better than Baker's', said *The Times* correspondent. 'There was a more fluent rhythm in his run-up and he always landed more comfortably than his English rival'. It is probable that Howard Baker had already switched from his primitive Scissors to the Eastern Cut-Off advocated by Knox and the technique was still at its teething stage. Unfortunately, another four years would pass before the polishing process could be further worked on.

Wesley Oler had been a youthful prodigy, clearing 6ft 3⅝in (1.92) for a US high-school record in 1912 which lasted for 14 years and competing at the Olympic Games that year. He was now a Yale University student and a member of New York AC and was to win the US AAU (national) title two years later. In a book entitled simply *The High Jump* written by the distinguished American coach, Richard ('Dink') Templeton, and published in 1926, Oler described his methods thus:

'Most of the spring in high jumping starts from the heel of the foot and not from the ball as is commonly supposed...I remember I used to compare my jumping with pole vaulting – imagining my take-off leg as the pole – and just as the vaulter jams his pole into the hole at the take-off board so I jammed my foot down. Then keeping the leg stiff rose on it as the vaulter rises on his pole, getting my upward swing just as he does, by kicking up the other leg'. Such thinking would most surely have never occurred to Baker in such terms, as he would have had very little opportunity to learn from pole vaulters; there had only been three British wins in the event at the AAA Championships since 1900, and in each instance that was simply because there were no foreign competitors.

Whatever his aesthetic failings then, and these were to be largely eradicated in post-war years, Howard Baker must have been a most imposing sight to see in action, either clearing a bar or defending his goalmouth. He was said to have stood 6ft 3¼in (1.91m) tall and weighed 14st 2lb (90kg), though his recollection for John Bromhead was of a slightly more modest 6ft 2½in (1.89m) and 12st 10lb (80kg) in his prime. Unquestionably, he was also of a cheerful disposition, and Captain F.A.M. Webster particularly remarked on this more than once in the numerous books which he wrote: 'I don't think I ever saw him jump without a smile on his face, but he was tremendously determined. To see Baker start on the slant and come bounding at the bar in a series of long leaps from one leg to the other was a joy to watch'. Webster also enthused of Baker that he 'was a born athlete and everything he attempted in sport not only prospered but was done superlatively well'.

Tim Carroll, whose Irish record lasted even longer than Baker's British record, surviving until 1954, was also described in wonderfully enthusiastic detail by Webster: 'Tim was a medium-sized, sturdily built fellow, with a perfect *oriflamme* of blazing red hair and fiery blue eyes. The sight of him in competition with B. Howard Baker would always delight a Stamford Bridge crowd, than whom none was more critical. Tim, eyes and mouth set, body bent forward from the hips and pitched right up on his toes, arms stretched down stiff as two pokers with hands on a level with his knees, and creeping towards the bar from straight in front, for all the world like a cat stalking a bird, made a picture. Then came three or four quick strides, a spring, and the sudden Sweeney twist over the lath'.

The Saturday following the AAA Championships the first triangular international match involving England & Wales v Ireland v Scotland was held at Hampden Park, Glasgow, and this was a commendable attempt to improve competitive opportunities for the leading British athletes. Could it have been one of Walter Knox's suggestions? England & Wales won six events, Scotland three and Ireland two, and Tim Carroll had a convincing win over Howard Baker. The Irishman got over 6ft 1¾in (1.87) and Howard Baker failed at 6ft 1in after clearing 6ft 0in. Willie Applegarth won both sprints for England, including another storming 220 yards in 21⅖ sec, and George Hutson took the four miles. The mile race would prove of historical interest in much later years because the Honourable H.R.L.G. Alexander finished second for Ireland. At that time he was a Lieutenant in the Irish Guards, and he rose to the rank of acting Lieutenant-Colonel during World War One and was awarded the Military Cross. In World War Two he became a Field-Marshal and was created Viscount Alexander of Tunis for his successes in the North African campaign.

There is actually evidence that Howard Baker was jumping rather higher that summer than he achieved at the AAA Championships. The *Liverpool Echo* newspaper for Saturday 13 June 1914 had published a photograph of him neatly attired in shorts and a white blazer with blue trimming (Liverpool Cricket Club colours, maybe?), which had been taken at the Cooper's Sports held at the city's Tramway Grounds, and it was said in the caption that he had cleared 6ft 4in (1.93m) at that meeting, presumably having taken place some days before. If indeed he did so, this performance supersedes two marks to be achieved by him in 1920 which have been regarded by the authoritative group of British athletics historians, the National Union of Track Statisticians, as the best by a British (but non-Irish) athlete. There is some confusion because the *Liverpool Daily Post* says of the occasion that 'B. Howard Baker gave a capital display of high-jumping and equalled the British championship record of 6ft 3in'. Quite what was meant by this obscure reference to a type of record which simply did not exist was not explained, though it seems likely that the writer had in mind the best achieved at the AAA Championships, which was 6ft 3in (1.91m) by the American, Sam Jones, in 1902.

Cooper's, incidentally, was in all probability I. J. & G. Cooper Ltd, who were straw-bonnet and hat manufacturers with factories throughout England, and the attendance for their sports day was no less than 25,000! Surrey Athletic Club thought the prizes attractive enough to send a team the 200 miles or so from London to win the one mile medley relay, and among the cycling competitors was Victor Johnson, from Birmingham; who had been an Olympic and World sprint champion in 1908.

Barely a month after his miling appearance for Ireland, Lt Alexander was on active service with the British Expeditionary Force as the Germans began their advance on the Western Front into Belgium on 14 August. Sport in Britain finally came to a halt on 31 August when the county cricket clubs decided to abandon their remaining fixtures. Jack Hobbs had just completed his 11th century of the season and an interval was taken which would last rather longer than usual – four years in all.

Sir Arthur Conan Doyle caught the national mood in a speech which he gave on 6 September 1914: 'There was a time for games. There was a time for business. And there was a time for domestic life. There was a time for everything. But there is time for only one thing now. If the cricketer has a straight eye, let him look along the barrel of a rifle. If a footballer has strength of limb, let him serve and march in the field of battle'.

A TIME FOR GAMES AT LAST, THOUGH
THE CASUALTY LISTS HAVE YET TO CLOSE

Even at the beginning of 1919, two months after the end of the 'war to end all wars' which had claimed the lives of 16 British Olympic gold-medallists, there were still casualties to be found among the ranks of former athletes; the death was announced of Major Miles Seton, a Scottish half-mile champion, who had given up his surgeon's practice to return to army duty in 1914 at the age of 40. There were other more transient repercussions, as there was not enough time to organise the major cross-country events of the winter. The National championships, which had first been held in 1877, would not take place, nor any of the regional races, nor the International race contested between the home countries and France.

Howard Baker had served in the Royal Navy Reserve during the war and the Reserve's officers and men had seen duty in some surprising and unwelcome theatres of action. It was decided that the majority of them, including more than 700 from the Mersey Division, would be formed into land-based brigades to defend harbours and other fleet bases, and this led many of them to the trenches of Northern France and then into the disastrous Dardanelles expedition, where among the Reserve officers who lost their lives in some far corner of a foreign field was Sub-Lieutenant Rupert Brooke. Some of the officers were luckier in being posted to sea-going ships, though perhaps 'luckier' is only a relative term, considering that Howard Baker spent the war on distinctly hazardous mine-sweeping duties. He survived unscathed all enemy action but broke his ankle when he fell in a passage-way, and this was to have some effect on his sporting interests for the rest of his life.

The pre-war experiences of the Mersey Division had not been without their share of black humour. The Division had been formed in 1904 and when the history of it came to be written on the eve of its centenary by a former chaplain to the Mersey Mission to Seamen, the Reverend Canon Bob Evans, two tales struck a note of pathos. The Admiralty had officially announced on the Division's formation that the Bishop of Liverpool, Dr John Charles Ryle, had been appointed chaplain but were forced to make a red-faced apology when they were informed that Dr Ryle had died four years before. In 1910 the Mersey division commander, Lord Lathom, was sent off on a health cruise to Egypt by his doctors, but their diagnosis was fatally at fault because their patient died at sea. The Reverend Canon Evans remains a character in his own right – a prolific author of seafaring tales whose entertaining autobiography was entitled *A Dog Collar In The Docks*.

The athletics debutants in 1919, the first full year of peace, were the Oxbridge men turning out for their winter-time sports, and as there was a healthy entry of 25 for the 100 yards at Oxford, won by the only pre-war 'blue' to have returned after military service, Bevil Rudd, it could be thought that a rapid revival of the sport was in the offing. Certainly, one of the rare benefits of the awful wartime experience had been that there was now a much greater awareness in the country of the benefits of physical fitness. When the first mass medical examinations for military service started in 1917, it was found that 10 per cent of young men were totally unfit, 41.5 per cent (nearer 50 per cent in London) suffered from marked disabilities and 22 per cent from partial disabilities, leaving only 26.5 per cent in a satisfactory state of health.

The British army had quickly realised the benefits of sport when the opportunity presented itself as a means of 'improving fitness, relieving boredom, providing distraction from the horrors of war, and building morale, officer-men relations and *esprit de corps*'. The familiar image of World War One is of the carnage in the trenches, but even the infantry servicemen in the thick of things spent on average 60 per cent of their time behind the lines, resting and recovering, and football matches, boxing tournaments, athletics meetings and even the occasional game of polo or a fox-hunt (officers only, of course) came to be seen as an important part of that therapeutic process. A graphic example of the talent uncovered by this initiative is provided by a soldier in the Royal Worcestershire Regiment, Walter Freeman, who took up running for the sheer joy of it on his days away from the front line, won his battalion half-mile, mile and three miles, joined Birchfield Harriers in 1919, and within two years was National and International cross-country champion.

Two eminent British sports historians, Eliza Riedi and Tony Mason, have examined the subject in great detail and they concluded, when their findings were published in 2006, that World War One 'marked the point at which sport, hitherto widely popular but unofficial in the armed services, became formally integrated into the military system, both as 'recreational training' and as an officially sanctioned form of leisure for other ranks…sport in the British army was transformed from a mainly spontaneous and improvised pastime in the early stages of the war into a compulsory activity for troops out of the line by the last months of the conflict'. For many of those 'other ranks', it would have been the first time in their lives that they had been given the chance to take part in an organised sport, and some of them would be keen to prolong the experience now that peace was restored.

One graphic account of wartime football was recalled by Charlie Buchan, subsequently a renowned player for Sunderland, Arsenal and England, who was a sergeant in the Grenadier Guards and organised a match against the Scots Guards not far from the Somme front line in July 1916: 'No sooner had we started than German shells began to drop perilously near the field. So we packed up and re-started on another pitch. The game had to go on'. In the early months of the war professional players had been prevented by their clubs from volunteering for military service, but League matches were suspended after the 1914–15 season and by the following June an ex-Glasgow Celtic player, William Angus, now serving with the Highland Light Infantry, had become the first professional footballer to win the Victoria Cross, losing an eye and part of a foot in the process. He was soon to be emulated as a VC hero by Donald Bell, whose allegiance had changed from Bradford City on the football-field to the Yorkshire Regiment in the battle-field.

Some 2,000 of Britain's 5,000 professional footballers joined the armed forces, and the Tottenham Hotspur club alone lost a full complement of 11 players killed in action. The

Football League competition and FA Cup were eventually suspended for the duration, and yet matches continued on a widespread scale with the London Combination, Lancashire Combination and Midland Combination absorbing the League clubs and maintaining full lists of fixtures.

As the war drew to a close, some semblance of domestic competition in athletics was started again, though each day the newspapers still carried long lists of casualties, and at Stamford Bridge on 7 September 1918, two months before the armistice, a good-humoured match was held between teams from the armed forces of Britain, the USA, Australia, Canada, New Zealand and South Africa. It was noted that an American soldier named Kirksey won the 100 yards, and *The Times* reporter commented wittily that 'even a generation to whom boy captains and colonels of 20 to 30 years are familiar might be struck with the sights of majors, captains and even a lieutenant-colonel running short-distance races, jumping and hurdling'. On another page of that same edition the latest catalogue of officers' deaths included the name of Captain W.M. Upjohn, who had set a half-mile record while at Eton.

Apart from the commanding officers and physical training staff who had encouraged the new-found participation in sport during the war years, there were civilians who also played a key role. One of the most prominent was Charles Otway, the honorary secretary of the English Cross Country Union, and a contributor to *The Sporting Life* newspaper, who organised almost single-handedly a race at Aldershot in December of 1914, and this led to the formation of a military committee which began to hold large-scale events for services' recruits throughout Britain. The army had started its annual athletics championships as far back as 1876, and the results from 1908 onwards show that the events were open to both officers and other ranks.

Otway had very clear ideas about the way in which athletics in Britain should function and had attracted the unstinted praise of *The New York Times* when in August of 1912 he devoted one of his columns in *The Sporting Life* to an in-depth appraisal of the American achievements at the Stockholm Olympics which had just taken place. Echoing strongly the sentiments of Henry Perry Robinson, Otway had written in condemnation of British officialdom: 'The one thing apparent in all this welter of criticism, inquiry and advice is that the existing organisation has failed most utterly. Those who really wish to see the honour of the national flag upheld will be sorry to find that even the Stockholm debacle has taught those mainly responsible therefor nothing. Even if it is no good asking them to 'wake up', it would be well to point out a few salient facts. The great factors in the success of the US in athletics, as in nearly every other thing our American cousins have taken up, is their capacity for organisation, their gift of spreading enthusiasm'.

Otway then went on to describe the US system of conducting its track and field athletics programme through the elementary schools, high schools, colleges and universities, and then in leagues, with overall control of numerous different sports in the hands of the Amateur Athletic Union and its district sub-divisions. This was clearly the model that Otway believed should be copied in Britain, and as he was such an eminent contributor to the existing English set-up himself he was better placed than anyone to make constructive public statements about its shortcomings. It must then have come as a shock to him when in May of 1919 the idea was revived in that most influential segment of the printed medium – the letters column of *The Times* – that it would be rather better for all concerned if Great Britain did not send a team at all to the impending 1920 Olympic Games in Antwerp. Even more of a shock for Otway, the signatories were the supreme Olympic champion of 1912, Arnold Jackson, now using his newly-acquired surname of Strode-Jackson, and his 1500 metres teammate at those Games, Philip Baker, already embarked on his diplomatic career.

Stating their belief that the refurbishment of athletics tracks and clubhouses neglected during the war years, and now in an advanced state of disrepair, was the greater priority in terms of any funds that might become available, Strode-Jackson and Baker wrote: 'It seems to us that it is both necessary and desirable to put our house in order at home before we begin to build castles in the air abroad. Olympic Games cost money, and our money is needed for other things first'. There was a lot of sense in what the distinguished duo listed as primary needs, such as the provision of help for clubs in the form of new tracks, improved existing facilities, updated changing-rooms and competent coaching guidance, and they emphasised that they continued to be supporters of the Olympic ideal, but their letter still seemed to leave some important questions unanswered.

Were they proposing a postponement of participation in the Games until a later date, 1924 presumably, when they reckoned their 'house might be in order'? Why should Great Britain stay away from the Games when other countries – Belgium, France, Italy, in particular – had been no less affected by the war? Would our absence not be seen as an admission of inferiority? What would be the view of the Americans regarding such a withdrawal after the unjustified but widely-publicised claims by much of the British press in 1912 that the US athletes weren't 'proper' amateurs? Could it be that Strode-Jackson and Baker, both of them highly intelligent men, were deliberately working up an anti-Olympic case in which they didn't really believe but which they hoped would galvanise the British Olympic Association and AAA decision-makers into action to put matters right on the home front? After all, both Strode-Jackson and Baker had enthused about their 1912 Olympic experience, and were presumably still committed to the principle of continuance of the Games.

Strode-Jackson's views carried rather more weight then just those of an Olympic champion – significant as that would have been – because his war service as the youngest Brigadier-General in the British army at the age of 27 had been exceptionally distinguished. He had been wounded three times while serving with the King's Royal Rifle Corps and was one of only seven officers to have been awarded the Distinguished Service Order and three bars.

There was naturally a spirited response by the British Olympic Council to Strode-Jackson and Baker, and the Reverend de Laffan's letter reads almost like one of those patriotic posters of 1914 which had barked out the message that 'Your Country Needs You!' Rally to the flag, support our cause, don't let our brave little Belgian allies down: that was the distinct tone of de Laffan's riposte. He particularly pointed out that Antwerp, having been chosen by the International Olympic Committee in 1914, had been offered the chance when the war ended to delay hosting the Games until 1924 but had insisted with royal backing that they could cope in the little time remaining to them. The Reverend de Laffan, who had acted as chaplain to the forces during the war, wrote: 'The question is not whether we can achieve a larger number of victories at Antwerp, but whether we are bound in honour to play the game by Belgium, as Belgium played the game by us in 1914'.

More concerned, understandably, with picking up the pieces of sporting careers interrupted or delayed by the war than with worrying at this stage whether or not there would be an Olympic opportunity for them a year hence, the athletes got on with their various competitions as the 1919 season began. There was no Inter-Varsity match in March – though there *was* a baseball game, largely played by American undergraduates, which Oxford won 6–4 – and so athletics competition at Oxford in the customary late-winter months was desultory and at Cambridge there seemed to be none at all. There was talk of holding the match later in the year, with the alluring prospect of brighter weather and better performances, but this only provoked an irritable note from a 'university correspondent' in *The Times*, who wrote: 'Is it too much to hope that at this 'reconstruction' meeting some reconstruction of the programme may be carried out? Is this not the very occasion on which 'Throwing the Hammer' and 'Putting the Weight' may silently vanish away? Are these two 'tricks' to play parts equally decisive as the final result of the mile and half-mile races?'

Unfortunately, such insularity all too readily found favour among the Oxbridge elite and when the Inter-Varsity match was revived in 1920 there was no pole vault, triple jump, discus or javelin, and nor was there a 220 yards, 440 yards hurdles, steeplechase or walk. There *was* a shot and hammer but the latter survived only a couple of years until that was dropped. The pole vault came back in 1923, but the discus and javelin were not introduced until 1938 and the triple jump was excluded until 1959. The hammer reappeared on the programme at last…in 1975!

Cambridge eventually held their university sports towards the end of May, the athletes having been allowed to train at Fenner's only in the morning or evening when the ground was not required for cricket, and a 'fine big strapping athlete', G.M. Butler, who had been the Public Schools' 100 yards and 440 yards champion of 1917, impressed by winning both those events. Undeterred by the carping of the 'university correspondent', a shot event was also held and was won by a Serbian, M. Yanjushevitch, who had reportedly achieved 45ft (13.70m) or thereabouts on his home soil, which was better than any Englishman had ever done, though he was far short of that distance on this occasion. A winner at the Oxford inter-college matches showed some considerable promise as a high jumper and was certainly of the right sort of physique, but the 6ft 5½in (1.97m) tall Sebastian Earl preferred to take his place in Oxford's crew in the Boat Race the next year, and though he suffered the indignity of losing on three successive occasions he was still selected for the Great Britain eight which took the silver medals at the Antwerp Olympics.

The athletics season in Britain in the 1920s was conducted in a very different fashion to that of the 21st century – haphazard was probably as good a description as any. There were no Leagues for the clubs to compete against each other at national or regional level. The regional championships (Northern, Southern, Midlands) and the AAA Championships were the domestic highlights for the leading athletes. The only international opportunities were at the Olympics every four years or in matches against France, which began in 1921, or Germany, which did not start until 1929. The run-of-the-mill club athletes competed week after week in local sports meetings; often hundreds of them in handicap sprints or middle-distance races, sharing the grounds – more often than not, the local football pitch – with racing cyclists, brass bands and brawny tug-of-war teams.

The 1919 AAA Championships were originally scheduled for the Queen's Club, in West London, but when the committee-men went to look at the track they found it in such a poor condition that they promptly moved their fixture back to Stamford Bridge instead. Queen's Club was where the Inter-Varsity match had taken place each year from 1888 to 1914 on its three-laps-to-the-mile track, and both Arnold Strode-Jackson and Philip Baker would have had fond memories of it, with eight wins there between them. Maybe it was their disappointment at finding the scene of their former triumphs in a state of such decay that had partly prompted their letter to *The Times*. Thankfully, a new track of conventional 440 yards circumference was to be installed at Queen's Club in good time for that first post-war Inter-Varsity meeting in 1920. Though no longer an athletics venue more than 90 years later, the grounds are still very much in use, containing 45 tennis courts and hosting an annual pre-Wimbledon tournament during which Rafael Nadal and Roger Federer smash and volley where Strode-Jackson and Lord Noel-Baker once strode in splendour.

Despite the alternative attractions of Henley, Wimbledon and cricket at the Oval, 15,000 spectators turned up for the AAA Championships, which were 'an unqualified success', according to *The Times*, though earlier rain had left the track and infield sodden and heavy. A dozen or so survivors from 1914 and earlier years figured prominently, but only four men again won titles – middle-distance runner Albert Hill, hurdler George Gray, walker Bobby Bridge and high jumper Howard Baker, and all of them except the Polytechnic Harrier, Hill, were, coincidentally, from Lancashire. To talk of an 'unqualified success' may have been true so far as the attendance and the general level of the track performances was concerned, but there were serious defects to be found by those who studied the full range of results closely.

Hill, whose previous title had been gained at four miles nine years before, was deservedly awarded the Harvey Memorial Cup as the outstanding champion, having won the 880 yards and the mile, and another double winner was his namesake, Billy Hill, of Surrey AC, in the sprints, who, like Howard Baker, was also a fine footballer and had played for Crystal Palace. Both Hills had served during the war – Albert as a signalman with the Royal Flying Corps; Billy as an army Lieutenant in France, Egypt and Gallipoli, and the latter had even had the occasional race, winning the South-Eastern Mounted Brigade 100 yards and 220 yards while posted to the Suez Canal region in 1916.

However, the AAA field events were a disaster for the home competitors, apart from Howard Baker's success in the high jump at 5ft 11in (1.80m) from a Swede, Karl-Georg Högström, with Tim Carroll third. After he had won Howard Baker had the bar put at 6ft 3in (1.91m), which would have equalled the Championship record if he had cleared it, but he didn't. The group of eight visitors from Sweden, enjoying the rapt attention of their Crown Prince from the VIP enclosure, took the pole vault (Högström), long jump and shot, and a Dane was successful in the hammer. Had the details filtered through to Walter Knox in far-away Ontario, he would not have been at all impressed as there were only two competitors in the pole vault and hammer, while the hop step and jump, discus and javelin were not held at all. For the five field events that did take place there was a total of only six British competitors. Carroll apart, the Irish were notably absent, and this was only to be expected as a violent Anglo-Irish conflict which would eventually lead to Irish independence had broken out during 1919.

The Times also devoted a fair section of its report to the comportment of the spectators, rather than the athletes they were watching, and the assessment would surely seem familiar to a 21st-century generation, though some of the phraseology would now be regarded as politically very incorrect : 'Those who go to the Athletics Championships are a very workmanlike body. There is a big proportion of old competitors who love to meet and talk of the giants of the past and compare them with their present-day successors, generally to the disadvantage of the latter. It is, moreover, a very knowing crowd. It can reel off the 'best' times and 'records' of athletes in a way that makes the average male dizzy and completely overwhelms any unfortunate female listener. Athletics meetings, however, always attract a large number of women. Perhaps it is the gay colours of the runners. Perhaps it is their youth and splendid physical condition. Women come in thousands and add brightness to the scene, even if their appreciation of the actual events is not always particularly intelligent'.

One of the reasons for the mediocre standard at the AAA Championships was that numerous athletes were scattered far and wide, still in uniform and awaiting discharge, and so some of the services' meetings offered rather better fare. At an 'Empire Day Athletic Festival' at Stamford Bridge, in which there were 1,500 competitors, the outstanding athlete was Sergeant C. Mears, of the Royal Army Service Corps, who won the 100 yards, 440 yards and 120 yards hurdles, and his time for the 'quarter', ahead of the Oxford undergraduate (and Olympic 400 metres champion-to-be), Bevil Rudd, was a brisk 50⅕ sec. Unfortunately, this was no new star emerging for Britain as Cyril Mears was an Australian *and* a versatile professional runner who was so highly regarded by the handicappers at the Powderhall meeting in Edinburgh that on the previous New Year's Day he had been placed off virtual scratch for both the 100 yards and the one mile. The stringent AAA rules regarding professionalism were waived for military sports events.

Howard Baker and Tim Carroll met again in the invitation high jump at the Manchester Athletic Club meeting at Fallowfield on 26 July, for which there was a crowd of 7,000, and the AAA champion was in tremendous form. *The Athletic News* gave extensive attention to him on the following Monday, and in the excellent report by a writer who identified himself only as 'W.L.S.' particular attention was drawn to the occupational hazards which Howard Baker faced. 'W.L.S' was W.L. Sinclair, a highly experienced athletics correspondent who had attended the 1912 Olympics for *The Athletic News* and would be at the 1920 Games for the *Sporting Chronicle*. His description of the circumstances of Howard Baker's jumping that day is worth quoting in some detail:

'Howard Baker cleared 6ft 1in and won the competition, whereafter he went for the British records. First of all, he polished off the best AAA championship performance, done by the lengthy American, S.S. Jones, at Stamford Bridge, in 1902, by clearing 6ft 3¼in and then he set about the endeavour to eclipse Carroll's British record of 6ft 5in (done in 1913, at Kinsale, and approved by the IAAA) by trying 6ft 5½in. He did not look like accomplishing the latter feat, for he never got high enough with his feet. However, he will have another go at Crewe next Saturday, and then he will compete at New Brighton, and at Leigh Harriers' games, where the Northern Counties High Jump will take place.

'Not nearly enough was made of Howard Baker's performance last Saturday as a spectacle, and with a man going after a record achievement it was certainly no incentive in the task to have bicycle races decided at the same time with, on the one hand, a brass band playing and, on the other hand, the lusty tones of the assiduous megaphone soloist proclaiming placings and times. In America or in Ireland, where high jumping is seriously regarded and properly appreciated, that event would not have any disturbing influences to divert the athlete from the task before him'.

'W.L.S.', having sprung so alertly to the defence of high jumpers, can be forgiven for not also pointing out that Howard Baker's achievement was of further historic importance because it beat the confirmed best by an Englishman, to the credit of the Honourable

Marshall Brooks 43 years previously! Worth noting at this stage is the fact that over the years 19 Irishmen had jumped 6ft (1.83m) or better but only five Englishmen and three Scotsmen had done so, as follows:

6ft 3¼in (1.92m) Benjamin Howard Baker (Liverpool Harriers & AC), 1919-
6ft 2½in (1.89m) The Honourable Marshall Brooks (Oxford University), 1876
6ft 2in (1.88m) George Rowdon (Teignmouth FC), 1887
6ft 0½in (1.84m) R.G. Murray (West of Scotland Harriers), 1904
6ft 0¼in (1.83m) John Parsons (Edinburgh University), 1883
6ft 0in (1.83m) Gerald Howard-Smith (Cambridge University), 1901
6ft 0in (1.83m) John Milne (Edinburgh University), 1902
6ft 0in (1.83m) Jack Probert (Polytechnic Harriers), 1918

The Crewe meeting referred to by 'W.L.S.' was the annual sports staged by Crewe Alexandra FC, and Howard Baker got over 6ft 3in (1.91m) in splendid style, according to one eye-witness, earning a prize worth four guineas (£4.20). It would seem that the Eastern Cut-Off technique first taught him by Knox five years before was starting to work to his advantage. At the Widnes Police Sports on 9 August Howard Baker contented himself with a 6ft clearance, attempting no higher, and maybe it was the fact that he had played a couple of days' cricket during the week, including a bowling spell of some 30 overs, according to *The Athletic News*, that curbed his energies. The unnamed columnist for *The Athletic News* added his opinion that Howard Baker 'is very keen about reaching the very top of his form next year, so that he may do well by the United Kingdom in the Olympic Games; and then I fancy he will have had enough of the sport'. He high-jumped each Saturday in August – so athletics was at least for the time being taking precedence over cricket.

The comments regarding Howard Baker's ambitions could have been pure speculation, but it seems perfectly feasible that it was based on a chat with Howard Baker. Very rarely were sportsmen quoted directly in newspaper reports in those years. The same writer continued: 'The Liverpool athlete, for a man who met with a nasty accident while serving in the Royal Navy during war time, and was told he need not expect to jump again, has been remarkably successful with a long string of performances over 6ft. Everywhere his work has been greatly admired, though in his own city there seems, for no apparent reason that I know of, a tendency to depreciate his worth. I could tell a funny story regarding the attitude of the Press, but I shall forbear'. What could he *possibly* mean?

The following Saturday Howard Baker went to the Leigh Harriers' Sports, for which the local newspaper had carried the previous day an advertisement which proclaimed in eye-catching capitals that 'HOWARD BAKER, ENGLAND'S CHAMPION HIGH JUMPER, WILL ATTEMPT TO BEAT THE RECORD'. The Lancashire town had long been a hot-bed of sporting activity, and this was a special occasion, as it was the first post-war meeting of a series which had begun in 1892. It was reported that 'the enthusiastic band of officers who had kept the club going during the long years of war worked hard to make the revival a success' and the 2,000 spectators who had paid a shilling each (or one shilling and sixpence for a better view) had their money's worth from the would-be record-breaker.

The high jump was one of nine events on the three-hour programme and incorporated the Northern Counties' title, which Howard Baker had already won on the four previous occasions, though these, of course, had been from 1911 to 1914. Whether he had actually signified his intention of breaking 'the record' – be it the British record or the Northern Counties' record – or whether the meeting promoters were indulging in journalistic licence is not known, but he cleared 5ft, 5ft 4in, 5ft 6in, 5ft 10in, 6ft and 6ft 2in in succession and then had a fine attempt at 6ft 4in 'which provoked loud cheering'. Among the numerous other events which was well received by the thronged spectators was the Leigh Harriers' 1,000 yards club championship won by Sergeant Harry Irlam, who had survived almost three years of fighting at the front with only a minor wound.

However, there were to be recriminations after the Leigh meeting. The regular columnist for *The Athletic News* who used the byeline, 'Strephon', and who may well have been the same man as that other contributor to the periodical, 'W.L.S.', published an article severely criticising the organisers of the high jump – to be more accurate, lambasting them unmercifully, as follows: 'To begin with, the tackle used in that event was most inadequate. That was probably not the fault of the Association, whose secretary had been assured that the standards were thoroughly satisfactory, though when the competition took place they were proved inadequate to test the merits of B. Howard Baker. The ludicrous sight of standards placed upon beer boxes for an attempt upon a record was seen!'

Howard Baker was officially credited only with his earlier jump of 5ft 4in, and the reason for that was not the improvised facilities for his winning jump but that the officials at the meeting decided on the spur of the moment that his use of a handkerchief tied to the cross-bar as a marker was illegal. 'Strephon' was roused to indignation: 'Does this mean that while in the Olympic competition, wherein at Stockholm the cross-piece was not only painted white with brightly-coloured spots marked for the aid of the leapers but the use of handkerchiefs was allowed, and in AAA championships, Inter-Allied Games, American and Canadian championships and Scandinavian championships 'wipes' were never objected to, such a thing was not permissible under the laws of the Northern Counties' AA, a divisional body of the AAA?'

Making use of a handkerchief was a common practice among high jumpers so that they could distinguish black-painted cross-bars against the background, in the same sort of manner as sight-screens on cricket grounds enabled batsmen to see the ball in flight better. Howard Baker had done just that on previous occasions at the Northern Counties' championships without any recriminations. The Leigh affair was apparently not an isolated incident because 'Strephon' had further words of criticism for meeting organisers: 'Howard Baker's high jumping last season was brilliant, but it was assuredly not improved by pettifogging official interference on certain occasions. Enthusiasm is one commendable thing and accuracy is another, but when officials seek to interpret for their own pleasure and for no other apparent reason the rules of competition, their zeal has bolted and has become unmanageable and generally unpleasant'.

On that contentious note, Howard Baker then changed his spiked shoes for football boots and his singlet for a woollen sweater to start out on his new-found career as a goalkeeper with the roving amateur team, Northern Nomads, but he was to have one more unforeseen high-jump competition before the year was out. The AAA arranged a match against Cambridge University, though the choice of date, 6 December, was more suited to chasing a ball, oval-shaped or round, than chasing opponents round a track. Even so, for the university Harold Abrahams ran a respectable 10⅕ seconds for 100 yards, beating Billy Hill, and Guy Butler inflicted a second defeat on the AAA speedster at the odd distance of 200 yards which was peculiar to the Fenner's track at Cambridge. The sprint win by Abrahams, still a few days short of his 20th birthday, would have come as no great surprise because he had shortly before won the 100 yards, 440 yards and long jump at the Freshmen's Sports despite a keen northerly wind and occasional sleet; 'His future career in University athletics will be watched with considerable interest', opined *The Times*.

The performance of the meeting, though, came from Howard Baker. The AAA champion beat the ground record with 6ft 2in (1.88m) despite no opposition at all to speak of – none of his opponents cleared better than 5ft 7in – and just failed with an excellent effort at 6ft 4in. This really was an achievement of the highest order, within an inch or so of his official best, and in the depths of winter at that. A photograph of his winning clearance was published in the next day's *Sunday Pictorial* and then in Monday's *Daily Herald* and rather suggested that he had a comfortable inch or so to spare. Howard Baker turned out again for a rare essay at 120 yards hurdles and finished within two yards of Major E. G. W. W. Harrison. The winning time was ordinary, 17⅕ seconds, but Eric Harrison was a very capable hurdler who had won the Inter-Services' title in September in almost a second faster and would eventually compete for Great Britain at the 1924 Olympics. He had been awarded the Military Cross in 1915 while in the Royal Artillery and would rise to the rank of Major-General and serve as aide-de-camp to King George VI in 1945–46, living to the age of 94.

Matches between the universities and visiting AAA teams would become a prominent feature of the domestic season for half-a-century or so to follow, and it would be at just one of these (Oxford v AAA on 6 May 1954, to be precise) that the most celebrated of all athletics achievements, the first sub-four-minute mile, would be achieved. In 1919 on that grey afternoon at Fenner's, when the World record for the mile stood at 4min 12⅗ sec (to an Oxford graduate from the USA, Norman Taber), and was thus still only a fraction faster than Walter George had done 33 years before, and a Cambridge undergraduate, W.R. Seagrove, had just won that event in 4min 35⅗ sec, the concept of breaking four minutes would have been unthinkable.

Lieutenant-Colonel Strode-Jackson, who presumably shared that view regarding potential mile times (though the lamented pre-war Olympic bronze-medallist, George Hutson, had reckoned it feasible), had penned a further letter to *The Times* in November calling for the British Olympic Association to 'undertake the complete reorganisation of athletics throughout the country', and so far as the next Games were concerned, now only eight months away, he proposed that the following commitments be made:
that every competitor who is up to the standard should be taken to the Games;
that no competitor not up to the standard should be taken to the Games;
that for every one who is taken adequate arrangements should be made and reasonable food and accommodation provided.

'At Stockholm', Strode-Jackson concluded, 'none of these principles were adhered to'. That must have seemed like a lifetime ago in the peaceful days before the war. Maybe Antwerp would be an improvement.

Keen to resume a rewarding football career which had taken him to the fringes of both the professional League and the England amateur team, Howard Baker had nevertheless joined the Northern Nomads as much for social reasons as for competitive ones. The Nomads were very much gentlemen, amateur to a man, dedicated to an open and entertaining style of play, and so had an obvious appeal to his sense of adventure. They were the Northern equivalent to the Oxbridge-dominated Corinthian club which had provided the entire England side on two occasions in the 1890s, and they also had a tradition to uphold, albeit not quite as illustrious.

Having already proved good enough as a centre-half to warrant a pre-war England amateur trial, Howard Baker now decided that he would become a goalkeeper because he believed that the ankle he had broken in his war-time accident would not stand up to the demands of playing in his former position. Who, then, could have been too surprised when in typical fashion this sporting man for all seasons very soon established himself as someone out of the ordinary in his new role? His reasoning for believing that he could cope with his impediment better between the posts than in midfield is not readily apparent, and there might have been a sense of sheer bravado in his decision. The early 1920s was a tough era for goalkeepers, subject to laws of the game which allowed constant harassment by opposing forwards, and Howard Baker would have been well aware of this. He was never one, of course, to avoid a confrontation, whether it was with a high-jump bar or a heavyweight opponent in the sparring-ring.

The Nomads had provided two players for Great Britain's winning team at the 1912 Olympics, Ronald Brebner and Arthur Berry, and both of them had links with Howard Baker. Brebner was a dental surgeon by profession who kept goal for his club and country, playing in 23 amateur internationals for England and he had turned out on a number of occasions for Chelsea during the 1910–11 season, 17 matches in all, and may have been an influence in Howard Baker's eventual decision to join the Chelsea club, as he was to do in 1921, but was certainly not instrumental in the matter. Tragically, Brebner had died at the age of only 33 in November 1914 from complications which set in after he was injured in a match. Berry, an Oxford graduate described as one of the most brilliant players of his generation, with a direct winger's style said to be 'a complete act without tinsel or gaudiness', had won 32 England amateur caps between 1908 and 1913 and had played League football for Liverpool, Everton, Fulham and Wrexham. He would certainly have known Howard Baker well, at least in post-war years, because he was also Liverpool-born on 3 January 1888, four years before Howard Baker, and his father had been chairman of Liverpool FC. Berry joined the family law firm in the city after serving in the Liverpool Regiment during World War One.

For England's first amateur international match for five years against Ireland at Derby County's ground on Saturday 15 November 1919, the Nomads duly provided the home team's goalkeeper. However, this was not a startlingly rapid rise for Howard Baker (to be delayed only a year or so) but a debut for the club's other goalkeeper, Jim Mitchell, who was a 22-year-old student at Manchester University, having already lived an eventful life, serving as an officer in the Liverpool Scottish Regiment during the war. Mitchell was also, incidentally a very capable high jumper, long jumper and hurdler. England won 5–0 and Howard Baker could have been excused for imagining that Mitchell's club and national place was secure for years to come and that a 27-year-old 'novice' would remain forever on the sidelines. In fact, the Nomads chose their teams in a somewhat haphazard fashion, as and when the players were free of other commitments to universities or old boys' clubs, and Howard Baker soon got his chance.

In the fourth round of the FA Amateur Cup (the quarter-finals) on 28 February 1920 the Nomads had Howard Baker in goal and put up a spirited defence against the formidable West London side, Tufnell Park, before losing 2–1 in front of a crowd of 3,000. The Nomads were left in something of a mess when one of their players, appropriately named Heap, kicked an opponent – most ungentlemanly conduct! – and was dismissed from the field by the referee, who was clearly not someone to argue with. He was Sergeant-Major H.M. Prince, who had himself appeared for England against Sweden in 1914 and was still an active player who would be in the Olympic squad in 1920. Incidentally, Tufnell Park went on to reach the FA Amateur Cup Final the following April, losing 1–0 to Dulwich Hamlet in front of a record attendance of 28,000 at Millwall's New Cross ground.

One of the Tufnell Park goals was certainly Howard Baker's fault because he left his line to clear the ball and it was collected by an opposing forward who shot it into an undefended net. This was to be a familiar occurrence every so often during Howard Baker's further dozen years of a flamboyant goalkeeping career but seemed hardly to matter so far as selectors were concerned.

The FA Cup Final that year was played between Aston Villa and Huddersfield Town on the Stamford Bridge turf with which Howard Baker was so familiar, and it makes a nice cameo to illustrate just how different a footballing era it was some 90 years ago that one of the principal advertisements in the newspapers during the lead-up to the game was for that homely drink, cocoa. Rowntree's ran an advertisement under the headline 'The Footballer's Food-Beverage' which depicted a group of players eagerly lining up to be served from an enormous china mug, and the accompanying text took the form of a verse composed by one E. Arkell, who could conceivably have been Reginald Arkell, the author of numerous comic novels and West End musicals, including an adaptation of '1066 And All That', or perhaps his actress wife, Elizabeth. Whoever was responsible does not matter too much, as a quick read through of the following jaunty but hardly timeless lines will confirm:

'The Football Cup – with nothing in it –
We hope to see the best team win it,
And when they've played the final round
Upon the famous Chelsea ground
With Rowntree's cocoa fill the cup
And cheer them as they drink it up'

Within 12 months Howard Baker would play in an England amateur trial, as he had done pre-war, and then make his debut against Wales. Higher honours were soon to follow, but meanwhile there was another Olympic Games to think about, and it was a shade too early to challenge for a place in Great Britain's football team, though his Northern Nomads teammate, Mitchell, would be one of the two chosen goalkeepers. Being the versatile sort of chap that Howard Baker was, there was always the possibility for him to defend his net in another Olympic context entirely – the swimming pool.

It's interesting to speculate whether he seriously considered challenging for Olympic places in two sports in Antwerp. His ability as a swimmer and his developing talent as a goalkeeper on the football field meant that keeping goal in water polo came even more naturally to him than the various other sports he took up. That he should be interested in playing what is now a relatively minor sport in Great Britain is not as surprising as it might seem because water polo remains to this day the longest-surviving team game contested at the Olympic Games and the British were then the World leaders, having won the gold medals in 1900, 1908 and 1912. Furthermore, the counties of Lancashire and Cheshire provided the hot-bed (or should that be hot-bath?) of the game. There were 40 affiliated clubs in Lancashire and the Inter-Counties' title had been won 13 times since the series had begun in 1896.

A Cheshire club, Hyde Seal, had been national champions seven times since 1902 and a Lancashire club, Wigan, had won in three other years. One of Hyde Seal's players, George Wilkinson, had taken part in all three Olympic triumphs. Wigan played in the Liverpool & District League, in which there were 21 teams in the three divisions, including those representing other such nearby towns as Chester, Runcorn, St Helens, Southport, Warrington and Widnes. Howard Baker was to recall in his latter years that it was a sport which was particularly popular with coal-miners – though presumably not coming to the pool straight from their shifts.

Howard Baker was also to say that he played two seasons of water-polo, but there is only tangible evidence of one at the top club level, and that was not until 1921. If he did have serious Olympic ambitions as a water-polo goalkeeper, and he may well have made some tentative and unannounced sorties in a local team during 1920, he would have realised full well the task that faced him. The Lancashire and England goalkeeper was Charlie Smith, whom Howard Baker would have known personally, having shared in pre war swimming exhibitions with him, and Smith had also been a member of the winning Great Britain team at the 1908 and 1912 Olympics. Such was his secure tenure as the country's No.1 that he was to remain England's automatic choice from 1902 to 1926 (!), and whenever an England trial was held both before and after World War One the selectors did not bother to include him, diplomatically informing the two goalkeepers nominated that for the ensuing international matches Smith would be 'considered when making the final selection'.

Curiously, Howard Baker did not actually like playing water polo very much, still calling to mind in his latter years the amount of fouling that went on, but maybe he simply could not resist a challenge – or simply had a spare evening to fill each week. So he had joined the Everton club which played in that thriving Liverpool & District League. Hardly surprisingly, this was a sport in which he would soon make a splash, and as if that wasn't enough to absorb his boundless energies he had also decided to take up yet another activity.

Anyone for tennis?

I SAY, HOWARD BAKER, WHY NOT HAVE A GO AT THE OLYMPIC JAVELIN WHILE YOU'RE ABOUT IT!

The euphoria of Stockholm was, as only to be expected, dismissed from memory during the appalling years of World War One. Then in peacetime, and by contrast to those previous Games, contentious issues surrounded Antwerp in 1920 which were to become more and more familiar in an Olympic context as the years went by. The city had been chosen as hosts by the International Olympic Committee at their congress in 1914 ahead of Amsterdam, Budapest and Rome, and the Games of 1916 had been scheduled for Berlin, but the onset of war a few months later put paid to those plans. The Germans were, of course, dismissed from the reckoning, and would not be back until 1928, but it was still with some misgivings that the IOC eventually agreed in April of 1919 to Antwerp going ahead with the first post-war celebration.

The IOC's concern was that the Belgians simply would not be ready in time. The worries though for Baron Pierre de Coubertin, the founder of the modern Olympic movement, were of a different kind. Back in the balmy days before the war the intention had been that the Games would form part of a 'World Fair', and that inevitably conjured up for him images of the flawed Olympics in Paris in 1900 and in St Louis four years later. In Britain rather more fundamental opinions were being aired. Just as had been the case in pre-war years, there were those who doubted the wisdom of competing at all, and they were now able to support their case by saying that it was far too soon after a war in which the country had suffered 994,000 dead and 1,663,000 wounded to contemplate another misguided Olympic venture.

This attitude was most forcibly expressed by no less than a prominent member of the British Olympic Association, Sir Theodore Cook, who claimed in a letter to *The Times* that the modern revival of the Games had become 'entirely alien to English character and thought', and he supported that statement by pointing out that the public had 'signified the national disapproval of the Olympic movement by utterly refusing to subscribe sufficient money to give our representatives in Belgium any chance of showing their best form'. This letter appeared on 16 August, when the Games were still under way, and it soon received a vigorous rebuttal in a reply signed by 40 members of the British athletics team, including Howard Baker, before they had even left Antwerp.

What a sensational media story this would have been in later generations – especially as Sir Theodore had been the author of the official 1908 Games report and was himself an Antwerp award-winner in the literary section of the Arts competitions! Yet the vociferous exchange of views seemed to pass off largely unremarked, and maybe that was because the public was already of the same mind as the querulous Sir Theodore. The fund-raising appeal launched in January of 1920 with a target of £30,000 had brought in no more than £2,000 by the following June.

The *Manchester Guardian* carried a lengthy and thoughtful leader article the very same day that Sir Theodore Cook's letter appeared and arrived at much the same conclusion, though clearly the timing was such that it could not have been influenced by Sir Theodore's theories. A number of reasons were presented why Britons were indifferent to the Games. One of these concerned what was described as the 'American attitude' towards sport, and this was defined as being 'a state of mind from which there has been squeezed the English amateur's traditional feeling that, after all, a game is only a game and not worth more than the place of a game among a man's interests'. If Howard Baker had later read these words, he would surely have nodded his head vigorously in agreement.

The 1920 athletics season in Britain had got under way back in March in its time-honoured and leisurely fashion. At the Inter-Varsity match Harold Abrahams had won the 100 yards and long jump for Cambridge, Bevil Rudd the half-mile for Oxford, and Rudd and Cambridge's Guy Butler had shared the quarter-mile, but no series records were beaten and the single one that was equalled – by Abrahams in the sprint – had first been set in 1868. As usual, the programme excluded several of those field events which were regarded with such contempt, though there was a happening of great significance after the traditional dinner for the teams that evening when it was decided to form an athletics club open to past and present members of the two universities. Lord Desborough was elected president, Philip Baker secretary, and Arnold Strode-Jackson, Butler and Rudd committee members.

The Achilles Club, as it was named, would become one of the major forces in British athletics for more than the next 40 years and it very quickly made its mark. A few days later a combined Oxford & Cambridge 4 x 880 yards quartet was sent off across the Atlantic from Southampton on board the steamship *Adriatic*, to compete in the annual Penn Relays. This was a meeting which had been first held in 1895 and remains in the 21st century the largest and most popular annual track and field fixture in the USA. The team of 'blues', dark and light, consisting of Wilfred Tatham, Henry Stallard, William Milligan and Bevil Rudd, won their event and in a World-record time of 7min 50⅖ sec, and there was inspiration on hand from two nicely contrasting sources. Accompanying the quartet were the 'natural' who had won Olympic gold, Arnold Strode-Jackson, and the newly-appointed Oxford coach, Alfred Shrubb, the legendary distance-runner of the turn of the century who in 1904 had become the first man to complete 10 miles in less than 51 minutes – still a highly reputable accomplishment more than a century later – and who trained harder than any of his contemporaries, at 40 or more miles a week.

An 'Olympic Trials' was held at Stamford Bridge on 12 June, but the meeting served even less purpose than it had in 1912. There was no justifiable need for it because the Olympic athletics would not begin until mid-August, leaving plenty of time for the selections to be made after the AAA Championships. Many of the athletes with Antwerp aspirations obviously realised this was so because they did not put in an appearance and the only performances of any real merit on a typical early summer's day of rainstorms were the 220 yards win in 22.0sec by Harry Edward, who had been born in British Guiana (now Guyana) and had been interned as a student in Germany throughout the war, and the three miles in 14min 58⅖sec by Oxford's Inter-Varsity winner, Evelyn Montague.

Howard Baker missed the high jump, but as it was won at only 5ft 7½in (1.71m) by R.A. Nicholas, of Southend Harriers, there was nothing for the AAA champion to concern himself about any possible new challenge from a fellow-Englishman. Nor, for that matter, had the Inter-Varsity match thrown up unsuspected home-grown high-jumping talent because the winner there at 5ft 9in (1.75) had been a Rhodes Scholar from the USA at Oxford, H.S. White. Howard Baker had begun his season instead with an 'Olympic high-jump trial' of his own which formed part of the Broughton Harriers & Athletic Club Sports at Weaste, Manchester on Whit Saturday 22 May, and he had displayed 'excellent form' according to the *Liverpool Daily Post*, clearing 6ft (1.83) and going no higher, which was scarcely surprising as he won by 13 inches (33cm)!

The description 'Olympic trial' had some official sanction to it because such promotions had been encouraged in the regions by the AAA, but the term seems to have been freely bandied about for events which in no way deserved such billing. There were further competitions carrying this title at Garston, in Liverpool, two days later, where the mile was won in a mere 4min 35⅖sec, the shot at 31ft 7in (9.62m) and the long jump at 17ft 7in (5.36m). Another long-jump 'trial' took place at the Sefton Harriers meeting in Liverpool the following Saturday and this was won at a rather more respectable distance of 20ft 1in (6.12m), though still, of course, by no means of Olympic calibre, by a newly-arrived Sefton member, William Childs, who would be Northern champion every year from 1920 to 1926. Childs was a Liverpool policeman and would have a long athletics career, still competing in 1933, more than a dozen years after Howard Baker had given up the sport.

On 5 June at the Salford Harriers Sports, staged on the local football ground, another five 'Olympic trials' were held, and Howard Baker won the high jump, long jump and triple jump, achieving a noteworthy distance of 43ft 8in (13.31m) in the last of these competitions. This was, in fact, a rather more significant performance than any of the officials and spectators, and even perhaps the perpetrator himself, may have appreciated on the day. The event, then known more accurately as the hop step and jump, was another which had long been dominated by the Irish, and universally so, as Peter O'Connor and Con Leahy had finished first and second in the 1906 Olympics and Tim Ahearne had won in 1908.

The best valid performance by an Irish-born Briton had been 50ft 11in (15.52m) by Dan Ahearne, younger brother of Tim, in 1911, though by then he had emigrated to the USA, where for some reason he amended his surname to 'Ahearn'. This distance was much superior – the length of a very tall man lying down, to draw an analogy – to the English best of 44ft 6½in (13.58) by Philip Kingsford, of London AC, in 1912. The event was grievously unappreciated in England then and for many years to follow, and it had not been held at the AAA Championships before 1914. There was no aspiring predecessor to Jonathan Edwards in that era, though the *Manchester Guardian* reported encouragingly that there had been eight doughty opponents in the hop step and jump that day for Howard Baker.

The reason that he was not in attendance at the so-called official Olympic trials at Stamford Bridge the next Saturday was simply that he was otherwise engaged, winning the Northern title in Manchester and equalling his Championship record from the previous year of 6ft 2in (1.88m). Again there was no opposition to speak of, as one R. Swindreth, of Rochdale Harriers, was second at 4ft 10in (1.47), but Howard Baker occupied himself fully throughout the afternoon by also taking the discus at 104ft 2½in (31.76m) and placing a close second to Childs in the long jump, 19ft 9in (6.02) to 19ft 5½in (5.93), and second again in the javelin. A couple of days later it was reported that Howard Baker and Childs were the only two athletes selected by the Northern Counties' AA for any of the field events at the AAA Championships. Nomination meant that the expenses for the journey incurred by Howard Baker and Childs would be met by the regional officialdom.

No doubt, though, Howard Baker still found time for one of his new-found sporting passions despite the demands of Olympic qualification. It was hardly surprising that he should have been attracted to lawn tennis because the Northern Championships tournament, taking place each alternate year on the courts at Aigburth alongside the Liverpool cricket club's ground, carried a great deal of prestige and attracted some of the World's leading players. Towards the end of 1917 he had married Christiana Fraser, who was herself an enthusiastic player, and their home was now in Mines Avenue, which was no more than 200 yards away. Taking the short stroll to the courts, they soon formed a lively mixed-doubles partnership.

The Northern Lawn Tennis Association had been founded in 1880 and their championships were considered second only in importance to Wimbledon. The singles winners at the 1920 event, held as always in early June, were Theodore Mavrogordato and Elizabeth Ryan, and Mavrogordato was an Oxford 'blue' of Ukrainian descent who went on to play in the Davis Cup for Great Britain, while Miss Ryan, US-born in 1892, a week before Howard Baker, became one of the finest players of her era, winning 30 Grand Slam titles for the ladies' and mixed doubles. She and her legendary French partner, Suzanne Lenglen, were to win all of their 31 matches at Wimbledon. When the authoritative *Manchester Guardian* tennis correspondent, A.E. Crawley, listed his top 50 male players of the year in no specific order 18 were British (including Mavrogordato), 11 American and nine from Australia & New Zealand.

On 19 June there were 7,000 spectators at the annual Crewe Alexandra FC Sports which Howard Baker favoured and he won the high jump without difficulty at 5ft 9in (1.75m). More significantly, the AAA honorary secretary, Harry J. Barclay, later to be Sir Harry Barclay, was in attendance and he and Howard Baker clearly had a lengthy conversation because the following Monday Barclay wrote a letter from the AAA offices in John Street, Central London, which more or less assured Howard Baker of his place in the Olympic team. Barclay must have expressed some concern to Howard Baker that he might want to contest too many events in Antwerp, judging by the following words, 'I am very glad to hear you are looking to the High Jump as the event at Antwerp in which you will represent Great Britain. I see no reason why we should not enter you for the Hop Step & Jump, and should this event be arranged to take place after the High Jump you might have a fair chance of scoring, if you were able to beat 48 feet. It has been won with about 48 ft. 11 ins. But only consider this event as quite secondary'.

One can only wonder what Howard Baker made of such a bold prediction that he could even win a medal (as one can justifiably interpret the phrase 'fair chance of scoring') in an event which he had contested seriously no more than a couple of times and for which his best performance was some five feet less than Barclay thought he could do. It might also have been wondered why it was that Barclay had not checked the readily available schedule of events at Antwerp before making his suggestion, which showed that the hop step and jump did indeed follow on after the high jump with a day to spare in between. As it happens, there was a change of heart by the AAA within the next fortnight or so.

At the all-important AAA Championships on 3 July – though perhaps no longer so all-important for those athletes who had already been taken into Harry Barclay's confidence – Howard Baker was in supreme form and won the high jump at 6ft 3¼in (1.91m), equalling his personal best of the year before and beating the championship record which had been held since 1902 by Sam Jones, the 6ft 8in (2.03m) tall American who was the Olympic champion in 1904. *The Times* was effusive in its praise: 'Nor, for that matter, could anyone approach, let alone excel, B. Howard-Baker as a high jumper. Howard-Baker has a magnificent physique and that mysterious quality of muscle that enables a man to leap higher than his own stature'. There was, though, a commendable qualifying footnote that Baker was 'still some inches short of the fabulous springs of 6ft 7in made by two Californian athletes'.

There was no mention of Howard Baker's performance also being a British record for the simple reason that the term 'British record' at that time signified the all-comers' best, and in any case the partition of Ireland was not to take place until May 1921 and so Tim Carroll, who was a distant joint second to Howard Baker at 5ft 9in (1.75) at this meeting, was still the best in Britain with his 6ft 5in (1.96) of seven years before. Baker's jump was the highest ever by an Englishman, apart from his unconfirmed 6ft 4in (1.93) of 1914 and the unapproved performances by the Devonian, George Rowdon, in the 1890s.

There were double successes for Harry Edward in the 100 and 220 yards and for Bevil Rudd at 440 and 880 yards, but Rudd would be running for South Africa in the Games and other titles which went overseas were the mile, pole vault and shot won by Frenchmen and the high hurdles, long jump, hammer and javelin won by Americans – none of whom were considered as serious Olympic medal prospects. The AAA organisers did the middle-distance men no favours by putting the newly-formed Achilles Club and Polytechnic Harriers in the same heat of the medley relay on the Friday evening, with only one team to qualify, which was ridiculous, not to say irresponsible. Albert Hill, for the Poly, who had won the 880/mile double at the previous year's Championships, held off Philip Baker by a yard in the opening half-mile stage and chose to defend only his title at that same distance the next afternoon, losing to Rudd by five or six yards.

The following Wednesday Howard Baker was sent two letters by Barclay, including an invitation to compete in that Saturday's home countries' international at Crewe (rather short notice, one would have thought), but much the more important was the one telling him that the 'Special Olympic Committee' of the AAA had named him for the high jump and the hop step and jump at the Antwerp Games. Barclay wrote helpfully, 'I shall be glad to hear immediately whether you will be able to leave for Antwerp about the 9th, 10th or 11th of August, or if you anticipate any difficulty in getting away from business whether a letter from this Association or any other source would be of assistance to you'. Howard Baker, who needed only to check with his father that it was alright to take time off for the Olympics, was also informed that 'a firm of outfitters has generously offered to equip the British Team with Blazers and flannel trousers' and that he should either contact Messrs. T.H. Downing & Co Ltd of 3a Wood Street, London E.C.2, or provide the AAA with details of his height and his chest and waist measurements. Howard Baker, always the picture of elegance, would certainly have made a personal call on the Olympic tailors.

The AAA win must have given him considerable confidence for the Olympic final to come in Antwerp on 17 August, and that feeling could only have been enhanced the next weekend when he and Carroll did well to tie at 6ft 1½in (1.87m) in heavy rain at the England & Wales v Ireland v Scotland triangular match at Crewe. On a track flooded to a depth of four inches, Billy Hill was reduced to 10⅗ for 100 yards, Harold Abrahams to 23⅕ for 220 yards and Bevil Rudd to 51⅗ and 1:59⅕ for his 440/880 double. At the Widnes Police Sports on 31 July Baker retired 'after easily negotiating 6ft 2in'.

The British team for Antwerp was rather smaller than it had been in 1912, 40 in all, largely due to the fact that entries were now restricted to four per country. Financial constraints may also have played a part because even for the 800 and 1500 metres, considered as Britain's elite events, only three had been chosen in each case. The total complement for the eight field events was seven, and just one of these was a thrower, Tom Nicolson, the veteran Scottish farmer who had placed fourth in the hammer back in 1908. Howard Baker and Tim Carroll were joined in the high jump by a recent Edinburgh University medical graduate, Willie Hunter, who had first emerged before the war and who had won that event with 5ft 9½in (1.76m) at the Scottish championships, and Lieutenant E.V. Dunbar, of the 13th Hussars, who had tied for the army title at 5ft 8in (1.73m). Hunter was also in the long jump with Harold Abrahams and Charles Lively, of the Birmingham club, Sparkhill Harriers, and in the high hurdles.

Howard Baker was additionally named in the triple jump (hop step and jump, if you prefer) with the AAA champion, Lively, and that decision was clearly based on the performance at the Salford Harriers meeting in June. What must have surprised Howard Baker, and perhaps even astonished him, was to read that he was also selected for the javelin, for which his only competitive experience of the year had been his modest second place in the Northern Championships. None of the regional javelin winners – Kenneth McLennan in the North, F.A.M. Webster in the Midlands or sprinter Victor D'Arcy in the South – had managed to approach even 120ft, and Northern Ireland, Scotland and Wales had not bothered to hold the event at all. So maybe the British selectors thought they might as well fill a place with someone who would already be in Antwerp, anyway.

Clubs from the London area provided 16 of the team, Oxford and Cambridge Universities seven, the Midlands five, Ireland and Scotland four each, and the North three. The Northerners were Howard Baker, hurdler George Gray (Salford Harriers) and cross-country runner Chris Vose (Warrington AC). Attentive readers will note that there is one selection not accounted for, and he was the high-jump colleague of Baker's, Eric Dunbar, who was an Australian army officer who happened to be on attachment to England that year and was chosen by Britain on the strength of winning the army 120 yards hurdles as well as that share of first place in the high jump. It is not recorded as to what the view was of officials of the Australian team which took part in the Olympic Games!

The winner of the US trials was John Murphy, from Portland, Oregon, who had also been national champion for the past two years, and he cleared 6ft 4¼in (1.94m) in the qualifying meeting at Cambridge, Massachusetts. Harold Muller and Richmond Landon were second and third at 6ft 3½in (1.92), and six others, including the 1912 champion, Alma Richards, cleared 6ft 2½in (1.89). Murphy, Muller, Landon and Walter Whalen were selected for Antwerp, and as Whalen had needed to go over 6ft 3¼in (1.91) in a jump-off to take the fourth place in the team all the Americans had performances equal to or better than

Howard Baker – but an inch or less difference meant little or nothing as a form guide. The best of the continental Europeans was of the same calibre; Bo Ekelund held the Swedish record at 1.93 (6ft 4in).

A notable absentee from the US team was the unrecognised World record-holder, Clinton Larsen, who had cleared 6ft 7⅞in (2.03m) in an unofficial meeting in 1917, though he was only 5ft 9½in (1.76) in height, and had won the national title that year. Larsen, who was a student at Brigham Young University in Utah, as had been Alma Richards, was close to his best form again in 1919 and was still active in 1924, when it was said that he had cleared 6ft 9½in (2.07m), again in excess of the World record, but he missed out on selection in each Olympic year. This was a pity because his style of jumping would have caused as much of a sensation in Antwerp as would Dick Fosbury in Mexico City 48 years later – he ran at top speed from a 45-degree angle and cleared the bar feet first and flat on his back.

There were 20 competitors in the high jump, all of them from Europe except for the four Americans, as follows:

Belgium: Rudolphe Jean Henault, Georges Henrion, Jean Mahy.
Czechoslovakia: Frantisek Stejskal.
France: Pierre Guilloux, René Labat, Pierre Lewden.
Great Britain: Tim Carroll, Eric Dunbar, Benjamin Howard Baker.
Greece: Dimitrios Andonidas.
Luxemburg: Henri Pleger.
Sweden: Bo Daniel Ekelund, Hans Rudolf Jagenburg, Thorvig Svahn, Einar Thulin.
USA: Richmond Landon, Harold Muller, John Murphy, Walter Whalen.

The Olympic qualifying round took place on the opening day, 15 August, and before it started there was a long discussion among the officials as to whether to use the available cinders or the turf as a take-off area, and it is some clear indication of how poor the facilities were in Antwerp that the cinders were so loose that it was felt that even the soft turf was preferable. Still, 12 athletes cleared the required height of 1.80m, of whom Howard Baker and Tim Carroll were the only two who had also competed in the 1912 final. Not surprisingly Dunbar did not figure among the qualifiers, as his personal best was only 5ft 8in (1.73) and he went no higher than 1.70 in Antwerp, and the fourth of the Britons, Hunter, did not take part, presumably because he preferred to concentrate on the hurdles and long jump still to come.

Only four countries were represented among the dozen finalists: Landon, Muller, Murphy and Whalen for the USA; Ekelund, Jagenburg, Svahn and Thulin for Sweden; Labat and Lewden for France; Carroll and Howard Baker. Labat was the brother of a 1912 high-jump competitor. The javelin preliminaries were decided the same day and Howard Baker understandably gave them a miss, but as a throw of 56.77m (186ft 3in) was required for the 10th and last qualifying place, and that was more than 40ft beyond the British record and 60ft beyond Howard Baker's best, it could hardly be said to have been an Olympic chance gone begging.

Though blessed by favourable weather, this opening session of the Games athletics had at first seemed hardly an occasion to stir the Olympic spirit. *The New York Times* described the circumstances: 'The day was one of wonderful beauty, the sunlight being tempered by a little breeze which was most agreeable to all competitors. The attendance, however, remains absurdly small. The stands were not half filled, and the whole great Olympic game, except for the babel of languages, has the character of club sports'. Yet the report 'by special cable' ended on a much more optimistic note: 'The whole day's proceedings were of a most enjoyable character and the absence of any appeals or friction between the nations competing showed much more of the ideal spirit of the League of Nations than any meeting of politicians'. Philip Baker, winning his 800 metres heat that afternoon, would have savoured that opinion, and there was further encouragement for British hopes as the war veteran, Albert Hill, and a 19-year-old Cambridge undergraduate, Edgar Mountain, also came safely through in that event and both Harry Edward and Billy Hill won their 100 metres quarter-finals.

The javelin was completed later that day and resulted in a clean sweep of the medals for Finland, and by the time the high-jump final began two days later three other events had been decided, resulting in a virtual Finnish-American domination. At 100 metres the American World record-holder, Charley Paddock, had taken the gold medal, with in second place his teammate, Morris Kirksey (the same man who had won the 100 yards at the Inter-Allies' Games at Stamford Bridge in 1918), and Harry Edward third for Britain. The USA had its own 1–2–3 at 400 metres hurdles and a Finn had won the pentathlon from an American and another Finn.

The outcome of the high jump final must have been a grave disappointment to Howard Baker, though the syndicated report in the *Liverpool Daily Post* by F.A.M Webster merely contained the bald comment that 'the English record-holder, Howard Baker, failed and was only equal for third place with Weyland and Murphy'. For two reasons this is a curious statement for the usually knowledgeable Webster to have made: (i) it was wrong, and (ii) if Howard Baker had indeed tied for third place, and therefore won a bronze medal, it would have been a performance of great distinction, though he only cleared 1.85. He was actually placed sixth but could conceivably have been deprived of a medal by the incompetence of officials.

The title in Antwerp went to the American, Richmond ('Dick') Landon, who was 6ft 2in (1.88m) tall and possessed a 'perfect turn and layout', according to Webster. Landon cleared 1.94m, equivalent to 6ft 4¼in, and the second and third placed athletes – Harold Muller, of the USA, and Bo Ekelund, of Sweden – both cleared 1.90 (6ft 2¾in). But Muller, Ekelund and two other Americans, Whalen (not Weyland, as Webster had written) and Murphy, had been involved in a jump-off and Howard Baker should have been there, too, but either the high-jump organisers or the British management forgot to tell him and he had left the arena!

The situation is further complicated by the fact that Muller and Ekelund had cleared 1.90 in the competition proper and the others only 1.85, and the jump-off was presumably intended to decide separately the silver and bronze medals for the first two and fourth, fifth and sixth places for the others. But Whalen and Murphy then achieved 1.89, Muller 1.88 and Ekelund only 1.85! Had Howard Baker also got over 1.89 he could have had a claim to a medal, if the British officials had been wily enough to argue that the jump-off was a competition in itself between all five men. It would be charitable to suppose that they considered it far too unsporting to make such an appeal, but the likelihood is that they were blithely unaware of the entire situation. So Howard Baker was allocated sixth place. As it was, no British male high jumper was to do better at the Olympics until 1952 and the first medal in the event would not be won until 1996.

Muller, the silver-medallist for the USA, was only 19 and was also adept at the long jump, triple jump and discus but was much better known in his home country as an outstanding footballer (US-style) and would be named an 'All-American' in 1920 and 1921. Ekelund, the Swedish bronze-medallist, would have been an 'All-Swede', had there been such an accolade, as he was another all-rounder in the Howard Baker mould; he was a hurdler and decathlete and took part in figure-skating, ski-ing, shooting, swimming, football and tennis. He later became an eminent administrator, serving as honorary treasurer of the International Amateur Athletic Federation from 1930 to 1946 and then as an International Olympic Committee member from 1948 until his death in 1983 at the age of 88.

A detailed account of the high-jump final made a rather unlikely appearance nine days later in the issue of *The Liverpool Courier* newspaper for 26 August. The author was again F.A.M. Webster and he devoted the best part of a column to describing and praising Howard Baker's showing in Antwerp. However, had the story been written 90 years later it would have had a very different slant because it was not until midway through his article that Webster revealed the astonishing news that Howard Baker had not been informed about the jump-off in Antwerp and so had been marked down to sixth place in his absence! Questions, of course, should have been asked of the organisers by Webster, whether or not he was aware of this oversight on the day or only learnt of it later. He merely described the matter as 'unfortunate'.

Webster had begun his article by paying fulsome tribute to Howard Baker: 'Liverpool athletes have every reason to be proud of their champion, B. Howard Baker, who holds the English high-jump record. Things have not gone very well for him at the Olympic Games, but for that no one can blame him; for no man living ever received a more careful training than Baker has had at the hands of Fred Birkett. Neither of them has spared pains to ensure success'.

The qualifying round had been held from a firm grass take-off under a hot sun, and Webster said of Howard Baker that he had 'seldom seen jumping in better form or with more precise style' from him. The article continued: 'On the day of the final, however, the ground was a good deal softer, which favoured the two light men, Landon (USA) and Ekelund (Sweden), both of whom jumped from slightly to the right of the bar and so hardly cut up the ground at all. The other 10 finalists, however, all seemed to choose the same patch; indeed, Baker and Murphy, the USA champion, both heavy men, used identically the same spot and were very soon jumping out of a soft and very decided depression'.

Intriguingly, Webster said that at 6ft 2¾in Howard Baker 'cleared very easily'. Then Webster described Howard Baker jumping at 6ft 3¾in: 'At his first attempt he was unlucky to touch the bar with his knee, and at the second time of asking was well over and just grazed the bar with his shoulder sufficiently hard to bring it down'. Yet Howard Baker is credited with only 1.85m (equivalent to 6ft 0¾in) in the official results. It seems unlikely that Webster, with his abiding interest in field events, would have got his conversions from metric to imperial heights wrong. So could it be that the official results are wrong? Why not? After all this was the same athletics officialdom which had crassly placed all the best 800 metres runners in the same heat to give others a chance!

This third day of Olympic athletics competition produced Britain's first gold medal as Albert Hill won the 800 metres, with the Oxford-trained South African, Bevil Rudd, third and the youthful Edgar Mountain only a stride away from a medal in fourth place. The 5000

Proud to represent his country, B. Howard Baker poses in his plain but effective Great Britain team outfit. This photograph from the collection of memorabilia which he left to his descendants is undated but was probably taken in 1921, his final year of high-jump competition.

Ready, perhaps, for one of the celebration dinners that followed so many of his athletics competitions or the matches that he played for the Corinthian football club. He might have wished, though, that the suit had fitted a little better!

*Huddersfield B.A&C. 1914. B.Howard Baker.
just failing at British Record 6 feet 5 inches.*

J. SIMONS   T. J. LEARY   B. H. BAKER

The Huddersfield Cricket & Athletic Club Sports of 1914. B. Howard Baker fails in his attempt to set a British record of 6ft 5in. World War One broke out two months later and put a stop to so much sporting activity, but he would return to Huddersfield seven years later and at last get his record.

An interesting high-jump group chosen by the photographer at the 1914 AAA Championships because this is not, in fact, the first three, as one would expect. The line-up was John Simons, of the USA (left), who placed third; the Irishman, Tim Leahy (centre), who was equal fourth; and B. Howard Baker, who was second to another American, Wesley Oler.

Howard Baker demonstrates his acrobatic skills in what looks very much like a backward somersault. His agility had its uses on social as well as sporting occasions. A favourite party trick of his was a high kick which set the dining-room chandelier jangling.

Howard Baker's spectacular high-jump style. The Eastern Cut-Off technique which he learned from the Canadian coach, Walter Knox, was a marked improvement on the Scissors style with which he had started his competitive career at school. Yet within his lifetime greater heights would be achieved by Americans using the more efficient Western Roll which was regarded with suspicion in Britain. The stadium in this photograph is probably Fallowfield, Manchester, where Howard Baker competed so often.

EASTERN CUT OFF

Les Steers, of the USA, who was to set a World record in 1941 using the Straddle technique, was also a very capable exponent of the Western Roll, as shown here when he competed at London's White City Stadium in 1939.

STRADDLE

Howard Baker's English record lasted until 1949 when it was beaten at last by Ron Pavitt, employing the very much more effective Straddle style, as illustrated here. Pavitt, incidentally, also went one better than Howard Baker at the Olympics, placing fifth in 1952.

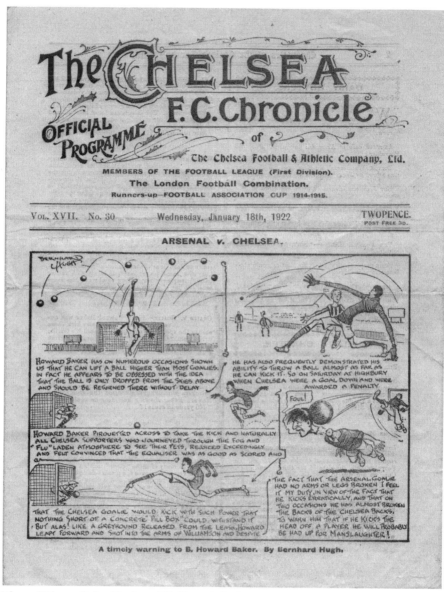

The edition of the Chelsea FC Chronicle for Wednesday 18 January 1922 when Bolton Wanderers were the visitors to Stamford Bridge. The tale told on the front page is of the previous Saturday's away game against Arsenal when Howard Baker was called upon to take a penalty, but his shot was saved and Arsenal won 1–0. Worse was to follow for he and his Chelsea colleagues because Bolton won the match that day 3–0.

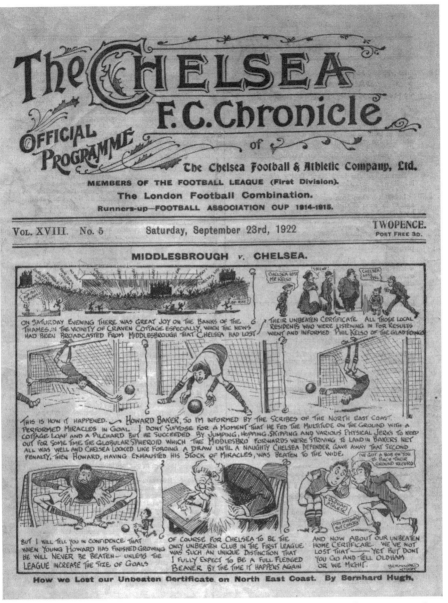

The Chelsea FC Chronicle for Saturday 23 September 1922. A happy occasion for the Chelsea players and supporters as Oldham Athletic were beaten 4–0. The previous Saturday Chelsea had lost 2–1 away to Middlesbrough.

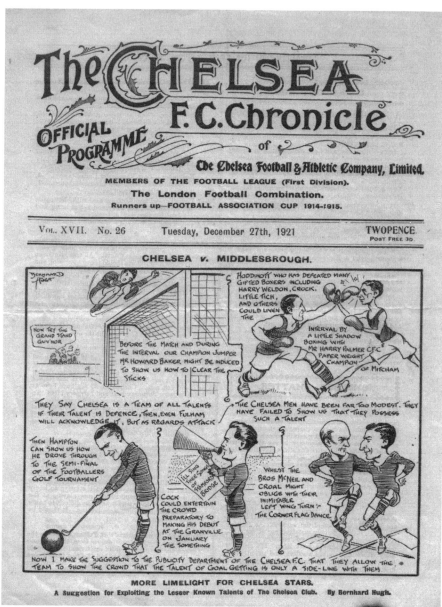

The Chelsea FC Chronicle for Tuesday 27 December 1921, when Middlesbrough held Chelsea to a 1–1 draw at Stamford Bridge. The previous day Chelsea had won at Middlesbrough 1–0. Howard Baker had been in goal for the first game, but was replaced by Wilson Marsh for the return fixture. The ingenious artist, Bernhard Hugh, neatly captures Howard Baker's twin skills as high jumper and goalkeeper and depicts a cloth-capped Chelsea supporter bawling, 'Now try the Grand Stand, Guv'nor!'

The Corinthians v Brighton & Hove Albion, January 1923. Left to right – Ashton, Bower, Doggart, Howard Baker, Knight, Moulsdale, Hegan, Hunter, Phillips, Blaxland, Creek, Sandy Tait (trainer). This was the first of three FA Cup-ties between the clubs in 11 days. After twice drawing 1-1 Corinthian eventually lost the second replay 1-0.

Cartoons were a popular feature of the newspaper sports pages in the years when action photography was still in its infancy. In this 1926 publication, the artist, 'Mel', depicts Howard Baker as a sort of Edwardian dandy. Some Chelsea supporters, wary of Howard Baker's extravagant goalkeeping manner, might have thought that the Mad Hatter was a more appropriate description.

A gathering of great Corinthians : 1 G.K. Foster, 2 A.G. Bower, 3 K.E. Hegan,
4 A.G. Doggart, 5 C.T. Ashton, 6 B. Howard Baker, 7 A.E. Knight, 8 F.N.S. Creek.

One of the best and most spectacular goalkeepers in the country. That was the wording of the caption to this photograph of B. Howard Baker which appeared in a publication called «Sports Pictures Photo Album » in the 1920s. The cameraman, though, has caught Howard Baker in restful mood, watching play at the other end of the pitch.

The Corinthians v Blackburn Rovers, January 1924. Back row, left to right – Phillips, Moulsdale, Howard Baker, Blaxland, Hegan ; Front row, left to right – Nicholas, Ashton, Morrison, Bower, Doggart, Creek. Corinthian won this FA Cup-tie 1-0, scoring their goal early on and then holding out in the second half as Howard Baker made some inspired saves.

We certify that B. Howard Baker of Liverpool H.a.C jumped 6 feet 5 inches in the High Jump at Huddersfield C & A C athletic Festival on Saturday the 25th of June 1921.

Sidney Foster Halifax Judge
Harry Gobby Manchester Starter + checker
Jno. Abraham V.P. a.a.a. Judge
E. Hoyle Referee A.A.A. x N.C.A.A.
F. E. Westin Judge A.A.A & N.C.A.A.
Albert Goodall N.C.U.
A. Fattorini V.P. A.A.A.
Howard Wheatley
Thos. Hy Lenton N.C.U.
W. H. Hird Secretary H.a.a.C

This was the note that was sent to the Amateur Athletic Association to support the application for B. Howard Baker's high jump of 6ft 5in as a British record. The signatories include four past presidents of the Northern Counties AA – Messrs. T.M. Abraham, E. Hoyle, F.E. Westin and A. Fattorini. Rather oddly, two officials of the National Cycling Union, which organised some events at the meeting, also added their names.

Newspaper cuttings from Howard Baker's collection. Goalkeepers in English League football in the 1920s were under constant pressure from opposing forwards challenging them for the ball, as illustrated by these photographs of Howard Baker in action. As he was to recall some 60 years later, 'Goalkeepers were anybody's target then. You were allowed two paces carrying the ball, and then you were attacked by everybody!' Not that he worried too much about that. He revelled in rushing out to save and launching massive clearance kicks to send the ball far down into the opponents' half.

Howard Baker at 90, and still looking spry and sparkle-eyed. Among his vast collection of trophies on display were his Olympic team badges and his England football team insignia.

metres was won for France by Joseph Guillemot from a promising young Finn named Paavo Nurmi, and Britain had Joe Blewitt of Birchfield Harriers, and William Seagrove of Cambridge University, a commendable fifth and sixth. Seagrove could truly be said to have been a wartime discovery because he had won the 880 yards at the 1916 Public Schools' Championships and then served as a lieutenant in the Worcestershire Regiment.

On the fourth day, 18 August, there was another British medal as third place in the 10,000 metres track walk was taken by Charles Gunn, who worked as a railwayman and would live to become Britain's oldest surviving Olympian, reaching the age of 98. Tom Nicolson was sixth in the hammer, and he is a classic example of an athlete achieving the highest levels in his sport despite the seemingly insuperable difficulties presented by his occupation as a farmer in the village of Tighnabruich, which is a Gaelic name meaning 'the house on the hill', on the Kyles of Bute facing across the sea passage leading into the Firth of Clyde. Even in the 21st century the one road out which eventually winds its way to Glasgow, 80 miles distant, is single track in places.

The author of the definitive history of Scottish athletics, John W. Keddie, points out that Nicolson missed many competitive opportunities because of work commitments, travel problems and limited funds and believes that in view of these circumstances he could be regarded as the best hammer-thrower in the World of his generation. It's an argument that is hard to refute, and even the Olympic authorities sympathised with Nicolson's plight because he was given special dispensation to go through to the final of his event in Antwerp after missing the qualifying round because of delays in his journey. The best throw of his life, 166ft 9½in (50.84m), had been achieved in Edinburgh many years before in 1908, and when almost half-a-century later in 1957 the first authoritative all-time rankings of British athletes were compiled by Norris and Ross McWhirter (the twins who later devised the *Guinness Book of Records*) Nicolson still ranked the 19th best ever, and only eight other Britons, four of them Scots, had by then thrown more than 10ft further than Nicolson's best.

As the best of the British long jumpers in Antwerp was only 13th and there were no contestants at all in the shot, it was further confirmation that the British were predominantly still a nation of runners and walkers, rather than jumpers and throwers (Howard Baker and Nicolson apart), when all three 1500 metres men comfortably qualified in their heats – Albert Hill, Philip Baker and the Scottish champion, Duncan McPhee, who was a clubmate of Tom Nicolson's at West of Scotland Harriers.

Two days after the high-jump Howard Baker turned out for the triple jump and was not far off qualifying among the first six who contested the final, achieving a best mark of 13.675m, which was equivalent to 44ft 10½in and thus beat Philip Kingsford's English record from 1912. This was a performance of genuine merit by Howard Baker as he was eighth overall, less than eight centimetres behind the sixth-placed former Irishman, Dan Ahearn, now competing for the USA. Not only that, but the conditions were all against any sort of record-breaking: rain had fallen throughout the previous night and continued unabated during the day. No British triple jumper was to do any better at the Olympics for the next 44 years until Fred Alsop was fourth in 1964, and Howard Baker achieved this is as a raw novice with only one reported previous competition in the event. So far as is known, he only ever attempted it on one further occasion!

Howard Baker attracted little attention from the British press for his efforts that day, but for once there was some justification. Albert Hill completed a magnificent Olympic double by winning the 1500 metres and Philip Baker was second after making much of the pace. It was only the second time in Olympic history that the same country had provided the first two at 1500 metres, and in St Louis in 1904 it had been the USA which had done so at a Games for which there had been very few overseas entries. The feat would not be achieved again until 1948, by Sweden…and then in 1984 by another British pairing named Coe and Cram.

By the completion of the athletics programme on 23 August the USA had maintained its supremacy, but not by much, as the Finns had won the same number of gold medals. Between them the USA, Finland, Great Britain and Sweden had shared 71 of the 87 available medals in 29 events, as follows:

USA - 9 gold, 12 silver, 8 bronze = 29 medals
Finland - 9 gold, 4 silver, 3 bronze = 16 medals
Great Britain - 4 gold, 4 silver, 4 bronze = 12 medals
Sweden - 1 gold, 3 silver, 10 bronze = 14 medals

The other gold medals had gone to Italy (two, by the walker, Ugo Frigerio), Canada, France, Norway and South Africa (the English-born and English-educated Bevil Rudd at 400 metres).

The British results had been significantly better than in 1912: twice as many gold medals and a total of 12 medals instead of eight. The Americans, by contrast, had lost a lot of ground, having won 16 golds in Stockholm. Yet the summary of the Olympic athletics composed by a correspondent for *The New York Times*, P.J. Philip, was headlined 'U.S. Athletes Win World's Title In Games At Antwerp' (Philip, incidentally, was to lead an adventurous journalistic life, being mistaken for a German spy during the headlong retreat of the British and French armies in 1940 and narrowly escaping being shot). According to the newspaper's calculations, the USA had scored 212 pts, Finland 105, Sweden 95 and Great Britain 85. Anyone who imagined that amid the euphoria of post-war camaraderie national rivalries would be forgotten was thus to be sorely disillusioned, and whatever might be the merits or de-merits of such flag-waving scoring-tables they were to become a regular and over-bearing feature of every Olympic Games to come.

The gold-medals table covering all the 20 sports contested in Antwerp was as follows: USA 41, Sweden 19, Finland 15, Great Britain 14, Belgium 13, Norway 13, Italy 13, France 9, Holland 4, Canada 3, Denmark 3, South Africa 3, Switzerland 2, Brazil 1, Estonia 1. The rankings were much the same as they had been eight years before except, of course, that Germany and Hungary had not been invited this time as aggressors in the war.

Altogether, including relays and team events, 14 British athletes were medallists in Antwerp: *Jack Ainsworth-Davis*, gold 4 x 400 metres relay; *Philip Baker*, silver 1500 metres; *Joe Blewitt*, silver 3000 metres team; *Guy Butler*, silver 400 metres, gold 4 x 400 metres relay; *Harry Edward*, bronze 100 metres and 200 metres; *Cecil Griffiths*, gold 4 x 400 metres relay; *Charles Gunn*, bronze 10,000 metres walk; *Frank Hegarty*, silver cross-country team; *Albert Hill*, gold 800 metres and 1500 metres, silver 3000 metres team; *Percy Hodge*, gold steeplechase; *Robert Lindsay*, gold 4 x 400 metres relay; *Alfred Nichols*, silver cross-country team; *William Seagrove*, silver 3000 metres team; *James Wilson*, silver cross-country team, bronze 10,000 metres.

Four of these 14 were products of Cambridge University – Ainsworth-Davis, Baker, Butler and Seagrove. Others came from a wide cross-section of society. Blewitt, Hill and

Gunn worked on the railways. Nichols was employed in a shirt factory. Wilson was a mechanical engineer. Edward was a former university student who qualified as a chartered secretary and would make his career in public relations. The facts, in effect, could be read almost anyway you liked in search of some sort of sociological revelation; almost a third of the medal-winners were from Oxbridge (actually, no 'Ox' and all 'bridge') and more than two-thirds weren't. Six members of the winning hockey team were from Cambridge or Oxford, but there were some interesting mixes elsewhere: the two boxing gold-medallists were Ronald Rawson, a Cambridge graduate, and Harry Mallin, a London policeman; the successful tandem cyclists, Tommy Lance and Harry Ryan, became a Brighton bookmaker and managing director of the family machine-tool business respectively.

Great Britain's footballers made a desperately poor showing, losing their opening match to Norway 3–1. Norway had been beaten in its first 27 international matches from 1908 through to 1918. The Olympic tournament finished in chaos when the Czech players marched off the field in protest at a series of referee's decisions, leaving the Belgian team to collect the gold medals by default. The British water-polo players maintained their unbeaten Olympic record to win the title again, but it was the end of an era as more than 90 years later no further medal has ever been won in this most durable of Olympic team sports.

Philip Baker, who because of his pacifist views as a Quaker had served in an ambulance unit during World War One, was fulsome in his praise of the organisation of the Games. 'By Herculean efforts it was admirably carried out', he later wrote – actually, it was 56 years later and his memories by then may have mellowed. 'With great difficulties to overcome, the Belgian organisers built a splendid stadium for the athletics and the association football, excellent pools for the swimming and diving, excellent grounds or sports halls for the contests, and they provided accommodation, living quarters, for the teams which I remember with lively pleasure still'. Baker drew an interesting comparison with another Olympics to be held 28 years afterwards: 'There was the same feeling of relief, of release, that there was to be at Wembley after World War Two. The four endless wasted years of battle were behind us. The World had turned, and we turned with it, to better happier things. So we all greatly enjoyed ourselves in Antwerp'.

Baker also fondly remembered that Brigadier-General R.J. Kentish, the commandant of the British team, had engaged some Scottish bagpipers who played 'on all probable and improbable occasions' and hired a dance orchestra for regular evening parties with other competing teams in the playground of the school where the Britons were staying. The lack of obvious partners for the waltzes and fox-trots was not recorded by Baker. Among the 2,582 competitors in Antwerp there were only 65 women – in five swimming and diving events and in lawn tennis, including Mlle Suzanne Lenglen, lauded by Philip Baker as seeming 'to us the greatest player, man or woman, we had ever seen'.

Mlle Lenglen won the women's singles, beating Britain's Dorothy Holman 6–3, 6–0, and shared the mixed doubles with Max Decugis against Kitty McKane and Howard Baker's Corinthian footballing clubmate, Max Woosnam, though Woosnam had his own success in the men's doubles alongside Noel Turnbull. Both Woosnam and Turnbull regarded tennis as no more than one of their range of recreational activities – just as Howard Baker treated his athletics. Woosnam had captained Cambridge University at cricket the previous year and had also been invited to lead Great Britain's Olympic football team but opted for the tennis tournament instead. Turnbull, who had won the Military Cross during the Battle of the Somme, gave up tennis for four years after his Olympic success and became a scratch golfer.

The recollections regarding the amenities in Antwerp of Albert Hill, the war veteran who won two gold medals, were somewhat at odds with his teammate, Philip Baker. Hill later wrote, 'Our quarters were in a school and we had to sleep on frail camp-beds with hard mattresses, some of which collapsed under the weight of some of the tug-of-war men. And great was the consternation when young women came into our sleeping quarters to tidy up and re-make the beds, some of which were still occupied. The food arrangements were rather poor and Britain's favourite beverage, tea, was undrinkable. After a couple of days of this I and a friend dined at an hotel until the food and cooking arrangements improved at our quarters. Our journey to and from the track was in an old lorry with wooden seats which almost shook everyone to pieces'.

It could hardly be supposed that Hill, whose official age then was 31 but who happily admitted to being 'the wrong side of 35', had been accustomed to a better standard of everyday living from his work as a railway guard than had Philip Baker in the course of his duties as a diplomat, or maybe Baker was comparing the Antwerp menus favourably with the Spartan fare that he had been used to at public school. On his return home Hill had been assured a comfortable night's sleep for many years to come with the presentation to him in recognition of his Olympic triumphs of a bedroom suite, along with other gifts, on behalf of Hill's 1,700 fellow-employees of the London, Brighton & South Coast Railway Company.

Confirmation of Albert Hill's memories of the poor facilities for accommodation and competition in Antwerp is to be found in a fascinating interview which one of the US team gave at the age of 90 in 1987 as part of a survey carried out by the Amateur Athletic Foundation of Los Angeles, which had been set up after the 1984 Games in that city. He was Walker Smith, who placed fifth in the 110 metres hurdles final, and he had served in the war even before the entry of the US in 1917, having volunteered to be a battle-field ambulance driver in a unit attached to the French army. Remarkably, he carried out those duties and then became an outstanding hurdler despite the fact that he had had one eye removed for health reasons at the age of 10.

Smith, whose second name was appropriately 'Breeze', vividly recalled the week-long transatlantic crossing to Europe for the Games in a troop transport ship with bunks in rows in the hold and meagre food rations, and his recollection of the arrangements when they arrived at the school where they were billeted was much the same as those of the Britons. 'We were just on cots without mattresses', he remembered, and as for the competition in the stadium, which was still being built while he and his teammates looked for somewhere to train, he said, 'We had a lot of rain that week and the track didn't drain well. We were almost running on mud'.

Had Howard Baker seriously bid for a water-polo place, he might not have been able to afford the time away as the tournament did not begin until 29 August, 12 days after the high-jump final. Having already won three Olympic titles, Great Britain maintained its record in Antwerp, beating Belgium 3–2 to take the gold medals yet again, and one of the members of the 1908 and 1912 teams, Paul Radmilovic, scored the winning goal to complete an Olympic title hat-trick. 'Raddy', Cardiff-born of a Greek father and an Irish mother, was to compete again in 1924 and at the age of 42 in 1928, and he was also winner of nine Amateur

Swimming Association freestyle titles, a scratch golfer and a capable footballer. He later became a licensee in Weston-super-Mare, where he had played his club water polo.

Such longevity was taken for granted in the water-polo pool as Howard Baker knew full well because his friend, Charlie Smith, of the Southport and Salford Swimming Clubs, who was now 41 and winning his third Olympic gold medal, would remain goalkeeper for the England team for another six years! Billy Dean, born in Manchester and a member of the Hyde Seal club which won the Northern title for 21 successive years, was a kindred spirit to Howard Baker as he also had goalkeeping aspirations on the football field, having been on Manchester United's books for two seasons. In the water he was a prolific goalscorer and played 18 times for England. Water-polo players of that era were successful in business as well as sport: Dean became managing director of an electrical engineering firm, while a Welshman in the team, Chris Jones, was later senior partner in a firm of coal exporters, and Noel Purcell, who also played rugby union for Ireland during 1920–21, was a solicitor.

Howard Baker had come into the sport at the very end of the era of British supremacy, and his interest in aquatic events was certainly spurred by the thriving local league system and by the fact that Liverpool was also a major centre for the swimming and diving events which he so much enjoyed. Austin Rawlinson, of the Garston club, who had been born in the affluent city district of West Derby, as had Howard Baker, had pioneered the backstroke technique in Britain as a teenager during World War One. He was a finalist at the 1924 Olympics and then devoted his life to the administration of the sport, receiving the MBE in 1961 for his services, and living to the age of 98. Hilda James, who was a member of the Cunard company's club in Liverpool, competed in the 1920 Olympics at the age of 16, and she was to win Amateur Swimming Association national titles at 100 yards, 220 yards and 440 yards and was twice long-distance champion on the Kew-to-Putney stretch of the River Thames.

A major advance in the provision of international competition for Britain's leading athletes was made with the staging of the first post-Olympic British Empire v USA match; this series would continue until 1967. The idea for it came from Arnold Strode-Jackson who was to emigrate to the USA soon afterwards, and Philip Baker; the 1920 meeting was held at the Queen's Club, in London, on 4 September. This date almost exactly celebrated the 300th anniversary of the sailing of the merchant vessel, 'Mayflower', from Plymouth – on 16 September 1620, to be precise – with 102 English immigrants aboard bound for Massachusetts, who would come to be known as 'The Pilgrim Fathers', and from whom seven presidents of the United States would be descended.

The schedule of events for the Queen's Club meeting was hardly comprehensive, based largely on assorted track relays with a few additional events: 4 x 100 yards (not 110 yards), 4 x 220 yards, 4 x 400 yards (not 440 yards), 4 x 880 yards, 4 x 1 mile, 2 miles team, 120 yards hurdles, 440 yards hurdles, high jump and long jump. Other American competitors gave 'exhibitions' of their skills in the pole vault, discus and javelin, for which British competitors of a kind could have been found if the will was there, and the impression remains that these events were deliberately excluded from the official scoring to make the match closer and more interesting.

The times in the relays were not particularly noteworthy, though the races were exciting, and much the best performances of the day came from the Olympic champion, Earl Thomson of Canada, who set a British all-comers' record of 14⅘ sec in the high hurdles, running on a grass track laid out in the infield, and from Howard Baker, whose defeat of Richmond Landon in the high jump was the finest of his career. Howard Baker set a further English record of 6ft 3½in (1.92m) to Landon's 6ft 2¼in (1.89) and the win gave the British Empire a 4–0 lead in the contest, though the eventual result was a 5–5 draw. Spectators clambered on to the roof of the Queen's Club building to get a view and others overflowed from the stands to mass along the grass edges of the track. They would have been much better accommodated, of course, at Stamford Bridge, but there would have been no room for them that day. The football season had begun and there were 42,000 people in that ground, watching Chelsea draw 1–1 with Derby County.

Previewed in *The Times* as 'the greatest International Athletic Meeting which has ever been held in this country', details had been given for the benefit of prospective spectators of seven 'motor-omnibus' routes which served the ground situated between West Kensington and Baron's Court underground stations. The newspaper's comprehensive report of the meeting was effusive in its praise but oddly gave Baker little credit for his win, preferring to dwell at length on Landon's sportsmanship in readily shaking hands with his British conqueror. The *Daily Telegraph* was much more appreciative of Howard Baker's contribution, describing him in the opening paragraph of their report as 'the Liverpool jumper with the figure of Apollo'. The newspaper's special correspondent continued in his report: 'The high jump was a magnificent contest, and not only Howard Baker but the Irishman, Carroll, excelled. It was great to note America's champion, Landon, rush up and congratulate Baker on his victory and walk away with his arm on Baker's shoulder – a curious pair, Baker a great upstanding figure, the Yale man a fragile youth in glasses'.

Asked more than half-a-century later by an interviewer from the *Liverpool Echo* to recall the occasion, Howard Baker – by then a silver-haired but erect 80-year-old – sparkled at the memory: 'Although it was not as high as the record I set up the following year at Huddersfield, I think it was probably the greatest jump of my career. It was pouring with rain, the conditions were all wrong, and the match was evenly balanced at five events each. It all depended on the outcome of the high jump. You can imagine how elated I was to win'. In reality, Howard Baker was slightly at fault in his remembrance about the effect of his win on the match result, but that matters not at all.

The Pathé cinema newsreel cameras covered the meeting in some depth and showed both Howard Baker and Landon in action, and then Howard Baker posing for the camera afterwards smiling broadly and looking positively dashing in his familiar white blazer with its blue trimming and an upturned collar. Howard Baker's jumping technique is depicted perfectly. With a massed crowd looking on intently from only a few yards behind him, he stands to the left-hand side of the take-off area facing the bar, takes four quick steps forward, then a couple of hops, swings to his right, taking four more urgent strides before driving his left leg upwards. He clears the bar – or, rather, in this instance knocks it off – in a half-seated position before landing on his feet and then his back in what looks to be not too deep a sand-pit.

The extensive *Daily Sketch* coverage of the match included five photographs, in one of which Howard Baker, still in his blazer, and Landon, wearing a sweater with a 'Y' for Yale emblazoned on the chest, were depicted strolling cheerfully out of the arena, and the caption read: 'R. Landon, the American (left), and his English conqueror in the high jump, Howard Baker, displaying the sporting spirit'.

During the long conversation which Howard Baker had towards the end of his life over such a wide range of topics with John Bromhead, the Olympics were scarcely mentioned at all. That was almost certainly because they seemed less important both at the time and in retrospect to Howard Baker than many other sporting contests of his. Difficult as that is to believe in the 21st century as the barrage of publicity leading up to the 2012 Games gathers force, the fact is that just as had been the case before World War One almost nobody in Britain thought too much of the Olympics in 1920. A thoughtful leader article in the *Manchester Guardian* by one of the foremost journalists of that era, William Crozier, caught the mood: 'It is not that many persons actually wish that there were no Olympic Games at all. The trouble is that they simply leave the general body of British sportsmen cold, or at best tepid'.

Crozier's opinion was not voiced from a narrow sporting perspective. Renowned for his wide range of political and social interests, he had joined the newspaper in 1903 and would be editor from 1933 until his death in 1944. He had gone to Cambridge University and his views were of the liberal kind that his newspaper – which would become *The Guardian* in 1959 – has long espoused. Reporting from Antwerp at the conclusion of the Games, his words have a startlingly familiar ring to them more than 90 years later: 'Whether the Olympic Games do any good to international relationships I could not venture to say. I could cite a good many reasons that suggest the contrary, but that would be helping a bad cause. With many people national feeling runs much too high for them to be able to pretend that they want to see the best man win'.

By the end of that 1920 Olympic athletics season, Howard Baker's thoughts were no doubt drifting elsewhere. The football season had begun and he had made an important decision which would lead to another phase of his sporting life to match in satisfaction that which had earned him two Olympic appearances. His high jumping was by no means over, but his diary of commitments was fuller than ever. Other sports had taken his fancy. The rough-and-tumble of water polo, in which his British Olympic teammates had again won the gold medals, presented a new and absorbing challenge. Football would occupy much of his attention for the next dozen years. Equally attractive was the prospect of honing his skills in the rather more gracious pastime of tennis.

FOOTBALL FOR ENGLAND. THEN OFF TO HUDDERSFIELD FOR SOME WATER-POLO...AND A HIGH-JUMP RECORD TO LAST 25 YEARS

Having pursued his new-found goalkeeping career in peacetime with the amateur club Northern Nomads, Howard Baker had then audaciously accepted an invitation to turn out for Liverpool towards the end of the 1919–20 season. It was on the face of it an obvious move, close to his family and business roots, but in fact he was taking on as tough a challenge as he could possibly find because the incumbent at Anfield was one of the most formidable goalkeepers in the country.

Elisha Scott had been the regular 'keeper since 1912 and was to play 467 matches in a career which lasted 22 years, remaining an Anfield legend to this day as he is one of only three players from prior to the 1950s among the 20 who have been honoured with a place in the club's 'Hall of Fame'. The understudy to Scott when Howard Baker arrived was Ken Campbell, himself a high-class player who was to win eight caps for Scotland while with Liverpool and then the Scottish club, Partick Thistle. Even so, Howard Baker joined the club with the express purpose of playing the following Saturday towards the end of the 1919–20 season, 13 March, for the simple reason that the goalmouths in the Scotland v Ireland match at Hampden Park that day would be defended by Campbell and Scott respectively.

A few days beforehand the *Liverpool Echo* had carried a report from their correspondent, 'Bee', to the following effect: 'By allowing Scott to play for Ireland, and Campbell for Scotland on Saturday, Liverpool left themselves in a quandary. It is not easy to find a deputy for both one's goalkeepers. However, 'Bee' learns exclusively that Liverpool have been in touch with Preston North End, who have Howard Baker's signature, for a reliable goalkeeper to assist them at Sheffield. The result is that Howard Baker will make his first League appearance at Hillsborough. He has been doing good work with Nomads. Baker is the famous Olympic jumper'.

But the plan went awry. The Preston North End secretary sent the wrong registration forms – those for the Central League in which both reserve teams played – and it was too late to rectify the mistake. Oddly, though, the same club, either generous to a fault or blessed with limitless manpower, was able to provide another goalkeeper instead named Tom Armstrong, who duly turned out and did well enough in the 2–2 draw against Sheffield Wednesday, actually known only as 'The Wednesday' until 1929. Howard Baker, seemingly unconcerned that his League debut had been scotched by administrative bungling, was content to help out Liverpool Reserves and was untroubled in a 3–0 win over Nelson. 'A clean sheet and a cool exhibition', said 'Bee' of him. Scott and Campbell returned from international duty the next week and Armstrong never played for the Liverpool first team again and was sent back to his previous club the following June.

It is not too surprising that Howard Baker was denied senior opportunities for his home-town club. His role was, in all probability, rather that of a local celebrity imbued with civic pride who could be called upon if necessary in an emergency. A further chance seemed to be in the offing when Scott was selected yet again to play for Ireland against England early in the 1920–21 season, on 23 October, by which time Campbell had departed to Partick Thistle for a fee of £1,750 which was regarded as sumptuous in those days, but even then there was no automatic selection for the gifted amateur.

There was yet another candidate, and the *Liverpool Echo* speculated in its 'Stud Marks' gossip column of the football edition for the previous Saturday as to who would be the replacement for the local derby with Everton: 'Neither Howard Baker nor McNaughton has sampled Football League proper, and whichever of the pair may be chosen, if Scott is away, the test is sure to be an abnormal one'. The Liverpool management was said to be 'very much disturbed to know what to do', but eventually it was Harry McNaughton, signed that season from an Edinburgh junior club, who was preferred, and he passed the test as Liverpool won 1–0. Howard Baker unpretentiously again played for the reserves instead that day and the following week. For McNaughton, like Armstrong the previous season, this was to be his only Liverpool first-team match.

Risking the wrath of many of his fellow-citizens, Howard Baker soon afterwards transferred his allegiance to the city's other League side, Everton. Though this was a matter which on Merseyside might have been thought tantamount to a Glaswegian player leaving Rangers for Celtic, *The Echo* made no song-and-dance about it and gave no explanation for the move, merely commenting that 'Howard Baker should prove a welcome addition to Everton's defensive forces'. His Everton debut on 4 December was for the reserves against Bury, and his decision to change clubs had certainly not been motivated by the prospect of a first-team place for the asking.

Just as Liverpool had the ever-reliable Scott to call on, Everton had a stalwart goalkeeper in Tommy Fern, who had joined the club from Lincoln City in 1913 and would go on to play 231 matches before his departure in 1924. Described as 'always in the thick of the action', Fern inevitably suffered injury from time to time in his bodily goalmouth clashes with marauding opposition forwards, and Howard Baker at last made his League debut on 26 February 1921. It was an away game but almost a home-from-home so far as he was concerned, because it was against Chelsea at Stamford Bridge, where he had so often won his AAA high-jump titles. Not only that but it was another triumph as Everton won 1–0 and he was commended for his 'agility and nice sense of anticipation'. There were 44,000 spectators that Saturday afternoon, which was rather more than had ever witnessed his summer-time appearances on the same turf, and one of the first to congratulate him as the players left the field was Chelsea's Danish half-back, Nils Middelboe, who had played in the 1908 and 1912 Olympic finals.

'Achates', the football correspondent for the sporting newspaper, *The Athletic News*, having dismissed the occasion as 'one of the most uninteresting games I have seen on the ground this season', nevertheless enthusiastically joined in the praise for Howard Baker: 'The British amateur high jump champion, B.H. Baker, was in goal for the first time in the League team, and I should say the Everton management were delighted with his display. A former well-known amateur goalkeeper declared that Baker was the best custodian who had been to Stamford Bridge this season. While scarcely going so far as that, I must say that he distinguished himself. With far more to do than Molyneux, his fielding of the ball was brilliant, and with long and high shots he was ideal, but I would like to have seen him tested with some low drives'. The original 'Achates' was the close friend of Aeneas in Trojan mythology and the name had become a by-word for 'intimate companion'.

Yet further plaudits were showered upon Howard Baker in the *Liverpool Echo* football special, as it was said of him that he 'had earned fine praise from all who have seen him more than once, and not only has a length of kick but also a safe pair of hands'. Reflecting on the match the following Monday, a correspondent named only as 'F.E.H' who had been at the match was in lyrical mood: 'Howard Baker made a highly successful first appearance in goal on behalf of Everton in a League match and acquitted himself admirably. I am not given to flattery – quite the contrary – but watching the Northern Nomad as he stood between the sticks I could not help recalling Kipling's lines about another sportsman, of whom he wrote:

'He trod the ling like a buck in spring.
And he looked like a lance at rest'.

(Readers may care to know that the quotation comes from Rudyard Kipling's *A Ballad of East and West*, written in 1899, which famously begins, 'Oh, East is East, and West is West, and never the twain shall meet').

In a bold-type announcement on the same page, the *Echo* promised readers: 'A STRIKING SNAP of HOWARD BAKER, with an arm towering over the goalpost, will be given in tomorrow's *Sporting Echo*, the first paper to indulge in the new phase of photography – action photographs'.

Despite all this flattering attention, it was inevitable that a fit-again Tommy Fern would be back in the side the next week for the FA Cup quarter-final at home to Wolverhampton Wanderers. Coincidentally, Everton lost 1–0, as did by the same scores two other clubs in which Howard Baker would have an interest – Chelsea at Cardiff City and Aston Villa at Tottenham Hotspur, who went on to win the Cup 20 years after their first success.

He was to have only one more League match that season, but his skills were much better displayed on behalf of another club and were soon to be recognised at the highest level. Having maintained his pre-war contacts with the peripatetic Northern Nomads, he also joined by invitation the most famous amateur team in the country, and one without a regular ground of its own, just as the Nomads. Howard Baker had become a Corinthian, though his social background did not make him an obvious candidate.

The Corinthian Football Club had been founded in 1882, preceding the legalisation of professionalism by three years, and was the creation of a man who has been described as 'one of the most industrious and enthusiastic of the game's earliest legislators'. He was Nicholas Lane Jackson, known affectionately as 'Pa', who was then the honorary assistant secretary of the Football Association, and who later explained his reasoning for forming Corinthian FC thus: 'Public school and university men provided most of the players for the England side, so I thought that by giving these plenty of practice together they would acquire a certain measure of combination'.

England lost all but one of nine matches against Scotland between 1872 and 1884, but the Corinthian 'measure of combination' eventually had its effect as in the next nine years England did much better, winning four times against the Scots, losing twice and drawing the other three, with 44 Corinthian members being awarded caps. For the matches with Wales in 1894 and 1895 Corinthian provided the entire England XIs. In those early days players wore cricket caps, billowing shirts and long trousers; the game was exceedingly rough; and teams formed up as goalkeeper, back, half-back and a pack of forwards who dribbled the ball all over the field rather in the manner of a rugby eight on the loose.

Jackson was a journalist by profession, editor of the magazines *Pastime* and *Cricket Field*, and like Howard Baker had an interest and an involvement in numerous different sporting activities in addition to football and cricket – athletics, boxing, golf, lawn tennis and rowing. Never more than a moderate performer himself, he played in only one football match for Corinthian but devoted an enormous amount of his time to the administration and encouragement of various sports and had been one of the originators of the Lawn Tennis Federation, which later became the Lawn Tennis Association. He lived to the age of 87, still playing golf in his 80s and giving one of the principal speeches at the Corinthian 50th anniversary banquet in 1932, five years before his death.

According to one of the club's historians, Edward Grayson, writing in 1955, 'If the immediate reason for the foundation of the Corinthian Football Club was to raise the prestige and standards of English international football against Scotland, its effect was of a far greater importance. Within 20 years the Corinthians were to become the greatest and most attractive team that football had then known. With an intelligent nonchalance, and in their tailored shirts and well-cut shorts, they brought a quality and culture to the game...Corinth produced a brand of progressive attacking football still wistfully remembered by those who saw it'.

For those two decades they often matched and even exceeded the very highest standards of the professionals, beating the FA Cup holders, Bury, 10–3 and inflicting a record defeat, 11–3, on Manchester United in 1904. They remained 'happy wanderers', without a ground of their own for more than a century of their existence, but from 1922 onwards played their 'home' matches at the refurbished Crystal Palace exhibition centre ground where FA Cup Finals had taken place in earlier years. The club's original rules stated that it 'shall not compete for any challenge cup or any prizes of any description whatsoever', but this stricture was later to be relaxed.

It was very much a case of Howard Baker not so much joining the Corinthians as of him being asked to do so. Since the club's formation, the etiquette had been preserved of the club's elders approaching 'anyone to play of whom they had heard good reports', and this had invariably meant that the recruits came from the older-established public schools and from the universities (Oxford and Cambridge only, of course, nothing red-brick) because these were the sort of people of whom the club had first-hand knowledge or whom members had already met and approved. The form then was that if the player satisfied scrutiny both on and off the field he was duly elected. Howard Baker was not even of red-brick stock, let alone Oxbridge, but he clearly must have passed the test, putting his hands to good use between the posts and then, presumably, never picking up the wrong knife or fork at the dinner-table.

Among Howard Baker's notable predecessors of international calibre in the Corinthian goalmouth had been Billy Moon, elegant of appearance, with his moustache waxed into fine points, who had played seven matches for England between 1888 and 1891, and Leslie Gay, who also went on England's cricket tour to Australia in 1894–95 as a wicket-keeper. Gay played in only one Test, but it was a memorable 'timeless' one, actually lasting six days, which England won by 10 runs after following on 261 behind! Gay made his contribution with three catches and a stumping. A rather more notable cricketer who had played in goal a couple of times for Corinthian immediately before World War One was Percy Fender, whose life-span was very similar to Howard Baker's, having also been born in 1892 and dying in 1985, by which time he was the oldest surviving Test player. He was a middle-order batsman but hit 21 centuries and at Northampton in 1920 reached his 100 for Surrey in 35 minutes, which is described as still the fastest century on record in 'normal' circumstances.

The tale is also told by another of Corinthian's goalkeepers of the 1920s named H. Murray which gives a further insight into the club's sometimes cavalier approach to the game. Among the leading public schools that Corinthian regularly played was Repton, which boasted a strong footballing tradition and held their illustrious visitors to a 2–2 draw early in the 1920–21 season. Murray recalled of one encounter with Repton in 1925–26, that when the action was all at the other end of the field and the Corinthians seemed to be able to do everything except score, he became absorbed in deep conversation (or perhaps was lured into conversation?) by the Repton master in charge of football, Colonel Morgan-Owen, a former Corinthian player himself and Welsh international, who was standing near his net, only for the discussion to abruptly end with the Colonel's aside, 'Oh, by the way, there's a ball in your net, Murray, I believe'. Despite Murray's lapse of attention, Corinthian won 5–4 that day.

The inherent 'intelligent nonchalance' of the Corinthians would have suited Howard Baker's temperament to a 't', especially as it was conducted in a neatly-fitting set of kit, but it has to be said that the Corinthian spirit was starting to be somewhat in decline by the time he joined. The amateur clubs had split with the Football Association in 1907 because of their concern at the increasing professionalism of the game and so were deprived of their regular fixtures against League teams. Then, too, improved training methods among the professionals had begun to place the part-time gentlemen players at too much of a disadvantage. The rift between the FA and the amateurs was ended in 1914, but by then many public schools had switched from association football to rugby football or hockey.

Yet it was not all gloom, as the historian, Edward Grayson, quickly noted: 'For a time during the 1920s the flames of life flickered on through such men as B. Howard Baker, A.G. Bower, A.G. Doggart, R.W.V. Robins and the Ashtons – Hubert, Gilbert and Claude. But they were exceptional. The age of specialisation and the increased premium placed upon success set in'. Howard Baker, Bower, Doggart (whose son, Hubert, was to be a fine footballer and played cricket for England) and Claude Ashton were all to make numerous amateur international appearances between them in the years to come, while Robins was to become 'one of the most dynamic all-round cricketers of his time', according to 'Wisden', playing for England and then becoming chairman of selectors.

'Specialisation' was not a trait that appealed to Howard Baker one little bit, and so he was at home with his new teammates, to the extent that over the next dozen or so years he was to make 210 appearances for the club – a total exceeded by only one other player, Tommy Whewell, with 259 – though he was not, of course, of the public-school or Oxbridge background from which most of them came, and he was to recall in later years that he was often the only 'outsider' in the team. One of his first Corinthian appearances had been against his other fellow amateurs, Northern Nomads, at Liverpool's Anfield ground on 30 December 1920, and the *Liverpool Echo* reporter singled him out for special praise, together with the centre-forward, J.E. Blair, who also played for Everton and scored a hat-trick for the Nomads in their 4–2 win.

The reporter was unimpressed by the visitors' overall showing: 'The present Corinthian footballers have a long way to go ere they reach the standard of their predecessors'. Yet he waxed lyrical about Howard Baker, while taking a sly dig at his less talented teammates, describing him as 'a mighty man...his kicks are in nearly every instance yards over the halfway line – an inestimable advantage to his side if the forwards will recognise what distance the ball can be expected to travel'. The newspaper's talented cartoonist, Fred May, contributed a marvellously graphic sequence of the 'mighty man' taking a goal-kick, and his caption wittily chided his apprehensive colleagues – 'half the Corinthians taking cover'. The team stayed at the St George's Hotel, in Liverpool, where no doubt Howard Baker was very well known and could ensure the best table and an expert guidance for his new colleagues through the wine list.

The match formed part of an exhaustive Corinthian end-of-year tour which had begun on Monday 27 December with a 3–1 defeat by the Isthmian League, founded in 1905 for clubs in London and the South-East and so firmly dedicated to amateurism that not even trophies or medals were awarded. This match was followed by Yorkshire Amateurs (lost 4–2), Manchester United (won 2–1), the Northern Nomads fixture, Scottish Universities (won 3–1) and the East Scotland League (won 6–5) on successive days during the rest of the week. The win in the last of these games on New Year's Day was surely a tribute to the tourists' powers of recovery from their sporting and social endeavours, but the 5–1 drubbing by Queen's Park was to come in retribution two days later. The great amateur all-rounder, Max Woosnam, who now played for Manchester City, was in the Corinthian side against Manchester United and then as a sort of honoured guest against his own club on 29 January, which didn't inhibit his City colleagues from putting two goals past Howard Baker without reply.

Amateur club affiliations were a free-and-easy affair in those days, and Howard Baker had taken no other part in the Corinthian excursion because on New Year's Day of 1921, two days after conceding four goals to the Northern Nomads, he was in the Nomad colours for their 4–1 FA Amateur Cup first round win! This was achieved against a club from across the Mersey on the Wirral peninsular, Harrowby, at the unpromisingly-named venue of the Ellesmere Port Cement Club. A fortnight later the Nomads moved their 'home' venue to Northwich and beat Leeds Calverley 3–1, but then lost 1–0 in the third round (the last 16) to the County Durham club, Willington, and it was another famous North-Eastern side, Bishop Auckland, who would go on to win the Final that year. The Nomads did not have to wait too long for their day of glory, winning the Cup themselves in 1926, and Willington were to eventually achieve the same feat in 1950.

Howard Baker actually played only three more matches for Corinthian during 1920–21 and just six more in 1921–22 but would soon become a regular in the side. He was one of six different goalkeepers employed by Corinthian in their 18 first-team fixtures and five more were called upon for the A team, including on one occasion R.C. Robertson-Glasgow, who was already establishing himself as a right-arm fast-medium bowler who would eventually take 464 wickets for Oxford University and then Somerset, and would gain wider appreciation as a cricket correspondent for the *Daily Telegraph*, the *Observer* and *The Sunday Times*. Of a convivial nature and with a humorous turn of phrase, he earned the nickname 'Crusoe', allegedly because an Essex batsman, Charlie McGahey, had returned to the pavilion after being dismissed by Robertson-Glasgow to announce to his teammates, 'I was bowled by an old ******* I thought was dead two thousand years ago named Robinson Crusoe!'

The eclectic Corinthian fixture-list for 1920–21 also included matches with Highgate School (won 10–1), Shrewsbury School (2–2), a Public Schools' XI (lost 5–3), Oxford and Cambridge Universities (losses to Cambridge 2–1 and 4–2, a 2–1 loss and a 2–0 win against Oxford), the Army (3–3), the Southern Amateur League (lost 3–2), and an occasional encounter with a Football League team when the latter was without a fixture. Thus Brighton & Hove Albion, who on the day were 15th-placed in Division Three South, were beaten 4–2 a week before Christmas.

There was no conflict of interests regarding Howard Baker's services to Northern Nomads and Corinthian because the latter had yet to waive their original policy of not taking part in any League or Cup competition. Despite this, and the unflattering description of most of the club's players by *The Echo*, there was still a prominent Corinthian presence among those named by England's amateur selectors for their international trial later in January, which took the form of a North v South match at Ayresome Park, Middlesbrough, and attracted 5,000 spectators. It is worth setting out the names of the two teams in full, as they give an interesting indication of the spread of amateur football at that time.

North: B. Howard Baker (Corinthian/Everton); H.P. Ward (Oxford University), J.S.F. Morrison (Corinthian); G. Atkinson (Bishop Auckland), A.H. Robertson (Northern Nomads), C. Painter (Yorkshire Amateurs); T.E. Evans (South Bank), D. Parsons (Eston United), J.E. Blair (Liverpool University & Everton), A.G. Doggart (Cambridge University), A.T. Davies (Cambridge University). South Bank, winners of the FA Amateur Cup in 1912–13, and Eston United were both based in Middlesbrough.

South: J. Munday (Leytonstone); D. Jarvis (King's Lynn), A.G. Bower (Old Carthusians & Corinthian); L.E. Wharton (Oxford University), C.B.G. Hunter (Cambridge University), F.V. Spiller (Oxford City); H.S. Buck (Millwall Athletic), H. Ashton (Cambridge University), C.R. Julian (Old Westminsters), R. Boreham (Wycombe Wanderers), A.V. Hurley (Oxford University).

The Oxbridge influence is obvious. Seven of the 22 players were undergraduates and the contribution did not end there. John Morrison was another of those multi-talented all-rounders who had captained Cambridge at cricket in 1919 and had once hit 233 not out against the MCC. In addition to football, he had also been awarded his 'blue' at golf and was to become a World-renowned golf-course architect. Eleven of the 22 had already played for Corinthian or would do so at some time during their careers. Howard Baker's Everton colleague in the Northern XI, Blair, was a Liverpool University student and also a very capable wicket-keeper and an athlete who competed against Howard Baker in hurdles races. Blair was one of the scorers as the North won the match 3–1.

Eight players – Howard Baker, Robertson, Blair, Doggart and Davies from the North; Bower, Spiller and Buck from the South – were selected for the subsequent match against Wales a fortnight later at Wolverhampton, but it was not an auspicious debut for Howard Baker as Wales won 2–0 with a spirited team made up from clubs the length and breadth of the Principality, namely Abergele, Barmouth, Buckley, Cardiff Corinthian, Colwyn Bay, Gresford, Holywell, Llanidloes, Pembroke Dock and Rhymney. The Liverpool newspapers, conscious perhaps of their wide readership just across the Wirral peninsular in North Wales, readily congratulated the Welsh on their first win over England:

'Of the Welshmen one cannot speak too enthusiastically over the way in which each man played for his side. The manner in which self was sacrificed for the common good was an object lesson to their opponents, and they had the immense satisfaction of achieving a victory over their Saxon rivals. At the same time it is but true that the English XI, as a team, probably gave as poor a display as has ever been given by an English amateur international side. The fly in the ointment so far as the Welshmen are concerned is that it was reported that some of the Welsh XI became professionals within a few hours of the close of the match. Amateur international games were not devised for this purpose'.

The writer used the pseudonym 'Tityrus' (in mythology the father of Helen of Troy, or a beast which led by authority, whichever you prefer) and was, in fact, the renowned sports journalist, J.A.H. Catton. He concluded of England's disappointing performance: 'Howard Baker proved himself a brilliant custodian. Maybe he is inclined to be spectacular, but he was by far the best man in the English eleven. Had he been less sure, England would have been thrashed; nothing less. Baker is alert and quick, has sound judgment, and kicks a very long ball. As no one can be offside from a goal kick he would be of real help to good forwards, and he husbands the energy of his backs. I have nothing but praise for Baker, in spite of the second goal'.

The England side lined up as follows: Howard Baker, E.H. Gates (London Caledonian), Bower, D.S. Long (Yorkshire Amateurs), Robertson, Spiller, Buck, E.I.L. Kail (Dulwich Hamlet), Blair, Doggart, Davies. Of these Howard Baker, Bower, Kail and Doggart were to become regulars in the England amateur side, but Long, Robertson, Buck, Blair and Davies were never selected again, which was to become a habit of the Football Association committee responsible for both the amateur and professional national teams throughout the 1920s.

Oddly, when the full England side met Wales at Ninian Park, Cardiff on 12 March their goalkeeper was also an amateur, Bert Coleman, of Dulwich Hamlet, who had played for the England amateurs on three occasions, including when they won 4 0 against Ireland the previous November in Belfast. So one can only wonder why he was considered good enough to appear alongside the professionals though he had been dropped from the amateur team and was not even selected for the trial match involving his unpaid fellows. The ways of selectors are perforce sometimes difficult to understand by the press or public, but this policy, or rather lack of it, smacked of anarchy. The same Saturday afternoon Everton were losing 2–0 to Tottenham Hotspur at White Hart Lane, with both Spurs' scores coming in the first 20 minutes, but it was said in *The Times* of Howard Baker, again deputising for Tommy Fern, that he 'kept goal well'. The result left Everton fifth in the First Division table and Spurs seventh.

The following week Howard Baker was commended for his performance in one of his rare outings for Corinthian in the 0–0 return match with the renowned Scottish amateurs, Queen's Park, at the Queen's Club ground in West Kensington where he had beaten the Olympic champion in the Empire v USA high jump the year before. This match was one of the regular home-and-away fixtures with Queen's Park and was very much a social highlight of the footballing year, scarcely demeaned on this occasion by the fact that it was a goalless draw and a somewhat disappointing spectacle for the 4,000 spectators. When the Scots had won 5–1 at Hampden Park the previous January the unfortunate H.C.D. Whinney had been in goal for Corinthian.

The splendidly sporting nature of the occasion at the distinctly patrician Queen's Club was perfectly caught by the laconic report in *The Times*: 'There was a certain amount of neat and tidy dribbling – the Corinthians provided the former and the Scottish amateurs the latter – a certain amount of clever half-back play, some lusty tackling by A.G. Bower, and some fabulous punting from goal by B. Howard Baker. The most exciting moment occurred after Howard Baker had been penalised for carrying the ball, but the free-kick was very friendly and slow and Baker stopped it with ease'. *The Sportsman* newspaper, based a few steps away from Fleet Street, devoted a full column to the proceedings despite the lack of scoring. The Corinthians missed three chances to win in the last five minutes, but the reporter was yet another to be beguiled by Howard Baker's goalkeeping clearances: 'Baker's kicking – he was always a good ten yards over the halfway line with his punt – was not the least feature of the game'. The teams and their officials met for dinner that evening at the Café Royal to round off the day in convivial manner

The Queen's Park club was even longer-established than Corinthian, having been founded with very much the same principles in mind in 1876, and the polite refusal of the visiting Scots to take advantage of a misdeed by Howard Baker was typical of the attitude to the game adopted by both clubs. Howard Baker was to recall cheerily of Corinthian games when he was interviewed more than 60 years later that 'if the opposition was awarded a penalty I would lean against the goalpost and let them tap the ball into the empty net', though he later admitted that he only did that in his first season with Corinthian. He also remembered with some feeling: 'The goalkeeper was anybody's target then. We were only allowed to take two paces carrying the ball and then we were attacked by everybody!' It was not until 1931 that the rule was changed to allow goalkeepers to take four steps unchallenged, and that – ironically – was the year of Howard Baker's retirement from the game.

Football continued to occupy Howard Baker's attention as his athletics career drew to an end. His greatest footballing honour so far came about when he was one of only two amateurs to be named in the full England side against Belgium at the Oscar Bossaert Stadium in Brussels on 21 May, the other being Albert Reade, of Tufnell Park. The match was to take place exactly three months after Howard Baker had made his debut League appearance! It was the first time England had gone to the Continent since undertaking tours in 1908 and

1909 in which they had played seven matches against Austria, Bohemia and Hungary and won them all with an aggregate score of 48 goals to seven! The team to face the Belgians was largely experimental in nature as eight of the players were being awarded their first caps. Maybe the England selection committee believed they could afford some latitude to modest opposition or that a full-strength side would humiliate a nation which had so recently suffered severely alongside their allies in wartime. Whatever the considerations, the match was won comfortably enough by 2–0.

The line-up was as follows: Howard Baker; Jack Fort (Millwall), Ephraim Longworth (Liverpool) captain; Reade, George Wilson (The Wednesday), Percy Barton (Birmingham), Archie Rawlings (Preston North End); Jimmy Seed (Tottenham Hotspur), Charlie Buchan (Sunderland), Harry Chambers (Liverpool), George Harrison (Everton). The only previously capped players were Longworth, Wilson and Buchan, while Longworth was the first Liverpool player to lead an England side. Seed and Buchan were among the numerous World War One veterans in the team, and Seed had suffered the awful experience of being gassed in the trenches, which should in all conscience have ended his League playing days. Yet he went on to a long and highly successful career – first as a player with Spurs and then leading Sheffield Wednesday to successive League championship titles in 1928–29 and 1929–30; and subsequently as manager of Charlton Athletic for 23 years, including their FA Cup win of 1946–47. Buchan, to be described by the renowned footballer/journalist Bernard Joy, as 'the finest inside-forward of his day', later joined Arsenal and retired in 1928 to also become a journalist, giving his name to Britain's first football magazine which was published from 1951 to 1974.

Belgium were to become regular opponents of England's during the 1920s, and in all England would play 18 matches against Continental opposition throughout the decade, winning 16, drawing on one occasion with the Belgians, and eventually losing 4–3 to Spain in May of 1929. Howard Baker's debut was in jeopardy for a while because the management of the amateur club for which he played, Northern Nomads, was under investigation for undisclosed irregularities and according to the *Manchester Guardian* the secretary had been ordered by the Amateur Football Association to submit the minute-book and accounts. Whatever the problem, it was soon resolved and the suspension was lifted in early May. One can only surmise that this had something to with money!

Though numerous leading footballers, cricketers and athletes of this era took part in more than one sport as a matter of course and at a high level, there were not actually that many who had represented England or Great Britain in two disciplines. Of the 12 men who throughout history have played cricket and football for England, those from the pre-World War One era included from the Corinthian club C.B. Fry, Leslie Gay and Reginald Foster (a brother of the club secretary), but during the 1920s and 1930s there were only two cricket/football 'double' internationals for England – Andy Ducat, Aston Villa and Surrey, and Johnny Arnold, Southampton and Hampshire, and they played in just one Test each. The one athlete who stands comparison in the inter-war years with Howard Baker as a double international is Eric Liddell, the Olympic 400 metres champion of 1924, who also played for the Scottish rugby-union XV on six occasions.

When the *Encyclopaedia of British Football* was published in 2002, edited by a trio of eminent academics, Richard Cox, Dave Russell and Wray Vamplew, one of the sections was devoted to 'All-Rounders' and only two candidates were put forward as the supreme examples. It was said of Max Woosnam that he 'can make a strong claim to being the most versatile British athlete of all time'. It was then stated that 'similar claims to the title of sporting polymath could have been made by Howard Baker'. These two eminent Liverpudlians, born only six months and a few miles apart, were thus judged to still stand alone 80 years after their greatest sporting achievements.

Three weeks on from his England debut Howard Baker, not at all debilitated by a long hard winter of football and then his first ventures into League water polo in the spring-time, was in his very best form for yet another Northern high-jump win at a Championship record height of 6ft 3in (1.90m) which was to last until 1938. No Englishman, other than Howard Baker himself and possibly George Rowdon, had ever jumped higher, and this was achieved despite a strong wind blowing across the Fallowfield grounds in Manchester and with no serious opposition, but then Howard Baker would have been well accustomed to such minor inconveniences.

He also won the 120 yards hurdles by three yards from his footballing teammate, J.E. Blair, of Liverpool University, in 18.0sec, which does not sound too impressive, but the race was run into a strong head-wind – presumably the officials gave no thought to helping the athletes by changing the direction of the event. As a measure of comparison, the Midlands title the same day was won in only 17.0sec by a patriotically named Birmingham University student, William St George Hombersley, and it is worth noting that a timing of 16.5 was good enough to rank 40th best in Europe for the year and that only two Britons broke 16 seconds.

Also at the Northern Championships athletics meeting Howard Baker was again a close second (by only half-an-inch) in the long jump to the regular winner, William Childs, and was put forward for the AAA Championships by the Northern Counties in four events – the hurdles, high jump, long jump and triple jump. Childs was to eventually set a Northern meeting record of 22ft 9in (6.93m) which also lasted until 1938 and was to represent Great Britain against France in 1922 and 1925, winning on the latter occasion. Howard Baker cleared a respectable 21ft 7½in (6.59), but in his biographical entry in Burke's Who's Who In Sport and Sporting Records, published in 1922, which he presumably contributed himself, an 'Olympic trial' win in 1920 is claimed at an inch further, and he told John Bromhead dismissively of his long-jumping efforts throughout his career that he 'only did 22-and-a-half, and they had that new style of walking in the air, and I was too heavy for that'.

If Howard Baker did, indeed, clear well beyond 22ft it would be a performance of great merit as up to the end of 1921 only a dozen Englishmen had ever beaten 23ft, including the great all-rounder, C.B. Fry, and a future Olympic 100 metres champion, Harold Abrahams, and his brother and fellow-Olympian, Sidney. Harold Abrahams did not join that select company until late in 1921 with 23ft 0½in (7.02), achieved at the Cambridge University inter-college championships in the depths of November. That leap equalled the ground record set in 1900, and Abrahams defied his brother's injunctions not to spread his talents too widely by winning the 100 yards, 440 yards and high jump during the afternoon and finishing second in the 120 yards hurdles.

England's goalkeeper on a winning side and then Northern high-jump champion yet again within three weeks – what a splendid demonstration of Howard Baker's versatile and seemingly readily interchangeable talents, but that was by no means all! At the beginning of May he had made his water-polo debut at the season's start for the Everton club at the

Margaret Street Baths, stepping (or perhaps one should say, more accurately, 'dipping') straight into the first team goalmouth and helping in a 4–3 win over Edge Lane. 'He played brilliantly in the deep end, despite strange surroundings and lack of practice', reported *The Liverpool Courier*, and the *Liverpool Echo* swimming correspondent, 'Leander' (not the most sensible of choices for a pseudonym; in ancient mythology Leander nightly swam the Hellespont to meet his lover but eventually drowned on one stormy crossing), reckoned Howard Baker was good enough 'to warrant hopes that he will prove a tower of strength to the club'. His progress in this new sport was to be startling, to say the least.

There was more and better high-jumping still to come from Howard Baker. A fortnight after the Northern championships, on Saturday 25 June, he achieved the best performance of his life at the Huddersfield Cricket & Athletic Club Festival, clearing 6ft 5in (1.96m). The meeting was previewed in *The Huddersfield Daily Examiner* newspaper on the previous day with an impressive list of star names among the 720 entries for the athletics events, including the Olympic steeplechase champion, Percy Hodge, and three other current AAA title-holders – Joe Blewitt (four miles), Charles Clibbon (10 miles) and Howard Baker. The advertisement for the meeting also promised 'a splendid cycle entry', and the admission fee to the ground was one shilling and three pence for adults (equivalent to some six new pence) and ninepence for children, or three shillings for adults and one shilling and sixpence for children in the grandstand. Membership of the Huddersfield C & AC Supporters' Club was offered at the bargain price of one shilling, which entitled card-holders to free entry to the festival. Sadly, 90 years or so later, the grounds are dilapidated and only used for amateur rugby league games, and a cinder track which existed at the town's Leeds Road Playing Fields has been replaced by an all-weather football pitch. Thus there are now in the 21st century no specific facilities at all for athletics in Huddersfield, the population of which is 146,000.

On the following Saturday, 2 July the town's other newspaper, *The Weekly Examiner*, carried a splendidly fulsome report of the annual festival, which had first been held in 1865. Howard Baker's high-jump record was rightly hailed by the *Examiner* reporter as the highlight of the afternoon. It was said that he 'received a tremendous ovation when he accomplished this at the second attempt, and the height was certified by representatives of the three premier athletic associations…as a memento of the fact that the record was set up at Huddersfield, Mrs Horace Broadbent, who distributed the prizes, promised Baker a special trophy upon which is to be the Huddersfield coat of arms and motto, with an inscription'. Neither the facilities nor the opposition that day were in any way superior to what Baker customarily encountered at the local meetings in which he competed. The high-jump takeoff was from grass and his 'rivals' were far outdistanced – J. McGuire, of Bolton, was second at 5ft 2in (1.57m).

There was particular mention of McGuire in the report, as if to emphasise the superiority of Howard Baker, but neither here, nor for that matter in almost any account to be found of Howard Baker's various appearances in smaller meetings over the years, is there any indication of when he actually started his competitions. Did he come in at the puny heights of less than 5ft attempted by the others and then patiently work his way up, an inch or so at a time, to beyond the 6ft mark? Or did he – in the manner of the great pole-vaulters, Sergey Bubka and Yelena Isinbayeva, of many decades later – sit it out until most or all of the rest had been eliminated?

In fact, his son Philip, remembered his father telling him that he would patiently wait while his lesser opponents attempted and eventually failed at their heights, and he would then have the bar set at what he considered a rather greater challenge. To emphasise the point, he was not averse to walking up to the bar when it was at 6ft or more and standing alongside it to demonstrate to his vanquished rivals and to the public just what was entailed. This is confirmed by the report of a meeting at New Brighton in 1921: 'Howard Baker had no trouble in the high jump; he wouldn't, of course. He simply waited till the other competitors had finished, asked for the bar to be raised a mere 12 inches, and then showed us all how easy it is to clear 6ft 3in'.

Maybe at Huddersfield that day it was the exceptional weather which contributed significantly to the record being broken. It was so hot that the *Examiner* noted that 'a goodly number of the spectators appeared to be made somewhat uncomfortable by such unusual conditions, and many gazed enviously at the young athletes, who were more fittingly clad for their exertions in that simple one-piece garment, the bathing costume'. The attendance was precisely registered at 6,029, and in addition to the 25 events on the programme, including a 100 yards for which there were no less than 17 races, there was no lack of other entertainment for the spectators: 'The prizes, upon a table near the track, flashed out their attractions with the aid of the ever-present sun, and the Linthwaite Band, under Mr J.W. Schofield, filled in enjoyably the few spare moments there were with popular selections'.

The Olympic gold-medallist, Percy Hodge, who was introduced to the admiring throng as 'the World's champion steeplechaser', gave 'a clever exhibition of hurdling and trick hurdling'. Hodge's favourite crowd-pleaser was to clear hurdles carrying a tray complete with bottle and glasses and not spill a drop, but in more serious vein that afternoon he won the 1000 metres invitation scratch race by five yards in 2min 37⅗ sec.

The fact that Howard Baker had travelled as far afield as Huddersfield to compete is intriguing in itself, though he had been to the same meeting in pre-war years and had attempted a British record there in 1914. The journey by motor-car or by train across the Pennines from Lancashire into Yorkshire would have presented no difficulties, but he usually confined his appearances at athletics meetings – maybe no more than half-a-dozen or so a year – to those held near Liverpool, with the exception of the AAA Championships or the Northern event, or if he was invited to a representative match. The explanation for this venture is to be found in the taped interview which he gave more than 60 years later. The previous evening Howard Baker had played water-polo for Everton against the local town side at Huddersfield Baths, and he had entered the athletics meeting as an afterthought simply because he would be in the town anyway!

In such chance circumstances was the British record set that would last for a quarter-of-a-century, and yet *The Liverpool Evening Express* expressed little enthusiasm in its cryptic reaction: 'Howard Baker appears to be making for improvement in his jumping abilities'. He attempted a further record of 6ft 6in (1.98m) at Huddersfield, as he was also to do on other occasions, and it might have been on this occasion that he could have achieved such a height but for an unfortunate interruption in mid-event. As previously mentioned, he often tied a handkerchief to the cross-bar, as was a widespread custom of the era, to serve as a marker point for his clearance, and it is recorded, though not specified exactly when, that a meticulous official took exception to the practice and called Howard Baker to a sudden halt during his run-up. His shoe burst and that was the end of that competition.

Howard Baker related the tale to John Bromhead in his taped interview in 1982 that his Swedish adviser, Hjalmar Mellander, had remonstrated with him after the Huddersfield meeting, telling him that he would have had his 6ft 6in clearance had he not wasted energies playing water-polo the previous evening. Mellander had been a fine all-round athlete who had won the 'Greek pentathlon' at the 10th anniversary Olympic Games in Athens in 1906, involving a standing long jump, a race over a distance of 192 metres (as contested at the Ancient Olympics), discus-throwing, javelin-throwing and Greco-Roman wrestling. He had also placed fourth in both the long jump and the javelin events, and he was already living in Liverpool then, having set up in business there as a trainer and masseur in 1902. He won the Northern Counties' high jump in 1905, 1906 and 1908, and Howard Baker frequently used his services.

However, in this instance, Howard Baker's memory was at fault. Mellander could not possibly have been present in Huddersfield for the tragic reason that he had died in October of 1919 at the age of 38, attempting to save a drowning person in the sea off the Isle of Man. It could be that it was Fred Birkett, another of Howard Baker's confidantes, who was in attendance at the record jump instead. Birkett, a fellow member of Liverpool Harriers, had himself been a very capable high jumper, placing second at the AAA Championships of 1907 to the Irishman, Con Leahy, with his personal best of 5ft 10½in (1.79m) and winning the Northern title the same year. Birkett emigrated to Canada later in 1921, and it is to be wondered whether his departure was another factor in Howard Baker's retirement from high jumping.

A massive crowd of 30,000 gathered for the 1921 AAA Championships on 2 July and was thrilled by a British record of 4min 13⅕ sec in the mile for Albert Hill, who had triumphed in both the 800 and the 1500 metres at the previous year's Olympics. The field-event results were much less encouraging for home interests as visiting Swedes won the pole vault, triple jump, shot, discus, hammer and javelin and an American took the long jump. The one exception, you will notice, is the high jump, in which Howard Baker triumphed for the sixth and last time in clearing 6ft 2¾in (1.90m) and beating Pierre Guilloux, of France, by a full two inches, with Bertil Jansson, of Sweden, third at 5ft 11in (1.80).

Howard Baker also took part in the triple jump and placed second, but his mark of 43ft 8¾in (13.33m), though very respectable by English standards, was a long way behind the 46ft 6¾in (14.19) of Sweden's Folke Janson. It should be noted that Janson was one of the World's foremost exponents of the event, having lost the Olympic title the previous year by no more than an inch, but even so the AAA result vividly illustrated the yawning gap between international and British standards. Howard Baker might well have achieved much more impressive triple-jump distances had he been given the opportunity to do so, but the event was so little thought of in England that it had not even figured at the AAA Championships until 1914, and at the 1921 meeting there were only five competitors and the third-placed athlete was the Norwegian-born Hans Odde who barely cleared 40ft! To be fair to Odde, he did improve with time and represented Great Britain at the 1924 Olympics.

While on the subject of Howard Baker's all-round abilities it is a vain but diverting exercise to consider what he might have done in the 10-event decathlon which had first figured in the Olympics in 1912. He would obviously have coped very adequately with the 100 and 400 metres, the 110 metres hurdles, high jump, long jump, discus and javelin, and had some experience of the pole vault, which would leave only the 1500 metres and shot for him to work on. He never had any pretensions to being a middle-distance runner, but then that is true of virtually everyone who has ever taken part in the decathlon, World and Olympic champions included, and his agility and his strong arm which he was reputed to put to such good use as an out-fielder in cricket for the Liverpool club would surely have enabled him to produce something respectable as a vaulter and shot-putter.

The decathlon was another of those athletic disciplines regarded with disdain in Britain for the entire first half of the 20th century, and it was not staged as a AAA championship event until 1928, and then only for one year until being revived in 1936. A rough rule-of-thumb guide, based on the scoring system then in existence, suggests that Howard Baker might well have finished in the top 10 of the 23 competitors at the 1920 Olympic decathlon…and it was not until 1952 that a Briton actually achieved that level of performance when Geoff Elliott, who was primarily a pole vaulter, placed ninth.

It took almost 30 years for Howard Baker's AAA high-jump performance to be improved by any significant margin at the championships. Pierre Lewden, of France, cleared 6ft 4in (1.93m) in 1923 and this height was equalled by the Olympic champion, Harold Osborn, of the USA, in 1925 but not again until 1947 and 1948 when Prince Adegboyega Folaranmi Adedoyin, of Nigeria, and Howard Baker's successor as British record-holder, Alan Paterson, were the respective champions. Paterson cleared 6ft 5in (1.96) at the championships of 1950, and Howard Baker's effort of 29 years before would still have been good enough for second place that year!

He was selected for both the high jump and long jump in the England & Wales team to contest the home countries' international against Ireland and Scotland at Windsor Park, Belfast, the following Saturday, but for whatever reason he was absent on the day. So, too, were several other leading English athletes, and Scotland, led by the future Olympic 400 metres champion, Eric Liddell, at 100 yards, won the match rather easily. Howard Baker competed only sparingly during July and August of 1921, and maybe retirement from athletics was uppermost in his mind and his attention was being distracted by his water-pool excursions and was also turning towards the football season to come.

He was, however, persuaded by the promoter of the Rangers FC Sports in Glasgow, who was the Rangers' manager and a former professional sprinter of some repute, Bill Struth, to travel up to the city for the hugely popular annual meeting on 6 August. Howard Baker told John Bromhead that Struth had tried before to lure him into taking part, and there was always a special financial incentive for those who accepted the invitation. True to his amateur principles Howard Baker declined the cash but settled for being provided hospitality for a week's sailing on the River Clyde instead. Before taking to the waters, he fulfilled the hopes of Struth by setting a Scottish all-comers' record for the high jump of 6ft 2¾in (1.90), and that was still better than any other European would achieve that year.

The features on the Hampden Park grass track were the defeats of the English Olympians, Albert Hill and Harry Edward, by local heroes. In the threequarter mile handicap Hill could not make up 20 yards on Duncan McPhee, while Edward lost at 100 yards, unable to pull back the 1½ yards' start given to a promising young medical student named Eric Liddell, who would win the Olympic 400 metres three years later. Even so, the Glasgow press concluded that 'distinction was lent to the meeting by the high jumping of B. Howard Baker, who came within a quarter-of-an-inch of his championship record'.

Later in life Howard Baker would recognise that he had not competed as often as perhaps he should have done during his career. 'A lot of people thought you had to go to more meetings', he recalled, 'and I could have gone up to the Rangers' or Celtic Sports in Scotland for years, but I would never go until that one year when they said, 'Come up and get the all-comers' record and then have a week's sailing on the Clyde'. There was always money in the boot for those meetings, but I got a gold watch instead'. There were other temptations, too, and on one occasion he was approached by bookmakers to lose a contest with his Irish rival, Tim Carroll, but reported the matter immediately to the meeting organisers.

One of his rare appearances in this final season of high-jumping was close to his city of birth at the Hoylake Football & Athletic Club Sports, on the Wirral peninsular across the Mersey from Liverpool, on 20 August. There is a lengthy article in the weekly *Hoylake and West Kirby Advertiser* on the following Friday which provides us with a splendidly elaborate and sometimes amusingly contradictory eye-witness account, though Baker's clearance of 6ft 3in (1.90m) yet again in the makeshift conditions on the Melrose Avenue football pitch was referred to only in passing as 'a fine exhibition of high jumping'.

In favourable weather some 3,000 or 4,000 spectators (according to which page of the newspaper you read) turned up, and the reporter observed that 'most of them found the magnitude of the sports and their almost flawless management far in excess of expectation', though it was later remarked that because so 'much time was wasted, many good people were quite bored before the end was reached at 6.45'. The delays were understandable because heats and finals were held for three different 100 yards events and there were also two races at 220 yards, an 880 yards and one mile, plus numerous cycle races and various motor-cycle record attempts. The mile handicap had 49 starters and was won, interestingly, by a one-armed miner, P. Reevey, of the Lancashire club, Makerfield Harriers, in a time of 4min 21⅖ sec off 168 yards. Back in the bunch, as was often the case, was Albert Hill, the British record-holder, but as he would have had to have run in the order of 3:57 to win in an era in which no man had yet broken 4:12, he could have been forgiven for soon abandoning the hopeless chase!

The final competition of Howard Baker's athletics career was a dramatic one, to say the least. He won the high jump for England against France in the first international match between the two countries which took place at Stade Colombes, in Paris, on 11 September. The French had much more experience of such encounters, having begun a series against Belgium in 1912 which was resumed in 1919, and during 1921 had met Switzerland and Belgium at home and Sweden in Stockholm.

In prospect, the high-jump at Colombes was one of the most enticing events on the programme with three Olympic finalists involved: Howard Baker and the Frenchmen, Pierre Lewden and Pierre Guilloux. However, Baker needed only a clearance of 1.80m (5ft 11in) to win by two centimetres from Guilloux, whom he had also beaten a couple of months before at the AAA Championships, and the modest height may well have been due to the unruly behaviour of the crowd who were said to have 'clapped in unison to distract our high jumpers'. No doubt this was so, though in the 21st century that sort of crowd reaction would be regarded as supportive and would be enthusiastically encouraged by the competitors!

To add to the fraught atmosphere, stones were thrown at the bus carrying the English team and several thousand spectators had broken into the ground without paying. The match itself was 'conducted with an abundance of ill-will', including a change being made in the scoring system by French officials without consulting their English colleagues, and one of the British athletes had particularly unpleasant memories of the occasion. Rex Woods, who had graduated from Cambridge the previous year and competed throughout the 1920s for Great Britain as a shot-putter, was to recall in later years: 'The home feeling ran very high and 'fouls' and booing from our hosts were the order of the day'.

Fortunately, no lasting damage was done to the *entente cordiale* and fixtures between the two countries would continue to be amicably held for another half-century or so until this type of two-a-side or three-a-side competition between national teams regrettably fell largely out of favour in a more commercialised age.

The French champion, Lewden, was one of the most technically proficient high-jumpers of his era – only 1.68m (5ft 6in) tall, he achieved a career best performance of 1.95m, almost precisely the same as Howard Baker's. He was to win the AAA high jump in 1922 and 1923, setting a championship best of 6ft 4in (1.93) on the latter occasion which was not beaten until 1951, and he would also be Olympic bronze-medallist in 1924. Yet he had no illusions about his event. He later wrote in a training manual published by the Fédération Française d'Athlétisme: 'The high jump is a member of that important group of field events that one tends to think of as the poor relations of athletics. Don't laugh: you will never see the start of a race delayed to allow a field event to take place. You will see, even for the needs of a national championships, the high jumpers forced to rest for many minutes, even if they have got to the point where the least cooling down could prove fatal to their chances, so that the 100 metres can start or the steeplechasers can circle the track'.

There were only three field events in this match, but it was more or less an arbitrary matter during the 1920s and 1930s as to what the schedule would be for these Anglo-French meetings, and it would not be until 1951, and the 20th in the series, that all eight standard field events would be included. France had first and second in the long jump and shot on this first occasion, but Howard Baker's success and six wins in the nine track events gave England a narrow overall victory by 123 points to 118. His colleagues in the high jump were both serving in the Royal Air Force – Frank Nuttall, an 18-year-old cadet at the RAF college at Cranwell, and the Irish-born Sergeant-Major J. Miller, of whom so little is known that his first name remains unrecorded to this day. Nuttall, who had placed fourth in the AAA Championships, commendably tied with the French champion, Lewden, for third place at 1.75 (5ft 9in), and though Miller only cleared 1.64 (5ft 4½in) he still managed to beat the third Frenchman.

The youthful Nuttall could clearly then have been considered as Howard Baker's potential successor, but it never quite happened like that, though Nuttall's career was a long one. While still at Cranwell in 1922 he achieved the best ever jump by a British junior (under 20) with 6ft 0in (1.83m) and he won at the same height against France in 1925, when the match was held in Brighton. He was also the RAF title-winner six times up until 1933 as he gradually moved through the service ranks to Flying-Officer and then Flight-Lieutenant, but his jumping heights did not improve accordingly and his best was to be a fractional improvement to 6ft 0¼in (1.83) in 1926. The Frenchman, Lewden, would win at the Anglo-French matches of 1922, 1925 and 1927, setting a record of 6ft 3in (1.90) in 1922 which stood for 24 years, and would be the Olympic bronze-medallist in 1928.

None of the performances at the 1921 match were particularly distinguished, and the best of them was probably that of the French Olympic gold-medallist at 5000 metres, Joseph

Guillemot, who won his event in a time which was exactly half-a-minute slower than he had produced in Antwerp to beat the legend-to-be, Paavo Nurmi, of Finland. *The Times* carried the full results of the France-England match but only a brief report which gave no further details of any events and mainly remarked on the fact that two Olympic champions from the previous year, Bevil Rudd and Albert Hill, together with Harold Abrahams, had apparently declined invitations to compete for England because the match took place on a Sunday, though this may have been a matter of convenience rather than religious scruples. No mention was made of the crowd other than to say that it was 'enormous'.

Howard Baker's final athletics appearance in Paris was, in fact, his second sporting visit to the city in successive weekends, as the Corinthian football club had played matches in Paris and Lille the previous Sunday and Monday. It may be, of course, that he was unable to resist the temptation to prolong his stay for the rest of the week for sociable reasons. These matches marked the resumption of a long-standing tradition of overseas tours by Corinthian which had come to assume missionary status, having begun with a visit to South Africa in 1897. There had been further expeditions to South Africa again in 1903 and in subsequent years to Czechoslovakia, Denmark, Germany, Holland, Hungary, Spain and Sweden, and to Brazil, Canada, South Africa once more and the USA. A second venture to Brazil in 1914 was cut short before a single game had been played when the team received news of the outbreak of war while still on the high seas three days out from Rio de Janeiro.

For this first post-war outing to France the Corinthian party left Victoria Station at 11am on the morning of Saturday 3 September and travelled via the Dover-to-Calais cross-channel ferry and then by train to Paris, staying the night in the Hotel de Grande Bretagne. The match against the French champions, Red Star, the next afternoon was memorable if only for the fact that, in the words of F.N.S. Creek's history of the club, published in 1933, 'There was not a blade of grass to be seen on the playing pitch, which in addition to being very small was covered with small stones and bits of glass'. Corinthian won 2–1 and 'Baker's kicking, as usual, thoroughly pleased the crowd'. He was again in splendid form on the Monday afternoon in Lille against the local Olympique club, and in much better playing conditions the tourists easily won 4–0. Staying the night at a hotel in Calais, the party – with or without Howard Baker – was back at Victoria before 11 o'clock on the Tuesday morning.

Throughout this athletics season Howard Baker had also been pursuing his water-polo ambitions to such good effect that after only two months in action for Everton he was on the verge of the England team! On 14 May 'Leander', in his *Echo* column, reported from the Birkenhead v Everton match that 'the goalkeeping on both sides was of the highest order and Howard Baker, for Everton, saved many terrific shots'. On Monday 6 June the Everton players set off by motor charabanc in the late afternoon towards Manchester for their English Championship first-round match against Tyldesley, and though they lost 5–3 it was said of Howard Baker (by 'Leander' again) that he was 'in magnificent form and made splendid saves repeatedly…on changing ends the home crowd accorded Howard Baker an ovation for his display, which he repeated in the second half'.

He was one of only two Liverpool players among the seven selected for Lancashire against Cheshire at Southport on Monday 11 July, but as had been the case for the triangular international athletics match in Belfast at the weekend he withdrew from the team. Later in the month (20–21 July), within 10 days of winning his sixth and last AAA high-jump title, he took part in representative water-polo matches on successive nights to decide which

Northern players would be put forward for the England team trials and who would be in the Lancashire team to defend the inter-counties' title which they had won so often in previous years. The reason why he did not subsequently add water polo to athletics and football as a third sport in which he had represented his country can be summed up in two words — Charlie Smith.

For the Northern trial on the first evening at Wigan, Smith was in goal for the 'Whites' and Howard Baker in goal for the 'Blues', and as Smith's team won 7–4 the honours clearly went his way, though the ever-present 'Leander' pointed out regarding the goals for the 'Whites' that Howard Baker had 'little chance of saving any of them'. Smith was duly nominated for the national trial. The next evening at Southport the Lancashire County Association 'Probables' met the 'Possibles' and at the last minute the selectors switched Howard Baker, Liverpool's only representative in the match, to the 'Probables' and Smith to the 'Possibles'. Apart from Smith, five of the players in that trial had had or would have Olympic experience stretching from 1900 through to 1928, including George Wilkinson (three Olympic gold medals, 1900, 1908, 1912), George Nevinson (two, 1908, 1912), Billy Dean and Charles Forsyth (one each, 1908 and 1920 respectively). As the Probables won 6–2 Howard Baker could then point to a 10–9 advantage over his opposite number.

Even so, Howard Baker probably knew from the outset that it was a lost cause. Smith was selected for Lancashire and Howard Baker had to settle for the knowledge that he was not only No.2 in his county but also probably No.2 in his country. Smith, winner of Olympic gold medals in 1908, 1912 and 1920, would continue to play for England through to 1926, by which time Howard Baker had long since given up the game. When Smith was at last replaced as Great Britain's Olympic goalkeeper in 1928, it was a Liverpool player, Leslie Ablett, a member of the city police force, who took over.

Howard Baker's Huddersfield high-jump record would rank third best in the World for the year behind two Americans, R.P. Chamberlain and Dewey Alberts, who cleared the fastidiously precise heights of 6ft 5⅝ (1.97) and 6ft 5⅛ (1.96) respectively. The seven men in the rankings immediately after Howard Baker were all Americans, including the Olympic champion, Richmond Landon (fifth), and the silver-medallist, Harold Muller (sixth). Also behind Baker were the two other Americans against whom he had declined a jump-off in Antwerp, John Murphy and Walter Whalen. The next best European was the Frenchman, Pierre Lewden, ranked 11th at 1.89, who had lost to Baker in the France-England match, and the only other Briton in the top 50 was the Polytechnic Harrier, Jack Probert, who was equal 36th at 6ft 0in (1.83).

Dewey Alberts, who was a Chicagoan, was the US champion that year and had five of the 15 best performances at 6ft 3⅜ (1.91) or better. A competition between him and Baker would have surely been enthralling, but it would not be until the 1930s that the sport's ruling body in the USA, the Amateur Athletic Union, would start sending teams to Europe for international meetings after the American domestic season had been completed. In 1921 the idea of the champions of Great Britain and the USA meeting up – other than in Olympic year for the post-Games British Empire v USA contest which had been first held the previous year – would have been entirely fanciful. There was, though, an opening for Oxbridge men as occasional Anglo-American inter-university meetings had been held in each country alternately since 1894 with Harvard and Yale, and in 1920 Oxford had met Princeton at the Queen's Club, in London, losing by six events to four.

Apart from its importance in the year's World rankings, and its long life as the best by a British athlete, Howard Baker's record was also a height which was not to be exceeded by anyone other than Americans until 1930 when Simeon Toribio, of the Philippines, beat Katuo Kimura, of Japan, 2.00 to 1.96, in a competition in Tokyo, and not by another European until Jerzy Plawczyk, of Poland, cleared 1.96 in 1932. Toribio was the Olympic bronze-medallist in 1932, with Kimura sixth and Plawczyk equal seventh. Toribio and Kimura had also been fourth and sixth respectively at the 1928 Games.

Incidentally, there is a curious sequel to Howard Baker's performance in an English context. As Alan Paterson, the man who became the next British record-holder in 1946, was Scottish, Howard Baker's performance lasted as an English native record even longer – but was then beaten three times in a single meeting. At the London v Gothenburg match at the White City in August 1949 Peter Wells and Ron Pavitt both got over 6ft 5¼in (1.96), but then Pavitt settled matters by clearing 6ft 6in (1.98), only for Wells to respond a fortnight later in a meeting at Bristol with 6ft 6⅜in (1.99). Paterson and Wells both employed the Western Roll technique and Pavitt the Straddle.

The reason for Howard Baker's retirement from athletics was simple enough. He was by then 29 years of age, and in his recollection of 60 years later he 'had so many other things to do', which is what he told both John Bromhead and his interviewer from *The Times*, David Miller. There is, however, some evidence that Howard Baker continued high jumping in 1922. F.A.M. Webster, the coach who took such an interest in Howard Baker's career, says that he had a clearance of 6ft 3in (1.91m) that year, and he certainly gave exhibitions of his prowess at local meetings and had thoughts of taking part in something more serious because he entered his name at the Northern championships in June for the high jump and the hurdles.

There are clear indications of some sort of serious falling-out between Howard Baker and athletics officialdom. In describing the 1922 AAA Championships the *Liverpool Echo* reporter, 'Marksman', wrote aggrievedly: 'The high jump was principally noteworthy in Liverpool people's eyes for the absence of Howard Baker, holder and record-breaker. Many conjectures were put forward as to why he was not there, but all that I heard were far from the truth. What I am assured, on very good authority, is the real reason reflects very badly on certain actions of more than one of our local NCAA officials at the back end of last season, and if they can now feel satisfied with their handiwork and the full results we have a great deal to be sorry for in the Liverpool district'.

Clearly 'Marksman' was in the know but was not prepared to tell all, which must have been a shade frustrating for his readers. A fair assumption is that the business with the handkerchiefs tied to the cross-bars as marker points or simply to improve vision was the cause of the dissension. Again this was a matter on which Howard Baker was never to comment publicly in later life, and maybe that was another reflection on his inherent sportsmanship. Or it just didn't seem very important to him.

In any case, tennis was now occupying an increasing amount of his time and enthusiasm. The day before those Northern athletics championships for which he had entered he played a second-round men's doubles match at the Northern lawn-tennis tournament on his home courts at Liverpool Cricket Club's Aigburth grounds, and he and his partner were beaten. Had they won, it is unimaginable that he would then have decided to go high-jumping and hurdling instead, leaving his partner stranded. That certainly would not have been playing the game in his book.

The Times reported in its preview of the AAA Championships that 'B. Howard Baker is presumably to defend his title', but it is not apparent as to whether this claim was based on the fact that his name was in the list of entries, or whether it was no more than wishful thinking on the part of the correspondent. As for Howard Baker's thoughts, it may be that on the day in question they were focussed instead a few miles away across South London. The Wimbledon tennis tournament had started and Borotra, Cochet and Suzanne Lenglen were all playing that weekend, and a future doubles partner, Billy Radcliffe, was losing in straight sets in the third round of the singles.

Howard Baker also took part in the occasional game of cricket for Liverpool during the summer of 1922 and had an innings of 44 on one occasion. His overall record of 82 runs in six matches was not too impressive, but he may well have been a rather better player than those figures suggest. Certainly, Jack Sharp had a high opinion of his abilities, and as Sharp had played in three Tests for England his opinion was well worth heeding. Additionally, he had been Everton's right-winger from 1900 to 1909 and an international on two occasions and later became a long-serving director of the club.

Without Howard Baker at Stamford Bridge it was his cross-Channel rival, Lewden, who won the AAA title at an ordinary 5ft 11in (1.80m) from two Norwegians, and the best Briton was the Southend Harrier, R.A. Nicholas, who cleared only 5ft 7in (1.70). Not that the high jump was any worse from the British point of view than the other field events at those Championships: in the three other jumps and four throws there was only one Briton placed in the first three. He was Malcolm Nokes, second in the hammer, who was to be the Olympic bronze-medallist in 1924, and who with his fellow hammer-thrower, Tom Nicolson, and Howard Baker was one of the only three Britons of the inter-war years to achieve World class in any of these technical jumping or throwing disciplines.

British high-jumping remained largely in decline for much of the next quarter-of-a-century. After Howard Baker there was not to be another home winner of the AAA high-jump title until Arthur Gray, of Polytechnic Harriers, succeeded in 1931, though a British Guiana-born undergraduate at Oxford, Colin Gordon, had won the previous year and had represented Great Britain at the 1928 Olympics. Gray was another who was thought of as a special prospect for the future, also making his debut against France in 1926 at the age of 19, and though he never fulfilled those expectations he deserves every credit as a rarity in British field events in that he was a product of a secondary school, and he won the Essex county high-jump title 10 times between 1925 and 1935 and shared the bronze medal at the 1934 British Empire Games with a personal best 6ft 1in (1.85m). Gordon was the silver-medallist for British Guiana at the inaugural 1930 Empire Games in Hamilton, Ontario, and stayed on to teach in Canada and subsequently in Australia, thus depriving British athletics of his services at the age of 22.

Actually there *was* a lone Briton who approached Baker's standard, and even equalled his record of 6ft 5in (1.96m) in 1931, and he, too, was a Lancastrian – Geoffrey Turner, who was a member of the Earlestown Viaduct club at Warrington. Turner had also competed at the 1928 Olympics but without making the final, and he had no chance to fully develop his talent as he died of septicaemia in 1932 at the age of 24. Encouraged by Howard Baker, Turner had emulated his adviser by winning the Northern title every year from 1927 to 1931 with a best height of 6ft 2in (1.88). He also twice tied for first place in matches against Europe's most powerful athletics nation, Germany, in 1929 and 1931, and like Howard

Baker he was a very capable 120 yards hurdler, winning the Northern title in 1929. Already the best high jumper in Europe at the age of 21, his tragic early death was a grievous loss.

The memory of the end of Howard Baker's high-jumping career was still clear in his mind more than 50 years later when he told the *Liverpool Echo* that 'I had always wanted to set up a British record in the high jump, and having achieved that ambition I put away my spikes and never jumped again'. He would continue for the rest of his life to take a keen interest in the sport which had brought him so many records and titles, but – to quote his own words of so many years later – 'There were other games I wanted to play'.

CHELSEA? WHY CHELSEA?
WELL, THERE'S SOME JOLLY NICE
ANTIQUE SHOPS NEARBY

As high-jump competition was now a thing of the past for Howard Baker, the figures '6–4' would in the future have more significance for him as a win on the tennis courts or an unlikely football result than as a record in the athletics stadium. If he harboured any long-term regrets regarding his comparative failure in the Olympics, then he had the satisfaction of a British record in his final season, which placed him far ahead of his contemporaries, and a victory for his country as his swan-song. There was plenty else to do, and he was about to take a new direction in his footballing career.

Quite why he should decide to join Chelsea is an intriguing mystery, for which there is a variety of possible explanations. He might have been influenced by the advice of his Liverpudlian contemporary and fellow-Corinthian, Max Woosnam, who retained fond memories of the club, having played 11 matches for them immediately before World War One, then returning to Cambridge University. After war service Woosnam had remained on Chelsea's books until taking up an engineering management appointment in Manchester and joining Manchester City.

Also a likely advocate would have been another illustrious amateur, Vivian Woodward, who played 116 times for Chelsea from 1909 to 1915 and was described by Howard Baker's friend and fellow-athlete, Philip Baker, as 'the living embodiment of the finest spirit of the game'. Woodward, who farmed at St Osyth, in Essex, some five miles from Clacton-on-Sea, had also been an Olympian in 1908 and 1912, and the only flaw in the argument regarding guidance by him in favour of Chelsea could have been that he was now a director of Tottenham Hotspur, and so would supposedly sing their praises in preference, but he did have Chelsea's interests also at heart because he joined that club's board of directors in 1922.

Howard Baker was certainly in demand because he was approached by the secretary of Aston Villa, George Ramsay, in April of 1921 with a view to joining the Birmingham club as successor to their renowned England international, Sam Hardy. Ramsay remains a major influential figure in the club's history, having been captain in the 1880s and then secretary for 42 years until 1926, which in effect meant that he managed the club, and during his tenure the FA Cup and the Football League championship title were each won on six occasions. Thus Ramsay was one of the most eminent club officials of the early 20th century, and to receive an invitation from him was a rare honour. Howard Baker understandably relished the prospect but eventually decided against, as his splendidly eloquent letter to Ramsay on 3 May explained:

'I regret the delay in replying to your letter of the 16th *ultimo*, more especially as I find myself unable to write in the strain I had ardently hoped to do. Everton F.C. would not stand in my way, and I personally am very anxious to play for you, realizing the great honour of succeeding the Great Hardy, and believing that I could make good for you.

'I must explain that I am associated in business with my father, there being only the two of us in the firm. While he does not utterly prohibit my engaging to assist you, he feels strongly that having regard to all our circumstances – personal and commercial – the present moment is not an opportune juncture to take a step which in other circumstances he would – as would indeed all my friends – applaud as much a privilege as a pleasure.

'I can only hope that ere next season all will be clear for me to accept a position which I believe to be the pinnacle of Association Football fame. I would get in touch with you at the earliest possible moment'.

Maybe the proximity of Chelsea to the London branch of the Howard Baker companies was the deciding factor, or perhaps it is the remembrance of Howard Baker's son, Philip, that his father was attracted to the Chelsea club simply because there happened to be some attractive antique-shops in the vicinity! Certainly, the very name 'Chelsea', then as now, had a rather more stylish ring to it than, say, prosaic Arsenal or Tottenham…or Aston Villa. The Chelsea Arts Club had been founded in 1891, with the painter, James McNeill Whistler, as one of its prime movers, and the Arts Club Ball, held from 1908 onwards, had lent the district a distinctly raffish air. Others of distinction – artist J.M.W. Turner, engineer Marc Brunel, politician David Lloyd George – lived close by, though there was a mix of every type of housing and social level from the richest to the poorest in the neighbourhood, and the irony of it all was that the Chelsea football ground was not in Chelsea at all but in the neighbouring borough of Fulham! Maybe, too, the attraction for Howard Baker was Stamford Bridge itself, scene of so many of his high-jump exploits, and the memory of having made his League debut there only a few months before.

Since 1877 Stamford Bridge had been the headquarters of London Athletic Club, loosely named after the nearby Stanford Creek, but the existing basic stadium and an adjoining market-garden, 12.5 acres in all, had been bought up in 1904 by the brothers Gus and Joe Mears, who were wealthy building contractors, and after considering their acquisition as a site for housing or for railway development they decided instead to build a sports arena 'for the masses'. Glasgow already had two such venues, Celtic Park and Hampden Park. London had only the remote and ill-designed Crystal Palace. The Stamford Bridge grandstands and terracing were re-developed to accommodate an eventual capacity of 85,000 – the standard of work by the Mears's men was not competent, but that is another story – and all that remained was to find and get elected to the Football League a team which would bring in the crowds.

Fred Parker was the man who achieved that aim. He was the honorary financial secretary to London AC and a coal-merchant's agent by profession, which no doubt was a lucrative business in those days when every household in London had grates to fill. He was also blessed with an eloquent tongue and it was his spirited canvassing of delegates on behalf of the Mears brothers at the Football League meeting in May of 1905 that won Chelsea, having changed its name from Kensington FC two months previously, its place in the Second Division. Parker, who was the same man who later became chief technical adviser to the Amateur Athletic Association, suggested to the Mears brothers that they form their own team after Fulham had turned down the chance to play at the ground because they thought the annual rent of £1,500 was too high.

Recruiting players was no problem, and it was very much a forerunner of what was to become commonplace practice in much later generations when Chelsea took the field for one of their first fixtures later that year with only one Englishman in the side, though in this instance the other 10 had come from no further than Ireland and Scotland. Chelsea's first manager was a Scot, John Tait Robertson, though his stay was a brief one because of interference in decision-making by the directors. Familiar story?

In their debut season of 1905–06 Chelsea finished third in Division Two, and the next year they were second and therefore promoted. The remainder of the pre-World War One era was something of a roller-coaster existence: 13th, 11th and then 19th in the next three seasons to be relegated back to Division Two, only to finish third in 1910–11 – when a ground record of 77,952 was set for an FA Cup tie with Swindon Town – and second in 1911–12 to regain Division One. In 1914–15 they were 19th and would have been relegated once more but were reprieved because fixtures were suspended in wartime and the Division was extended from 20 clubs to 22 afterwards. Yet they also reached the FA Cup Final in 1915 – and would not do so again until 1967! Such mixed fortunes were already becoming part of footballing folklore and were eagerly seized upon as material for his stage act by George Robey, the most famous of music-hall comedians of that era, who had formed an early affection for the club and had even proved himself a capable inside-forward in a charity game which he organised in 1907 for the widow of the Chelsea trainer.

A dozen Chelsea players won international honours during those formative years, of which Vivian Woodward was the most famous. Before World War One the club's first England caps was earned by their centre-forward, George Hilsdon, who played eight matches and scored no less than 14 goals – no Chelsea player was to do better for England until Jimmy Greaves more than half-a-century later. Two others, Ben Warren and Jimmy Windridge, had nine and eight appearances respectively for England, and there was even an early recruit from the Continent in the person of Nils Middelboe, who was a qualified lawyer and had captained Denmark in their losing Olympic final against Great Britain in 1912. He joined Chelsea in 1913 at the invitation of his most esteemed opponent that day, Woodward, and as he was 6ft 2in (1.88m) tall he was inevitably immediately dubbed 'The Great Dane'. He stayed on in London until 1936, working as a banker, and continued to take a close interest in Chelsea's affairs.

The secretary-manager of the club, David Calderhead, had been in the post since 1907 and was to remain until 1933, presiding over more than twice as many games (1,117 in all) as any other manager in Chelsea's history, but it was certainly not his force of personality which kept him in the job. Scottish by birth, he was so monosyllabic and expressionless that he was known as 'The Sphinx', and in the recollection of Nils Middelboe 'he only showed up in the dressing room a few times' – maybe, of course, that was the reason for his longevity! Rick Glanvill, whose official biography of Chelsea FC, published in 2006, contains a wealth of valuable data and entertaining anecdote about the club, candidly summed up Chelsea's comportment during Calderhead's long reign as one of 'attractive, talented individuals under no discernible instruction'.

In their first post-war season of 1919–20 Chelsea had risen to the best position they were ever to achieve under Calderhead in the First Division – third, with 49 points, to West Bromwich Albion (60) and Burnley (51) – and had reached the FA Cup semi-finals, but in the next season they had slipped to 18th, as Burnley led a Lancastrian clean-sweep with 59 points, ahead of Manchester City (54) and Bolton Wanderers (52), and Howard Baker's arrival could be said to have been timely. His predecessor in the Chelsea goal was Jim Molyneux, who had played 253 times for the club since 1910–11 (still the third highest total by a goalkeeper in Chelsea's history to Peter Bonetti, 1959–70, and Vic Woodley, 1930–45), including the first nine fixtures of the 1921–22 season, but 'Moly' was already well into his 30s by then and the club won only one of those matches. As it happens, he was not the man most at fault as there had been five draws, and the problem was lack of goalscoring; only six goals in all, which was less than any other team in the Division.

Whether 'Moly', who was formerly a near neighbour of Howard Baker, having been born in Port Sunlight, directly across the River Mersey from Aigburth, was injured or dropped has not been recorded, and though he did not play again for Chelsea's first team he left the club in 1923 with a highly respectable career record total of 77 'clean sheets' (no goals conceded in a match) which 84 years later had still only been surpassed by three of the 16 goalkeepers who have played 100 or more times for the club – Bonetti; Carlo Cudicini, from 1999 onwards; and Sam Millington, who was Howard Baker's successor from 1926 to 1932. A description of Molyneux's style was that 'though not prone to theatrical displays, like some 'keepers he did take risks'.

The other goalkeeper on Chelsea's books with whom Howard Baker was to mainly share duties was Colin Hampton, also a very capable golfer, who was to play 82 matches between 1914 and 1925 and had the distinction of having won the Military Medal for gallantry during army service in Mesopotamia (now part of Iraq). A wartime connection of sadder memory was provided by another of Chelsea's former 'keepers, Bob Whiting, who was so famous for his enormous upfield kicks – soon to be a speciality of Howard Baker's – that he was nicknamed 'Pom-Pom' after the rapid-fire Maxim machine-gun which had been used in the Boer War. Whiting, who only conceded 34 goals in 38 games during 1906–07, was ironically the one Chelsea player to be killed during World War One, serving as a private in the 17th Middlesex Regiment, known as the 'Football Regiment'.

Whiting had followed into the Chelsea team in 1906 the remarkable Willie Foulke, who weighed 22st 3lb (141kg), which was only one pound less than both his regular full-backs put together, but was so nimble on his feet that it was said of him that 'when people first come to Chelsea they fall to admiring the proportions of the ground, then the proportions of Foulke, and next his unquestionable skill as a goalkeeper'. Foulke had previously been with Sheffield United and had been involved in a farcical sequel to the drawn FA Cup Final of 1902 against Southampton. He disputed Southampton's equalising goal and after the game he ran out of the dressing-room stark naked to chase the referee into his cubicle. Only the intervention of FA officials prevented Foulke wrenching the locked door off its hinges! Bob Whiting's successor was Jack Whitley, who played 138 times from 1907 to 1914 and had then become the club's trainer, and he would remain so until 1939, presumably passing on his expertise to Howard Baker and his fellow 'keepers.

Back from the brief Corinthian tour of France at the beginning of the 1921–22 season, Howard Baker was again in goal for the amateur club against Tottenham Hotspur in a midweek match on 6 October which was lost 2–1, and he then assumed his Chelsea duties, making his debut in the away match with Newcastle United on 15 October, and though that was lost 1–0, and the following Saturday five goals were put past him at Burnley, he stayed in the side and results started to improve. The next match was the return home fixture with Burnley and to the delight, and no doubt bemusement, of their supporters Chelsea beat the League champions 4–1. The turning-point in the game was provided by Howard Baker, as *The Times* reported. Burnley had been awarded a penalty, and unlike the generous nature of the Corinthian approach to the game which so appealed to him there was no question on this occasion of his standing aside and letting the ball be tapped into the empty net. The Stamford Bridge crowd would not have understood that at all. The scenario was described in *The Times*:

'Boyle took the kick, and he would score nine times out of 10. This time he shot a little too straight at Howard Baker, and the latter just managed to stop the ball, knock it up, and get rid of it. It was an exceptionally fine save, and only possible to a man of his height and reach. If Burnley had led 2–1 at this point there might have been a very different story to tell at the finish. The unexpected let-off, however, encouraged Chelsea immensely, and for the rest of the game they were easily the better side'.

A third win of the season, 2–1 away to Sheffield United on 12 November, was again much of Howard Baker's doing as it was reported that his goalkeeping was brilliant. Chelsea still languished fifth from the bottom of the table, but the following week's match programme was characteristically ebullient in tone. The programme appeared at each home game in the form of a four-page magazine entitled *The Chelsea F.C. Chronicle* and was filled with jokes, anecdotes, witticisms, cheerful comments on the team's performances and informed pen-portraits of each player in that afternoon's visiting team, for which the editor was the versatile Fred Parker, whose financial expertise had also proved such an asset to the club. One Saturday, after a series of misfortunes had befallen team members during the week, the match to be played against Manchester City was labelled 'Chelsea v Superstition'. It was, if you like, a 'fanzine' some three-quarters of a century before the concept was devised, and the snap appraisal of one particular win the previous Saturday along the lines of 'once again Chelsea have confounded the critics' was followed by a clever parody of the story-lines in various weekly boys' comics of the era which delighted in featuring a fictitious version of the club's activities:

'Chelsea are now losing about three matches every week – in serial stories. The handsome centre-forward of, say, the Mossgrown Ramblers, gets badly burned in rescuing the pretty daughter of a club director on the Thursday night, gets knocked about in a fierce fight with a couple of ruffians who try to bribe him on the Friday morning to lose the game at Stamford Bridge on the morrow, dives into a river or two to save a drowning dog or a would-be suicide, and then turns up at Chelsea on the Saturday covered with glory and bandages, and scores three or four goals before falling exhausted from the combined effects of bronchial catarrh, housemaid's knee and writer's cramp. Poor old Chelsea every time. But as long as the boys in blue can keep getting a few League points what does it matter?'

The following week, again at Stamford Bridge, Howard Baker achieved lasting renown. The match against Bradford City was not a very inspiring one as there was still no score with five minutes to go, even though the visitors had had one player sent off and another was injured. Then their desperate defenders gave away a penalty, and the Chelsea captain, Jack

Harrow, apparently surprised everyone, maybe even including his 10 teammates, by calling Howard Baker the length of the field to take the kick. He scored the goal – it was only Chelsea's 13th in 15 matches. It was not entirely an act of desperation on Harrow's part because Howard Baker had experience of taking penalties from his pre-war spell as a centre-half in the Blackburn Rovers reserve team.

Remarkable as it is for a goalkeeper to have converted a penalty in League football, thereby hangs a tale which is well worth the further telling, even if Howard Baker's recollections of 60 years later were by no means accurate. In his taped interview with John Bromhead in 1982 he related with relish: 'Before my second match for Chelsea I was asked 'Are you any good at taking penalties? We've missed our last five'. Well, 10 minutes from the end – I forget who we were playing – we duly got a penalty, and I'm sure everybody in the crowd must have been saying, 'What's this new boy going to do?' I scored the goal, and so I took penalties for a long time after that'.

It was not, of course, his second match for Chelsea but his sixth – though the fact matters little – and his penalty-taking duties were very much shorter in duration than he remembered because he certainly didn't score any more from them, and nor did he do so for Corinthian. The official Chelsea history records that a half-back, Tommy Meehan, and later a centre-forward, Andy Wilson, were the main penalty-takers in the early 1920s. A very good reason why Howard Baker's penalty-taking didn't last long was that later in the season when he was given the duty against Arsenal he missed.

It's not entirely certain that it was the captain's decision that Howard Baker should be tried on that occasion against Bradford City, as the report in *The Athletic News* that 'there were loud cries for Howard Baker' when the moment came rather suggests that it was the stentorian voice of the Chelsea director, Joe Mears, from the sidelines which was heeded. There is, though, another version to be found in an unattributed newspaper cutting in the archives which Howard Baker bequeathed to his descendants. In an elegantly written report headlined 'Howard Baker's Penalty Goal' the reporter states: 'Baker walked so leisurely the length of the ground that he seemed uncertain that Harrow wanted him to take the kick. After the trifling delay Baker put such power into his shot that the ball went along the ground into the net so rapidly that Ewart did not attempt to stoop to save'.

Howard Baker could still recount the story in further detail at the age of 91 when he was interviewed by the *Liverpool Echo* in 1983: 'Jack Harrow turned to me, which was awful because in those days the professionals were on a £2 win bonus and I realised that if I missed that was that. Then Ewart, the City goalkeeper, ran off his line to me, and later everyone asked what he said. Well, it was 'For chrissake don't kill me'. Anyway, I scored'. The contributor to *The Athletic News*, 'Achates', added intriguingly after Howard Baker's success, 'I was particularly pleased when he converted the penalty kick to see the spontaneous congratulations of his colleagues, which publicly, and better than in any other way, refuted the rumours that his advent has not been popular with the team generally'.

Three further wins improved Chelsea's situation by the end of November, and Howard Baker soon began to figure regularly in the columns of *The Chelsea F.C. Chronicle*. The programme's resident cartoonist, interestingly named Bernhard Hugh, whose work was always featured on the front page, depicted the club's goalkeeper combining both his favoured sports by high-jumping over the cross-bar, while a cloth-capped spectator cried out encouragingly, 'Now try the grandstand, Guv'nor!' For the home fixture with Arsenal on

Wednesday 18 January 1922 the entire page was given over to Howard Baker's exploits, though not without amicably chiding him for the penalty he had missed against Arsenal at Highbury the Saturday before when Chelsea were 1–0 down.

The editorial coverage expanded on the theme: 'When Howard Baker was advancing to take the penalty kick those among the spectators who had witnessed his terrific drive from 'the spot' in the Bradford City game two months ago audibly expressed their 'sympathy' with Williamson in the ordeal he was about to undergo. A minute later everyone was vociferously cheering the Arsenal custodian for his magnificent save. It was perhaps fortunate that a corner-kick and not a clearance resulted. In the latter event the onlookers would have witnessed the spectacle of Howard Baker showing how near he could get to 100 yards in evens!'

At the end of January Everton were the visitors to Stamford Bridge for a friendly match which had come about in unwelcome circumstances because both sides had made an early exit from the FA Cup. By this stage of the season neither thus had much left to play for – Everton 15th in the table and Chelsea 17th – and the programme editor recalled a similar situation 10 years before when a verse composed about Everton's misfortunes was deftly adapted to describe Chelsea's plight:

'At Stamford Bridge spectators sit
Upon the grand-stand, resting;
In angry mood they loudly call,
The finest men requesting.
They roundly blame 'the powers that be',
And ask of what they're thinking?
To let the famous team, Chelsea
Keep sinking, sinking, sinking!'

In February Chelsea won by three clear goals at Oldham Athletic, which was only their second away victory by such a margin since the 1907–08 season, and the *Chronicle* waxed lyrical: 'There must be something in the air of Lancashire which the 'poor old' Pensioner finds so bracing, and Saturday's visit to Oldham afforded him another opportunity of returning from the County Palatine wearing a smile of satisfaction akin to that of the celebrated tiger after 'entertaining' the young lady of Riga. Seven visits to Lancashire this season have yielded seven points'.

By mid-March Chelsea had moved up to 13th in the table and in the end the season turned out to be very much better than could have been imagined the previous November. Howard Baker played 24 matches in all through to April, occasionally replaced by Hampton and on one occasion by Wilson Marsh in one of his dozen appearances for the club until 1924, but after those four early-season successes Howard Baker was on the winning side only four more times and the FA Cup first round tie had been lost 4–2 at West Bromwich Albion. This was a striking contrast to the previous year when Chelsea had played eight Cup matches in all, beating Reading and Plymouth Argyle only in second replays. When Hampton returned in goal for the last five matches of the 1921–22 season four of them were won, and the final League position was a reasonable ninth.

It was a tribute to Howard Baker's skills, not those of Hampton, that *The London Evening News* chose to feature in the columns of one of their editions in early March, with an explanatory theory of their own: 'Football spectators usually squirm and murmur, 'That's risky', when a goalkeeper runs out and kicks at a moving ball. Howard Baker does that, as will have been noticed by many frequenters at Stamford Bridge, but he does it all so accurately that there is no squirm. There is a reason for this. What is not generally known is the fact that Howard Baker started football as a centre-half. On two occasions he has represented Lancashire Soccer in that position, and he played in the middle of the North team against the South in the last amateur international trial game before the war. This is why the ex-Northern Nomad has such confidence in himself when, on those occasions that make waste of time dangerous, he runs out and kicks the ball up to the halfway line without first gathering the object in his hands'.

The crowd attendances at Stamford Bridge naturally reflected the club's fortunes. The previous season 76,000 had turned out for a visit by their London rivals, Tottenham Hotspur, but the Christmas Eve match of 1921 between the two, in which Howard Baker played and his side lost 2–1, attracted a rather smaller following of 60,000 and the best for the season was 67,000 three days later for a 1–1 draw with Middlesbrough. Could it be that even back in the 1920s family shopping took precedence before the holiday, but the menfolk were only too glad to get out of the house as soon as they could afterwards? The smallest crowd of the year was 15,000 for a midweek game on 18 January 1922, and it was perhaps as well that there weren't more as Chelsea ignominiously lost 3–0 to Bolton Wanderers. The season's average 'gate' was 38,000.

A highly entertaining and informative 21st-century perspective regarding Chelsea's fortunes in the early 1920s, and Howard Baker's contribution to them, is to be found on a website devised by the club's tireless historian, Rick Glanvill. Writing in 2009, and striking a note that will be familiar to football supporters through the ages of whatever persuasion, Glanvill remarked of the 1921–22 season:

'The team boasted the necessary glamour, too, in Great Dane Nils Middelboe, the dashing Jack Cock, trainee medic and able right-winger Dr John Bell, and the colourful amateur keeper Ben Howard Baker, a former high-jump champion whose party-trick was to kick light bulbs out of chandeliers. Much like Chelsea sticksman Petar Borota six decades later, HB seemed disdainful of the 18-yard box, often rushing out into midfield in pursuit of the ball. He would play basketball around the box, flicking the ball over an opponent, while the coach was barking through a loud-hailer for him to 'Get on with it!' And like a Bruce Grobelaar or Fabien Barthez he would spend ages joshing around before facing a penalty kick himself. He was an absolute hero, the epitome of the old Chelsea. Chelsea finished ninth in 1922, but what an entertaining place the Bridge must have been'.

The 1921–22 season's record was Played 42, Won 17, Drawn 12, Lost 13, Goals For 40, Goals Against 43, Points 46. Liverpool won the title with 57 points out of a possible 84, with Tottenham Hotspur second (51) and Burnley third (49), and though only three points further back, Chelsea's problem was self-evident: their forwards couldn't get the ball in the net. They scored fewer goals than any other club in the Division except Oldham Athletic, 19th, with 38, and even Manchester United in 22nd and last place (imagine that!) scored 41. That 4–1 victory by Chelsea over Burnley and the defeat of Aston Villa in the last-but-one fixture of the season by the same score had been aberrations. The surprising fact was that Chelsea actually had four international forwards on their staff – Jack Cock (England), Jimmy Croal (Scotland), Jim Ferris (Ireland) and Frank Hoddinott (Wales) – and Cock, in particular, was a player of outstanding talent.

Born in Cornwall, he had won the Military Medal during the war, like his goalkeeping colleague, Colin Hampton, and is described in the official biography of Chelsea FC as a 'superstar who took football to a different level…supremely skilled and graceful, he had a powerful shot in either foot and was great with his head'. He was renowned for the stylish suits which he wore off the field – described as 'the snappiest dresser of his day' – and he endeared himself to the Chelsea faithful by stepping on to the pitch for every match singing at the top of his voice. He played the starring role in a 1920 silent film entitled *The Winning Goal*, but unfortunately, despite all this praise lavished upon him, he hit few of those in real life during the 1921–22 season, though his total of 13 was almost twice as many as any other of his teammates.

Yet neither he nor the newcomer, Howard Baker, had need for any regret when the campaign was over. Chelsea had finished in the top half of the First Division, and had he cared, Howard Baker might have noted that only the two leading clubs in the Division had conceded fewer goals – Liverpool 36, Spurs 39. In any case, he would surely have been the first to commend the support he received from the defenders in front of him: the full-backs, Jack Harrow and George Smith, were each to play more than 300 times for Chelsea (304 and 351 appearances respectively), while the centre-half, Harry Wilding, was not far behind at 241 despite carrying pieces of shrapnel under his heart as a forcible reminder of war service. Another regular was Tommy Meehan, the penalty-taker, commended as 'a clever, stylish, tenacious but constructive left mid-fielder or wing-half', but he was to die tragically of a brain disease in 1924 at the age of 28.

Amateur football was thriving and the correspondent for the Sunday newspaper, the *Observer*, identified only as 'W.H.L.' had previewed the 1921–22 season with this enthusiastic observation, 'With an unprecedented influx of new players joining up, practically all the best amateur organisations are running three strong elevens, and public interest has never been so great'. Corinthian had 34 fixtures and Howard Baker managed half-a-dozen appearances, including a 4–0 defeat of Oxford University in early December and a commendable 1–1 draw with Queen's Park in Glasgow at the start of the new year. Still, he seems not to have been considered by England's amateur selectors, despite his impressive League credentials and the fact that he had already played for the full England XI. The chosen goalkeeper for the match against Wales at Swansea in February had been H.P. Bell, one of four Cambridge University undergraduates making his debut in the team. Bell had also played in goal for Corinthian in their 7–2 win over Derby County on 28 January, which could not have harmed his selection prospects, but it was to be his one and only cap, as happened to so many players selected by committee for the England amateur and professional XIs during the 1920s.

Corinthian finished off their season with a five-match tour of Denmark and Holland, starting on 14 April. Norman Creek, the club's future historian, was one of the party of 16 players, also including Howard Baker and such stalwarts as Claude Ashton, Bower, Doggart, Hegan, Morrison and Moulsdale, accompanied by the club secretary, Geoffrey Foster, which set off from Liverpool Street station on a Monday evening for the Harwich ferry. Creek's diary dutifully recorded the details of the voyage and its mixed blessings: 'This jolly party left Harwich at 6pm that evening on board the 'King Haakon'. An excellent dinner was followed by a sing-song, with Doggart at the piano. By this time the ship was in the open sea, and one by one the songsters left the piano and unostentatiously slipped away until – we only have the steward's word for this – Doggart himself noticed that the piano was conforming to the movements of the ship. Twenty-four hours of really bad weather followed, and it was a languid and listless collection of Corinthians who stepped ashore at Esbjerg'.

Spectating at a professional tennis match and then a 15-round heavyweight boxing contest between a Briton, Harry Reeve, and the Danish champion, Emil Andreasen, which Reeve lost narrowly on points, occupied the recovering tourists for a couple of days in Copenhagen. Reeve's social background was the very opposite of his Corinthian supporters at the ringside as he was from the East End of London and a docker by trade when he could get work. He once beat the British heavyweight champion, Joe Beckett, in a non-title fight and had 149 professional bouts in a career which lasted from 1917 to 1934 – in between times he fathered 14 children. Howard Baker, with the experience of the pummelling he received and no doubt gave in his sparring sessions with the Liverpool pugilists, would surely have kept his teammates well informed about the finer points of the fistic exchanges that night.

The next day, Good Friday, Corinthian played their opening fixture, which attracted a crowd of 25,000 and in which a combined Copenhagen XI was outclassed 5–0. Creek reported that 'Howard Baker had only a few opportunities to show his cat-like agility, but he soon became the idol of the crowd'. A second match in the city against the same opponents on Easter Sunday was won 3–1, and there was plenty of time to spare for another round of less strenuous activities: visits to a horse-race meeting, art galleries, the zoo and a tea-dance, culminating in a banquet and then a lunch given in honour of the visitors at the Royal Yacht Club overlooking the harbour.

On the Tuesday the Corinthians left Copenhagen to take the steamer to Kiel and the train to Groningen, in Holland. There they beat the Dutch champions of two seasons before, Be Quick, even more easily than the 5–2 score suggests. Then a 5–3 win against the Dutch Universities in The Hague, where 'the referee's interpretation of the rules caused a little trouble', was followed by a match in Amsterdam against De Zwaluwen ('The Swallows'), which was in effect the Dutch national side, and there the faults which Creek had readily admitted were the cause of the FA Cup defeat the previous January came to the surface again. 'While the Corinthian defence was in good form, the forwards never really got going' – and the Swallows darted to a 1–0 win.

Some consolation was to be found at the nearby Nordwyck golf course on the last day in Holland, where the footballers who were also adept on the fairways and the greens had the better of their Dutch hosts. There is no evidence from Norman Creek's account that Howard Baker turned his hand to yet another sport that afternoon, but it would be surprising if he managed to resist the temptation.

'Swiftly, skilfully, dramatically', Howard Baker charms Chelsea and the Corinthians

Chelsea's start to the 1922–23 season must have satisfied even their dour Scots manager, David Calderhead. After four matches they topped the table for the first time in their history with three wins and a draw, but the editor of the club's *Chronicle* wisely cautioned supporters that 'it would be unwise to chortle prematurely'. By their 12th match at the end of October Chelsea had still lost only three times, had drawn on four occasions, and had beaten Stoke City (twice), Birmingham City, Oldham Athletic and Sheffield United, but the *Chronicle* was proved right.

It was a fool's paradise as only the last-named of these clubs which Chelsea had beaten would finish their League programme with some distinction, in 10th place, and Birmingham would be 17th, Chelsea 19th, and Stoke and Oldham relegated in 21st and 22nd positions. Before the end of November, during which month they failed to score a single goal in their four matches, Chelsea had already slipped to 15th in the table, and the *Chronicle* mournfully recorded the situation in verse, though the composition was as ragged as the club's form:

'No points, no goals, no longed-for win.
No single bit of luck that we remember;
No glad-hand, no 'bulging' of the *others'* net; November.
Never mind; let us hope for a Decent December'.

Even in one of those rare early-season defeats by Middlesbrough in September, Howard Baker had excelled himself and the *Daily Sketch* summary of the match was full of praise for him: 'A fine exhibition of goalkeeping by Howard Baker, the famous amateur, which will long be remembered at Ayresome Park, failed to avert defeat for Chelsea. He saved a penalty taken by Andrew Wilson and dozens of scoring shots from the Northern sharp-shooters'.

It did not turn out to be the 'Decent December' hoped for by the versifier for the *Chronicle* until Boxing Day, when Nottingham Forest were beaten 4–0 to at last end a sequence of 10 matches without a win. In celebration of two successive wins in which the centre-forward, Jack Cock, had played a major role, a more polished literary allusion was made use of as Shakespeare was the author and Act I Scene II of *The Tempest* the reference:

'Hark, Hark! I hear
The strain of strutting Chanticleer,
Cry cock-a-doodle do!'

Well, it *was* Chelsea, the bohemian borough, and the editor of the *Chronicle* was no doubt perfectly justified in assuming that there would be much appreciation of the Immortal Bard on the terraces.

In between his Chelsea outings, Howard Baker again figured in a 2–1 defeat for Corinthian against Tottenham Hotspur at the start of the 1922–23 season, and though this was not quite the first match that Corinthian had played at their new Crystal Palace headquarters – they had met Cambridge University there the previous year – it was a significant occasion because it attracted 10,000 spectators and marked the real beginning of a largely successful 14-year association with the ground. The Corinthian secretary, Geoffrey Foster, and his opposite number at the like-minded Casuals FC came to an agreement with the Crystal Palace company to use the facilities, and the clubs jointly renovated the stands and dressing-rooms. The venue had a resonant history; the FA Cup Final had been held there on 20 occasions up to 1914, watched by crowds of as many as 100,000.

Howard Baker played in 17 of Chelsea's first 18 fixtures, missing only the home match with Preston North End on 11 November (a 1–0 defeat) when Colin Hampton took over for the very good reason that Howard Baker was back in the England amateur team that day, playing alongside four other Corinthians. This was for the match against Ireland at Crystal Palace which England easily won 3–0 for their 10th success in 13 encounters since the first in 1905–06.

Their side was Howard Baker, J. Thompson (South Bank), A.G. Bower (Corinthian), J. Lamb (Bishop Auckland), C.B.G. Hunter (Corinthian), F.V. Spiller (Oxford City), M.

Howell (Corinthian), S.J.G. Earle (Clapton), W.H. Minter (St Albans City), F. Hartley (Oxford City), Lieutenant K.E. Hegan (Army/Corinthian). Six of them – Thompson, Lamb, Hunter, Earle, Minter and Hartley – were making their debuts, and Wilfred Minter has a particular claim to a dubious distinction, having once scored all seven goals for his club in an FA Cup tie but still finishing on the losing side as Dulwich Hamlet had replied with eight!

Howard Baker did not appear in the Chelsea line-up after 9 December, when Hampton again replaced him and then stayed for the rest of the season. As Howard Baker conceded 22 goals in his 17 appearances and Hampton 29 in his 25, there was really very little to choose between their handling abilities at the season's end, and it can only be surmised that the 3–0 away defeat at Huddersfield in Howard Baker's last game had perhaps counted heavily against him. *The Times* reported of Chelsea that 'the moral of the team seems to have been poor'. Presumably, the writer meant 'morale', but can one be sure? Hampton, too, was to have his trials and tribulations, and most notably among them a 6–1 annihilation at Cardiff City in March. Actually, only seven other clubs conceded fewer goals than Chelsea, but scoring remained elusive. The season's record was Played 42, Won 9, Drawn 18, Lost 15, Goals For 45, Goals Against 53, Points 36. Liverpool won the title again with 60 points, from Sunderland (54) and Huddersfield Town (53).

Maybe, though, it was for business or personal reasons that Howard Baker simply preferred to take a break from League football for a while, and the decision certainly did not affect his reputation because he was now attracting the sort of attention which was the ultimate accolade of recognition for a British sportsmen of those years. His portrait or a stylised action shot of him started to appear in the issues of cigarette-cards which were so intensely popular with youngsters. One of these sought-after sets was a series of 100 cards issued by the cigarette-manufacturers, Gallaher's, under the title of 'Famous Footballers'. Howard Baker was also featured in a weekly publication for young men entitled *Jack's Paper*, which chose him among 11 players for their series, also called 'Famous Footballers', during the 1922–23 season under the headline 'He's A Football Thrill!'

He was regularly called on by Corinthian, playing 15 matches for the club, and this must have been with Chelsea's approval because it was to involve an historic FA Cup appearance. Before that, though, Corinthian lost 3–1 in their annual New Year's Day match against Queen's Park in front of a 20,000 crowd at Hampden Park, and yet Howard Baker was still singled out by *The Times* for special praise. The Scots, it was reported, 'found a magnificent goalkeeper against them in B. Howard Baker. This famous player distinguished himself by clever anticipation and coolness in stopping shots, but he often came out boldly to pick up and clear with tremendous kicks'. The Corinthian side was, as usual, filled with internationals – Baker, Bower, Hunter, Creek, Morrison, Doggart and A.T. Davies – but Queen's Park, who were members of Division Two of the Scottish League, had their own array of talent…and maybe clearer heads on the day.

Later in that January of 1923 the Corinthians had a rather more serious commitment to fulfil as the club management had decided to break the rule of a lifetime and enter the FA Cup competition, and this could have been another incentive for Howard Baker to have renewed his Corinthian connection. With 22 clubs now playing in each of Divisions One and Two of the Football League, no free dates were left for Corinthian to arrange friendly games, and so the reason for the change of heart, according to the club's latter historian, Edward Grayson, was 'the difficulty in obtaining professional opposition and in order to give the club the stimulus which was necessary to enable it to rebuild its strength and public standing'. The Corinthians took this prospect seriously enough for 17 players to actually train together for the first time for three days under the direction of a former Spurs' captain, Sandy Tait.

For their debut match they travelled on 13 January to Brighton & Hove Albion to fulfil a first round proper tie – equivalent to the third round in modern terms – having been generously exempted from qualifying by the FA. Before the end of the month the host club were to beat the Division Three Southern leaders, Bristol City, and move to sixth in the table. Not, demonstrably, the most formidable of opposition it would seem, but still tough enough, in all conscience, for the public-school amateurs and their interloper, Howard Baker, to view with respect. Undaunted, Brighton's gentlemanly guests forced two successive 1–1 draws on a Saturday and the following Wednesday before eventually losing the second replay by 1–0 on Monday of the next week. It was said of Baker in the first replay that he 'had much more to do than Hayes, at the other end of the field, and he did it swiftly, skilfully, and dramatically, as in fact he never fails to do'.

Of the opening match the club's player/historian, Norman Creek, who scored Corinthian's equalising goal, commented, 'Considering that nobody beforehand could be quite sure what was going to happen, it was altogether a very satisfactory start'. The first replay was high drama even before the kick-off – fog blanketed London; the ground was frost-bound and iron-hard; two of the Corinthian players, Knight and Hegan, were held up in trains and did not arrive in time to play, and the referee was also delayed by the weather and had to be replaced by the senior of the linesmen. The deciding match of the three was disappointingly tame and Creek concluded: 'The lesson of the three Brighton cup-ties was that while the amateurs' defence was well up to the professional standard the forward line was as yet not quite good enough'. Creek, who had played at centre-forward only in the first of the three matches, was one of Howard Baker's numerous Cambridge University graduate teammates, and in addition to compiling a wonderfully comprehensive club history he later became a Football Association official in charge of the England amateur team and a BBC radio commentator, and in 1954 he was to diversify into another sport by writing a useful athletics training manual for beginners.

The public interest in this dramatic series of Cup matches was astonishing, as a record attendance of some 25,000 was set for the first encounter at the Albion's Hove ground, and *The Times* understandably commented wonderingly in reference to the second replay at Crystal Palace that 'few people can have anticipated that over 45,000 followers of Association football would find time on a Monday afternoon to watch a Cup tie in which an amateur team was engaged'. Howard Baker was described as 'that great athlete...an untiring player'. More than £5,600 was taken in gate receipts at the three matches, of which some £1,800 would have been the Corinthian share. Taking the Retail Price Index as a comparison, that sum would be worth £395,000 in 21st-century terms – a useful boost for the finances of an amateur club with no wages to pay!

Five days after his FA Cup marathon had been completed, Howard Baker was in the England amateur side to play Wales at Middlesbrough's Ayresome Park ground, and though it was reported of him that 'he made mistakes which gave Wales two out of their four goals', England scored twice in the last 15 minutes to force a draw. It was the first such result in the 11 matches played between the two countries since the series had started in 1907–08, and of the 10 previous England had won all but one, including a 7–0 thrashing of the hosts at Swansea the season before. England fielded much the same team as they had against Ireland the previous November:

B. Howard Baker (Corinthian), J. Thompson (South Bank), A.G. Bower (Corinthian), E. Nattrass (Ilford), W.E. Barnie-Adshead (Birmingham University), F.V. Spiller (Oxford City), W.S. Lucas (Ilford), H. Douthwaite (Cambridge University), W.H. Minter (St Albans City), F. Hartley (Oxford City), Lieutenant K.E. Hegan (Army/Corinthian). These were the one and only appearances for Nattrass, Barnie-Adshead, Lucas and Douthwaite, but then until fixtures were started against Scotland in the 1928–29 season the only two international matches which England's amateurs regularly played each season were against Ireland and Wales. Barnie-Adshead, who was also a capable cricketer who played a dozen first-class matches for Worcestershire between 1922 and 1928, became an eminent gynaecological surgeon but died at the early age of 49.

Corinthian managed to find some professional opposition as the season continued and held Crystal Palace, then third from last in Division Two, to a 3–3 draw on 3 February, and though Howard Baker was not in goal that day he still attracted press attention. He featured, perhaps surprisingly, in the 'By The Way' column in *The Illustrated Sporting & Dramatic News*, which was published each Saturday from offices in the Strand in Central London, and paid much more attention to the high society activities of golf, rugby football, hockey, hunting and coursing than it did to the more plebeian sporting exertions. Their diarist, writing under the name, 'Shan', drew some comparisons between amateurs and professionals in various sports, most notably billiards and lawn tennis, and related, without any obvious link, what had obviously been a recent convivial encounter with Howard Baker:

'I doubt if any athlete of the moment is more full of vitality than B. Howard Baker, champion high jumper as well as goalkeeper for the Corinthians and Chelsea. His dark eyes light up as he talks, and he is a ready talker, and he laughs openly and naturally. He is, as one would say, full of life'.

Howard Baker was on call against the Army a fortnight later but was for the most part an interested spectator because Corinthian won 15–2 and Creek, at centre-forward, scored 10 of them! The unfortunate Army 'keeper was the splendidly-named Sergeant Quelch of the Royal Army Medical Corps, who at least would presumably have had some expert psychological care from his military colleagues afterwards, had he needed it. Those readers with memories of boyhood weekly comics will surely remember that the crotchety cane-wielding school-master in the Billy Bunter series was also named Quelch. 'Cavey chaps! Here comes Quelch!' was one of Bunter's stock phrases; the dog Latin term, 'Cavey', meaning 'Look out!'. In this instance it was more a matter of 'Cavey Quelch! Here comes Creek!'.

The return match against Queen's Park was won 2–1, played on Monday 26 February, with a 3.30pm kick-off, but still attracting a crowd of 5,000, and for the Corinthians Howard Baker, Bower and Morrison were described as 'that trinity of defensive giants'. The Wednesday (later to become Sheffield Wednesday, and then placed 12th in Division Two) narrowly beat Corinthian 3–2 at Sheffield on 10 March, with 15,000 spectators present, and it was a typically flamboyant gesture by Howard Baker, rushing out to intercept but failing to do so, that let the professionals in for the winning goal. Nobody really seemed to mind too much, and Corinthian found some top-class opposition again a fortnight afterwards on the day of the FA Cup semi-finals. It was an occasion which also enabled Howard Baker to resume old acquaintanceships.

Everton were the visitors to Crystal Palace, and Corinthian were without their two outstanding full-backs, Bower and Morrison, who were instead elsewhere in town fulfilling their obligations to the Old Carthusians (former pupils at Charterhouse) who were playing Old Malvernians in the Final of the Arthur Dunn Cup at the splendidly named 'Spotted Dog' ground at Forest Gate. This competition for public-school old boys' clubs had been started in 1902 and Old Carthusians were to make it a ninth success in 10 appearances in the Final, winning resoundingly 5–1.

Corinthian were down to 10 men in the second half against Everton after an injury to Graham Doggart, but they still won 3–2. Some cheerful banter must have been shared after Everton's first goal because the scorer of it was Howard Baker's former Chelsea teammate, Jack Cock, and when the Corinthian defender, Arthur Knight, was penalised the ball was 'kicked straight at Howard Baker, who saved'. Bearing in mind Howard Baker's Corinthian policy of standing aside in such circumstances, it rather seems as if this was a penalty which was not too seriously treated by the man who took it, Everton's inside-forward, Wilf Chadwick.

The Everton team that day was no token presence as, in addition to Cock, two other internationals on show were Neil McBain, of Scotland, and Sam Chedgzoy, who was to play 300 times for the club and eight times for England. Chedgzoy, born across the Mersey in Ellesmere Port, has his place in football history, as he was to score a goal against Spurs a year later by dribbling the ball in from his own corner-kick as the defenders watched bemused. The Everton players had been alerted by a quick-witted *Liverpool Echo* journalist to the fact that there was a loop-hole in the recently-changed law regarding scoring direct from a corner. In retaliation the authorities quickly re-wrote the regulations. McBain subsequently had a managerial career lasting 34 years, including a spell in South America, and even stepped into the breach as goalkeeper for New Brighton when they suffered an injury crisis in March of 1947. He set a League record as the oldest ever player, aged 52. There was no fairy-tale ending to that story, though, as his club lost 3–0 to Hartlepool United.

No doubt Howard Baker enjoyed meeting up with all these accomplished players from his home town, and maybe it caused him to hanker after the greater challenge of League football as the 1922–23 season came to an end. With his other local club, Liverpool finishing the season as the champions, Everton had placed fifth, and of the three London teams in Division One the best of them had been Arsenal, 11th. Chelsea were back to their familiar 19th – Played 42, Won 9, Drawn 18, Lost 15, Goals For 45, Goals Against 53, Points 36.

The Corinthian Easter tour of 1923 was to Belgium and Holland and had been largely arranged by the club's honorary secretary, Geoffrey Foster, through the connections he had made when he was organiser of sport for the British Expeditionary Force in Belgium after the war had ended. He was one of the remarkable Foster cricketing family of seven brothers, all of whom played for Worcestershire, and had scored 1,000 runs in a season in both 1907 and 1908. The Corinthians, not at full strength, joined other travelling English football teams on the Dover-to-Ostende ferry, which must have made for a convivial channel crossing, and the first serious business the day after installing themselves in the Hotel Terminus at Brussels was conducted at the Royal Belgian Golf Club, where the singles were lost 4–2 and the foursomes 2–1, but the hospitality of the hosts, including Prince Edmond Ruspoli, son of the Italian ambassador, more than made up for the reverses on the course. No mention of any exploit on the greens or fairways by Howard Baker.

Howard Baker and H.P. Bell shared the goalkeeping duties. The opening engagement as regards footballing commitments was on Easter Sunday against FC Daring, in Brussels, and was won 1–0, watched by a crowd of 35,000, but in the next two outings, against Union St Gilloise the following day and the Willem II club at Tilburg on the Wednesday, the Corinthian half-backs and forwards were again found wanting ('completely outclassed', said Creek), and losses of 5–1 and 5–2 were sustained. The next day the tourists took the train to The Hague, meanwhile having urgently telegrammed for reinforcements, and Bill Blaxland, Norman Creek and Colin Hunter arrived by aircraft from Croydon to meet up with their teammates. Creek promptly scored both goals in the 2–1 win over a Dutch Universities' XI and did the same against De Zwaluwen ('The Swallows') in Amsterdam the following Sunday for another success, 2–0.

Norman Creek's remembrances almost relegated the football to second place. His account leaves the distinct impression that the highlights of the tour for all concerned were a banquet and dance arranged in specific honour of the Corinthians by the British Embassy in The Hague; a Brussels night-club foray which featured 'a most amusing solo turn and then going round with the hat' by one of the Corinthian forwards, Miles Howell; and a perilous road journey to Rotterdam in a fleet of high-powered cars 'whose drivers vied with each other in the speed at which they took the many hair-pin bends across the canals'

Not surprisingly, the nerve-wracked Corinthians lost their closing match 2–1 but arrived back safely in London on the morning of Thursday 12 April, having travelled via the Hook of Holland and Harwich, after what Creek described as 'one of the jolliest fortnights imaginable'.

A time for re-evaluation in 'that dazzling decade' of British athletics

'That dazzling decade, the Twenties, saw athletics transformed into a major sport as stars like Nurmi, Abrahams, Liddell, Lowe and Burghley burst into prominence'. The perceptive comment was that of Peter Lovesey in his history of the Amateur Athletic Association, published to celebrate the centenary in 1980, and he enthused of 'a legend-making era…achievements of heroic quality…the stuff of schoolboy fiction'. Actually, the pity of it from Howard Baker's point of view was that much of this bedazzlement was only effected from 1923 or so onwards, by which time he was retired from high jumping at the age of 31.

The legendary 'Flying Finn', Paavo Nurmi, had begun to construct his pantheon of titles and records in 1920, but the others, all of them Britons, were several years later in developing. Harold Abrahams, Eric Liddell and Lord Burghley were to win gold medals at the Olympic Games of 1924 or 1928, and Douglas Lowe outstripped them all by winning at both. The other feature which they shared in common with Nurmi was that they were all runners. Had Howard Baker been born a few years later, or not had numerous other sporting interests to consume his energies, he might well have added a much needed field-event presence to the elite group. But this, of course, is no more than idle conjecture.

In October of 1923 the British Olympic Association announced an ambitious action programme which they claimed would be 'of a far-reaching nature and of vast importance to the future of British athletics'. This was based on what they said would be 'the opening-up and exploiting to the fullest possible advantage of training centres throughout Great Britain like the White City and the Crystal Palace, which have recently been placed at the Association's disposal through the generosity of their owners'. The White City Stadium, at

Shepherd's Bush, in North London, had been used for the 1908 Olympics but for not much else since, though it would eventually become the 'home' of the AAA Championships and other major athletics fixtures for almost 40 years from 1932. Crystal Palace had never staged the AAA meeting but would, ironically, succeed the White City as the major venue in 1971.

The Olympic officialdom wisely decided to seek the counsel of various dignitaries of the sport before loosening their purse-strings, and the list of invitees to the Association offices was lengthy and impressive, 18 in all, including such notable athletes of the recent past as Albert Hill, Philip Baker, Howard Baker and Percy Hodge, together with coaches Ernest Hjertberg, Alec Nelson and Sam Mussabini and the former miler, Joe Binks, who was now a prolific journalist and sponsorship entrepreneur. Less obviously qualified, though no doubt somebody on the committee thought that he was worth listening to, was the coach to Derby County FC.

The chairman of the committee was Lord Decies (pronounced 'Dee-shees'), an Eton-educated former Hussar officer, whose sporting interests seemed peripheral at best to the subject of inquiry – polo, show-jumping, horse-racing, pig-sticking, membership of the Royal Yacht Squadron – though maybe his function as director of the British Income Tax Payers' Association commended him as someone who would keep a tight hold on those purse-strings. He had also been military press censor in Ireland during World War One, and so presumably he could be relied upon to ensure that nothing out of place was revealed about the committee's deliberations.

The 10-man committee was Earl Cadogan, General R.J. Kentish, Sir Emsley Carr, Morley Brown, Colonel R.C. McCalmont, Major Hartley, Colonel Percy Laurie, Air Vice-Marshal J.F.A. Higgins, W.E.B. Henderson and Gordon C. Innes. Earl Cadogan was chairman of the British Olympic Council and General Kentish honorary secretary of the British Olympic Association. Sir Emsley Carr and Morley Brown were editors of *The News of the World* and *The Sporting Life* respectively. The two Colonels, the Major and the Air Vice-Marshal represented the various sports bodies of the armed forces and the police. Gordon Innes, while a vice-president of the AAA had been involved with the sport for some 40 years, and Walter Henderson was simply described as 'late Oxford University Athletic Club' and was the one active athlete among the assembly. A versatile and durable field-events man, he had competed in the Olympic Games of 1908 and 1912, and had represented Great Britain against France in the discus less than three months before the committee first met. The joint honorary secretaries were Evan Hunter, of the Scottish AAA; Harold Abrahams, ex-president of Cambridge University AC; and the renowned coach, Captain F.A.M. Webster.

It may even have been that the committee was targeting the field events, as they had the expertise on hand of Henderson, in addition to that of Abrahams, who was an exceptional long jumper as well as sprinter, and of Captain Webster, who had made it his life's work to promote interest in those sadly neglected aspects of the sport. All of these respected establishment figures had been entrusted with the task of taking into consideration 'not merely the training of the Olympic competitors for the Games next year, but the facilities which can be obtained for the thousands of boys and young men of London who today have no possible chance of training or recreation of any kind...the committee is also requested to ascertain what other similar centres exist in other parts of the country'.

Too much to do? Too little time to do it in? It would be easy to scoff, with all the benefit of hindsight and the knowledge of so many other such well-meant but inevitably fruitless enterprises to transform British athletics which followed over the decades to come. The fact is that the 1924 Paris Olympics would begin in less than nine months, and that was far too short a gestation period for even the Olympic elite to benefit, let alone those notional 'thousands of boys and young men' starting completely from scratch. The only British athletes at the end of 1923 who could be regarded as serious Olympic medal contenders were Abrahams and Liddell in the sprints, Cecil Griffiths and Henry Stallard at 800 metres, and Malcolm Nokes in the hammer. There was not a single Briton in the World's top 50 for the pole vault, shot, discus, javelin and decathlon, and the best of the high jumpers, Robert Dickinson, was lower placed than 22 Americans and others from Czechoslovakia, France, Germany, Norway, South Africa and Switzerland.

Howard Baker made his appearance before the committee on 18 October, the fourth day of the interviews, and to the great advantage of inquiring souls from later generations a complete transcript has survived, which gives a remarkably comprehensive insight into what he had learned during his competitive career. Much of this is produced below, with the identities of individual questioners shown. Otherwise the questions were those which had been formulated beforehand and then read out to him.

Question. From your own experience would you tell the committee how long you think it takes on average to produce a first-class field-events athlete.
Howard Baker: 'Three to four years. To do that he must, of course, have natural ability, keenness, opportunity and time for training, expert advice, massage and frequent competition, and finally a proper preparation of, say, a month or six weeks before an Olympic contest. If we are to produce athletes of Olympic Games standard, we must find the right type of recruit to begin with. At present, most of our athletes, apart from the varsities, army and navy, are brought from the working classes who have not the opportunity or facilities for training under the right conditions.

'How many of them do their training when they are in an absolutely unsuitable physical condition after a day of strenuous manual labour and, more than possible, after a hurried evening meal? Under such conditions it could hardly be expected a man could make rapid improvement, and assistance in such cases would be of great help to the athlete. Assistance could be given in many ways. Their employers might be approached with the request to grant facilities for training during the afternoon, and arrangements made to provide the necessary impedimenta, if not available in the district. Massage and correct food are problems which the committee would have to consider some months before the athlete had to compete.

'Many men who undoubtedly would make excellent field-event athletes have never had the opportunity of taking part in them at school and a special appeal ought to be made to the public schools to encourage and to create an interest in the field events. The majority of public-school boys take very little part in athletics after they leave school, whereas it is from this source that the American and Continental athletes are largely recruited. While at our schools people are playing cricket and football, but they are *not* jumping, hurdling, throwing the discus or javelin, as the case may be'.

Question (chairman). You say they take very little interest after they leave school. Do you think they take interest when at school?
Howard Baker: 'No, but they should take an interest when at school. Very few take up field events afterwards. With regard to this, I would suggest that among the police might be

found the right men for field events. In Liverpool many of them, had they the opportunity, would be only too glad to take part in javelin, discus, hammer, etcetera'.

Question. As a first-class high jumper will you tell the commission what sort of training you regard as essential for a field-events man for the Olympic Games?
Howard Baker: 'Except for certain general principles beneficial to an all-round athlete, it would very much depend on the man himself. In the event of a man being found whom it was thought would make a champion, three months or longer, providing he has been practising and training himself for two or three years and is not absolutely in the rough. Careful consideration and study of the man is essential – his work, time available for training, his build and constitution, and the particular event he was being prepared for.

'With the exception of our varsity and service athletes, most of our men have to work in all kinds of employment, and while six weeks is considered sufficient time to devote to a special preparation for a big event, three months or even longer would be better and would allow sufficient time for building up the strength of the athlete over a steady preparation, provided he is properly advised against the possibility of getting stale. Proper diet, good food, which all of our athletes don't get, and an occasional scratch competition as a try-out. Steady practice without great effort three or four times a week and sometimes twice a day if possible. A little and often is far better than crowding a week's work into a couple of days'.

Question (Abrahams). Do you think that the fact of your record jump in 1921 was in any way due to seeing the jumpers in 1920?
Howard Baker: 'In my own case, having studied by films and photographs etcetera, I noticed my faults and corrected them'.

Question (Captain Webster). Have you not learned anything from foreigners?
Howard Baker: 'Yes, I think I have learned a good deal from Mr Knox, the coach. I used to jump Scissors style, but he evolved the other style which I adopted. This is an instance where a coach helps'.

Question (Henderson): Is it your opinion you do not necessarily learn by seeing a first-class performer?
Howard Baker: 'When you watch a man jump you may think at the time you know exactly how it is done, but you find out afterwards that you have not grasped it'.

Question (Abrahams): Undoubtedly a mental picture helps?
Howard Baker: 'To a certain extent, but you cannot retain it'.

Question (Webster): Would you consider a coach essential or non-essential?
Howard Baker: 'Decidedly essential'.

Question: Would you tell the commission very briefly your impressions of the Olympic Games at Antwerp (a) as to organisation and (b) as to the spirit of the British team?
Howard Baker: 'With reference to (a) the conditions were not helpful. The best was made of a bad job. The conditions of living in the school at Antwerp were quite unsuitable for

highly-trained and highly-strung athletes. The beds were terrible, sanitary conditions worse, and the cooking was not good. The dormitory system was very trying. People who wanted to get to bed early were bound to be disturbed. The Belgian organisation was very bad, the programme badly arranged, people having to compete as early as 9.15am. The stadium was closed to our team, no opportunity being afforded for practice. The poor substitute, the hockey ground adjoining, being quite unsuitable for 200 athletes jumping, hurdling, hammer throwing etcetera. It was quite impossible.

'With reference to (b) had it not been for the excellent spirit of the teams, and the heart-to-heart talks with General Kentish, things would, without a doubt, have been much worse. The spirit is splendid, but there is undoubtedly a very strong feeling that the controlling athletic bodies – more especially the district associations and committees – should be more representative of the younger generation of athlete with progressive ideas. All schemes and work in connection with the Games should be in the charge of younger men who have not long ceased their athletics and having a known standing and influence with the athletes themselves'.

Question (Abrahams): How long do you think the athlete should arrive there before competing?
Howard Baker: 'At least 10 days or a fortnight, and provided conditions are alright'.

Question: Assuming that a chief coach is to be appointed, and recognising the entire deficiency of a field-events coach in this country, do you think the employment of a foreign coach would be acceptable to the British athletes as a whole?
Howard Baker: 'I think a good man is always acceptable by the majority of British athletes, apart from his nationality, if he knows his job. The short time available between now and the Games would not give a coach a chance to get immediate results. He would certainly do much good work in finishing off our best performers, but to produce an Olympic field-events team a coach, in my opinion, would require at least four years in which to do the work. Let him appoint the best available man in each district to work under his instructions and have frequent try-outs in which he could be present to advise and correct failings where necessary. I can vouch in my own case for the great assistance I have received by the advice of such an experienced and practical athlete as Fred Birkett, of Liverpool, and also from the few occasions I was able to turn out under the eye of our late coach, Walter Knox'.

Responding to a series of other questions, Howard Baker told his listeners that there were only three cinder tracks for athletics in his home town of Liverpool, and though he had identified a local park as a suitable setting for a corporation sports ground nothing had so far been done about it. Asked where a training centre for athletes in the North of England would be best placed he suggested Manchester, Leeds or Huddersfield. General Kentish commented that he had a candidate in mind as a field-events coach and gave his name as Starkey, who was about to leave the army. 'He is a professional and would have gone to France to represent Great Britain had he not been', the General explained. 'He is good all-round and available at present. He could be placed in any centre'.

All of what Howard Baker had to say was sound advice. Athletes for the jumping and throwing events could not be produced overnight. They needed expert coaching, proper facilities to practise their event, and the free time to do so. His underlying message was perfectly clear, however unpalatable it might have been for his audience: that whatever Lord Decies and his committee decided to recommend it was already far too late to have much bearing on the forthcoming Olympics. In some instances, what was of particular interest in Howard Baker's responses was what he did *not* say. He was readily forthcoming in his praise of the briefly-appointed chief coach from before the war, Walter Knox, and of his Liverpool Harriers colleague and former Northern high-jump champion, Fred Birkett. Yet was there really not a single one of the many fine high-jumpers against whom he had competed over the years – a dozen or more Americans among them – who had impressed him sufficiently by their style and technique for him to have recalled their names?

There is no evidence whatsoever that the retiring soldier, Starkey, in whom General Kentish had such faith, was ever engaged in the future in any coaching capacity of national significance, though he clearly had some credentials for the task. Sergeant-Instructor R.K. Starkey, of the army's Physical Training School, had won the shot-put event on three occasions at the army championships from 1920 to 1922 and also the discus and hammer in the last of those years. Neither is there obvious indication of *any* recommendations from the committee being taken up, and it was to be another decade before real progress was made in coaching, with the establishment of the AAA summer schools at Loughborough from 1934 onwards, the organisers of which included Captain Webster and Malcolm Nokes, who was to be the bronze-medallist in the hammer at those Olympics of 1924.

Yet it is a moot point as to whether any substantial progress had been made before the disruption of World War Two. In 1938 members of the Achilles Club, under the editorship of the Olympic 400 metres champion of 1920, Bevil Rudd, produced a detailed training manual for which there was a stellar line-up of contributors, including other Olympic gold-medallists in Harold Abrahams (1924 100 metres), Bob Tisdall (1932 400 metres hurdles for Ireland), Godfrey Brown (1936 4 x 400 metres relay) and Jack Lovelock (1936 1500 metres for New Zealand). Malcolm Nokes, in his capacity as assistant director of studies at the Loughborough summer schools, contributed the chapter on the hammer throw and summarised the continuing 'Cinderella' status of the English field events in ironic but obviously heartfelt fashion:

'In this country the various athletic events have different values. Running and hurdle racing are fine spectacles and are deservedly popular. High-jumping and pole-vaulting are good spectacles, provided a not too deliberate record-breaker has been billed to appear. Long-jumping is of some historic but not much box-office interest. The throwing events are regarded as rather tedious, sometimes dangerous, and slightly comic. This estimate of the worth of athletic events has been fostered by the Press and readily accepted by the great body of athletic onlookers, to whom every deference should be paid as it is they who supply the sinews of athletic war'.

The staid thinking in England regarding techniques in the high jump was unconsciously illustrated by the fact that the Achilles manual had not one chapter on the event but *two,* and the brief biographies of the authors were most revealing for those who were astute enough to read between the lines. A chapter on the Eastern Cut-Off was written by Gerald Moll, whose prime achievement had been to set a Bedfordshire county record of 5ft 11¼in (1.80m) at the age of 17 but who had never improved because of a recurrent ankle injury. The other chapter was concerned with the Western Roll and came from the pen of the most accomplished exponent of it in Britain in the 1930s, Charles Stanwood, who had done a mere 5ft 8in (1.73m) with the Eastern Cut-Off at school and then improved to 6ft 3in (1.92) with the Western Roll.

Unfortunately for any hopes of a significant British presence in the 1936 Berlin Olympic high jump, Stanwood happened to be an American who had made the transition in high-jumping style while at college in the USA and had then come to Oxford University as a Rhodes Scholar and was the outstanding athlete in the Inter-Varsity matches of 1933 and 1934, winning the 120 yards hurdles, the 220 yards hurdles and the high jump at each. The best that Moll could say of his preferred method was that 'properly performed it is the neatest and cleanest style there is', whereas Stanwood was able to point out that the Western Roll which had been popularised – at least in the USA – by George Horine in 1912 had since been used 'by most of the World's record holders'. This is apparent from the following all-American progression of the official record:

6ft 7in (2.007m) – George Horine (USA), Stanford, California, 18 May 1912. Western Roll.

6ft 7⁵⁄₁₆in (2.016m) – Edward Beeson (USA), Berkeley, California, 2 May 1914. Western Roll.

6ft 7¾in (2.03m) – Harold Osborn (USA), Urbana, Illinois, 27 May 1924. Western Roll.

6ft 8⅝in (2.04m) – Walter Marty (USA), Fresno, California, 13 May 1933. Western Roll.

6ft 9⅛in (2.06m) – Walter Marty (USA), Stanford, California, 28 April 1934. Western Roll.

6ft 9¾in (2.07m) – Cornelius Johnson (USA), Randall's Island, New York, 12 July 1936. Western Roll.

6ft 9¾in (2.07m) – Dave Albritton (USA), Randall's Island, New York, 12 July 1936. Straddle.

6ft 10¼in (2.09m) – Mel Walker (USA), MalmUo, 12 August 1937. Western Roll.

The precise metric conversions of the first seven of the records listed above are those of the International Association of Athletics Federations (IAAF) as published in their official list. All of those seven jumps were originally measured in feet and inches. One other performance of particular note is that of yet another American, Clinton Larsen, who cleared 6ft 7in (2.029m) at Provo, Utah, on 1 June 1917, but this was never recognised by the IAAF. Larsen used his own modified form of Eastern Cut-Off. It needs hardly adding that the British record, first set by the Irishman, Tim Carroll, at 6ft 5in (1.96m) in 1913, and then equalled by Howard Baker in 1921 and by Geoffrey Turner in 1929, was still the same in 1938.

However reluctant the acceptance in England of proper coaching, one aspect of the British Olympic Association's deliberations of 1923 did, oddly, stand the test of time. General Kentish's belief that the army could provide the man for the job eventually became reality almost a quarter-of-a-century after he had voiced the idea. Geoff Dyson, who had been a fine hurdler and a student at the pre-war Loughborough summer schools and then a Major in the army's physical education corps during the war, was appointed chief coach by the AAA in 1947 and among his own group 'spearheading an improvement in events unfashionable in Britain', as the historian for the AAA, Peter Lovesey, was to put, it would be the country's best ever exponents of the pole vault, the shot and the discus. Dyson, coincidentally, had been born in 1914, the year of Walter Knox's brief tenure of office in Britain. A 33-year gap between the two appointments was rather longer than Howard Baker had hoped for!

By the time that Howard Baker made his appearance before the Olympic committee, his Chelsea FC teammates were in trouble. They had played 11 matches of the 1923–24 season and won only two, and it was a depressing sequence that was to be continued until well into the new year. By 16 February Chelsea had still won only five of 30 fixtures, and Colin Hampton had been in goal for 22 of these and Wilson Marsh for the other eight. The nadir had been reached the previous Saturday when the lowest Stamford Bridge crowd of the season, 15,000, watched aghast as Notts County put six goals past Marsh without reply. Howard Baker was recalled for his first match for the club in some 14 months and stayed in place for all but one of the remaining 11 games. Of these, Chelsea won four and drew four, and as the team was otherwise much the same as it had been all season the return of the Corinthian goalkeeper had clearly been a major factor in the revival. The four victories, all at home, were achieved in the last four matches of the season against Liverpool (2–1), Newcastle United (1–0), Sunderland (4–1) and Manchester City (3–1), by which time the attendance was back to 40,000.

Unfortunately, the revival came too late and Chelsea finished 21st of 22 ahead of only Middlesbrough, and both were relegated. Only goal difference separated Chelsea and the 20th-placed club, Nottingham Forest. Chelsea's record was Played 42, Won 9, Drawn 18, Lost 15, Goals For 45, Goals Against 53, Points 36. It was much their worst season since they had been founded. But it's an ill wind…the next season, with Chelsea in Division Two, would see Howard Baker installed once again as the regular goalkeeper. Wilson Marsh had left the club and Colin Hampton would do so soon afterwards.

Despite his Chelsea commitments, Howard Baker played in 20 of Corinthian's 25 matches during the 1923–24 season and his finest hour undoubtedly came at the FA Cup first round proper tie against the famous old club, Blackburn Rovers, on 12 January, drawing a crowd of some 20,000 to Crystal Palace. Corinthian won 1–0, adopting a simplistic style of game which the professionals never got to grips with until the closing minutes when Howard Baker distinguished himself by first of all fisting out 'a horribly curling centre' and then by making 'a brilliant save from a free-kick taken on the edge of the penalty area', in Norman Creek's recollection. To add to the spectacle, Howard Baker also launched one of his length-of-the-pitch clearances. 'On the whole, the defence was good, and the halves and forwards fair', wrote Creek. 'Bower was the outstanding player on the field, and his display was more than masterly, it was heroic, for at times he was doing three men's work. Baker and Hunter also gave fine displays'.

It was vintage stuff and *The Times* was lavish in its praise, saying of Howard Baker that he 'must have been very cold and almost bored in the first half but had an enormous lot to do and had to use his astonishing powers of anticipation to save the game'. More than 30 years later a subsequent and widely respected football correspondent for *The Times*, Geoffrey Green, was to enthuse in a summary of the club's history, 'Here in opposition once more were the champion enemies of old; here was an echo of those exciting far-off days of the eighteen eighties. It was on Blackburn's backs that Corinth had first jumped to fame. Now they were to repeat the dose. When the news was out that night that A.G. Doggart's goal had given the amateurs a great victory, the acclaim of the country was general and sincere'.

However, Corinthian joy – probably, of course, expressed as no more than murmurs of satisfaction – was short-lived. The Cup run soon ended. Corinthian were well beaten in the next round 5–0 by West Bromwich Albion, who were then in the lower reaches of the First

Division, though the prospect of the encounter drew 50,000 people to The Hawthorns. The Corinthian inside-forwards lacked power, the wing-halves were outpaced, and the backs did not show their usual soundness, according to Creek, who played in the game. An 'injudicious advance' by Howard Baker – criticism so delicately phrased! – gave away the last of Albion's goals, but Creek did not blame him for the score being so large. The cameraman for the Pathé cinema newsreel coverage rather unkindly but not unreasonably concentrated entirely on the Corinthian goalmouth, and so Howard Baker is seen for the most part retrieving the ball from the back of the net in an understandably disconsolate manner.

Such was still the reputation of the Corinthians that the tie against WBA had been regarded as the most interesting of the round, and the defeat was a rare setback for the amateurs. They played 31 matches during the season, including 'A' team fixtures, and won 22, drew three and lost six, scoring 83 goals against 40. Of their nine matches against professional League teams other than in the FA Cup they won five and drew two. Their victories were 3–1 against Queen's Park Rangers, 1–0 and 2–1 against Southampton, 2–1 against Preston North End and 2–0 against Chelsea. There were draws with Heart of Midlothian (1–1) and Bolton Wanderers (2–2). The losses were by 2–0 to Swansea Town and 2–1 to Plymouth Argyle. Even so, the most satisfactory successes of the campaign were against their long-standing Scottish amateur rivals, Queen's Park, who were beaten both home and away by the same score, 4–1, before the usual thronging crowds. Further evidence of the pulling power of the amateur game was that 32,000 people turned up for the FA Amateur Cup Final at Millwall's New Cross ground in April to see Clapton beat Erith & Belvedere 3–0.

The first of the hallowed series of matches between Corinthian and Queen's Park had been played in 1886, 10 years after the founding of the Glasgow club, and Norman Creek explained in his club history: 'It was almost inevitable that a keen and friendly rivalry should develop between the two clubs, the one in England and the other in Scotland, for both had found bodies of players inspired with the same purpose and having the same attitude to the game of Association football'. The sequence had been broken in 1907, by which time Corinthian had won 23 matches, Queen's Park 13, and there had been seven draws, and had then been revived in 1920 and over the next 11 years would produce an even share of fortunes which must have left everybody satisfied: 20 matches, eight wins each, four draws, 36 goals for Corinthian, 34 for Queen's Park.

Numerous dramatic and comical incidents had marked the matches over the years. On one occasion fog delayed the arrival of the Corinthian players at Hampden Park on New Year's Day by more than an hour and one of their officials already at the ground apologised profusely for keeping the home team waiting. 'It doesn't matter about the team', replied his anxious opposite number. 'It's the crowd that's getting out of hand'. It was then suggested that someone walk round with a notice-board explaining the situation, but back came a swift response on behalf of Queen's Park: 'That wouldn't be much use. There are over 20,000 people here and half of them are drunk already'. Another year the Scottish hosts had a player named Dr Paul on the wing, and after he had scored the one goal that had decided the match the newspaper placards around the Glasgow streets proclaimed, 'Paul's Message To The Corinthians'.

Howard Baker was passed over for England's amateur international matches during 1923–24 which were won 2–1 at Llandudno and 3–2 in Belfast, though he played for the

South against the North in a trial match. Instead the England selectors opted for another goalkeeper with League experience, and a friend of Howard Baker's. This was Jim Mitchell, the former Manchester University student who now played for Manchester City. He was the same man who had been preferred to the then novice Howard Baker for the England amateur XI in 1919–20 when both were playing for Northern Nomads and had then been one of the two goalkeepers in Great Britain's 1920 Olympic team.

This was apparently justification enough for Pathé to have featured on their newsreels sent to cinemas throughout the country Mitchell's wedding in 1921 to a Miss Marjorie Broadhead. He is shown coming out of the church in top hat, tails, striped trousers and spats, his bride on his arm. He was good enough to turn out once for the full England XI and achieved the rare feat (perhaps even unique?) of having worn spectacles when he played in an FA Cup Final – that of 1921–22 for Preston North End when they lost 1–0 to Huddersfield Town. The less discerning supporters must surely have revelled in the opportunity to vary their habitual cry of 'Where's your glasses, ref?' with the occasional 'You need stronger glasses, goalie!'

MIXED FORTUNES IN THE OLYMPIC ARENA AND THEN IN THE SECOND DIVISION

Howard Baker's thoughts in the summer of 1924 must surely have turned across the Channel to the Stade Colombes, in Paris, where he had finished his high-jumping career three years before by beating the French. In July the Olympic Games were taking place there, and on the face of it Great Britain's athletes were doing rather well. These were the 'Chariots of Fire' days which were to be immortalised on the cinema screen 60 years later, and Harold Abrahams at 100 metres, Eric Liddell at 400 metres and Douglas Lowe at 800 metres all won gold medals. Yet these, of course, were the glamorous short-distance and middle-distance runners, and maybe Howard Baker was set to wondering if the advice he had dispensed to the British Olympic committee-men regarding the under-valued field events would ever be heeded.

Apart from the bronze medal by the hammer-thrower Malcolm Nokes, every one of Great Britain's 11 medals was earned on the track. Of the 14 athletes who contested the various jumps and throws and a pentathlon and decathlon, only Nokes and a long jumper, Charles Mackintosh, who was sixth, emerged with credit. Both of them were Oxford University products; Nokes having learned the rudiments of the hammer at Oxford, though his main sporting interest had been water polo, at which he played in goal in four inter-varsity matches; Mackintosh having also represented the university at rugby football, association football and ski-ing. The latter, who went on to play rugby for Scotland, stayed active in sport for many years afterwards and was a member of Great Britain's four-man bobsleigh team which won the World title in 1937. His two daughters were both to be Olympic skiers after World War Two.

The British high jumpers in Paris, of which there were three, were frankly dismal. Robert Dickinson, Harrow and Oxford educated and later to be a governor at his old school, was equal 15th. Neither Arthur Willis (Repton and Cambridge) nor Crawford Kerr, the Scottish champion who was the son of an Isle of Arran crofter, cleared any height at all, and none of the three of them ever did better than 6ft 1in (1.86m) in their years of competition. At the British Empire v USA post-Olympic match at Stamford Bridge, where Howard Baker had won so memorably four years before, the Empire high jumpers were humiliated by the

Americans. The Olympic champion, Harold Osborn, and his silver-medallist teammate, Leroy Brown, both cleared 6ft 4in (1.93m); Lawrence Roberts, of South Africa, did no better than 6ft 1in and the English pair, Dickinson and Willis, a paltry 5ft 9in. *The Times* did absolutely nothing to promote the field events, which their correspondent considered worthy of only the last five lines of his report, having devoted the first 118 to the track races!

Howard Baker may well have been a spectator at this meeting, wondering at the ineptitude of his successors, and he was certainly at Huddersfield – scene of his British record of three years before – the following Saturday in his capacity as a high-jump judge for the visit of some of the American athletes. A somewhat enigmatic report of the meeting in *The Sporting Chronicle* suggests that there was a controversy that afternoon regarding Osborn's Western Roll technique. Readers will recall from the earlier chapter in this book concerning the history of the high jump that there was some scepticism in Europe about the legitimacy of the Western Roll, based on the belief that it was a form of 'diving' head first. So far as Osborn in particular was concerned, there was a further suspicion that he had the habit of holding the bar in place with his hand as he cleared it.

According to the description of the afternoon's event, Howard Baker called a halt to his officiating duties after Osborn had cleared 6ft (1.83), and the implication is that he did not regard the American's style as being fair. Osborn won the event at 6ft 2in (1.88). Howard Baker's departure would, of course, have had all the makings of a dramatic headline story in the 21st century – 'British Record-Holder Says American Olympic Champion Cheats' – but the local newspaper coverage of domestic sport in the 1920s usually avoided any form of dissension concerning competitors and officials, and so we can only guess as to what were Howard Baker's motives that day.

A couple of weeks after the Olympics ended Howard Baker was doubtless at the Liverpool quayside waving a regretful goodbye to many of his Corinthian fellow footballers. They were sailing away aboard the SS *Montrose* for a pleasurably extended tour of Canada and the USA, during which they would play 22 matches and enjoy much generous hospitality, but as they were not returning until 19 September it was understandable that Howard Baker and some of his teammates were unable to afford the time away from their business commitments. Such England amateur internationals as Morrison, Chadder, Creek and Hunter were among those for whom spending 50 days on a Transatlantic jaunt seemed to present no problems of conflicting interests between their indulgence in leisure and their having to earn a livelihood. A future Olympic steeplechaser and subsequently a renowned journalist, Vernon Morgan, also travelled but was injured in the second game.

It was the third visit to North America by the Corinthians and in the tours of 1906 and 1911 they had lost only twice in 38 fixtures, but this time there were eight defeats, all of them in Canada, and Howard Baker's absence cost dearly because none among the 18 players had any goalkeeping experience. Creek, who was a member of the party, reflected in his club history that 'had Howard Baker or any Corinthian goalkeeper been able to make the journey there is little doubt but that all the matches except two would have been won'.

While the athletes had been seeking Olympic honours and the Corinthian footballers were revelling in their agreeably sociable transatlantic idyll, Howard Baker had been honing his lawn-tennis skills. It was the turn of his home courts at Aigburth to host the Northern championships in early June and he had a solid run through to the quarter-finals of the men's doubles in between showers of rain throughout the week before he and his partner, W.

Napier, were well and truly beaten 6–1, 6–4 by A. Conway and T.N. Wrench. Howard Baker's future doubles partner, Billy Radcliffe, had a good tournament, winning the mixed doubles title with Miss E.M. Beckingham and reaching the men's singles final.

No doubt these matches were all conducted with the utmost sense of fair play. Decorum rather than dynamism was the order of the day, and the biographer of Max Woosnam, Howard Baker's comparably versatile sporting all-rounder, caught the mood of the era perfectly. Mick Collins was to write: 'In the 1920s tennis looked and was played very differently from the game we know today. Men wore long trousers, women long skirts, and things proceeded with a certain dignity. Serving and charging into the net was unheard of, as a step backwards to commence a baseline battle was the standard tactic. Coming off court, the men would don threequarter-length smoking jackets, straighten their cravats, and make sure they looked properly respectable'. For Howard Baker it was simply a matter of applying the familiar Corinthian style and spirit to a summer game, and much more was to be heard of his tennis-court exploits in later years.

However, he had no more than a few weeks to develop his back-hand and to muse on his country's mixed Olympic fortunes. Football began again in August, and the Second Division must have come as a bewildering experience for the newer Chelsea fans, though maybe the players were bewildered, too. The opening match of the 1924–25 season, at home on 30 August, produced a reasonably satisfactory 1–0 win over Coventry City, but what could anyone make of the next three results – losing 4–0 away to Leicester City and then beating them a week later by the same score at home, with a 5–0 win at Oldham Athletic in between? By the end of the year Chelsea seemed destined for an early return to the top division, as they had only lost once more in their next 19 matches, though there was actually a far greater number of draws (11) than wins, and the crowds stayed away. There were no more than 8,500 spectators for the home fixture with Hull City on 1 November which produced the first win in almost two months.

Howard Baker had played throughout this sequence, with one exception, and had conceded only 15 goals in 22 appearances. His single absence had been on 8 November because he was back in the England amateur side for the meeting with Ireland at the Cliftonville club ground in Belfast which England won 3–2. This was the ninth win in the 11 matches which England's amateurs had played against Ireland or Wales since 1919 and in the process they had scored 45 goals, which was a considerably better record than the English professional XI against the same opposition – three wins in 10 matches, and 12 goals scored. Howard Baker had replaced his former Northern Nomads teammate, Jim Mitchell, in the side, which was as follows:

Howard Baker, E.G. Spencer (Bishop Auckland), A.G. Bower (Corinthian), A.F. Barrett (Leytonstone), W.I. Bryant (Clapton), F.H. Ewer (Corinthian), R.G.C. Jenkins (Polytechnic), E.I.L. Kail (Dulwich Hamlet), W.V.T. Gibbins (Clapton), F. Hartley (Oxford City), I.M. Hamilton (London Caledonian).

Chelsea's other goalkeeper was now Peter McKenna, like Howard Baker a Liverpudlian, who had joined the club the previous season. At 5ft 10in (1.77m) tall, McKenna was not of Howard Baker's stature, but he took his place capably enough on 12 occasions during 1924–25 and would appear intermittently through to 1930–31. One of Howard Baker's three absences during November was when he produced 'some truly wonderful goalkeeping' as Corinthian beat the South African touring side 4–1. He then drew even more fulsome praise from *The Times* the following Saturday as Corinthian thrashed Cambridge University 7–0: 'Howard Baker is in wonderful form this season. He shows an almost uncanny intuition as to where the ball is going and knows to an inch where his goal posts are'.

The following Wednesday he was in goal for England against the South Africans at Tottenham Hotspur's White Hart Lane ground, along with eight of his teammates from the win over Ireland, as C.S. Caesar (Dulwich Hamlet) replaced Barrett and Lieutenant K.E. Hegan (Army and Corinthian) took over from Hamilton, but it was only a last-minute goal from his clubmate, Ewer, that got England home 3–2. This was exactly the same margin by which England had beaten South Africa in a previous match in Southampton the month before when Howard Baker's persistent England rival, Jim Mitchell, had been in goal. The South Africans – all of whom, judging by their surnames, were of British and not Afrikaans ancestry – also beat Ireland 2–1 and lost to Wales 1–0 during their extended visit.

Coincidentally, by the end of their Chelsea careers Howard Baker and McKenna would have exactly the same record of 38 per cent of 'clean sheets' (no goals conceded in a match): Howard Baker 36 in 93 matches, McKenna 25 in 66. Chelsea's momentum was continued into the new year and by mid-February they were joint second in the table with Leicester City and Manchester United, only two points behind Derby County. But then something went seriously wrong and a 4–0 away defeat at Stockport County – hardly the most formidable of opposition as they were to finish 19th in the table – was followed by six more losses and only three wins in the closing dozen games. Chelsea finished the 1924–25 season 10 points away from a promotion position, as the leading five clubs in the Second Division were as follows: 1 Leicester City 59pts, 2 Manchester United 57, 3 Derby County 55, 4 Portsmouth 48, 5 Chelsea 47.

The attendances at Stamford Bridge inevitably fell away as the chance of promotion disappeared. The average through to mid-April was 33,000, except for the oddity of only 8,500 for the Hull City game in November, but against South Shields (1–1), Barnsley (0–1) and Stoke City (2–1) in the last three fixtures of the season the totals were only 24,000, 20,000 and 25,000.

Howard Baker reached agreement with Chelsea that he would be available for Corinthian in the FA Cup, but it did neither him nor his club much good. The first round proper draw brought Corinthian up against Sheffield United at Bramall Lane in January and the match was duly lost 5–0. The consolation was that no one else could beat the Yorkshire club either in any of the succeeding rounds and they duly registered their first win in the Final since 1902, 1–0 over Cardiff City.

The prompt report in *The Sheffield Evening Telegraph* football edition (familiarly known as the *Green 'Un* because of the colour of the paper on which it was printed) is a gem, a classic of its kind, typical of the Saturday afternoon newspaper coverage of football throughout that era and for many decades to follow – telephoned over from minute to minute during the course of the match by their football writer, merely identified as 'Looker-On', and then set in print and rushed out on to the streets so that the spectators at the match could even buy copies on their way home.

'Looker-On' set the scene admirably: 'In the past the Corinthians came to Sheffield a number of times for friendly contests, but to-day the celebrated amateur club visited the city on more serious business, that of contestants for the Cup. This made the match at Bramall

Lane unusually interesting, and all the world of football would be anxious to know how the last and greatest of the amateur clubs had fared with Sheffield United. There are famous players in the present Corinthian team, as in the days of yore, and the many Internationals gave a strength to the side which suggested that the home team would not find their task an easy one…United were the first out and were warmly received, but an even heartier welcome awaited the amateurs'.

Then followed a ball-by-ball account of some 1,400 words, and it was made obvious from early on that the United were the better side. Yet 'Looker-On' was generous in his treatment of the Corinthian performance, and as the teams went off at half-time he remarked: 'Baker, in goal, had been one of the busiest of the amateurs. Shot after shot he had passed in excellent style and well deserved the extra cheer which greeted him as he retired'. The bank of headlines to the finished report summed the game up succinctly – 'Four For Johnson. United Too Good For Corinthians. Baker Splendid'.

On another page of the same newspaper J.T. Howcroft, who had refereed the Cup Final of 1920, and had officiated at a Corinthian fixture prior to the match with Sheffield United, told a charming tale: 'It is 25 years ago since I first saw this clever combination; hence my delight was great in once more seeing the side that has for so long stood for all that is good in the world of football. Really, the play of those clever amateurs was fine, and I do not remember a game for many 'moons' where the charging was so robust. The way Bower, the back, got through his work was a splendid sight, and even the professional side had a good word for all that he did. One of the amateur players last week made me smile at one of his remarks. He had run half the length of the field through terrible mud and slush, with the ball at his toes. When he got to the goal he was 'beaten' and shot very poorly. To my astonishment he cried out, 'Damnation!'. On seeing me close up he at once came to me and whispered, 'Forgive me, Ref, but the wretched shot deserved even stronger language'.

England's amateur selectors kept faith, nevertheless, with Howard Baker and he was in the side against Wales at Plymouth on 21 March. A trial had been held at Middlesbrough a fortnight before in which the South had beaten the North 2–1 (the latter also including players from the Midlands), and Howard Baker, in goal for the winners, had 'made no mistakes with the few shots he had to deal with'. England also won 2–1 with a team that included regulars Howard Baker, Twine, Bower, Armitage, Ewer and Kail. There were three new caps, L.F. Cooling (Birmingham University), G. Sparrow (Barnet) and R.S. Donald (Bishop Auckland), in the forward line, though none of them were ever selected again; Sparrow's failure to convert a penalty perhaps being the reason in his case.

Writing in the *Daily Telegraph*, the newspaper's football correspondent, B. Bennison, was moved to ponder on some wider issues raised by what he thought was a disappointing match: 'It confirmed what is a popular impression – that the difference in the football of the amateur and professional is considerable; that the paid player rules the roost. Which impression, I like to feel, is wrong. The difference is not so marked as is generally supposed, though I am afraid that for the bigger internationals our side must continue to be built up largely, if not wholly, of professionals'. Ironically, the one Welsh goal was almost entirely of Howard Baker's making, as Bennison explained: 'Howard Baker took a chance in the way of trying to boot it; and it happened that he twisted the ball into his own goal'. Having said that, Bennison then added much commendation: 'Let it be said that Howard Baker played his part manfully; without the least question, he is a goalkeeper of the highest class. Mannerisms he has, and in plenty, and he would at times appear to revel in taking risks. But, nevertheless, he stands for safety. I like his unconventionality and his daring. And I know of no goalkeeper who can kick such a prodigious length as he can'.

From a 21st-century perspective, the most interesting aspect of the football coverage that Monday morning of 23 March 1925 in the *Daily Telegraph* is that their chief football writer should choose to attend the England-Wales amateur international rather than any of the First Division games at a critical stage of the season when Huddersfield Town were the leaders but only six points separated the seven leading clubs. Furthermore, his report and those for the other amateur fixtures taking place that day occupied the first two columns of the page, and the four divisions of the professional league, 44 matches in all, were condensed into the next two columns, with particular attention given to Southern clubs. Maybe it is churlish to make such a suggestion, but could it be that Mr Bennison's choice of destination that afternoon was also conditioned by the fact that six of those clubs at the head of the Division One table were from the North of England and the seventh from the Midlands, and a visit to Plymouth seemed rather more appealing than one to Huddersfield, where fourth-placed Bolton Wanderers were the visitors?

There was a distinct graciousness to the reporting of football by B. Bennison and his press-box colleagues in those days and maybe this reflected the general attitude of those they watched playing. In February the Burnley centre-forward, Tom Roberts, has fractured his pelvis in a collision with the Tottenham Hotspur goalkeeper, Bill Hinton, and a few days later the *Manchester Guardian* printed a letter which the hospitalised Roberts had received from Hinton. 'I cannot say how sorry I am that our collision on Saturday has had such a serious result', Hinton wrote. 'Had I thought this was going to happen I should certainly not have made an effort to reach that ball when it was centred, even though you were bound to score had I not done so. I sincerely trust you will make as steady and complete a recovery as possible. The 'boys' join me in expressing sympathy'.

Maybe that gesture by Hinton and his teammates was truly characteristic of the era. Maybe, though, *The Guardian* printed the letter because they thought it was so *un-characteristic*.

Despite his commitments to Chelsea, Howard Baker managed to appear in 11 of the Corinthian's first team's 20 domestic fixtures, and he was on call again for the end-of-season expedition overseas, which was to be one of special significance. Norman Creek recorded his recollections in fulsome manner: 'That the Corinthians were privileged to visit Germany and Austria, our late enemies, with the definite intention of cementing the peace, was indeed an honour; and it is certain, though the details of the tour may fade from their memories, that the general impression of hospitality and good-will must always remain with those members of the club who were fortunate enough to take part in this historic tour'.

The bridges across the Rhine were still being guarded by the British army of occupation and there were many soldiers among the crowd of 10,000 which saw the Corinthians beat Cologne 4–2. Earlier that day the visitors had been conducted round the site of what Creek described as 'the vast new stadium in course of erection, with all the wonderful accessories for the various Continental sports', which maybe gave some of the party food for thought as to why a defeated country should be building such a multiple-use structure when nothing like it was in existence in the visitors' home country. The usual round of sightseeing, celebration banquets, dances and theatre visits filled such spare time as the tourists had in between beating Hamburg 4–1 and drawing 1–1 with Berlin. There is some British Pathé newsreel footage surviving of this Berlin match, and though as usual the camera-shots of the action on the field tend to be rather distant there is a dramatic moment when Howard Baker, resplendent in what appears to be a cricket sweater (Liverpool CC, presumably?), unleashes one of his towering down-field goal kicks.

When the Corinthians arrived at the Vienna railway station shortly before midnight on Wednesday 15 April they were astonished to find an enormous crowd waiting to greet them and then accompany them in triumphant procession to their hotel. The next morning they were surely even more gratified to read over breakfast an editorial eulogy, in English, to their presence addressed directly to them in the leading Viennese newspaper:

'For the first time after the Great War we have to-day the opportunity to welcome a British amateur team within the city of Vienna. This fact is in itself sufficient to be called a mark-stone in the history of Austrian sport, but it is still more important when it is realised that the first British amateur team to visit Vienna after the war is none other than you, Corinthians of England, most prominent representatives of the amateur idea in sport, who stand foremost for the cry 'sport for sport's sake', you who have been identified in the eyes of the football world, with a class of amateur sport which for decades has been able to hold its own against the professional sport of your country.

'To you, Corinthians, who come to us not only as real sportsmen, as true champions of fair play and high-class scientific football, but also as carriers of a mission of peace, as standard-bearers for the spirit of international sport and for the reconciliation of nations through sport; to you, esteemed guests, our greetings are extended. In a time when unrest and unsettled conditions prevail you, Corinthians, have come to Vienna to play a picked team of our professional footballers. By acting in this manner you have once again shown the world-wide outlook of British sporting spirit'.

Unfortunately, the match – which had been postponed 24 hours because of incessant rain, and for which 50,000 people turned up at 3.30 on a Friday afternoon – entirely failed to live up to any criterion of 'high-class scientific football'. The pitch was hard-baked sand entirely devoid of grass. The ball was far smaller than the Corinthians were accustomed to, and when the full-back, John Morrison, deliberately booted it over the stand in the hope that it would be lost it was replaced by one even smaller. The referee disallowed any form of charging, which was an integral part of the Corinthian style of play, and so numerous free-kicks were conceded, and the outcome was a 2–0 defeat.

No matter. Motor excursions and yet more dances and banquets organised by the hosts ensured that a good time was had by all, and Norman Creek was hardly to be blamed for being eventually proved wrong in his assessment that the 12-day visit 'had really helped to cement the peace'. This was an unfortunate claim which was to be recalled more than half-a-century later in a typically stylish column by the renowned *Daily Mail* sports-writer, Ian Wooldridge, composed on the eve of the last FA Amateur Cup Final to be played before the competition was abandoned in the face of all-embracing professionalism. 'At least World War Two didn't break out until 15 years later', he scoffed.

Wooldridge chose the example of the Corinthians to illustrate his disparaging view of amateur football in the 1970s. 'The Corinthians didn't need to fiddle their expenses, of course, because they weren't exactly born to sweep chimneys', he wrote. 'They were the sort of men who took cold baths, shooed their wives out of earshot after dinner, and later led their troops into the Hun guns on the Somme armed with nothing more than a Malacca cane and a Webley revolver. They were all public school chaps who thought nothing of keeping 20,000 crowds waiting while they finished lunch and then make up for it by kicking everything that moved above ground level'.

The next season of 1925–26 would prove to be equally frustrating for Chelsea and yet it would be the most rewarding of Howard Baker's goalkeeping career. It began startlingly well for the club with 14 unbeaten matches through to after Christmas, including crushing wins over Port Vale (6–0), Fulham and Hull City (both 4–0) and Preston North End (5–0). The last three successes were all at home, and the Chelsea staff had obviously found a way to count precisely the number of spectators coming into the Stamford Bridge ground because there were reported crowds of 49,379, 47,428 and 40,539 respectively. Howard Baker was in goal for all of those matches except the game against Preston, when Peter McKenna came in. This was on 24 October and Howard Baker's absence was explained by the fact that he was back in the full England team for the first time since his debut against Belgium in May of 1921. The England team chosen to play Northern Ireland (no longer Ireland since the 1921–22 season) in Belfast was as follows:

Ben Howard Baker (Chelsea), Tom Smart (Aston Villa), Frank Hudspeth (Newcastle United), Fred Kean (Sheffield Wednesday), George Armitage (Charlton Athletic), Tom Bromilow (Liverpool) Sam Austin (Manchester City), Syd Puddefoot (Blackburn Rovers), Claude Ashton (Corinthian), Billy Walker (Aston Villa), Arthur Dorrell (Aston Villa).

An amateur goalkeeper from a Second Division club? This was a remarkable choice, indeed, but it is one that is readily explained. On Monday 5 October – two days after Howard Baker had kept his goal intact for the fifth time in eight Chelsea matches – he played for the Amateurs against the Professionals in the FA Charity Shield at Tottenham's ground, and the result was sensational. The Amateurs won 6–1! Admittedly, the Professionals had a player limping with an injury after the first 20 minutes and he did not appear at all for the second half, but the correspondent for *The Times* offered his opinion of the Amateurs that 'one cannot help believing that they would have won, and won decisively, in any circumstances'. As the match kicked off at 3 o'clock on a weekday afternoon, it goes without saying that all the amateurs would have needed to be of independent means, self-employed, or engaged in some sort of professional occupation with indulgent management to be able to take part.

The Amateur line-up that day was the following: Howard Baker, Sgt F. Twine (Army), E.H. Gates (London Caledonian), C.S. Caesar (Dulwich Hamlet), G.H. Armitage (Charlton Athletic), W.I. Bryant (Millwall), R.L. Morgan (Clapton), E.I.L. Kail (Dulwich Hamlet), C.T. Ashton (Corinthian), Cpl F. Macey (Army), W.R. Bellamy (Dulwich Hamlet). The half-back, William Bryant, who was an established international, later wrote a column for *The Daily Mirror* newspaper in which he described the Amateur teams of both 1925 and 1926 which beat the Professionals as 'the finest I have ever played in'. The Professional selection for 1925 was based on the Football Association team that had gone to Australia during the previous summer and won all its 25 fixtures, scoring 139 goals to 13. Of course, the cohesion fashioned among the professionals during that tour may well have been offset by their need of a good rest from the game. Two days later Howard Baker was in goal at Anfield in the Football League's 5–1 win over the Irish League – and 16,000 people turned up to watch despite the 3pm kick-off. Surely they couldn't all have been shop assistants benefiting from early closing day?

Armitage, from a Division Three South club, and Howard Baker's Corinthian teammate, Claude Ashton, were two others from the Shield-winning Amateurs to be selected for the full England XI, and the latter, who had scored four goals in that game, was made captain. This, perhaps, gives the impression of an enterprising selection policy, drawing on skills from a wide spectrum, but the truth is much more mundane. The England selection committee's only consistency was that they certainly had no idea of continuity. Though the match was a goalless draw, and Howard Baker and the Ireland goalkeeper, Elisha Scott, of Liverpool, were both commended for 'some wonderful saves when close-range shots had to be dealt with', Howard Baker was not to be chosen for the further England games that season against Wales and Scotland in March and April of 1926, and nor, for that matter, were any of the others in the England team except Puddefoot and Walker! England thus used 29 players in three matches. Ashton and his two successors that season were the 18th, 19th and 20th centre-forwards to have been selected in 24 matches over a seven-year period.

Walker was, in fact, the only England player of the mid-1920s who seemed reasonably assured of his place. An ex-miner from the Black Country, he won 18 international caps and was to score 244 goals in 531 appearances for his club from 1914 to 1934, being described in the following terms by that most observant of player-writers, Bernard Joy: 'Billy Walker had an angular, awkward build which was deceptive. He moved with surprising speed, had deft ball control, and was very dangerous in the air'. After his retirement as a player Walker promptly became a highly successful manager with Sheffield Wednesday and then a long-serving one with Nottingham Forest, taking both clubs to FA Cup Final wins in 1934–35 and 1958–59 respectively. England's team continued to be selected by a committee until 1939, and the first manager, Walter Winterbottom, was not to be appointed until 1946.

A fortnight after the English professionals – with help from their three amateur auxiliaries – had been held to a draw in Belfast, the amateur teams from the two countries met at Maidstone and in a remarkable game England eventually won 6–4! At halftime they led 4–1, but the visitors scored three times in as many minutes, and the correspondent for *The Times* remarked that 'the small Irish forwards at this stage quite ran the burly England defenders off their feet'. The highly detailed but staid manner of reporting in those days meant that the temptation was resisted to say that the Englishmen had been tied up in knots – one of their full-backs was named Twine.

Making their mark in footballing history that day alongside Howard Baker by representing England against both Ireland's professionals and amateurs within a fortnight were Armitage and Ashton. It was to be Ashton's only appearance for the full XI though he was to win 12 amateur caps in all, starting in 1921–22, and he was another of those remarkable all-rounders who had captained Cambridge University at cricket, with his two brothers in the side, as well as winning hockey and soccer 'blues'. He was to be killed while serving with the RAF in 1942. Other Corinthians on the field at Maidstone were Bower, who captained the England professionals twice and played five matches in all, and Ewer, who was spiritedly described by the Corinthian historian, Edward Grayson, as a left-half 'with tons of pluck and courage'. The selectors were the same for England's amateur and professional teams, though in this instance they seemed for once to have abandoned their usual capricious manner:

Howard Baker, Sgt F. Twine (Army), A.G. Bower (Corinthian), C.S. Caesar (Dulwich Hamlet), G.H. Armitage (Charlton Athletic), W.I. Bryant (Clapton), Lt K.E. Hegan

(Army/Corinthian), E.I.L. Kail (Dulwich Hamlet), C.T. Ashton (Corinthian), Cpl F. Macey (Army), W.R. Bellamy (Dulwich Hamlet). The only new cap was Bellamy.

Chelsea were beaten for the first time in 15 matches of their 1925–26 campaign when they lost 1–0 at home to Swansea City on 21 November and then went down again at Sheffield Wednesday the following Saturday by the decisive margin of 4–1. This result confirmed the home club as joint leaders of the table with Middlesbrough. Chelsea were third only one point behind, and by the end of the season the positions were much the same. Sheffield Wednesday finished top with 60 points. Middlesbrough slipped away and Derby County came through to second with 57 points. Chelsea were again not in proper sight of promotion, third with 52 points, winning 19 matches, drawing 14, losing nine, scoring 76 goals to 49.

Howard Baker did not play again that season for Chelsea after the defeat by the eventual champions in November, and this seems a curious turn of fortune for a man who little more than a month before was good enough to have superseded all the professionals in the England goalmouth. He had conceded just 10 goals in 13 Chelsea games, while 39 were scored against the club in Peter McKenna's 29 appearances. Presumably, it was not a question of dropping Howard Baker but of him having the Chelsea's management approval to return to Corinthian, as his form continued to be outstanding. He played in all but one of the 18 Corinthian fixtures from mid-December onwards, starting with a visit by Derby County, no less, who were then in third place in Division Two but were held to a 1–1 draw at Crystal Palace. This was a match which, incidentally, received more attention in *The Times* than had any of Chelsea's fixtures, and Howard Baker was remarked upon for saving 'some hard and difficult shots'. Even by their own exalted standards, the Corinthian team was a star-studded one that day: nine of them were England amateur internationals, including Bower, Ewer and Claude Ashton.

On Boxing Day Corinthian for the first time in six post-war meetings beat the representatives of the Isthmian League, a competition in which many of the leading amateur clubs in the London and home counties' area played, and Howard Baker was described as 'again quite brilliant in goal'. The score was 3–0 and it must have been an exhilarating post-Christmas match to watch because Corinthian had an entire team of England amateur caps as their line-up and the League had eight. The post-Christmas tour began with a 3–3 draw at Manchester United on 28 December and then a visit to Preston North End two days later, where the 5–3 defeat was the first that the Corinthians had suffered in their 15 first-team and 'A' team matches of the season so far, in the process scoring 66 goals (an average of more than four a game) and conceding 33. Corinthian were, in fact, victims of their own generosity because they allowed their opponents to replace an injured player and the substitute repaid the gesture by scoring twice! On New Year's Day Queen's Park and Corinthian drew their regular encounter 1–1, and Corinthian had Howard Baker to thank them for avoiding a beating – 'he never erred in anticipating shots and meeting the ball', said the Scottish correspondent of *The Times*.

Corinthian was then one of three amateur clubs to take part in the first round proper of the FA Cup and at Crystal Palace a 3–3 draw was forced with the Division One side, Manchester City. Admittedly the professionals had a player hampered by injury for much of the game – though that didn't prevent him from scoring a goal – but Corinthian drew yet more praise from *The Times* in the lengthy report by their correspondent which occupied an entire column of the Sporting News page. Taking a dig, perhaps, at a certain cynicism in the professional game, he wrote: 'The Corinthians always play strong football and fast football without employing any of those sly niggling little tricks which infuriate even if they do not hurt'. Howard Baker kept goal splendidly, though he was responsible for one of the visitors' goals when he took four steps with the ball instead of the two allowed and a free-kick was given against him. Four of the goals came in the last half-hour and Norman Creek, who scored twice, remembered it 'as undoubtedly one of the most thrilling matches in which the Corinthians have figured since the Great War'.

The following Wednesday more than 40,000 people turned up at Manchester City's new ground for the replay, but the Corinthians failed to reproduce their form of the weekend and were beaten 4–0. Howard Baker's display was not dissimilar to the first game: 'He had made practically every kind of save known to goalkeeping, except the save at full length. He let one ball through that he should not have done – and it was the important second goal, too – but most of his hand work and his long kicking were as good as ever'.

Later in January the RAF were beaten 7–2, though Howard Baker was at fault for the airmen's first goal, being caught completely out of position. Such occasional lapses were all part of his flamboyant manner and the amateur selectors paid no heed because they put him in goal for the England v The Rest trial at Wimbledon on 6 February. Out of the reckoning for the full England side, Howard Baker was replaced by Dick Pym, of Bolton Wanderers, against Wales on 1 March, though Pym, too, had no better luck, as England lost 3–1 and he was never chosen again – for which another good reason would be that he was in goal for The Rest when they were beaten 7–3 by England in a trial match in January 1927. Pym's lifespan was almost exactly the same as Howard Baker's; born in 1893, when he died in 1988 at the age of 95 he was the oldest surviving England football international.

Less expectedly, the selectors decided they wanted the Cambridge University goalkeeper, A.M. Russell, also a Corinthian-to-be, for the England amateurs against Wales at Wrexham on 20 March. Russell had certainly impressed in the trial – 'a lot to do and he did it extremely well' – but England had won 2–1 and Howard Baker had made no mistakes on his team's behalf. So it seemed perverse to pass him over. Anyway, with only four players from the senior trial team, England again won 2–1.

The 1925–26 season was reckoned to be the finest in the Corinthian history – played 31, won 22, drew five, lost four, goals for 126 (maintaining that four-a-game average), goals against 56. In March and April there were wins against Queen's Park (4–2), Yorkshire Amateurs (3–0) and Division One team Birmingham (1–0), though Birmingham won the return fixture 1–0, while the regular visits to public schools included a 13–1 win at Eton which must have caused some heartache among the Old Etonian members of Corinthian. Howard Baker's fine form was maintained through to the end of the season, and when Corinthian beat the Royal Navy 3–1 at Crystal Palace in their closing game on 17 April, for example, he was described as having 'distinguished himself by bringing off several brilliant saves'.

There is no question that Howard Baker was an outstanding goalkeeper at his best. He was also an unashamed showman whose speciality at Chelsea was to delight the home spectators and enrage those of the visiting team by bouncing the ball around the penalty-area and over the heads of opponents as if playing basketball while one of the club's co-founders, Joe Mears, bellowed instructions through a megaphone from the sideline. In his 1982 taped interview with John Bromhead, shortly before his 90th birthday, Howard Baker reminisced once again in familiar vein about his playing days. 'Goalkeepers were anybody's target then', he recalled. 'You were allowed two paces carrying the ball and then you were attacked by everybody! I could never resist fooling about, and I would bounce the ball with two or three forwards charging at me, and Mears from the chairman's box would bawl, 'Get rid of the bloody ball!'.'

Howard Baker's habit of kicking the heavy leather ball the length of the field had its inherent dangers – on one occasion an opposing full-back unwisely headed it and was carried off unconscious – and he often could not resist the temptation to leave his goal and run the length of the field to add his height and weight to the attack when the opposition conceded a corner. Whatever risks his opponents were subject to when Howard Baker fired off one of his soaring kicks, it was a tough era for goalkeepers. The offside law was changed in 1925, reducing to two instead of three the number of opposing players required to be between an attacker and the goal when he received the ball, and scoring immediately became more frequent. In the 1926–27 season George Camsell, of Middlesbrough, set a record of 59 goals as his club won the Second Division title by eight points, and in 1927–28 Dixie Dean scored 60 in Everton's First Division Championship success, which total has still to be surpassed more than 80 years later. It was not until 1931 that goalkeepers were given more latitude and protection when the number of steps which they could take with the ball was increased from two to four.

Athletics still figured in Howard Baker's thoughts and he met up socially on occasions with Harold Abrahams, who had been an Olympic teammate in 1920 but whose active career had been brought to a premature end the year after his 1924 Olympic 100 metres triumph when he seriously injured himself long-jumping. Now Abrahams was embarked on a legal career which he would combine with a continued involvement in the sport for more than another half-century as an administrator, writer and broadcaster for which he was widely respected, though in the latter years conflicts of interest became increasingly evident. Both Abrahams and Howard Baker got a favourable mention when an American contributor to the edition of *The British Olympic Journal* for the summer of 1926 wrote an article comparing athletics in the two countries.

Hugh Baxter had been US pole-vault champion on four occasions in the 1880s and had then become an executive of the New York Athletic Club, which had produced many Olympic champions over the years. During 1926 he was in England on holiday and generously offered his services as a coach, and he then recorded his impressions for the Olympic officials and members. His message was politely expressed but chastening: 'My experience in England has been that year after year a wealth of good athletic material goes to waste…in field events England has always done badly and America has done well. The reason is not far to seek. The American starts to high-jump, pole-jump or put the weight with a fixed idea in his mind as to the mechanical principles involved. The nearer he can succeed in applying the principles the greater is his success. They have all been worked out over and over again. There is one way to pole-jump and one way to put the weight, and 95 per cent of the record-holders have adopted these ways. But in England you see every conceivable method employed. Such fine performers as Abrahams, Howard Baker and Nokes have done much for field events here, but after all they appear to be the exception and not the rule'.

Unfortunately, the well-intended remarks of the American visitor seemed to pass entirely unheeded. Howard Baker's would-be high-jump successors in Britain were still caught up in what Americans would regard disdainfully as an Eastern Cut-Off time warp, and it would be 20 years before any discernible change would take place.

'THIS IS LONDON 2LO CALLING. NOW WE TAKE YOU OVER TO CRYSTAL PALACE FOR COMMENTARY ON THIS AFTERNOON'S FA CUP TIE'

No doubt Howard Baker thought that the most significant aspect of the 1926–27 football season for him was that it marked, oddly, both his last prolonged spell as a League player and his return to the England teams, professional and amateur. From a broader viewpoint, though, it was another match entirely, when he was in goal for Corinthian, which stands out as of greater historical importance. 'Broader' is a word not lightly chosen in this particular context.

He was back in Everton colours more by chance than design. The club's regular goalkeeper, Henry Hardy, had sprained an ankle in pre-season training and the reserve goalkeeper had also gone down with injury. Howard Baker offered his services as a temporary replacement, though it has to be said that it was not to be one of the more memorable spells of his career among the professionals. Everton made a dismal start, and after 12 matches by mid-October they had won only once (though that was against Liverpool 1–0), had drawn four times and lost seven, conceding 27 goals, which was more than any other club in the First Division.

Howard Baker had figured in all but one of those games, but the match reports clearly indicate that he was not to blame for the series of disasters. Away to Bury on 1 September (Everton lost 5–2) *The Echo* concluded that 'but for Baker's clever goalkeeping the score would have been a very big one'. Away to Sheffield Wednesday on 11 September (Everton lost 4–0) he was 'holding the fort like a sentinel'. Away to Blackburn Rovers on 2 October he 'saved a certain goal' which enabled Everton to draw 3–3 and at last stumble out of bottom place in the League – though not for long.

Matters scarcely improved after he ended his spell of emergency duty. His successor for a few weeks was Arthur Davies, born across the Mersey in Wallasey, and signed from the Welsh club, Flint, who played 10 matches; Hardy managed only seven when he returned; and a Liverpudlian, Ted Taylor, the former England international and a pre-war amateur teammate of Howard Baker's, who had been recruited from Huddersfield Town rather in the twilight of his career, played out the last 14 fixtures. By the end of the season Everton had scraped their way to 20th, avoiding relegation by four points as Leeds United and West Bromwich Albion were the two clubs that went down. Newcastle United won the title resoundingly with 56 points to Huddersfield Town's 51 and Sunderland's 49.

The amateur contribution to League football was rapidly diminishing as Howard Baker's withdrawal from League football meant that only one unpaid player was still appearing regularly in the First Division – Vivian Gibbins, the West Ham United inside-forward, who was a headmaster and would make 138 League appearances for the club, scoring 63 goals – and there were no more than half-a dozen or so amateurs playing throughout all the divisions.

The habitual late start which Corinthian made to their season enabled Howard Baker to appear in their opening fixture on 6 October – a 4–1 win at Crystal Palace over the Southern Amateur League – and The Times reported that he was at his best: 'There are days when a goalkeeper seems to attract the ball, and so it was with Baker on Saturday. It is true that he was beaten once but only after saving four times and having to leave his goal'. The visitors had two future Corinthians in their side in Vernon Morgan, also later to be an Olympic steeplechaser and then a distinguished sports editor, and N.W.B. Stone, of the Bank of England. Five other players were from the Midland Bank or the Bank of England, including the goalkeeper and both full-backs, but irony was not a feature of newspaper reporting in those days, and so there was as usual no tongue-in-cheek reference to debiting accounts or adverse balance sheets.

Though Howard Baker was nursing a persistent knee injury he missed only three of the 24 matches throughout the season. One of those absences had cost his club dear as the heaviest defeat in its 44-year history was suffered, 9–1 by the Athenian League, and the luckless chap between the posts that day was one E.G.C. Harlow, who was making his debut and was not asked by Corinthian to keep goal again until six seasons later.

Newcastle United already led the First Division at the turn of the year, and as luck would have it the FA Cup draw for the first round proper on 29 January brought Newcastle's name out of the hat immediately after that of Corinthian. Opinion as to whether this was the worst of ill-luck or a plum attraction was probably divided among the Corinthian hierarchy; since its inception the club's management had been noted for its hard bargaining over the share of gate receipts, and no doubt the treasurer's eyes glinted at the prospect of such eminent visitors to Crystal Palace. Hours before the match had even kicked off, he would have been agog with delight.

This would be an encounter which would attract by far the biggest 'attendance' for any which Howard Baker and his clubmates had ever played in. Such was the fever of interest in this fixture that the gates of the Crystal Palace ground were opened at 10 o'clock in the morning and an enormous crowd of 56,338 was packed in, many of them brought by the dozens of special trains laid on from central London, but there were yet vast numbers more who were able to follow the game in its entirety. One of the very first live commentaries by BBC radio on a sporting event was arranged for that afternoon.

Sports broadcasting was so much in its infancy that it could be said that the delivery was still taking place, or at least the umbilical cord was yet to be cut. The first such programme had been transmitted only a fortnight before when Captain H.B. ('Teddy') Wakelam, a voluble club cricketer and rugby player, described the action from the England v Scotland rugby union match at Twickenham. He had then covered the Arsenal-Sheffield United League football fixture the following Saturday to general acclaim from the listening public. So the BBC management enterprisingly decided to broadcast four of the Cup ties a week later from their various transmitter stations and hurriedly called in a number of Fleet Street football writers for a midweek microphone test at an Arsenal reserve game. Three days later George Allison was at Crystal Palace for the Corinthian-Newcastle United match, and he was no doubt racked with nerves as the 2.35 starting-time for the programme approached and the band of the Irish Guards completed their hour-long rendering of popular and stirring airs to entertain the spectators as the latecomers streamed in for the 2.45 kick-off.

No recording of these pioneering broadcasts has survived, but whatever might have been the shortcomings of Allison's commentary that day he learned fast. He was to become the leading broadcaster at football matches for the next dozen years. Having started his journalistic career in the north-east, he had then moved to London, covering Arsenal's matches and taking over as the club's programme editor. Remarkably, as his radio career blossomed, he also rose through Arsenal's chain of command to be appointed secretary-manager. Interviewed in 1931, and now with the experience of four years of commentating behind him, he said, 'You just repeat what you see happening, talk as the words come into your head. Something instinctive inside does the rest...listeners want to know what is happening and they also want to share in the game as it goes on'. Such a philosophy would be surely echoed by every radio sports commentator down the years since.

The Radio Times had carried a full-page preview of the match the previous day, illustrated by photographs of the captains – for Corinthian it was Alfred Bower, educated at Charterhouse, who spent his working week as a member of the London Stock Exchange; for Newcastle it was Scots-born Hughie Gallacher, whose upbringing had been shaped by the somewhat different experience of being a 15-year-old coal-miner working 10-hour shifts. An ingenious idea by *The Radio Times* editor was to print a chart of the pitch divided into numbered squares so that listeners could follow the movement of the ball as George Allison's assistant intoned the appropriate figures in the background. Two very notable broadcasters of the future, John Snagge and Derek McCulloch, began their radio careers fulfilling such a humble but helpful function.

Radio coverage extended to some 70 sports events during 1927, and half of them were football matches, including the FA Cup Final when Cardiff City beat Arsenal 1–0 to take the trophy out of England for the first time. This exposure was an immensely important innovation for football, as previously the only source of information for the fans had been the newspapers, and though there were to be problems in the future for the BBC in getting agreement for coverage of the matches from the clubs – fearful of losing spectators who might prefer to stay at home and listen in rather than pass through the turnstiles (and maybe brave the worst of the weather on windswept terraces) – radio was here to stay.

The story of how that happened was to be told in an immensely entertaining and highly informative book by Dick Booth, published in 2008, and his detailed researches lead him to suppose that the radio audience for that Corinthian-Newcastle United match could have numbered hundreds of thousands, tuning in to their nearest transmitters in London, Daventry, Cardiff, Swansea and Edinburgh. More than two million licences had been bought by the public in 1926 (2,178,259, to be precise), and excited listeners to football commentaries that afternoon would also have included those within range of the stations in

Birmingham (Wolverhampton Wanderers v Nottingham Forest), Stoke-on-Trent (Port Vale v Arsenal) and Sheffield (Sheffield Wednesday v South Shields). Are you sitting comfortably? This is London 2LO calling.

As for the Corinthian match itself…well, they lost, but the way in which they did so could scarcely have suited radio better had the whole affair been carefully scripted. The amateurs led 1–0 for two-thirds of the game, but then their centre-forward, R.G.C. Jenkins, was injured and had to leave the field, and his remaining 10 teammates succumbed to the might of their visitors. The equalising goal by Newcastle was fortuitously scored from a free-kick deflected into the net off the shoulder of a Corinthian defender, with Howard Baker left hopelessly unsighted, and before the end two more goals were added. The correspondent for *The Times*, whose exhaustive report of the proceedings ran to some 1,600 words, provided a doleful post-mortem: 'The Corinthians again played the part of the heroes, and the leading professional side of the day, if hardly the villains, represented the stern material forces of acutely developed technical skill, team work and rigorous training'.

Howard Baker, it was said, 'performed prodigies', and he and his defenders well needed to as Hughie Gallacher, at centre-forward for Newcastle, was one of the finest players of his generation, though he was of diminutive stature, only 5ft 5in (165m) in height. An expert assessment of him was that he 'could shoot with either foot, dribble with the ball, head, tackle and forage'. He was to score 463 goals in 624 League games and 23 goals in his 20 appearances for Scotland, forever enshrined in Scottish football folklore as one of the 'Wembley Wizards' of 1928 who gave the English a 5–1 hammering. Norman Creek, whose adroit cross-kick led to Claude Ashton scoring the goal by which Corinthian had led at half-time, recalled of his teammates: 'In a side where every one played his hardest and best, Baker, Ewer and Hegan all played fine games. It was generally agreed that the BBC could not have chosen to broadcast a more thrilling and exciting Cup tie'.

The Corinthian team on this occasion was as strong a one as ever put out in the 1920s – B. Howard Baker, A.G. Bower (captain), A.E. Knight, J.R.B. Moulsdale, A.H. Chadder, F.H. Ewer, A.E. Taylor, F.N.S. Creek, R.G.C. Jenkins, C.T. Ashton K.E. Hegan. Every one of them was or would be an England amateur international except Moulsdale, and he had played for Wales. In addition to Gallacher, Newcastle United's other professional internationals were full-back Frank Hudspeth, centre-half Charlie Spencer (both England) and inside-forward Bobby McKay (Scotland). On the wing for them that day was Stan Seymour, who over a period of 56 years from 1920 would serve the club as player, manager, chairman and president.

Corinthian would continue to take part in the FA Cup competition until the 1938–39 season, but of the 27 ties which they played only five were ever won, and two of those were against non-League clubs. Accordingly, Edward Grayson, in his history of the club, wondered if the whole enterprise had been worthwhile: 'The Corinthians wrote the greatest pages in their history in about 40 years, during which they did not bother about cups. Their name lost a lot of its significance – let there be no mistake about this – during the period which included their Cup adventure. The Cup was never anything more than incidental to their survival. Perhaps the mistake was made of thinking that it might be used as the means'. Grayson is perhaps being a trifle dismissive of the Corinthian efforts, particularly as he later noted in his book that the average attendance at the 19 Cup games in which they were involved from 1923 to 1934 was over 30,000, reflecting the widespread interest in the Corinthian style of game, but then he was a barrister who thought in precise and unemotive terms though still passionate about sport. He was later responsible for establishing much of the framework of sporting law and was still attending court in his 80s, dying in 2008 at the age of 83.

Norman Creek, who would eventually accumulate the experience of being a Corinthian and England forward, a noted journalist, an author of coaching manuals, and the England amateur team manager, took a more benevolent view of Corinthian Cup exploits, or at least the earlier ones. In his 1933 club history he wrote: 'It was only in three of their contests that the Corinthians were definitely outclassed – by West Bromwich Albion, Sheffield United (1925, and winners that year) and Manchester City (a replay in 1926, and beaten finalists that year). All the other games produced hard struggles, and in the ties against such first-class sides as Blackburn Rovers, Newcastle United, Manchester City and Sheffield United (1932), the amateurs fully held their own'. Maybe it would be fairer to say that Howard Baker and his Corinthian colleagues went down with all flags flying. The Corinthian club eventually amalgamated in 1939 with the Casuals, formed four years earlier than Corinthian in 1878, and with much the same ideals. Corinthian-Casuals survive to this day, having at long last acquired their first ground at Tolworth, in Surrey, after a further merger with the local club in 1988.

One of the best FA Cup performances over the years by Corinthian had come in the previous round three weeks before the Newcastle match when they beat Walsall – then in mid-position in the Division Three North table – by 4–0, though even on this occasion it was reported that 'B. Howard Baker had an immense amount of work to do, and luckily for the Corinthians he played a magnificently safe game'. Between Christmas and the New Year the club had departed on its usual tour, taking the overnight train to Glasgow after losing 2–0 in a match against Tottenham Hotspur which must have given Howard Baker a feeling of *déjà vu* because he had also been in goal at White Hart Lane when Everton lost in their opening match of the season.

On 6 November, while the Corinthians were conceding nine goals to the Athenians, Howard Baker had been in Belfast with the England amateur XI against Ireland, and though the England players were still suffering the after-effects of a rough ferry crossing of the Irish Sea from Fleetwood on the previous Thursday evening they won comfortably enough, 3–0. The side was as follows:

B. Howard Baker (Corinthian), Sgt F. Twine (Army), E.H. Gates (London Caledonians), Cpl A. Cartlidge (Army), Dr R.W. Fairbrother (Northern Nomads), J.G. Knight (Casuals), A.E. Taylor (Corinthian), E.I.L. Kail (Dulwich Hamlet), W.V.T. Gibbins (West Ham United), F. Macey (Kingstonians), W.R. Bellamy (Dulwich Hamlet). Macey was the former army player.

Edgar Kail and Vivian Gibbins were both also to win full England caps during their careers and could lay claim, together with Howard Baker, Claude Ashton, and Max Woosnam to being the outstanding England amateur players of the 1920s. Kail was a salesman of wine and spirits by occupation who played 18 times for the England amateur XI and scored 427 goals in his career for Dulwich Hamlet, which lasted from 1919 to 1933. Later in life a successful football writer, primarily with *The Daily Sketch* newspaper, he became so much of a legend as a player that the road leading to his club's ground in

Southwark, South-East London, was re-named 'Edgar Kail Way', and his memory is further preserved in the anthem still sung by Hamlet supporters:

'Edgar Kail in my heart, keep me Dulwich,
Edgar Kail in my heart I pray,
Edgar Kail in my heart, keep me Dulwich,
Keep me Dulwich 'til my dying day'.

Gibbins, who won 10 amateur caps, was lavishly praised in the report for *The Times* of one match in October of 1927, when he scored both goals in a win over Burnley which took West Ham United to the top of the First Division: 'Gibbins is one of the old-fashioned centre-forwards, a player with resource and craft, and not merely one who stands far down the field waiting for the ball to be sent through to him and then setting off with a dash in an attempt to squeeze between the backs for a shot at goal. He keeps his place in the line and is never so good as when he joins with the other forwards in a united attack. In fact, he is just an inside-forward placed in the middle, and that was how the most successful men of a former era regarded themselves'.

Against the Royal Military College Sandhurst in November, designated as an 'A' team game, Howard Baker had little to do in a 14–2 win, as one might suppose, with 11 of the Corinthian goals coming in the second half, though he did make one unusual contribution by laying on a 'pass' which led directly to a goal. On one of the rare occasions that the ball came in his direction he launched 'a prodigious kick which landed clear of everyone, and Doggart raced the full-back for the ball, took it on the bounce and scored'. Officer Cadet K.K. Denton, in the Sandhurst goal, was far from disgraced, 'brilliantly saving a great many shots'. Even so, it is easy to imagine an irate Regimental Sergeant Major haranguing the hapless cadets as they trailed off the field. 'What *do* you think you were playing at, gentlemen?'

The following Thursday Corinthian ran up another massive score at Westminster School, winning 16–3, before Howard Baker figured in a rather more significant match against Millwall two days later which the amateurs won 4–3. This was a highly creditable result considering that Millwall would eventually finish the season third in Division Three South, and the report of the game in *The Times* was singularly informative about prevailing contrasts in playing methods: 'It is always interesting to see a strong side of amateurs opposed by a good professional side, and on Saturday this was particularly the case. The difference in style is so marked. Whereas the amateur goes the shortest way for goal, taking and giving straightforward passes, the professional will indulge in all kinds of tricks and give square and even backward passes in order to attain the same end'.

The Corinthian players also had something of a reputation for another sort of directness. When the club had been formed almost half-a-century before, the strategy was to dribble the ball until shoulder-charged off it, when hopefully there would be a teammate close behind to continue to progress in that fashion. The idea of passing the ball was not highly regarded – dismissively, passing was known as 'sneaking' – but shoving an opponent unceremoniously off the ball was perfectly acceptable. The professionals had gradually given up that ploy in the interests of self-preservation, but it was still an occasional part of the Corinthian repertoire, and in one match when a player was sent sprawling (a Corinthian, as it happened) some of his supporters shouted, 'Foul!', only for one of the club's elder statesman to retort, 'Foul, be hanged! We love it!'.

England met Scotland at Leicester on 18 December in the first ever match between teams from the two countries chosen specifically as amateurs, though the fixtures from the first in 1872 onwards had, of course, involved only amateurs until the legalisation of professionalism in 1885. Howard Baker was replaced in goal by A.M. Russell, of Cambridge University, who had played the previous season against Wales, and the reason for that change may well have been that Corinthian had lost a return match to the undergraduates 3–0 on 4 December, though a reasonable excuse for the Corinthians was that they had only 10 men for most of the first half because of the late arrival of one of their half-backs, J.G. Stevenson. Russell had also made an odd debut for Corinthian two days after Christmas, conceding five goals to the Isthmian League while his forwards scored six in reply.

A second member of the Cambridge University side awarded an England place at inside-forward was R.G.H. Lowe, who was yet another of those prolific varsity cricketer/footballers and had had his days of glory in the summer of 1926, taking eight wickets against Oxford, including a hat-trick, but it was not a happy afternoon for the Cantab men as the Scots won 4–1. Russell was given only two more caps over a period of four years, and Lowe was never picked again, but whatever the size of England's defeat old values still held good because their centre-forward, Gibbins, deliberately took a half-hearted kick after a Scottish defender had been penalised for a handling offence by the referee, whose decision had mystified even the English players, and the shot was easily saved.

Seven of the visiting team were from Queen's Park and they must have wondered why the goalkeeper who had foiled their efforts so often on behalf of Corinthian was not playing. Instead Howard Baker was at Crystal Palace, saving 'one or two seemingly impossible shots' as his club beat the Royal Navy 2–1. Everton, incidentally, were buried in their slump that day, losing 5–1 at Burnley.

After the exciting FA Cup venture, Corinthian resumed normal service with a 7–1 drubbing of Winchester College and a commendable 2–2 draw with the professionals of Portsmouth. Against the Army at Aldershot at the end of February Howard Baker very nearly scored a spectacular goal as his massive clearance, with the wind behind it, forced the Army goalkeeper, Corporal Lewis, into saving. Corinthian still won 5–2 and a couple of days later the players went off to Paris for a charity game against Red Star Olympique, three times French Cup winners in the 1920s, which took the place of the customary end-of-season tour, and won 2–0, with Howard Baker saving a penalty. The Parisian club had been co-founded in 1897 by Jules Rimet who was to become president of FIFA, the international ruling body of football, and whose name was given to the trophy awarded to the World Cup winners.

The match took place at the quaintly-named Stade Buffalo in Montrouge and attracted 12,000 spectators, though the banked cement cycling-track which surrounded the pitch meant that most of them had only a distant view. Far from being charitable, the action was alive with incident and controversy, and the evening newspaper, L'Intransigeant (the translation is *The Uncompromising* and reflects its entrenched right-wing editorial policy), which sold as many as 400,000 copies an issue, devoted much of its sports coverage on Thursday 3 March to the previous day's encounter. A detailed report was provided by Gabriel Hanot, who had become a highly respected coach and journalist after playing a dozen times for France before and after World War One. This was accompanied by a complimentary profile of Howard Baker by an even better-known writer, Gaston Bénac, who is remembered in France as 'un des créateurs du grand reportage sportif' – a description which really needs no translation.

Interestingly, Monsieur Hanot took up the Corinthian cause and was extravagant in his praise for what the French would call *sang-froid*, though the word wasn't actually used, and was highly critical of the home side. In so doing he neatly summed up what was, in effect, a regrettably outmoded style of play and conduct. 'The English amateur aristocrats were there for nothing, I hasten to say', he wrote. 'Punished for hypothetical faults more or less minor in character by two penalties, pulled up for off-the-play incidents which were sometimes imaginary, penalised for shoulder-charges said to be irregular or for unlikely handling of the ball, they showed at no time their surprise or their disagreement. They stoically played the game, sticking by the rules, and nothing else.

'Inheritors of a long-established sporting tradition, chosen from the intellectual elite of the former students at Oxford and Cambridge, united by their shared memories and preferences, the phlegmatic Corinthians more readily represented heroes of antiquity than our players, who come from more varied backgrounds and are more inclined to express their naturally demonstrative temperament, giving in to their first impulse and reacting violently to everything they considered as a mistake or an injustice'.

The article went on to describe at length an incident in which a Red Star goal had been disallowed for offside and three of their players – including a future national team manager, Paul Nicolas, who would be in charge when France placed third in the 1958 World Cup – had immediately surrounded the referee in protest. The tale continued thus in a distinctly ironic manner, contrasting Gallic fervour with English stoicism: 'Chayriguès, the coolest head in French football, then left his goalmouth (*the splendidly flowery phrase actually used by M. Hanot was 'maison de bois', or 'house of wood'*) and headed at a swift pace towards the incident. 'Good', I said to myself, 'he's going to make his teammates see reason. He's going to tell them it's not a French Cup match or the Championship Final, but a demonstration of the purest values of sport, no matter how many goals are scored'.

'What a mistake on my part! My former colleague in the French team, who I've never ceased to regard as the living example of calmness and insight, was about to commit a puerile act. Bitten by I know not what bug on this showery day in March, he ran off towards the changing-rooms in protest against the goal being disallowed. While the Corinthians impassively waited for the argument to end, a little man with white hair climbed over the barrier of the official seating, ducked under the hand-rail surrounding the pitch and hurried towards Chayriguès. It was Monsieur Jules Rimet, no less, who combines in one personage the triple titles of honorary president of Red Star, president of the French Football Federation and president of the International Football Federation. His entreaties, together with those of the directors of Red Star, cooled the temper of Chayriguès, who went back to his place'.

Pierre Chayriguès was no hot-headed novice. On the contrary, he was a seasoned international who was to be chosen 25 times for France between 1911 and 1925 and gained such renown that he was offered highly favourable terms by Tottenham Hotspur to join them in 1913, but he preferred to remain an amateur with Red Star. His style of play was one of which Howard Baker would have heartily approved. He was the first French goalkeeper to develop the art of leaving his line and diving fearlessly at the feet of oncoming forwards, and the injuries he sustained in the process eventually brought about his retirement soon after this dramatic match against Corinthian.

Gaston Bénac's tribute at the top of the page in that day's copy of *L'Intransigeant* was headlined 'Le grand athlète Howard Baker', and the subject of it took home a cutting for his collection which he eventually had translated, though not too accurately, as it happens. Inevitably, the precise comments which he is quoted as having made to his interviewer sound a shade stilted in translation, but the article still gives a genuine feel for the impression which the illustrious English visitor made on an astute and expressive Frenchman with much experience of writing about the star performers in a number of sports:

'He causes a sensation in front of his goalmouth with his canary-coloured jersey draped from the impressively athletic breadth of his shoulders, and he has a very fine style in clothes and also wears an elegant white sweater, this gentleman millionaire from Liverpool who plays football purely as an amateur. There are few who are as representative of athletics, in fact, as this tall dark-haired amateur whose name is Howard Baker, whose smile every time reveals his impeccable set of teeth. Still the English high-jump record-holder with 1 metre 95½, a competitor in the Olympic Games at Antwerp, an athlete of repute, Baker has dedicated himself body and soul to football, and he occupies with admirable enthusiasm the position of goalkeeper for the Corinthians, having played for Chelsea and Everton and given his services freely to a number of impoverished clubs.

'Yesterday evening, in the grand hall of the Cercle Interallié, while he was being congratulated by Henry Paté (*a radical socialist deputy in the French Parliament who would serve as under-secretary of state for physical education in four French governments between 1928 and 1930*), he told me, "I play football for my personal satisfaction, but like the other Corinthians I don't believe that that is enough. One must think of others, of those who are less fortunate, and it's to help poor clubs or to support other causes that we put on shorts and jersey. And when the match is over, we can enjoy ourselves doubly, having done a little bit of good. I don't understand any other reason for playing".

'Howard Baker is truly the type of British gentleman of the old school, and it is a type which has not been made redundant by commercialism, professionalism, stadiums with large receipts. He carries his 35 years well, this athlete who stands some 1 metre 90 tall, and if he is proud to be one of the finest ornaments of an exclusive club where they admit only the purest of the pure he displays neither haughtiness nor excessive pride when he talks to us about his perceptions of this superior school of football whose members pay all their own expenses'.

Howard Baker went on to tell M. Bénac, 'We must always seek to improve our own play and that of the game in general. We must remain worthy of a game which brings us so much pleasure, so many emotions. The result matters little, and the criticism which anyone can make if we score relatively few goals doesn't really affect us'. Having been informed by Howard Baker that he no longer high jumped but rowed and ran for pleasure, as well as playing football, Monsieur Bénac added that 'this amateur super-athlete forgot to say that he also dances the Charleston brilliantly'. Clearly, the evening's social gathering was less fraught for the 11 eligible Corinthians than had been the afternoon's footballing.

All differences having presumably been amicably settled, the teams met for dinner at Le Cercle de l'Union Interalliés – the Inter-Allies' club which has been set up in 1917 to foster harmony among the allied nations, and which included prominent politicians, diplomats and business leaders among its membership. Top-table places alongside Monsieur Rimet were occupied, most notably, by 76-year-old Marshal of France Ferdinand Foch, the president of the Cercle, who had been supreme commander of the Allied armies in World War One, and the Marquess of Crewe, who was the British ambassador in Paris. The speeches afterwards may well have received a mixed reception. Foch was reputed for an apt turn of phrase, having remarked prophetically at the war's end, 'This is not a peace. It is an armistice for 20 years'. The Marquess, by contrast, was a poor speaker and it was wittily said of the Marchioness by her father, Lord Rosebery, when she was in labour, 'I hope that her delivery is not as slow as Crewe's'.

For the final amateur international of the season against Wales at Elm Park, Reading, on 19 March there were, unsurprisingly, half-a-dozen changes in the England team and Howard Baker was back in goal for his ninth amateur cap. The team, more than half of them Corinthians, was the following: Howard Baker, A.G. Bower (Corinthian), F.J. Gregory (Wimbledon), Cpl A. Cartlidge (Army), W.I. Bryant (Millwall), F.H. Ewer (Corinthian), R.G.C. Jenkins (Oxford University/Corinthian), R.A. Smith (Stockton), R.C. Dellow (Ilford), C.T. Ashton (Corinthian), Lt K.E. Hegan (Army/Corinthian). Only Howard Baker and Corporal Cartlidge survived from the team which had beaten Ireland the previous November. England scored twice in the first eight minutes and won 4–0, and even that result 'absurdly underestimated the superiority of the England side', though Howard Baker had plenty of saves to make and *The Sunday Times* even headlined their opinion that Wales were unlucky not to score.

Bower, who turned out very occasionally for Chelsea in the mid-1920s (nine matches in three seasons), had also played for the full England side in a 3–3 draw against Wales at the Racecourse Ground, Wrexham, the previous month when there was a record attendance of 16,000 and gate receipts of £1,790. To expand on the financial theme, it was reckoned that most professional footballers at that time, even in the First Division, earned no more than £5 a week during the season, and less in the summer, and that only a few exceptional players received the maximum £8 a week in winter and £6 in summer. The record transfer fee then stood at £6,500 for the England international inside-forward, Bob Kelly ('a sinuous dribble and a flashing shot', according to the future amateur international and writer, Bernard Joy), when he had moved from Burnley to Sunderland in December 1925, though the record-breaking goalscorer (59 in all) for Middlesbrough during the 1926–27 season, George Camsell, had cost only 'a few hundred pounds' when signed from Durham City.

The change in the offside law, reducing the number of defenders required between the ball and their goalmouth, was largely responsible for the scoring trend, but *The Times* was not over-impressed by the development, commenting that it had 'made the game faster than ever, reduced the number of stoppages, and resulted in a good many more goals being scored, but the greater pace has driven out some of the craft and there is less art and science in the game than before'. Corinthian made their contribution to the proceedings with an 8–4 win over the RAF on a prolific day of contrasting Second Division fortunes for two neighbouring clubs when Nottingham Forest scored seven against Preston North End and Notts County conceded nine to Portsmouth.

Howard Baker was close to home for a match between the Northern Nomads and Corinthian at the Cadby Hall ground, in Wavertree, Liverpool, which the Nomads won 3–2, with the hurdler, J.E. Blair, at centre-half. It was a rare reversal – not that any of these gentleman amateurs got too excited about the result – and Howard Baker's winter, which had seen him play for both England sides, was neatly summarised in the account of the fixture which Corinthian arranged with West Ham United, then in the top half of Division One, on the day of the sixth round of the FA Cup. Corinthian won 4–3 and *The Times* said, 'Howard Baker, who always has a great deal to do with a Corinthian victory, was at his best. He has, in fact, kept goal exceptionally well this season'.

There was to be nothing 'exceptionally well' about Howard Baker's high-jump successors in Britain during the summer of 1927, with another Olympic Games to come the following year, as all of them had been eclipsed by a sprinter, the British Guiana-born Jack London, who on a rare dalliance with the event had cleared 6ft 2in (1.88m). At the AAA Championships the winner was a Swede, Herbert Adolfsson, at a mere 6ft (1.83m), and so Howard Baker remained the only non-Irish Briton to win the event since 1908. The French, led by Howard Baker's old rival, Pierre Lewden, had taken the first three places in the match against Great Britain at Stamford Bridge. Only six athletes in the World during 1927 cleared higher than Howard Baker's best of six years before, and they were all Americans. No European would surpass Howard Baker until 1932.

Anyone for tennis? Well, not quite *anyone*

Howard Baker at 35 years of age could very reasonably have decided to pack away his football-boots and concentrate on his rapidly expanding business interests. He had gradually taken over from his father greater and greater responsibility for the day-to-day running of the commercial activities, and there was always his tennis to provide a respite, keep him in trim, and no less importantly add another dimension to his social life. Nevertheless, he would happily keep turning out each winter for Corinthian through several more seasons to come, and his League and international adventures, though reduced, were by no means over.

Within a couple of years of discovering tennis, he had been confident enough of his abilities to start entering tournaments, deciding that because of his knee ailment, which was a legacy of his high-jumping days and had caused him further trouble as a goalkeeper, he would concentrate on doubles. The main attraction for him was the Northern Lawn Tennis Association tournament, which alternated between Manchester and the Liverpool Cricket Club courts across the road from Howard Baker's home at Aigburth throughout the 1920s and 1930s and which had drawn such a quality of entry over the years that it had justifiably come to be known as the 'Wimbledon of the North'. The Northern mixed-doubles event actually carried the 'All-England' title with it for many years until it was eventually transferred permanently to Wimbledon, and in 1924 Howard Baker's future partner, Billy Radcliffe, and Miss E.M. Beckingham were the winners. Howard Baker himself progressed to the third round of the men's doubles that year before going out.

A glance through the entry-lists for Wimbledon and other tournaments of the early 1920s is enough to show that lawn tennis appealed to a much narrower section of society than it does in the 21st century. Among those figuring, at least in the earlier rounds, in major tournaments of the late 1920s were such military men, serving or retired, as Colonel H.G. Moyes, Major C.F. Scroope, Lieutenant-Commander P.F. Glover and Lieutenant-Colonel A.N.W. Dudley, together with an array of aristocrats – Baron H.L. de Morpurgo, the Honourable Cecil Campbell, Lady Cholmondley and Baroness Van Reznick among them.

Baron de Morpurgo, from Italy, was adept enough to be seeded No.7 in the Wimbledon men's singles one year, but the titles went to the likes of Jean Borotra, the 'Bounding Basque' of France, and 'Big Bill' Tilden, of the USA, who had the resources to play wherever and whenever they wanted without the need of prize money to keep body and soul, forehand and backhand, together. Occasionally, players used pseudonyms, for whatever reason, and one of the most inventive was 'Fuller-Hope'.

The American academic, William J. Baker (no relation to Howard Baker), who in 1982 wrote a perceptive book about the development of sport in the Western world, explained of that era of the game, 'Even more than golf, tennis also continued to cater for the upper classes. Most tennis courts in the 1920s were still privately owned or attached to socially exclusive clubs. All the major tournaments were strictly amateur, a sure sign that players possessed independent wealth'. Like their counterparts in football and cricket, the tennis authorities were not at all averse to amateurs and professionals mingling, but there was not much real competition between them, and when a team of amateurs from Lancashire and Yorkshire met the professionals in their annual match in 1930 it was the amateurs who won 5–4. Jack Chamberlain, Jack Harrison and Henry Burrows, of the amateurs, had all played at Wimbledon but not with the greatest of distinction. Dan Maskell, who was a teaching professional at the Queen's Club, in London, and was later to gain fame as a television commentator, led the defeated team. Oh, I say!

There was only one international tournament of consequence for professionals in the early 1920s, and that was played in France, either at Beaulieu or Cannes, and has been described by the American writer, Ray Bowers, a shade dismissively as an event which 'provided entertainment for the Riviera's well-to-do seasonal population', with attendances of no more than 400 or so. It was won on six occasions by Karel Koželuh, who had been born in Prague in 1895 when it was part of the Austro-Hungarian Empire. Koželuh was an all-rounder in the Howard Baker mould, having played at centre-forward for the Austrian national football team and then after World War One for Czechoslovakia.

During the 1920s there was no Federer or Nadal, Williams sisters or Clijsters, or hundreds of other dedicated professionals touring the world, winning vast sums of money, watched by packed crowds and millions more on television. The idea of professional tennis as a highly competitive spectator sport was virtually unheard of until towards the end of the decade, and such professionals as there were made their living teaching the members of private clubs. One of them from the Queen's Club, in London, R.A. Nash, had enterprisingly been recruited to Liverpool in 1919 to help improve standards in Lancashire and Cheshire. 'If Northern lawn tennis was to be brought to something like the level of the game as played in the sunnier south, practical coaching was essential for the younger players', one of the Cheshire organisers sensibly told the local press, and Nash later wrote a series of articles in the *Liverpool Daily Post* which highlighted the particular needs for the game locally.

Nash said that the first priority was the provision of covered courts. The only ones in Liverpool were at the city-centre Racquets Club, and as he pointed out, 'That club is not for the many and cannot do a tithe of the work to be done if any real attempt is to be made for Liverpool to do the share in regaining British prestige in the lawn-tennis world'. Does this strike a familiar chord? The perceptive Mr Nash *was* writing more than 90 years ago! Even access for the general public to watch the game was limited, and Nash wondered, perhaps more in hope than expectation, 'if the days are about to dawn when the clubs, instead of keeping their grounds private, will make more suitable provision for spectators'. The *Liverpool Daily Post*, which gave an immense amount of coverage to the local tournaments, listing all the results from the first rounds onwards, enterprisingly took up this refrain and pronounced in an editorial in July of 1922: 'Up until recently the game was played almost exclusively by the leisured and professional classes. The clerk, the typist and the artisan had no opportunity of playing without involving a heavy expenditure in the provision of gear and the laying-out and equipment of courts'.

The grounds of Liverpool Cricket Club at Aigburth, which included the grass and hard-surface tennis-courts, had been opened up on Sundays – somewhat contentiously – but this, of course, was only for the benefit of the members. Some significant steps were being taken to redress the balance elsewhere in Liverpool as two of the major shipping concerns, Cunard and Cammell Laird, had set up sports clubs for their employees, bringing the game to a wider appreciation, but there was at the same time aggrieved correspondence to the press regarding limited facilities for the general public. One letter-writer, signing himself 'Old Racket', complained of having to start queuing at 5.30 in the evening to book a public court for the following afternoon at Harrison Park, in Wallasey, across the Mersey from Liverpool. Another frustrated player pointed out that two of the four public courts at Central Park, also in Wallasey, were permanently let out to a private club and often stood empty. The number of municipal tennis courts in Liverpool increased from 170 to 400 between 1921 and 1930, but clearly this was not enough to meet the growing demand.

The president of the Lancashire LTA was Lord Rochdale, later to be chairman of the council of the British Olympic Association and an arch-opponent of any form of financial compensation for taking part in sport. He was a prime mover in the BOA's resolution of 1927 that it was 'unanimously opposed to the participation in the Olympic Games of competitors who accepted broken time payment'. The Lancashire LTA had 36 affiliated clubs, which does not seem to be a great number for a county of that size, but the standard of play was high. Four of the men – Max Woosnam, Alexander Brew, Billy Radcliffe and Leslie Godfree – had reached the last 16 of the men's singles at Wimbledon in 1921 or 1922. Woosnam, as previously related, was one of the best known sportsmen the length and breadth of Britain, while Godfree shared in Wimbledon titles for the men's doubles and mixed doubles.

As a fellow-Liverpudlian of Howard Baker's and virtually the same age, Woosnam pursued a sporting career which was uncannily similar: most notably, footballer for England, Manchester City and Corinthian and Olympic and Wimbledon doubles champion. The two men came to know each other well in the 1920s and they shared the same philosophy. In his absorbing biography of Woosnam, published in 2006, the journalist, Mick Collins, wrote: 'He would never play sport for money, but we should not confuse that Corinthian ideal with the assumption that he never played for the glory. His desire to succeed and to triumph was as strong as that of any professional'. Howard Baker would have cried out, 'Hear! Hear!', had he read those words.

Woosnam won his Olympic gold at Antwerp in 1920, but after the 1924 Olympics, when the USA took all the titles, lawn tennis disappeared from the Olympic programme until 1988. The international tennis authorities' version of events is that they withdrew from Olympic consideration because they did not agree with the way in which the tournament was run. It's probably equally true that the International Olympic Committee were concerned that tennis was not as amateur as it purported to be.

Maybe one of the attractions which lawn tennis held for Howard Baker was that it was in the process of dramatic changes as the 1920s wore on. Players such as Borotra, Tilden and Suzanne Lenglen were transforming the game. The BBC featured tennis from its very earliest pioneering radio sports outside broadcasts in 1927. The weekly cinema newsreels familiarised the hundreds of thousands of film-goers with the appearance and style of the champions. The Wimbledon tournament was starting to attract sell-out crowds. One of the iconic photographs in a history of Wimbledon written by John Barrett in 2001 is of dozens of messenger-boys in natty uniforms and rakish pill-box hats queuing up outside the Wimbledon gates to collect entry-tickets on behalf of their well-heeled customers who didn't have the time or inclination to get there themselves. It was in that same year of 1927 that the first professional 'circuit' was set up in the USA, starring Madameoiselle Lenglen.

Tilden, according to John Barrett, 'introduced a new element of majestic technical authority in every department of the game, together with a commanding presence on the court, that ushered in a new era. He was the complete player – tall, athletic, capable of every shot in the game, a master of spin, a match player of unsurpassed skill and judgment'. Howard Baker would have appreciated all that expertise. With slight amendments, it's a description which could have been applied to his own skills as a high jumper and goalkeeper.

Borotra's forte (again according to John Barrett) was 'his charm, his liveliness, his sense of fun and his great respect for the traditions of the game'. He was 'the most charismatic player of the decade' and his party-piece was to occasionally complete one of his energetic leaps about the court by landing in the lap of any pretty girl who happened to be seated in the font row. Mlle Lenglen 'caused a sensation not only for her outstanding brand of free-flowing graceful tennis but also for her daring decision to discard the stays that were *de rigeur* among the women players of the day'.

Writing almost 30 years later, the tennis correspondent for *The Daily Mail*, Stanley N. Doust, himself a Southern men's doubles title-winner before World War One and a Northern winner in 1921, recalled with ardour the dramatic fashion change: 'Suzanne adopted the one-piece sleeveless dress. Material was silk; the skirt pleated and short – just below the knee. There was nothing that could go wrong. No worry about safety pins nor falling petticoats. It gave her freedom for her limbs, which the English costumes did not. She also introduced the bandeau to keep her hair tidy while playing. How I remember those bandeaux! Every day a different one, superbly chosen as to colours – and nobody could ever make a bandeau look so neat as Suzanne'.

Tilden turned professional and played a marathon series of matches against the Czech, Karel Koželuh, in the USA during 1931, winning the series 50 to 17. Sadly, both Tilden and Mlle Lenglen came to an unfortunate end. Tilden was a homosexual in an age when the subject was not even talked about in polite society, let alone tolerated, and died penniless and almost alone. Mlle Lenglen's life was cut short in 1938 by leukaemia.

By 1928 Howard Baker had improved his game sufficiently to play regularly alongside Woosnam and Radcliffe in the Lancashire team, and he would continue to be a mainstay of the county team for 10 years, by which time he was 46 years old. One of his most notable victories would be in partnership with Radcliffe at the Welsh covered-courts' championships in October of 1929. This tournament was held at the Craigside Hydro hotel in Llandudno, and the Radcliffe-Howard Baker pairing swept through their first three matches in straights sets and then beat Dr Ali Hassan Fyzee and Vincent Allman-Smith, who had played in the Davis Cup for India and Ireland respectively, in an intensely exciting and long-drawn-out final 8–6, 6–3, 6–8, 3–6, 6–3. 'One of the finest doubles games ever seen in the tournament', enthused the *Liverpool Daily Post*.

Having also played in the singles that week but losing in three sets to a former title-winner, H.V. Mander, Howard Baker was still as tireless as ever, turning out in goal for the Amateurs against the Professionals in the FA Charity Shield match at New Cross, Millwall, two days after his doubles success. Though the Amateurs lost 3–0, *The Times* said of him that he was 'as spectacular as ever and particularly fine in his dealing with the high shots'. There was plenty more football to come for him – but more of that later. Meanwhile, back on the Centre Court...

Again partnering Radcliffe, Howard Baker was to win the Welsh covered-courts' title at Craigside for a second time in 1931, and throughout the 1930s he continued to play regularly with a degree of success in the Northern outdoor event at Aigburth. The reference which had been made when the professional, Nash, had visited Liverpool in 1919 to the advantages of playing tennis in the 'sunnier south' had a grim irony to it because the Northern 'Wimbledon' was frequently disrupted by rain, and on occasions the finals could not be played and so the titles had to be shared. Aigburth had only three hard courts, and even by farming out matches to neighbouring clubs when the grass was too wet for play it was sometimes difficult to complete the programme.

Max Woosnam himself had figured prominently at Aigburth, winning the men's singles in 1926, and his spirit of 'playing for the glory' was often in evidence from his successors in later years. For the 1931 tournament there were entries from Belgium, Canada, Egypt, France, Germany and India, and Howard Baker was joined in the men's doubles by a fine player named Donald Greig, who had partnered Woosnam in the doubles at Wimbledon in 1923, but Greig could only get to the tournament by travelling overnight on the train from London. That day, to catch up on schedule, he played three singles matches, two doubles matches and a mixed doubles match and won all but the last – 110 games in all! The first two singles had taken place back-to-back and then Greig had snatched a brief nap before going back on court with Howard Baker. Despite all this, the pair won both their matches in straight sets, conceding only one game in the latter.

Greig and Howard Baker eventually lost in the semi-finals in three sets to a pair named D.A. Hodges and A.M. Wedd, and because of the rain only two finals could be decided on the Saturday. The men's singles was due to have been between the holder, John Olliff, who regularly ranked in the top six in England, reaching the fourth round at Wimbledon on five occasions, and later became lawn-tennis correspondent for the *Daily Telegraph*, and another leading player, Nigel Sharpe. Olliff generously conceded the title, and the two of them beat the conquerors of Howard Baker and Radcliffe in the doubles final. Howard Baker and his wife joined forces on a number of occasions for mixed-doubles matches and were regulars at the Northern tournament.

A splendidly graphic idea of Howard Baker's comportment on the tennis court was given by the correspondent for the *Liverpool Daily Post* when he covered the 1932 Northern tournament at Aigburth. The writer, whose name was so unlikely – V.A.S. Beanland – that it could surely only have been his real one and not a pseudonym (perhaps confirmed by the fact that he wrote a book entitled *Great Games and Great Players* under the same name), described a second-round doubles match in which, for once, Howard Baker and Radcliffe were on opposite sides: 'It was cut and thrust, volley and smash throughout, and some great shots were intermingled with not a few that illustrated keenness and enthusiasm rather than beauty and craft. Still, it was a rollicking match that was good for the solemnity of the centre court'. In other words, it would seem that Howard Baker played tennis rather like he did football – full of dash and fire, sometimes reckless, never dull.

The star that year was the Dutchman, Henk Timmer, still regarded more than 70 years later as one of the best players ever produced by his country, who was in regular attendance in the latter rounds at Wimbledon, having reached the last eight in 1927 and 1928, and who figured in three finals in an afternoon at Aigburth, playing 11 sets and 109 games in the course of 5½ hours! One of his earlier wins had been in the third round of the mixed doubles against the Howard Bakers. By 1934, which was the jubilee year of the Northern tournament, Howard Baker had started on what would be a highly distinguished administrative career in tennis by taking on the secretaryship, and in a rather stilted interview with the *Daily Post* (the reporter's transcription being the likely fault, rather than Howard Baker's mode of expression) he was quoted as saying: 'The number of entries in the championship events seems to indicate that the Northern lawn tennis tournament will revive this year those former glories which entitled it to be termed 'The Wimbledon of the North'.

Howard Baker also competed in the singles and doubles that year, and it didn't seem to effect his stewardship of the tournament, though as a highly successful businessman such duties would presumably have come as second nature to him. V.A.S. Beanland reported that 'it is a tribute alike to the interest in the 'Northern' of distinguished players, some of whom are old favourites at this meeting, while others are making their first appearance, and to the organising ability of the tournament committee, that every one of the 'billed' players has fulfilled the engagement'. Now into his 40s, Howard Baker was becoming an elder statesman of the courts, but he was by no means the only one, as an account of one of the 1934 doubles matches at Aigburth, again from the pen of Beanland, revealed: 'One wondered whether the guile of the 'old gentlemen' – one uses the term with great respect and only to indicate the handicap of forty odd years in one case and fifty in the other – would prevail against the stupendous 'kills' of the big men, who fought so strenuously that they were leading by five to three in the first set, but it was the younger pair who were worn down in the end'.

The 'old gentlemen' in this case were not Howard Baker and his partner E.A.G. Caroe, but the Indian pair who beat them, Dr Ali Hassan Fyzee, actually then aged 54, and Mohammed Sleem. The venerable Indians were a formidable combination, having reached the semi-finals of the Davis Cup and beaten Belgium, France, Greece, Holland, Romania and Spain over the years. Dr Fyzee, commended as the 'keenest of players and one of the most delightful personalities in the great world of lawn tennis', was a model of sartorial splendour on the court, wearing long trousers, as was the general custom among male players, and a long-sleeved shirt elegantly buttoned at the cuffs. By contrast, when a Jubilee celebration parade of tennis fashions through the ages was held at that same tournament, one of the ladies dashingly and daringly sported a pair of shorts.

Whatever impression she made, it paled into insignificance at the 1936 tournament when Howard Baker succeeded in enticing the World's leading player, Fred Perry, up to Aigburth to play an exhibition match on finals' day. Not only that but Perry brought with him his glamorous wife who was the Hollywood film actress, Helen Vinson. They had been married the previous September (and were to be divorced in 1940) and Mrs Perry had made a speciality on screen of playing the 'loose woman with an active romantic life' opposite Gary Cooper and Cary Grant, among others. Tall and distinguished looking, chic and elegant, with a pronounced southern drawl, she no doubt caused a sensation wherever she went during her weekend's visit.

Howard Baker's sumptuous house in Beechwood Road, so convenient to the tennis-courts, would have been the essential place to see and be seen in for every social climber in Aigburth that week of June 1936, and the gossip about Mr and Mrs Perry might even have taken a sensational turn. The couple were already drifting apart – she on call for the Hollywood studios, he on court no matter where – and when divorce proceedings were started she was to cite the 'extreme cruelty' of her husband in refusing to accompany her to parties, starting in May and June of 1936. Had it all happened 70 years later, *Hello!* magazine or *The Sun* would probably have made Mrs Perry an offer she couldn't refuse, but the Liverpool press politely ignored entirely the fact that a screen goddess was in their midst.

Fred Perry was the son of a Labour MP and had been born in Stockport and had played tennis for Cheshire against Lancashire in his earlier years. He and his family had lived briefly across the Mersey in tennis-starved Wallasey during World War One and he had attended the local grammar school. He actually lost his exhibition match to his fellow Davis Cup player, Pat Hughes, that afternoon at Aigburth, though no one worried too much about that. The World's No.1 since 1934, Perry controversially turned professional at the height of his career in 1937 and for many years afterwards was ignored by the lawn-tennis establishment, but he became reinstated as one of the universally-recognised great players of the game after the distinctions between amateurs and professionals had been ended. He lived to the age of 85, dying in 1995. Helen Vinson's film career came to a finish in 1945, but she had an even longer life than her ex-husband, dying in 1999 at the age of 92.

Perry was an all-rounder after Howard Baker's own heart. He had won the World table-tennis title in 1929 at the age of 19 and he was the first British tennis-player to train for that sport in a serious fashion. He joined the Arsenal football team at 9 o'clock every morning whenever he was in London, taking part in a physical-exercise programme which was more demanding than any other League club had adopted, and he regularly played in practice games and was adept at firing successful penalty-kicks past the regular Arsenal goalkeeper. Perry had been able to remain a World-touring amateur tennis player for so many years because the regulations were conveniently flexible and allowed him, for instance, to write and broadcast for payment so long as he wasn't commenting on his own games. 'Alas, we only had one Perry!', recalled *The Daily Mail* correspondent, Stanley N. Doust, of Britain's tennis fortunes in the 1930s. 'There was a terrific gap between him and the next best players'. Times never change.

Fred Perry's memorable appearance at Aigburth was something of a final fling not only for himself as an amateur player but for the tournament, and maybe there had been an element of wishful thinking on Howard Baker's part when he had talked bravely of reviving 'the Wimbledon of the North'. There had been an on-going controversy ever since 1925 when the organisers of the Manchester version of the Northern tournament played at the West Didsbury club had announced without warning that they wanted to take over complete control. The Northern had first been held in 1884 and it had become the custom that

Manchester and Liverpool – or more precisely, the West Didsbury and Aigburth clubs – would take it in turns to act as hosts, but in December of 1925 it was revealed by E.J. Sampson, the tennis correspondent of the *Manchester Guardian*, that West Didsbury had applied to the Lawn Tennis Association for permission to hold the following year's event even though Aigburth should by rights be the venue.

The West Didsbury bid was apparently supported by the Northern Lawn Tennis Council, and the club's honorary secretary, Walter Brownsword, claimed when asked about the matter a few days later for a follow-up report by Sampson that 'there was a greater reluctance among some of the best known players in the country to go to Aigburth than there was to come to Manchester'. Naturally, this side-swipe by Mr Brownsword was parried by the Aigburth secretary, E.J. Deane, who said he could produce 'letters from many famous players saying how they enjoy the Liverpool tournament'.

The solution offered by the LTA was that both clubs should henceforth hold separate events each year carrying the 'Northern' title, and as there were already some 200 open tournaments taking place annually in England this seemed at best an uneasy compromise. In any case, the dispute continued and for 1934 both clubs wanted the same dates in June, though the matter was resolved and the Aigburth event passed off happily enough with a good entry and some entertaining finals played in warm weather. Yet within five years the Liverpool connection came to an end, with the plans for 1939 shelved because of what E.J. Sampson reported as being 'lack of support and the difficulty of getting a sufficiently large entry of star players'. Ironically, the swan-song tournament of the previous year had enjoyed fine summer weather and the singles titles had both gone to World-ranked players: Kho Sin Kie, of China, who was also British hard-courts' champion that year and in 1939, was the men's winner; Hildegard Krahwinkel Sperling, described to this day as the second best German-born woman player in history after Steffi Graf, took the ladies' title.

Howard Baker's involvement with the game had already expanded to national level, as he was Lancashire's representative on the Lawn Tennis Association council from 1932 to 1936 and would be so again from 1945 to 1970. He was also a prominent committee-member for the British hard-courts' championships which had been instituted in 1924 and were to take place intermittently in Bournemouth from 1968 to 1995. The first of those Bournemouth tournaments was also the first of the 'open' era in the sport and Ken Rosewall, of Australia, received $2,400 for winning the men's singles, while Virginia Wade took nothing from her victory in the women's singles because she was still an amateur. In recognition of his contribution to the organisation of the game over so many years, Howard Baker was appointed an honorary life councillor to the LTA in 1971 and an honorary life vice-president in 1980.

Whatever the other fortunes of British tennis over the quarter-of-a-century or so since Howard Baker's death, he would have been heartened to learn that the game would be revived at international level in the city of his birth from 2002 onwards with an annual tournament in another leafy venue, Calderstones Park, less than two miles away from where he once lived and enjoyed so many of his own on-court ventures. He would certainly have enjoyed the range of conversation at the post-match socialising. The event would soon establish sufficient a reputation to provide a setting for one of the numerous successes of a future World No.1, Caroline Wozniacki. Her father had been a professional footballer in Poland who joined a Danish club. Howard Baker would have had fond memories, too, to relate of the five matches he had played on tour with the Corinthian club in Copenhagen in 1922 and 1928.

'WATCH IT, KING, YOU'RE DIVING', WAS THE WARNING, BUT THE WESTERN ROLL RULES ALL

British high jumping had not moved on at all perceptibly in the seven years since Howard Baker's retirement. As the 1928 Olympics in Amsterdam drew near, there was absolutely no prospect of any medal success in that event – or, for that matter, in any other of the jumps or throws. Captain F.A.M. Webster had persevered, continuing to produce a succession of training manuals which all conveyed the same message: that Britons were perfectly capable of mastering the necessary techniques, if only they had a mind to do so. Deaf ears?

The natural successor in the late 1920s to Howard Baker as a British high jumper ready to take on the Americans ought to have been Harry Simmons. He was spotted by the astute Captain Webster when sharing first place at the Public Schools' Championships at Stamford Bridge in April of 1927 aged just 16, and he improved five inches in a year under the Captain's tutelage to set a British junior record of 6ft 1in (1.86m) and then – still only 17 – was an Olympic finalist in Amsterdam.

Captain Webster later wrote at length about the coaching which he gave Simmons and said that on first sight the youngster had been 'simply a natural scissors jumper, which meant that he was relying upon such spring as he had been endowed with by nature'. Converted to a form of Eastern Cut-Off layout over the bar, Simmons was to continue competing for another seven years but never improved significantly after 1928 because of a knee injury which hindered his progress. This was a pity from the point of view of British athletics because he was one of the country's only two finalists in field events at those Olympics, placing equal 11th, and the overall results for Britain had a very familiar ring to them: two gold medals, two silvers and a bronze, and all of them earned on the track. Simmons took up a career as an RAF officer after learning the rudiments of high jumping at Taunton's School, in Southampton, and lost his life in a flying accident in 1944.

It seems that little consideration was given by Webster to the idea of teaching Simmons the Western Roll, though the evidence of its greater efficiency which had led to World records and Olympic titles was there for all to see. Webster makes little mention of this style of jumping in the complex and frankly somewhat pretentious book which he wrote in the late 1930s entitled, *Why? The Science of Athletics*, containing details of the training programme he devised by correspondence for Simmons. Webster simply describes the Western Roll as 'much discussed and often adversely criticised' but does not elaborate on this opinion.

The reason was most likely that Webster was concerned that some officials still regarded the Western Roll as a suspect form of diving over the bar, as Howard Baker may have done when he officiated at a meeting in 1925 at which the Olympic champion, Harold Osborn, competed. Even the next Olympic champion of 1928, Bob King, of the USA, had problems during his career convincing judges that his style was legitimate, and it rankled with him all his life. King, who had developed his skills on the West coast at Stanford University, in California, where the technique had originated almost 20 years previously, recalled shortly before his death in 1965: 'I never competed in an eastern meet that some official didn't badger me throughout the competition. They were always suspicious that a Western Roll jumper was slipping something over on them. I always felt I could have gone four or five inches higher if there wasn't an official always warning, 'Watch it, King, you're diving'.

The two other British representatives in the 1928 Olympic high jump were not much older than Simmons: Colin Gordon, also a finalist, was a 20-year-old Oxford undergraduate and Geoffrey Turner, 19, had already been twice Northern champion. Yet neither did these two fulfil their potential; as previously related, Gordon went abroad to teach at the age of 22 and Turner – after unofficially equalling Howard Baker's record 6ft 5in (1.96m) in 1929 – tragically died of septicaemia at 24.

Turner, who came from Warrington, in Lancashire, was 6ft 3½in (1.92m) tall and 12st 8lb (80kg) in weight, and so had the perfect physique for the event. His introduction to it had been remarkably similar to Howard Baker's, as he had first competed at a meeting at Broad Green, Liverpool, in May of 1926 and within three weeks had improved seven inches to take second place in the Northern Championships, just as Howard Baker had done 16 years before. Coached by the former RAF international, Sergeant-Major Miller, and encouraged by Howard Baker, Turner almost matched his mentor's feat by winning the Northern title for five successive years before his fatal illness. Turner also came from the same sort of entrepreneurial background as Howard Baker: his father owned a plumbing business in Leigh, in Lancashire, and the family could afford to employ a chauffeur.

It has ever been a scourge of the sport that youthful prodigies very often fall short of expectations when they graduate to the senior ranks, and there did seem to be a profusion of them in high jumping during the 1920s and 1930s, but then this was an event which required adequate facilities to hand and the opportunity to use them in daylight, and the situation in Britain in those decades was not much different to the one of half-a-century before described by Montague Shearman. Of the 32 high jumpers who represented Great Britain at the Olympic Games or in international matches during the 1920s and 1930s, 12 were university students and seven were serving in the armed forces or police. Only Howard Baker and Turner had graduated to that level from clubs in the North of England, though Scotland did rather better...and would eventually produce Howard Baker's successor as British record-holder. 'Eventually' meaning not until after World War Two.

As can be seen from the list which follows, there was no other Briton remotely in the same class as Howard Baker and Turner during the 1920s, and only one other man had surpassed Brooks and Rowdon from the previous century. The 'Oxbridge' influence is clearly apparent.

Best British High Jump Performers – as at the end of 1929
Excluding Irish jumpers from pre-1921
6ft 5in (1.96m) Benjamin Howard Baker (Liverpool H & AC) 1921
6ft 5in (1.96m) Geoffrey Turner (Earlestown Viaduct AC) 1929
6ft 3in (1.91m) Carl Van Geyzel (Cambridge University/Achilles C) 1925
6ft 2½in (1.89m) Marshall Brooks (Oxford University) 1876
6ft 2in (1.88m) George Rowdon (Teignmouth FC) 1887
6ft 2in (1.88m) Jack London (London University/Polytechnic H) 1927
6ft 2in (1.88m) Colin Gordon (Oxford University/Achilles C) 1929
6ft 1in (1.86m) Jack Probert (Polytechnic H) 1925
6ft 1in (1.86m) Arthur Willis (Army/Cambridge University/Achilles C) 1924
6ft 1in (1.86m) John Pendlebury (Cambridge University/Achilles C) 1927
6ft 1in (1.86m) Harry Simmons (London AC) 1928

Note: Carl Van Geyzel was from Ceylon (now Sri Lanka) and Jack London and Colin Gordon from British Guiana (now Guyana), but they all represented Great Britain at the Olympic Games. Van Geyzel was from a family of Dutch origin and was also a right-hand opening batsman who played twice for Ceylon and had a highest innings of 66 in 1927, though he had failed to gain his 'blue' in cricket while at Cambridge University.

If Captain Webster was not advocating the Western Roll in the latter 1920s, then probably no coach the length and breadth of the British Isles was doing so. There *were* coaches of exceptional ability such as Sam Mussabini, Bill Thomas, Alec Nelson and Albert Hill, all of whom were technically competent and dispelling the traditional image of the little man with a towel over his shoulder and a bottle of noxious liniment in his hand, but they were concerned with the track events, and most notably among them Mussabini, who died in 1927, had been adviser to Harold Abrahams. A typical case was that of Frank Wright, of the Birmingham club, Birchfield Harriers, who was appointed as a trainer to the Olympic teams of 1908, 1920 and 1924 and would be so again in 1928 and 1932, of whom it was said in his club's history: 'It would be wrong to assume that Wright and those like him were merely 'rub-down' men whose presence was of little importance. Those who knew him testify that he was a man of great presence who could instil confidence in the athletes'. Even so, Wright's forte was also the running events, as exemplified by Birchfield winning 16 of the 20 national cross-country team titles between the two World Wars – on the four other occasions the club had three second places and a fourth.

The earliest evidence to be found of a British high jumper using the Western Roll competitively is from the Olympic year of 1936 when an Oxford undergraduate, Arthur Selwyn, demonstrated it and later wrote about the event for an Achilles training manual, though it has to be said that his venture into 'Rolling' lacked conspicuous success. He had placed equal second in the Public Schools' high jump of 1935 at 5ft 5in (1.65m); the winner being a respected future administrator and coach, Arthur Gold, knighted in 1984 for his services to the sport, while Selwyn's best in inter-college competition was 5ft 6½in (1.69) and he was modestly equal third in the Inter-Varsity match won at 5ft 10in (1.77) by the Scotsman, Robert Kennedy, for Cambridge.

Selwyn then switched to the Eastern Cut-Off and cleared 6ft 2in (1.88) the next year before audaciously changing yet again to the Straddle in mid-competition during the Oxford

& Cambridge v Harvard & Yale match at the White City in 1939…and winning the event! Even so, he was not really of international calibre: 36 Europeans from 10 different countries cleared 1.90 (6ft 2¾in) or better that year, including two other Britons, John Newman, of Southgate Harriers, and Hubert Stubbs, of Polytechnic Harriers. The former eventually got over a respectable 6ft 4in (1.93) while serving with the RAF in 1943. The latter had set a Welsh record of 6ft 3in (1.91) in 1938 which stood until 1961.

Sir Arthur Gold had pre-empted Selwyn in attempting to learn the Western Roll when he was a pupil at Grocer's School, Hackney Downs, in London, though he never managed to use it in competition. Writing in 1963 in a most erudite fashion about the various techniques used in high jumping, he recalled with some amusement that he had 'learnt the Eastern Cut-Off in the early 1930s while trying to follow the Western Roll instructions in a text-book of the day, having at that time seen neither style outside the photos in magazines'. Sir Arthur was fond of recounting in later life the conversation he had after his competition against the American World record-holder and Western Roll exponent, Mel Walker, in Stockholm in 1937 which Walker, as one would expect, won rather easily. 'Arthur', remarked the victor consolingly, 'I sure like your style, but I sure like my height better'.

Sir Arthur had rather greater success as a coach than as an athlete. He was responsible for the progress of the two men who eventually beat Howard Baker's English record, Ron Pavitt (Straddle) and Peter Wells (Western Roll), and for the double Olympic silver-medallist, Dorothy Tyler, who changed from the Scissors to the Western Roll under Sir Arthur's guidance in 1951, 15 years after winning her first Olympic medal.

All credit to Selwyn for experimenting with the Straddle because on the eve of World War Two he had the chastening experience at the White City of watching a supreme 'Straddler', Lester Steers, of the USA, continue to clear height after height, finishing at 6ft 6in (1.98m) after Selwyn had done no better than 5ft 10in (1.77m). Hopefully, Selwyn had the consolation of coming to hear in 1941 while he was serving in the Royal Naval Volunteer Reserve that Steers had taken the World record up to 6ft 11in (2.11m). This would not be beaten until 1953. The face-downwards Straddle was another Californian invention, credited to a jumper named Norman Green as early as 1919, and known more familiarly in the USA by the less elegant description, the 'Belly Flop', but the successful development of it had not come about until 1930 onwards, initially by yet another Californian, James Stewart (not the film actor), and then by the 1936 Olympic silver-medallist, Dave Albritton, who had been a boyhood neighbour of Jesse Owens in Alabama.

Stewart set no World records and failed to qualify for the US team at the 1932 Olympics, but he clearly had a homespun way with words as effective as that of his Hollywood namesake. His renowned coach at the University of Southern California, Dean Cromwell, related a tale that Stewart had once told him about his upbringing. 'He said that he had been raised on a ranch and had needed considerable agility at the fences whenever the cattle went rampaging', Cromwell wrote. 'At first he took the barbed-wire fences with the scissors high-jump form, but he found this both destructive for the seat of his trousers and unpleasant anatomically. Finally, he was forced to use the technique of the belly roll, for with this form he could hold down the barbed-wire as he rolled over it. I never believed Jim's yarn, either!'

In the fullness of time it would be shown that the Straddle was clearly the most efficient form of high jumping before the advent of the Fosbury Flop, and maybe even its equal had it not been condemned to redundancy for the salient reason that the Flop is easier to teach and learn. The ultimate men's World record to be set with the Straddle would be in 1978 when Volodomyr Yashchenko, of the USSR, cleared 2.34m at the age of 19. The ill-fated Yashchenko never improved and sadly died of alcohol abuse at the age of 40. All of the records since his have been achieved by 'Floppers', and within a decade the only front-rank athlete still using the Straddle was the Olympic decathlon champion of 1988, Christian Schenk, from the German Democratic Republic. The women's record follows the same pattern because the supremely elegant Rosi Ackermann, also from the GDR, was the last of the 'Straddlers', taking the record up from 1.94m to 2.00m during the years 1974 to 1977. In more than 30 years since the performances of Yashchenko and Ackermann, the men's record has improved by 11 centimetres and the women's by nine. In other words, not a great deal.

Like so many of his contemporaries who found a less painful method of honing high-jump skills, Arthur Selwyn lost some of his best years to the war but had the distinction of equalling his personal best after a lapse of 10 years in 1947 and then again in 1949 at the age of 32. His excursions through the range of high-jump styles were assuredly no spur-of-the-moment decisions because the chapter which he contributed to the Achilles Club book, published in 1956, described the intricacies of the event in very great detail, though not, unfortunately, explaining how he came to try the Western Roll in the first place. He had been educated at Uppingham School, in England's smallest county of Rutland, and maybe there was an enterprising games master there who taught him the rudiments. Another possibility is that he learnt them from his university teammate, who was an American Rhodes Scholar, Milton Meissner, reputed to have 'jumped well over 6ft' before coming to Oxford. Meissner was an engineering graduate who presumably knew all there was to know about raising centres of gravity and had previously been a student at the aptly named LeHigh University in Pennsylvania.

Unfortunately for Britain's jumpers and throwers, a smoke-screen of success was thrown up by the runners at the Amsterdam Olympics. Douglas Lowe won the 800 metres for the second time. Lord Burghley won the 400 metres hurdles. The sprinters, Jack London and Walter Rangeley, each took silver and shared in a 4 x 100 metres relay bronze. There were top-six placings at 400 metres, 1500 metres, 110 metres hurdles and the 4 x 400 metres relay. The Americans, of course, did far better with 21 medals. Finland had 14, mostly from their distance-runners, and Germany – returning to the Games for the first time since World War One – had seven. Lowe and Burghley were both Cambridge products and London was, appropriately enough, at London University, while one of the 4 x 100 metres runners was an 18-year-old, Teddy Smouha, also at Cambridge, who embodied a devil-may-care spirit of the age by always wearing a monocle in competition, because he said it helped him to keep his head still, and trained by running behind his father's chauffeur-driven Daimler through Richmond Park. The other two relay medallists were, more prosaically, a bank employee (Rangeley) and a hotel worker (Cyril Gill).

Of the nine British competitors in the four jumps and four throws, only two of the high jumpers, Simmons and Gordon, qualified for finals. Sixteen years on from when Howard Baker had made his Olympic debut, nothing had changed regarding the balance of power in British athletics, and if anyone was hoping for a widespread improvement in the 1930s they were going to be sorely disappointed.

BENJAMIN HOWARD BAKER

At the 1932 Olympics in Los Angeles Great Britain's men and women athletes won two golds, four silvers and a bronze, and there was not a single competitor in any of the eight field events for men or three for women thought worthy of even sending to the Games. Of the 10 men involved (including the 4 x 400 metres relay runners), four were from Oxbridge and four from the armed forces. At the 1936 Games in Berlin, there were two golds and five silvers, but the only Briton among the 148 men from 25 different countries who qualified for field-event finals was a pole vaulter, Dick Webster, whose father was the coach, F.A.M. Webster. Yet the fact that there was talent to be found in Britain in those technical events was proven by a 16-year-old Dorothy Odam (later Mrs Tyler), who won one of those silver medals in the high jump and would still be competing at the Games 20 years later.

THE CORINTHIANS ON TOUR, AND EVEN DIOGENES WOULD HAVE LEFT HIS TUB TO SEE SUCH A MATCH

For another three seasons Howard Baker, as eager as ever for the fray, was to continue playing 20 or more matches a year for Corinthian. A record number of goals was to be accumulated by his teammates during 1927–28 – 152 in 31 fixtures, to be precise – but these figures were boosted by the customary 'cricket scores' against some of the lesser opposition. The season had started auspiciously with a 4–0 win in a Wednesday evening match with Arsenal, reduced to 35 minutes each way because of impending darkness (no floodlights in those days), and as it was a benefit game for one of the Highbury coaching staff it was probably not too serious an affair. Certainly, Arsenal fielded several reserve players, but the correspondent for *The Times* was adamant in his view of the game: 'It was a splendid performance on the part of the amateurs, and they gave as fine a display of football as one could wish to see'. Despite the score-line Howard Barker was still required to do 'some brilliant things in goal'. At the age of 35 his skills seemed to remain undiminished.

Corinthian were then chosen to play the FA Cup holders, Cardiff City, in the Charity Shield match at Stamford Bridge in October, again on a Wednesday, and did well to hold the Welsh professionals, who were on the attack for three-quarters of the match, to 2–1. In goal for Corinthian that day was A.M. Russell, the Cambridge graduate who would make three intermittent England amateur appearances in four seasons. Then followed a 45-goal avalanche for Corinthian in their next six fixtures, including wins over the Southern Amateur League (10–1), Oxford University (10–3 and 6–1) and Wiltshire (8–2). A 6–2 defeat of Cambridge University came next early in December in which, despite the margin of victory, Howard Baker 'performed wonders' in goal. The sporting news in his Monday-morning newspaper after that match would have made nostalgic reading for him because Everton were now leading Division One and Chelsea headed Division Two.

Against a Division Three South team, Millwall, at their New Cross ground on 26 November, Corinthian had lost 4–2 but had only 10 men throughout after one of their players was delayed by fog. Howard Baker 'kept goal splendidly, having absolutely no chance with any of the four shots that passed him', reported *The Times*, and running out to clear during a Millwall attack he was almost beaten by one shot 'which no one else but Howard

Baker could have reached'. Queen's Park Rangers, also in Division Three South, were beaten 4–3 in December and Howard Baker was at his best in goal as he 'fielded all kinds of shots with the greatest ease and on several occasions took the ball right off an incoming forward's foot'. Then after yet another huge win by 11–3 against Howard Baker's former club, Northern Nomads, the post-Christmas tour was cut short because of snow and frost and both matches that could be played were lost, to Queen's Park on a frozen ground and then to Manchester United.

The FA Cup draw for the first round proper took Corinthian to New Brighton, the Wirral seaside resort with which every Merseysider was familiar, and no doubt Howard Baker and his colleagues thought that there was a very reasonable chance of success. New Brighton were currently an undistinguished 15th in Division Three North, having lost the previous Saturday 3–2 to an even more modest side, Ashington, whose rare victory lifted them out of last place in the table. Because of a required change of colours, Corinthian were resplendent in shirts of gold, white and purple stripes instead of their usual plain white for the first time in their history, but the effect was rather spoiled by the heavy rain that fell throughout and by the performance of a particular player on the home side. It was a rare occurrence, but Howard Baker was outshone that day by his opposite number on a pitch that was 'a lake of grey treacherous mud'.

'Let it be said at once that one man, McHaffy, the New Brighton goalkeeper, was alone responsible for the summary ending of Corinthian Cup hopes in 1928, and his name is worthy to be placed on record in any history of the club', wrote Norman Creek, who did not play in the game. 'Throughout the whole of the first half, the Corinthian forwards and Chadder bombarded his goal, but only once did they succeed in placing the ball in the net. Two of his many saves, from Ashton, who had broken right through, were truly magnificent, and his anticipation and cat-like agility nullified all the fine approach work of the amateurs'. New Brighton won 2–1, though the Corinthian army officer, Hegan, was for once wayward in his shooting and missed a gift chance in the closing minutes which could have forced a draw.

'McHaffy' was, more accurately, Bertie Mehaffy, the thinning-haired New Brighton captain, whose background was steeped in a goalkeeping tradition. Born in Belfast in 1895, and christened Joseph Alexander Cuthbert, he had played as a teenager for Belfast Celtic in the Irish League and was in the championship-winning teams of 1914–15 and 1919–20. He had a single cap for Ireland against Wales in 1921–22 (a 1–1 draw in Belfast) and had trials with Everton and Tottenham Hotspur without ever playing in the first teams before establishing himself at New Brighton. All of his four brothers were also goalkeepers – two of them, like Bertie, representing the Irish League, and another was his understudy at New Brighton – and a cousin was the illustrious regular Ireland and then Northern Ireland goalkeeper in the 1920s and through to 1936, Elisha Scott.

Interestingly, Mehaffy and Howard Baker had distinguished themselves on opposing sides eight seasons previously in a Central League match in which Liverpool reserves had beaten Everton reserves 3–2. The *Liverpool Echo* had then reported that 'although two goals in arrears, Everton played hard to reduce the lead, and after Howarth got the second point Howard Baker alone kept them from equalising. This player played a great game in the last few minutes, and Everton's Irish recruit in goal also played well'. Regardless of his side's FA Cup defeat, Howard Baker had the lion's share of attention from the inventive Merseyside newspaper cartoonists: George Green, in The *Echo*, caricatured him in fancy dress, looking spick and span despite the downpour, and Bert Wright, in the *Evening Express*, struck a similar note, describing the Corinthian goalkeeper as looking like 'the Lord Mayor of football'.

The author of the daily sports column in the *Liverpool Daily Post* who signed himself 'John Peel', which could just conceivably have been his real name, had enthusiastically previewed the FA Cup match on the Saturday morning: 'New Brighton are fortunate in having Corinthian as visitors. Their fight against Newcastle United last season showed that they are worthy opponents for the best of the Football League clubs. The amateurs are deservedly popular and probably the Rake-lane ground will be taxed to-day as it has never been before. The traditional Corinthian game has a great appeal and New Brighton will find it a severe task to overcome the skilful, lusty and always sporting plan of campaign which the amateurs are sure to adopt. They revel in the grand shoulder-to-shoulder charge, and altogether the struggle is likely to be a memorable one'. This was a fine tribute, and nicely written, leaving little doubt in the readers' minds that John Peel thought that the Corinthians would win. D'ye ken?

The match summary on the following Monday by 'Bee' was a marvellous piece of journalism – thoughtful, balanced, informative, and again favoured towards the illustrious Londoners rather than the local team. 'Bee', whoever he was, also gave a great deal of attention to the Corinthian style of play, despite their defeat, and did he but know that his words were as much a requiem as a tribute. Corinthian, 'Bee' was saying, were beaten as much by their rigid adherence to old-fashioned principles as they were by the superior staying-power of the professionals, and the proof of his analysis was that while there were still one or two FA Cup flourishes to come from Corinthian in future years there was never to be an acclaimed 'Cup run'. This is what he wrote:

'The Corinthian had the misfortune to play on a cramped and confined space, with a pronounced slope, and on a heap of mud. They have a style all their own and it would be churlish to imagine that they could at a given moment change their style of play. They do not want to change; their main idea is to play football and to keep the ball where it should be – on the ground. The fact that it is heavy going is no justification for any Corinthian player adopting kick and rush methods for the purpose of gaining a victory. The essence of the amateurs' game is that the ball should be worked in rather close space, and that combination shall reign where pace in the ranks of the professionals is all too frequently the main test of ability.

'The amateur does not train in the accepted term. He honours his club by keeping fit, but the professional has to show his fitness by his ability to weather a storm of rain and mud such as we experienced on Saturday and play at full pace to the ninetieth minute. Keeping the ball on the ground was not, in such conditions, the wisest way of getting through an English Cup tie'.

There were 9,256 spectators packed into the rain-lashed Rake-lane ground that afternoon, paying on average the equivalent of about 80 new pence each, and altogether the attendance at the 32 FA Cup ties played that day was 771,092, which works out at just over 24,000 a game – including 28,500 across the Mersey at Anfield for Liverpool against Darlington. If these statistics don't sound too impressive, then remember that this was 1928 and 80 new pence would have represented a very significant proportion of a working man's weekly wage.

It was a measure of the abiding appeal of the Corinthians that Pathé should choose to feature this match in their weekly distributed newsreel which went to cinemas throughout the country – 1928 was the year in which the first all-talking feature film was produced, and UK cinema admissions per year would increase hugely to 903 million in the early 1930s, an average of about 22 per head of the population. The Pathé coverage of the New Brighton v Corinthian Cup tie lasts less than two minutes and is a miniature classic of its kind. As is customary, the opening shot is of the players running on to the pitch, though the variation to the theme this time is that they are led out, incongruously, by a man dressed in a white suit and matching hat and brandishing a black umbrella aloft to protect him from the downpour. Next is the obligatory panoramic view of the crowd – seemingly all men, and all wearing either flat caps or trilbies. The conditions underfoot are appalling; the playing surface is a mud-patch, pure and simple, with not a blade of grass to be seen, and yet the standard of football, or at least the brief snatches which are shown, is surprisingly good in spite of all that.

Corinthian demonstrated that they could still out-play League opposition a fortnight later, on 28 January, when they walloped 5–0 a full-strength Southampton side which would finish the season 17th in Division Two. Howard Baker 'was absolutely safe in goal and showed good judgement in coming out to save' and was then named for the England amateur trial at Ilford at the beginning of February, along with clubmates Chadder, Creek, Hartley and Taylor, but he was in the junior side, entitled The Rest, and the man who had made his debut in goal against Ireland the previous November, Norman Jones, of the Aldermere club in Manchester, was at the opposite end. With the match ending in a 2–2 draw, Howard Baker might then have thought after the final whistle that his chance of another cap had gone; though, as it happened, Jones was one of only three of the England team at the trial chosen against Wales the next month. There was a reference in the trial match report in The Times to Howard Baker having 'atoned for two bursts of recklessness by bringing off some remarkable saves', but that might not have been atonement enough for the selectors.

Having put their FA Cup setback behind them, Corinthian then lost only one more match all season, running up more of those 'cricket scores' – nine goals against the RAF, 12 against Charterhouse School – and beating Queen's Park by the widest margin since 1903, 5–1, aided by Howard Baker saving a penalty. Clearly, the ancient tradition of the goalkeeper stepping aside in such a situation and letting the opposition tap the ball into the undefended net had by now been abandoned as just a shade too sporting a gesture even for a Corinthian.

To set against that gratifying win, the season's six defeats included four against English League sides, and the club historian, Norman Creek, was to emphasise the point that there was now a growing divide between amateurs and professionals. Something of a shock wave was felt among the Corinthian ranks in February when for the first time one of their members actually turned professional. He was the inside-forward, Frank Hartley, who signed up with Tottenham Hotspur a week after captaining The Rest against England in the amateur international trial, having already played unpaid for the club over the previous two seasons. Hartley was clearly not drummed out of Corinthian in disgrace because his name still appeared on the list of members six years later. Hartley was from Oxford, but he was 'town' not 'gown', having played for Oxford City, not the university.

The end-of-season Corinthian tour was to Denmark and Germany, avoiding the Harwich-to-Esbjerg crossing which had been so turbulent six years before, and of which 'memories had become more vivid with the passing years', according to the club history. Instead the players took the shorter sea passage to Flushing and then continued by road to Copenhagen. As the only two among the party of 13 who had experienced that sea voyage of 1922 were Howard Baker and one of the full-backs, Colin Hunter, it seems likely that one or other of them had the say in opting for the different route this time. We can safely speculate that it was Hunter, on the assumption that Howard Baker's leisure-time sailing expertise and war-time naval service would have strengthened his sea-legs and the prospect of however protracted a ferry crossing would not have bothered him.

The opening match in Denmark was a 1–1 draw, but injuries to two players meant that all remaining 11 had to turn out for the second game and that was lost 6–3. If any zealous student of Corinthian history among the defeated team was counting, it was the first time in the 193 overseas fixtures which had been undertaken in 14 different countries since 1897 that so many goals had been conceded by Corinthian in a game. Still, it was also reported of the team's arrival that 'many were the greetings exchanged with old friends when the Danish capital was safely reached', and the evening's hospitality would have cheered everyone up. Boosted by late-arriving recruits, two subsequent wins and then a draw with a Hamburg team which ominously 'all looked splendidly fit, and included an international centre-forward who really was a first-class player' brought the tour to a satisfactory conclusion.

The Olympic Games in Amsterdam that summer seemed to indicate that Great Britain was steadily slipping down the sporting order of merit. There had been 14 gold medals for Britain in Antwerp in 1920 and nine in Paris in 1924, but there were only three this time round, and all of them to the credit of Cambridge University. In athletics two Cambridge graduates, Douglas Lowe and Lord Burghley, won the 800 metres and the 400 metres hurdles respectively, while the other win in rowing was achieved by the Trinity College coxless fours crew. Athletes contributed three other medals, all in the sprint events, but there were no British footballers in Amsterdam, and no Europeans at all in the final, in which Uruguay beat Argentina. In the other team game in which Britain had once been all-powerful, water polo, the title was won by Germany, back in the Games for the first time since the end of World War One, and Britain was fourth.

The Corinthian fixture-list for the 1928–29 season followed a familiar pattern, with 20 matches before the end of the year, including the customary midweek visits to the more reputable public schools – Repton, Shrewsbury, Malvern, Westminster, Wellingborough (11–5 to Corinthian!) and Winchester (14–0!) – and high-scoring wins against the United Hospitals (9–1), Northampton Town (4–3) and the familiar Cup tie rivals, Brighton & Hove Albion (6–4). Oxford University were beaten 7–2, with all six of the goals in the first half coming from N.W.B. Stone, who was a senior manager at the Bank of England. On Boxing Day against an Isthmian League selection including five England amateur internationals, at the 'Old Spotted Dog' ground in the east end of London, Corinthian registered all of their goals in the last quarter-of-an-hour to win 4–2 after Howard Baker had apparently 'performed miracles' to keep the score down before then. The really serious business began with the FA Cup tie at Norwich on 12 January.

It's to the credit of the administrators of both amateur and professional football in Britain that throughout this era they not only allowed but welcomed these regular interchanges between those who were paid to play and those who turned out only for the fun of it. This could not possibly happen in athletics, where the hierarchy continued to be dead set against any relaxing of the draconian rules regarding amateurism. Even such worldly men of influence as Harold Abrahams and Douglas Lowe, Olympic champions both, and now qualified in law and in the forefront of the management of the sport, led the virulent opposition to the simple and practical introduction of 'broken time' payments to compensate those athletes who, unlike Abrahams and Lowe during their active careers, did not have generous opportunities for training and competition. Sir Harry Barclay, the long-serving AAA honorary secretary, was to stand down in 1931 and propose Lowe as his successor. Lowe stayed in the job for the next seven years, ensuring that the amateur status quo was preserved, and nothing would change for almost half-a-century after that.

The contrast in attitudes between the two sports was exemplified when Norman Creek was to reflect at length about the Corinthian club's original radical decision to change their constitution and take part in Cup competition. 'All true lovers of football welcomed the resolve of the Corinthians, as the foremost exponents of the amateur game, to enter the field with the professionals', he wrote. 'It is not to the good of any game that amateurs and professional players of it should be entirely separated, for both stand to gain by playing more frequently together. The Cup is not entirely without romance, and it has, too, a fine simplicity. Here is no long-drawn-out pursuit of points throughout a whole season, but a battle of sudden death. It is, moreover, a campaign in which finesse is often counteracted by speed and dash; and in the eighteen cup-ties in which the Corinthians have taken part these qualities of enthusiasm have been well displayed'.

Even so, Edward Grayson, the subsequent Corinthian historian, described the years from as early as 1927 onwards as 'this period of the Corinthian twilight', and he explained this in technical terms: 'The old five-in-a-line frontal attack of the forwards mixing close and long passing still prevailed. Once they resorted to the 'W' formation and the third-back strategy in the thirties their distinctive style went, and with it their reputation'. Comparing the present Corinthian era with that of the beginning of the century, when the legendary centre-forward, G.O. Smith, was in his prime, Grayson added that the Corinthians 'were still a national asset, in more ways than one, but representatively in the main for only amateur occasions. In the thirty years from G.O.'s time, the professionals had so improved their standards as to well squeeze the amateurs from the full international sides, except against the continental pupils who were then in their soccer infancy'.

In what was tantamount to a final fling, Corinthian overwhelmed their Cup tie opponents, Norwich City, 5–0 despite playing most of the 90 minutes with only 10 men after their winger, Jenkins, was injured. The crowd was a record at over 20,000, packed so close to the touch-line that there was space for only two or three steps to be taken by the players assigned the corner-kicks, and there was no summary of the game more concise than Creek's opinion of Howard Baker that he was 'in fine form during the first few minutes when the issue was uncertain but afterwards had little to do'. A slightly divergent account in The Times was to the effect that he 'did not have a lazy afternoon but got through all his work with that gymnastic competence which is the delight of every crowd'. Graham Doggart scored the third goal and it was described by Creek as 'the finest individual one registered for the Corinthians in any Cup tie – after dribbling from left to right and beating three opponents in the process'. The Corinthian team that day was Howard Baker; A.G. Bower, Knight; Whewell, Chadder, F.H. Ewer; Jenkins, C.T. Ashton, Stone, Doggart, Hegan.

A fortnight later Corinthian – having revelled in a joyous romp the intervening Saturday, 15–4 against the luckless Army XI – met West Ham United, then fourth from last in Division One, in the next round of the Cup at Upton Park but came up against another superlative goalkeeping display, just as they had at New Brighton the previous season, and lost 3–0. The stumbling-block this time was provided by Ted Hufton, who was a contemporary of Howard Baker's, having been born in Nottinghamshire in the same year of 1892, and who was also one of those many players who suffered from the machinations of the England selection committee, having made his international debut at the age of 30 in 1923 and then being called up for the last of his six appearances in 1929. Against Northern Ireland in 1927 he had broken his forearm in a collision with another player.

Howard Baker, for once, was at fault for the first West Ham goal, losing his grasp on the ball after he had saved a slithering shot on the treacherous and heavily sanded pitch, and there is a sequence in the Pathé cinema newsreel coverage which catches the moment exactly as the ball inexplicably slips out of his hands and rolls into the net, and he turns to watch aghast. The overall conclusion by Creek, who had replaced Jenkins in the Corinthian side, was that 'West Ham fully deserved their victory, but the margin of three goals undoubtedly flattered them'. The report in *The Times* was positively apologetic in tone in its detailed description of what was considered to be the decisive West Ham goal:

'By inference it would be grossly unfair to a fine goalkeeper like B. Howard Baker to say that the difference in goalkeeping did as much as anything to decide the issue…but, certainly, it was a disastrous slip by their goalkeeper that started Corinthian on the downward track. Watson gave his right-wing man, Yews, a chance to shake off the defence just sufficiently to get in a fast daisy-cutting, or rather sand-disturbing, shot. Baker plunged at the ball, as it all but reached the goalpost nearest to Yews. He appeared to have well smothered it and had risen to his feet before the crowd saw the ball reappear from behind his elbow and then trickle slowly but surely over the goalline. It was a quite horrible moment'.

Howard Baker might thus have been pleasantly surprised, a month past his 37th birthday to find himself back in the England amateur team for the match against Scotland in Leeds on 16 March, especially as he had not played in the previous month's 1–1 draw with Wales in Brighton, nor even in the trial match beforehand in which England had beaten The Rest 9–1, but as Norman Jones had been in goal for The Rest that put paid to his international career. The chosen side against the Scots was as follows:

Howard Baker; F.J. Gregory (Millwall), E.H. Gates (London Caledonian); Paymaster Lieutenant-Commander C.E. Glenister (Royal Navy), A.H. Chadder (Corinthian), J.G. Knight (The Casuals); L. Morrish (Dulwich Hamlet), E.I.L. Kail (Dulwich Hamlet), C.T. Ashton (Corinthian), A.G. Doggart (Corinthian), Lieutenant K.E. Hegan (Army/Corinthian).

Thus four of the players were selected from Corinthian, but the club's influence on the English amateur game extended beyond that because Lt Hegan was, of course, a Corinthian when his military duties allowed and Lt-Cdr Glenister, from the cadet-training ship, HMS *Erebus*, at Devonport, and Knight also turned out occasionally for the club. As eight of the Scots were from Queen's Park it was almost an extension of the annual fixtures between the two bastions of amateurism, or rather compensated for it, because it had proved impossible to arrange a match between them that season. England won 3–2.

Corinthian played no more than another seven domestic matches in the last three months of the season, including a defeat in Liverpool by Everton, 2–1. The match with Everton came about because the sixth round of the FA Cup that day had left the League side without a fixture, but despite being almost at full strength their winning goal did not come until the very last kick of the match. The reporter for *The Liverpool Daily Post* sensed incentive lacking among the Everton players, and for once it was Corinthian who were the more workmanlike against professional opposition: 'Corinthian took the contest rather more seriously than did Everton, for they played with commendable earnestness and spirit throughout'. Howard Baker gave an admirable display and saved a penalty. As was so often the case in that era when football-pitches were at the mercy of the winter weather, the surface was entirely unsuitable for skilful play – half of it was treacherous icy slush and the other half bone hard. The Corinthians had arrived lacking one of their half-backs, but a Northern Nomad, H. J. Moore, who lived locally, generously stepped into the breach.

Enjoyable as that return visit to Goodison Park must have been, Howard Baker and his colleagues were bound to welcome a brief respite from the British weather at the end of March by heading off to a sunny clime. The fashionable Mediterranean resort of Cannes was the destination, and the Franco-British celebrations of the 25th anniversary of the signing of the *Entente Cordiale* political agreement between the two countries was the reason for the trip...or maybe, of course, just a cheerful pretext.

En route a match was played against Club Français, at the Stade Buffalo in Paris, but even the most gregarious of the Corinthians must surely have begun to wonder whether the delights of sightseeing and night-clubbing in the French capital were sufficient to compensate for yet another bone-hard and grass-less pitch set inside a banked cement cycle-racing track. The match was lost 2–1 and Norman Creek was to note in his club history that 'it must have been one of their worst exhibitions on the Continent'. No sooner had the overnight train journey to Cannes been completed by the party of 14, which included Howard Baker, Creek, Doggart, Hegan, the Reverend A. V. Hurley of Portland, Dorset, playing on the wing, and the future Test cricketer, R. W. V. Robins, than they were regaled by the sight on the tennis-courts in their hotel grounds of Mrs Phyllis Satterthwaite beating a future Wimbledon champion, Fraulein Cilly Aussem, of Germany, in the final of the ladies' singles tournament which formed part of the festivities.

Actually, this match might not have provided too exciting a spectacle for the Corinthian onlookers. Mrs Satterthwaite had played in a Wimbledon final, though that had been back in 1921 when she had had the dubious privilege of facing the invincible Suzanne Lenglen, and the English lady was a dogged sort of player with a preference for endless baseline rallies and the odd drop shot every now and then to briefly alter the tempo. Rather unkindly, the correspondent for *The Times* had described the vain struggle against the wiles of Mlle Lenglen by Mrs Satterthwaite as being like 'a slow bowler pegging away at Hobbs on a perfect wicket'. Once in a match in Italy, she had been involved in a rally which lasted 'something over 300 shots'.

Two matches in successive days – football, their *raison d'etre*, not golf or tennis – proved too much for the Corinthians, or maybe it was a matter of there being rather too much of the *cordiale*. After a 3–2 win over the Cannes club, Corinthian met a South of France selection which was made up of six French players, two English, two Italians and one Czech and lost 4–2. The football didn't amount to much, and for Norman Creek the abiding memory of the opposition was that 'although this cosmopolitan team spoke numerous languages, they one and all swore at each other and the referee in good solid English'.

For the post-match celebrations the director of the town casino provided a decorated carriage so that the players could take part in the traditional annual 'battle of flowers', and could it be that his benevolence was in recognition of the frequent visits which had been made to his tables by his Corinthian guests? A reception to view the fireworks and the illuminated battleships off shore was followed by a banquet at the Sporting Club that night and a leisurely train journey back to Paris and then on to London the next day. It was the last foreign tour that Howard Baker would make with the Corinthians.

When Geoffrey Green, the football correspondent for *The Times* came to write about the history of the Corinthian club at the time of its 75th celebrations in 1957 he waxed lyrical about the effect these tours had had on playing standards in the countries visited: 'Many of the countries were merely in the kindergarten stage when Corinth descended upon them with football, text book and code of behaviour. They helped to water the flower of football artistry which is so much a part of the continental and South American – certainly of the Central European people. That many of the nations did not fully imbibe the code of ethics was shown when the heat was on in after years. But of their playing skills and of their fount of inspiration there could be little question. After all, four of them in the last 25 years have reached the Final of the World Cup – Hungary (the losers of 1938 and 1954), Czechoslovakia (the losers of 1934), Brazil (the losers of 1950) and Germany (the World champions of 1954)'. A year after those words were written Brazil beat Sweden, another of the Corinthian destinations in the past, in the 1958 Final.

Overblown as Green's comments might be thought to be – and, after all, he did not mention that neither Uruguay nor Italy, who had each won twice in the first four World Cup tournaments from 1930 to 1950, had been graced with a visit by the Corinthians – there was no doubting the effect the club could have on its host countries. As an instance, a delightfully warm tribute to the continuing appeal of the Corinthians was to be made by the Swiss press when the club went there for the second successive year in 1931, with H.M. Garland-Wells as Howard Baker's replacement in goal, and again beat both of the country's leading sides, Young Boys Berne and Grasshoppers Zurich. 'Let us hope that the Corinthians will now, like birds of passage, return to our country every year', enthused one newspaper columnist. 'We prefer them by far to the professionals from their country, who for obvious reasons never take their Continental matches seriously, and who, unlike our guests of Easter Monday, never take the field with the motto 'Work while you work and play while you play'. Even Diogenes himself would have left his tub to see such a match'.

Monty Garland-Wells was Howard Baker's natural successor as goalkeeper in more ways than one because he additionally played for a League club, Clapton Orient (later to be renamed Leyton Orient), and had proved good enough to win an England amateur cap in 1930. He was also a capable cricketer for Oxford University and Surrey, scoring 6,068 runs and taking 185 wickets between 1927 and 1939. Like so many of his Corinthian colleagues, he had his contribution to make to society in a wider sphere – though in this case not of his own making. During World War Two the term 'Garland-Wells' was used as a code name for Field-Marshal Montgomery ('Monty', of course). Presumably no German intelligence experts had been socialising with the Corinthians in Berne or Zurich during 1930 or 1931.

The England professionals, of whom the Swiss observer was so dismissive, had won 17 successive matches against Continental opposition from 1920 onwards, though all but three of these had been against Belgium or France. Then England's fortunes had changed in the ensuing fixtures before the Corinthians had happily set off on their second Swiss tour – a 4–3 loss to Spain, draws with Germany (3–3) and Austria (0–0) and the first defeat by France (5–2). It was not until 1938 that Switzerland and England (with a youthful Stanley Matthews but no Corinthians in the team) met and the Swiss won 2–1 in Zurich. The 'birds of passage' flew no longer.

A couple of weeks before the Corinthians had gone off on their spree to Cannes towards the end of the 1928–29 season, Howard Baker had made a move which must have surprised everyone who knew him. He signed for yet another Football League team, and one which did not possess the *cachet* of those whose ranks he had previously adorned. This was no Liverpool, Everton or Chelsea. This was Oldham Athletic, then languishing at the foot of the Second Division. His friends and his fellow-Corinthians might well have chorused, 'Oldham!? Whatever possessed you!?'

The answer, it seems, was 'pure charity'. Despite their poor showing in the League, Oldham had provided England with their goalkeeper for the two previous home internationals of the season against Northern Ireland and Wales, and as these had both been won it seemed logical, even allowing for the eccentricities of the national selection committee, that he would be in the team again for the final match with Scotland. The man in question had a splendidly emphatic name which might have been more appropriate to a centre-forward in the earlier highly aggressive days of the game – Jack Hacking. He was duly chosen and a week beforehand the local newspaper had announced in conspiratorial terms Howard Baker's signing as a stand-in, though it had actually taken place almost a month earlier. Hacking's England debut against the Irish had been on a Monday evening the previous October at Liverpool's Anfield ground, and it seems perfectly conceivable that Howard Baker would have gone along out of interest to watch the match.

The correspondent for *The Lancashire Evening Telegraph*, under the pen name of 'Pilgrim', reported of Howard Baker's recruitment to Oldham: 'The secret known only to a handful of us has been well guarded, for Baker put his pen to the necessary forms rather late on Saturday night, March 16; the actual signing, I understand, being done at a Manchester railway station in the presence of Mr Robert Mellor, the Boundary Park secretary, and an official of the Athletic club who acted as witness. The papers were transmitted in time to the League authorities' offices at Preston so that the amateur will be available this season, if required.

'We understand that there is no intention that Baker shall become a reserve player for Athletic. The idea behind the move is that if the club, through an international call or sickness or injury, are deprived of the services of Jack Hacking, the amateur would step into the breach and fill the vacancy. Considering the dangerous position in which the team is in the Second Division table, it is felt that no risks can be taken, and there is justification for the implied fact that neither of Athletic's present reserve professional goalkeepers has yet arrived at a sufficiently high standard'.

'Pilgrim', clearly being fed the story by Oldham Athletic officials, and maybe as a coveted 'exclusive' for his newspaper, made the further observation, 'It was only after some persuasion that the well-known amateur consented to sign. However, now that it has been accomplished, the followers of the Boundary Park club will learn with satisfaction that Baker has come forward and in such a sporting fashion is willing to lend a helping hand if it is needed'. The economic situation in the town of Oldham suggests that Howard Baker's choice of what might have seemed to be a 'poor relation' of the Football League was not as unlikely as it may now seem. With a population of 140,000 in 1930, and situated some seven miles north-east of Manchester's city centre, Oldham was at the time situated in Lancashire and had been described as 'the textile boom town of the Industrial Revolution'. The cotton business was still thriving, with the largest textile factory in the UK built there in 1928, and there were 360 mills in operation locally.

As it happens, Howard Baker's services in goal for the local club were required only once, for the away match against Clapton Orient on 13 April, the same day as the Scotland v England game, and Oldham lost 2–0 but still managed to avoid relegation. The next season they did rather better, finishing third and missing promotion by only two points...to Howard Baker's old club, Chelsea. That one appearance for Oldham was to be Howard Baker's last for any club in League football.

The following week, and probably aware that his League career was now at an end, Howard Baker was back in goal a few miles down the road for Corinthian's closing match of the season against the Northern Nomads at the Belle Vue ground in Manchester, and was on the receiving end of a rare hat-trick against him from the nomadic centre-forward, George Smithies, as Corinthian were beaten 4–2. The enduring appeal of the amateur game, even if the professionals were drawing ever further ahead, was exemplified by the FA Amateur Cup Final which was played that day at Highbury and attracted 35,000 spectators for a local derby in which Ilford beat Leyton 3–1.

The Corinthian commitments completed for the season, Howard Baker turned his attentions to tennis and went off to Folkestone with the Lancashire team in the last week of May for the finals of the Inter-Counties' Championship, stopping off convivially for a match at Cambridge University en route. The undergraduates routed the Lancastrians by 13 matches to two, with Howard Baker one of the only winners for the visitors, valiantly getting through two sets of singles and seven of doubles during the afternoon. The Inter-Counties' tournament was played entirely as men's doubles, and Middlesex were the winners, which was not the least bit of a surprise to anyone as they had won every year but one since 1920 and would do so again on all but two occasions until the outbreak of World War Two. Their line-up included some of the country's leading players, all of them with imposing sets of initials – G.R.O. Crole-Jones, L.R.C. Michell and H.G.N. Lee – but Lancashire lost honourably 6–3, with Howard Baker and his partner, Billy Radcliffe, playing eight sets in a single day, and placed second overall.

The 1929–30 football season started with another representative honour for Howard Baker as he was named for the Amateurs to meet the Professionals on Monday 7 October in the FA Charity Shield match at Millwall's ground. This was just a few days after he had spent the best part of a week playing tennis and winning the Welsh hard-courts' doubles title with Radcliffe again alongside him, culminating in their five-set victory over a pairing with Davis Cup experience to which reference has previously been made. The majority of the Amateurs at Millwall were Corinthian, with five of Howard Baker's clubmates in front of him – Glenister, Chadder, Knight, Doggart and Hegan. The Professionals, with no more than one player from each of 11 clubs, included only four internationals, and interestingly *The Times* observed, 'There was no noticeable difference in style between the two teams. The amateur and professional methods have become very closely approximate'. This opinion rather conflicted with the general belief that the amateurs, even the Corinthians included, were no longer in the same class, though the fact that the Professionals won 3–0 that day does suggest that even if the methods were similar the execution of them differed somewhat.

England had two international matches within five days in November; the amateurs against Ireland at Crystal Palace on Saturday 16 November and the professionals against Wales at Stamford Bridge the following Wednesday. Howard Baker would naturally have had some hopes of selection for the first of these, especially as it was to be played at the Corinthian ground, but the unpredictable committee-men chose instead his successor with Corinthian, Monty Garland-Wells, who had been showing brilliant form in Oxford University's opening matches of the season, even including a 3–2 defeat by Corinthian the previous Saturday. Garland-Wells was one of four new caps and England ran up their highest score yet in 19 matches with the Irish since 1906, 7–2. The professionals won even more easily against the Welsh, 6–0, and making his debut in goal there was Harry Hibbs, of Birmingham, who would establish the place as his own, with 25 appearances over the next six years to become the first regular goalkeeper England had had in the full international side since Sam Hardy almost a decade before.

Garland-Wells was a product of St Paul's, one of the leading public-school practitioners of football, and his opposite number and captain at Cambridge, R.T. Vaughan, was educated at Repton, which had produced so many fine players since C.B. Fry at the turn of the century, and had the misfortune to catch Corinthian in one of their purple patches. Under a downpour of rain Corinthian put eight goals past Vaughan in their match on 23 November, having overwhelmed the Royal Military College Sandhurst 18–0 three days before, and the correspondent for *The Times* detected an element of ruthlessness in the onslaught: 'Whether they win or lose, the Corinthians are no flatterers to their opponents, and whoever meets them can expect no polite concealment of his blemishes'. Corinthian beat Oxford less easily 3–1, but honour was satisfied for all the Oxbridge men when the Inter-Varsity match a few days later in December was drawn. Of the 22 players, 15 came from the long-established major public schools (including Highgate and Winchester four each, Malvern three) and only one from a grammar school (Steyning, in Sussex).

During the devastating defeats of the Cambridge undergraduates and the Sandhurst cadets Howard Baker had played in goal – or perhaps it would be more accurate to say that he had for the most part leisurely observed the activities of the afternoon from the opposite end of the field – and he was to appear in all but three of the Corinthian first-team games through to the end of the season. The post-Christmas foray took the Corinthians to a hotel suitable to their sophisticated standards in Harrogate, and they played Yorkshire Amateurs in the town on the Saturday, losing 4–3 in the closing minutes, and then ventured to Middlesbrough, where they won 2–0, and to Newcastle, where they drew with United 4–4.

Middlesbrough, who would finish the season 16th in the First Division but only nine points short of third place, so close-packed was the table, put out their reserves against Corinthian and they gave Howard Baker little to do and the meagre crowd of 1,000 even less to cheer about. Newcastle United, at that stage only one point off a relegation place, provided a sterner test at St James's Park on New Year's Day and were three goals up at half-time, as both Howard Baker and the home goalkeeper, Albert McInroy, also an England international, were kept well occupied. The 5,000 spectators, no doubt in festive mood, gave vent to their loudest applause of the day when Claude Ashton got a late equaliser for the amateurs.

These were encouraging performances by Corinthian against seasoned professionals with the FA Cup to come and a tough tie against Millwall, then as now regarded as one of the most resolute of the London teams. This turned out to be a saga reminiscent of the prolonged series against Brighton & Hove Albion when Corinthian had first entered the competition seven years before, and the outcome was exactly the same – two draws and then defeat in the second replay. The first match at Crystal Palace ended 2–2, watched by a crowd of 45,000, though the snowstorm which swept across the ground in the latter stages meant that many of them saw little of the action. Howard Baker found himself facing a centre-forward he knew well from his Chelsea days, the dapper and tuneful Jack Cock, who very nearly won the game for Millwall late in the game, but his header scraped over the cross-bar. In his customary form, Howard Baker sent one of his towering goal-kicks so far – despite the sodden ball and no wind to help him – that the Millwall goalkeeper had to field it direct.

Pathé featured the match in its nationwide cinema newsreel with the title, 'Bravo Corinthian!', and their sequence starts with the Corinthian players, led by Howard Baker, emerging from the dressing-rooms in a somewhat laconic fashion, either with hands thrust deep in the pockets of their knee-length black shorts or rolling up the sleeves of their white shirts in a manner which seemed more concerned with a stylish dress sense than purposefulness. One of Howard Baker's siege-gun kicks from his goalmouth provides the most vivid action of the minute-and-a-half or so of coverage.

Four days later there was another draw at New Cross, 1–1, with extra-time played, and when the two teams had their third encounter in nine days at Stamford Bridge an immense crowd of 58,775 turned up, to the astonishment of the correspondent for *The Times*, who commented: 'When it is remembered that the match was played on a Monday, that one side consisted solely of amateurs, and the other occupies a lowly position in the Second Division of the League, these figures are amazing'. This was, of course, an afternoon kick-off, and one can only conclude that the crowd was made up of people of independent means or with indulgent employers…or were there really that many out-of-work football fans with some cash to spare? The national unemployment figure was 1,534,000 in January 1930, though this figure would almost double in the next three years, and the UK population at the 1931 census was 46,074,000.

Tom Webster, the famed sporting cartoonist for *The Daily Mail*, produced a series of drawings for a subsequent Millwall match programme which affectionately took Howard Baker to task and provided a witty, but highly implausible, explanation for the huge turn-out. 'Howard Baker came out of goal when he should have stayed in and stayed in when he should have come out', Webster captioned his drawings, and he then added, 'The crowd was the astounding thing. They broke in. They surged in. Everyone thought that they were football enthusiasts. Nothing of the kind. Somebody in Scotland had heard that the gates were open. So they ran excursions from Aberdeen'.

The score was still 1–1 at half-time, with Howard Baker's indecision responsible for the Millwall goal, but the Corinthians had shot their bolt, and with two of their players virtual passengers because of leg injuries four more goals went past Howard Baker, though he was really only at fault on that first occasion. Millwall's style of play was fully committed, to say the least, and the Corinthian historian, Edward Grayson, was to conclude a shade aggrievedly, 'The Corinthians' battered defence cracked, four goals were surrendered, and the score of 5–1 registered Millwall's superiority as the better and more effective team of the day, although not necessarily as well the better footballers'. More than £4,000 was taken in gate money at this match alone, providing another windfall for the Corinthian bank-balance.

Only five days later Oxford University thoroughly avenged their defeat of earlier in the season, and by exactly the same score as Millwall's, though in Howard Baker's favour it was said that he 'had not the slightest chance with the five shots that beat him'. As if conceding 10 goals in two matches was not enough penance, he was then on the receiving end of an avalanche in the amateur international trial at Ilford on 1 February. England were beaten 7–0 by The Rest, which must have caused the selectors some palpitations, and judging by the press reports Howard Baker actually managed to keep the score down. George Smithies, who played Division Two League football for Preston North End and would also later make three appearances for Corinthian, hit a hat-trick, as he had done against Howard Baker for Northern Nomads the previous season.

Not surprisingly nine of the winning team, including Smithies, were then awarded caps against Wales at Aberystwyth a fortnight later, with a Liverpool policeman, A.E. Millington, in goal – his one and only appearance on the beat, so to speak. England won 2–1, with Smithies scoring both goals, to remain unbeaten against the Welsh since Howard Baker's debut on the losing side nine years before. Smithies, who was training to be a teacher, had a meteoric League and international career, scoring 16 goals in 20 matches for Preston during 1929–30, but never seemed to find that form again. He eventually became headmaster of a school at Broughton, four miles from Preston, and was to be fondly remembered more than 70 years later by one ageing former pupil as 'seeming like a man from another planet' because he had once upon a time played for Preston North End.

The feature of the Wales v England match was a remarkable display of generosity by the Welsh captain, Jack Nicholls, appearing for the eighth consecutive time in the series, who persuaded the referee to allow the England winger, G.S. Watson of Charlton Athletic, to play on after he had been ordered off the field for a foul. Nicholls' deed can perhaps be explained by the fact that he was of the Corinthian frame of mind – he played for Cardiff Corinthians, founded in 1898 and as dedicated to the ideals of amateurism as their London forebears. His international career was very similar to Howard Baker's as he remained an amateur throughout in winning four caps for the Welsh professional XI in 1923–24 and 1924–25 and 10 with the amateur side from 1922–23 to 1929–30, also playing for Newport County and Cardiff City in the Football League.

The most notable Corinthian performance in the remainder of the season was a 2–1 win against Portsmouth at Fratton Park on 1 March, in which yet another accomplished footballer/cricketer showed his mettle. The Chelsea-born George Kemp-Welch, who scored both Corinthian goals, had been Cambridge's captain and centre-forward in the previous December's Inter-Varsity match and as a batsman had hit 270 runs in his three matches against Oxford. He scored 4,170 runs at an average of 24.82 during his first-class career for the university and for Warwickshire, and after marrying the daughter of Stanley Baldwin (later Earl Baldwin of Bewdley), who served three terms as prime minister between 1923 and 1937 and was a noted football enthusiast, he gave up a lucrative business career on the outbreak of war to take a commission in the Grenadier Guards. He was killed in 1944 during a German bombing raid on London which destroyed the Guards chapel.

Corinthian ended their programme on 29 March with a 6–0 thrashing of their long-term rivals, Northern Nomads, in front of a 3,000 crowd at the Cadby Hall ground, Penny Lane (*the* Penny Lane, later to provide a refrain for the Beatles), in Wavertree, a few miles across Liverpool from Howard Baker's home, and he had only one shot of mention to deal with throughout the game. The Nomads had a long and honourable tradition behind them, having been founded well before Corinthian, in 1862, and had won the FA Amateur Cup in 1925–26 by a 7–1 margin over Stockton. They had also taken the eventual winners in 1929–30, Ilford, to a semi-final replay only 12 days before the Cadby Hall match. Might the Corinthian officials have had cause to give thought to what could have been achieved over the years had they entered this competition? Corinthian had beaten the Nomads in six of their eight matches.

The overall record for the Corinthian season was 24 wins, three draws and seven defeats, which was more or less par for the course, but it had been an unusual campaign in the professional Leagues. New names appeared as the winners of each of the four divisions, though in the case of the First Division this was only a technicality because Sheffield Wednesday, resounding champions with 10 points to spare over Derby County, had been known as simply The Wednesday until 1929 and had also won the title in that guise the previous season. For those who like to dwell further on the changing fortunes of clubs from generation to generation, it should be interesting to note that Liverpool finished 12th that year, Arsenal 14th and Manchester United 17th. Genuine newcomers to title-winning were Blackpool, three points ahead of Chelsea in Division Two, and Port Vale in Division Three North and Plymouth Argyle in Division Three South. Oh, and Arsenal won the FA Cup for the first time in their history and England beat all three other home countries for the first time in 21 years.

Another footballing 'first' for 1930 was the staging of the Fédération Internationale de Football Association (FIFA) World Cup, which had been awarded to Uruguay, in recognition of the country's independence centenary celebrations and their victory in the two preceding Olympic Games football tournaments. England had been invited, though not members of FIFA, but had declined, and it was only late in the day that four European teams – Belgium, France, Romania and Yugoslavia – were persuaded to go; their reluctance was not a matter of money, as the organisers had offered to pay the expenses for all teams.

The European teams, officials, three referees and Jules Rimet with his trophy sailed off together in the SS *Cape Verde* on the fortnight's voyage. Eight of the other competing countries were from South America, while the ninth was the USA, and Uruguay beat Argentina in the Final, with Yugoslavia and the USA as the beaten semi-finalists, both by devastating margins of 6–1. Yugoslavia was by no means a leading team in Europe, and their surprise 2–1 win over Brazil in the group round raised them only to 25th in the World rankings.

The chairmanship of England's Football Association had been held by 80-year-old Sir Charles Clegg ever since 1890 even though he was a vehement opponent of professionalism, believing it to be a corrupting influence, and he was fond of advising anyone who cared to listen that 'nobody gets lost on a straight road'. In this instance the rest of the world could be forgiven for thinking that Sir Charles and his committee-men could not see the way ahead.

FROM SOMETHING VERY LIKE FUTILITY
TO SOMETHING VERY LIKE
MAGNIFICENCE

The most recent of the histories of the Corinthian Football Club, published in 2007 and enthusiastically written by Rob Cavallini, has headlines for the successive chapters concerning the years 1925 to 1930 and then 1930 to 1936 which neatly sum up a sequence of rapidly contrasting fortunes. 'FA Cup Glory' is followed by 'The Decline Of Corinth'. Delight to dejection is a dramatic turn of emotions, but the attendance figures for Corinthian's home ties in the FA Cup tell the sorry tale: from 45,000 v Millwall in 1930 to 16,000 v West Ham United in 1933 to 2,000 v Bristol Rovers in 1936 and Southend United in 1937. Not even the fact that the first two of these matches had the extra attraction of being 'local derbies' could explain away those figures.

Of course, the Corinthian amateurs could no longer match the League teams in serious competition, but it didn't help matters that the club was parting company with its supporter base. There had been 15 first-team matches at Crystal Palace in 1931–32 but no more than seven in 1932–33, and for the next three seasons the only cup-tie matches were those against Bristol Rovers in November of 1936 – the last fixture to be played by Corinthian at the ground they had graced for 14 years – and the visit of Southend United a year later was to the other side of London at the White City Stadium. This was the refurbished venue for the 1908 Olympic Games now in use for greyhound-racing and for the major British athletics fixtures, which had been packed to the rafters with an estimated 83,000 people at the 1936 post-Olympic British Empire v USA match.

Edward Grayson, who wrote so passionately about the Corinthian club in his anecdotal 1955 history, was an eye-witness of that White City Cup tie, and his memory of it was weighed down with sadness:

'I shall never forget a dull November afternoon in 1937 at the White City, itself a legacy of Edwardian London, when the Corinthians, themselves then nothing more than a legacy in name of Victorian and Edwardian soccer, made their final FA Cup appearance in London, against Southend United. Any resemblance to the old greatness, even of the twenties, had completely gone. A miserable crowd of 2,000 sprinkled round the empty stadium gave an eerie atmosphere to what resembled a memorial service rather than any parade of soccer talent, or at least of amateur soccer talent, by what had once been the country's premier amateur club. As the thumps of the ball echoed round the deserted stands, with the occasional whisper, 'Play up, Corinth', filtering through the murky air like some haunting cry that one snatches to retain but always slides away, the forward-line of the Third Division team showed clearer shades of the combined Corinthian forward style than their ghostly opponents who bore the famous name'.

The retirement of Howard Baker after the 1932–33 season and of other stalwarts such as Alfred Bower (180 matches), together with increasingly rare appearances by Claude Ashton, Harvey Chadder, Graham Doggart, Fred Ewer and Kenneth Hegan – the backbone of the side in the 1920s – contributed to the depressed standards. Howard Baker respectably faded away, playing 17 games in 1930–31 for the first team and the A team, 11 in 1931–32 and four in 1932–33, and even approaching 40 years of age he could still reproduce his form of old. The three-fold Cup opponents of seven seasons before, Brighton & Hove Albion, were visitors to Crystal Palace in December of 1930, and this time Corinthian won with ease, 4–1, and Howard Baker, well supported by his full-backs, Chadder and W.B. Goulding, 'showed that he was in his best form', according to the man from *The Times*.

England's amateur selectors, unimpressed by Howard Baker's longevity, had given their goalkeeping place for the visit to Ireland to a Birmingham University student, K.C. Tewkesbury, and though England lost 3–1 for only the second time since 1906 he was retained against Scotland and Wales later in the 1930–31 season and for the same three fixtures the next season. Tommy Whewell, centre-half and captain, was the only Corinthian in the England team as even his perennial half-back partner, Fred Ewer, was dropped after 13 appearances in six years. Consolingly, Howard Baker and Ewer were in the Corinthian team that ran rings round Yorkshire Amateurs at Bracken Edge, Leeds, 7–1, the same day, having beaten Northern Nomads very nearly as convincingly 7–2 at Crystal Palace the previous Saturday.

Another 7–2 victory was run up against the Royal Navy on the Saturday before Christmas, and the football coverage in *The Times* the following Monday morning makes interesting reading. The Arsenal–Newcastle United match occupies much of the first column, but none of the other 10 Division One fixtures get a mention, other than in the list of results, and nor do any of those in Division Two, Division Three South and Division Three North. Instead, there are detailed reports of Old Citizens v Old Carthusians, Old Bradfieldians v Old Reptonians, Old Wykehamists v Old Cholmeleians, Old Westminsters v Old Etonians and Lancing Old Boys v Old Hurst Johnians. The explanation is that this was Arthur Dunn Cup day, when the leading old boys' clubs met, and the top people's newspaper knew where the loyalties of its readers lay. At least a dozen Corinthians turned out for the various Cup teams, which makes the club's resounding triumph over the naval men, among whom was yet another Corinthian, Lieutenant-Commander Glenister, all the more noteworthy.

A 2–0 win in Glasgow over the 'auld enemy', Queen's Park, on New Year's Day, helped by three fine saves by Howard Baker late in the game, led nicely up to the FA Cup tie at Crystal Palace against Port Vale on 10 January. Port Vale is one of the few Football League clubs not named after a town or city and had been founded in Burslem, in Staffordshire, six years before Corinthian in 1876, though their home ground had actually been located in another Potteries' town, Hanley, since 1913. They represented formidable opposition because they were eighth in the Division Two table at the time of their visit and would finish the season fifth, having won the Division Three North title the season before. Their manager was an ex-player named Tom Morgan who despite these achievements was to be dismissed in 1932 – some things never change.

The Times previewed the match on the Saturday morning in the affectionate belief that 'the thoughts of all those who are interested in amateur football will be at the Crystal Palace this afternoon', and almost 13,000 people replaced the thought with the deed by turning up at the gates. This despite the fact that the ground was blanketed with thick fog until shortly before the kick-off and that in other Cup ties Arsenal were at home to Aston Villa (50,000 spectators), West Ham United were playing Chelsea (21,000), and Tottenham Hotspur, Brentford, Fulham and neighbours Crystal Palace were also drawn at home. The fog lifted, but the ground was frozen, and Port Vale always had 'much more resource and were quicker on the ball'. They won 3–1 and Howard Baker had no chance of saving any of the goals.

There had been a considered assessment of Corinthian's 4–2 win over the Athenian League the previous Saturday by the football correspondent of *The Times* which went a long way towards explaining the disparity between amateur and professional levels of play: 'The Corinthians are a curious side in that, for no apparent reason, they can swing in the course of a single game from something very like futility to something very like magnificence. There were moments in the first half when they were playing football which belonged in speed, accuracy and cleverness to an altogether lower class than that played by the League, but there were more moments when the intelligence of their scheming and the precision of their foot-work made the scoring of goals seem not only easy but the logical and inevitable sequel to their work'. One of the Corinthian goals came from a towering goal-kick by Howard Baker which reached Doggart deep in the Athenian half and Hegan scored from the pass.

Charles Wreford-Brown, now in his 60s and one of the bastions of the Corinthian club, having played for them 161 times, having captained England, and having turned out at county cricket for Gloucestershire, concluded of the Cup tie defeats that 'the vigour and keenness of the professionals in these matches is difficult to counter'. His views were understandable, but it was some irony that it wasn't so very many years since the amateur vigorousness of the Corinthians, rather than that of their paid opponents, was the matter at issue. More objectively, Wreford-Brown said in an interview with *The London Evening News*: 'Our difficulties are great when you realise that the members of our team come from all parts of England, and that they have no central training ground. Few can spare much time for football, and that is one of the reasons why I, personally, am not in favour of employing a professional coach. Our players would have little opportunity to benefit by it'. Wreford-Brown was to serve on the FA Council for 59 years, including chairmanship of the selection committee, and was also, incidentally, a good enough chess player to be invited among the dozen who played in the British championship of 1933.

A fortnight after the Cup tie against Port Vale, Howard Baker injured his knee so seriously in a match at West Ham United that he had to be carried off the field, and that put paid to his season. The next Saturday England beat The Rest 4–0 in the amateur international trial at Watford, and Ashton, Hegan and Whewell, of Corinthian, were selected for the match against Wales, as were R.G.C. Jenkins, now of the Casuals, and W.H. Webster of Cambridge University, both of whom had also played for Corinthian. England won 5–0 at Bournemouth to bring their tally to 16 wins and two draws in the 19 Anglo-Welsh encounters since 1908. Furthermore, England would win all the eight following matches in the series up to World War Two, averaging more than five goals a time.

Considering that he had carried a knee problem ever since his high-jumping career had ended a decade before, Howard Baker might well have thought for a while that his goalkeeping days were now also over, but he recovered well enough to be back in action again from the very start of the 1931–32 season. By the beginning of November he had appeared in five matches for Corinthian and had not had a great deal to do as Corinthian won them all, scoring 27 goals to six. A return meeting with Oxford University at Crystal Palace put him to the test, and though Oxford won 3–1 the conclusion of *The Times* was that but for him the score would have been higher. Corinthian were without Ashton, Hegan and Whewell, all in the England side beating Ireland 3–2 at York. One of the Oxford full-backs was K.S. ('Sandy') Duncan, who would later play a few games for Corinthian and become a Great Britain long-jump international from 1933 to 1937 and then an avuncular secretary-general for the British Olympic Association from 1948 to 1974.

A fortnight later Corinthian were at Southport, and though they lost 4–2 the amateurs put up a good showing against a useful side which would finish seventh in Division Three North that season, with Howard Baker having another fine game. A few miles south his old club, Everton, were at home to Leicester City and in the process of achieving a 9–2 victory, which still remains their biggest League success 80 years later. The peerless Dixie Dean scored four of the goals and Everton moved five points clear at the head of Division One – and they would hold that place until the season's end, by two points from Arsenal.

For the next nine matches through to mid-January Howard Baker gave way in the Corinthian goalmouth to a Cambridge undergraduate, Rolph Grant, who would later captain the West Indies at cricket, and would go on to play 21 times that season. On 23 January Howard Baker was back in the side for a visit to much stronger League opposition, West Bromwich Albion, then in second place in Division One, and the match programme that day, entitled *The Albion News*, paid effusive tribute to the contribution which Corinthian had made to the history of the game, while making the realistic comment that 'although the Corinthians still claim pride of place among the amateur clubs of this country and are capable of holding their own with all but the strongest professional sides, they are not the power in football they used to be in the vintage period of this famous organisation'. No spokesman for any League club was better placed to make such an observation because this was the 11th meeting of the clubs since 1892, of which Albion had won five, Corinthian four, and the other two had been drawn, though the last Corinthian success dated back to the 1913–14 season.

WBA won this time 4–0, but the match report in *The Times* finished with the comment that 'before Baker ran off the field to the cheers of the crowd he had been forced to save brilliantly with one hand from both Sandford and Fitton'. As had happened so often before, whether Corinthian had won or lost, it was Howard Baker who attracted the most attention from the spectators, however partisan, and the press. *The Times* thought that Howard Baker was as good as ever just a month short of his 40th birthday: 'Baker, perhaps, sometimes takes undue risks, but he can rarely have been more justified or played better than he did on Saturday, when some of his saves were almost miraculous'.

He was going out in style and he finished off his career the next season with three matches in 10 days during October and November and then a final appearance early in the New Year. The most notable of these games for various reasons was the charity match against Arsenal at Highbury for the Sheriff of London Shield on the afternoon of Wednesday 26 October for which 10,000 people found the time to attend. The proceeds went to the National Playing

Fields Association, which had been set up in 1925 and for which Howard Baker's illustrious Olympic athletics teammate, Harold Abrahams, was the legal executive. By 1933 the NPFA had overseen the construction of 1,000 recreation grounds throughout Britain.

Arsenal were without Alex James, one of Scotland's legendary 'Wembley Wizards' who was on international duty that day, but still fielded seven capped players: between them Cliff Bastin, Eddie Hapgood, Joe Hulme, David Jack, George Male and Frank Moss would play 92 times for England, while Bob John played 15 times for Wales. Not surprisingly, Arsenal were overwhelming winners, 9–2, though it was not quite the first time that Corinthian had conceded that number of goals in a match – it had happened in 1890–91 against a Scottish Select XI and as recently as 1926–27 against the Isthmian League. It would even happen again early in 1933 when Preston North End also won 9–2.

The further significance of the occasion was that it was the 50th anniversary, to the very day, of the first match played by Corinthian – a 2–1 victory over St Thomas's Hospital on 26 October 1882 – and so the charity outing against Arsenal was followed in the evening by a jubilee banquet at the Dorchester Hotel. Some details of the occasion are given in an article on the society page of *The Times* the following day, and among the dignitaries present were Sir Frederick Wall, secretary of the Football Association since 1895, together with Jules Rimet, president of FIFA and an old friend of the club, and representatives of the football ruling bodies of Belgium, Denmark, Sweden and South Africa. Occupying the newly-appointed post of president of the club was Major R.T. Squire, who had played in the 1880s and had served on the committee for 48 years, 30 of them as treasurer.

The report of the evening's proceedings is as interesting for what is left out as what is said. It is not clear whether the newspaper's football correspondent was in attendance, or whether the information was provided by a Corinthian member such as Major Squire or the secretary, Geoffrey Foster, but the references to the speeches are tantalisingly brief.

One of the letters of congratulation from absent members which was read out was from G.O. Smith, who had played 137 matches for the club and 21 for England around the turn of the century and was now joint headmaster at a preparatory school with another esteemed ex-Corinthian, William Oakley. Smith's message to the assembly was described mysteriously as an 'inverted tribute', and his absence was remarked upon – 'a Corinthian dinner without so illustrious a name must still be great, but it lacks Hamlet' – but it may be simply a matter that school commitments took precedence; his colleague, Oakley, was certainly among the guests. Nicholas Lane Jackson, now 82, the founder and the guest of honour, expressed in his speech the fervent hope that the club would never consider applying to enter the Football League. Lieutenant Kenneth Hegan, oddly, thought that it was 'at least a creditable performance' that Corinthian had managed to score two goals against Arsenal that afternoon.

This choice of such brief extracts from what was said by the speakers seemed to strike an apologetic note, rather than reflecting the joyful celebration of half-a-century of sporting achievement that one might have expected. 'Pa' Jackson's comments – or at least the emphasis placed on them by *The Times* – suggests that the idea of playing regular League football, either exclusively amateur or against the professionals, was being seriously discussed among Corinthian members. Lt Hegan's remarks struck a sort of 'we're not as bad as you think' tone.

Whatever the mood of the messages from the top table, for Howard Baker it would have been an enjoyable social occasion touched by nostalgia, rather than an analytical appraisal of the state of the club, because he certainly now had retirement from the game in mind, and maybe the memory of having conceded nine goals that afternoon for the first time in his life concentrated his thoughts wonderfully on the prospect! His final appearance for Corinthian was not, unfortunately, in the most auspicious of circumstances because he was roped in for a match against Manchester United reserves during an extended – over-extended, perhaps – early January tour in the North of England which involved 40 players and five games in three days.

The previous day one of the other goalkeepers in the party which had based itself at the Hotel Metropole, in Blackpool, F.E.H. Gibbens, had been on the receiving end of those nine goals by Preston North End, ironically also celebrating their 50th anniversary, and A.M. Russell, the Cambridge graduate, had played in goal in the A team's 3–3 draw with the Lancashire Amateur League. Only 500 spectators were there to see Howard Baker's farewell appearance, but he left them with some fond memories as he made a series of spectacular saves to keep the score down to 2–1. That was not actually the end of his association with Corinthian that season because he then went on the tour to Holland, Germany and Denmark in April, but there did not seem to be any question of him playing.

A few amateurs still commanded places in Football league teams after Howard Baker's final departure from football. One of them was his clubmate, Howard Fabian, who had 77 games for Corinthian in between appearing for Derby County and winning six amateur caps in the early 1930s. In 1960 he co-edited with Geoffrey Green, of *The Times*, a four-volume history of the game. J.C. Burns, of Queen's Park Rangers and then Brentford, played 16 matches for the England amateur team through to 1934–35. Maurice Edelston, a London University student and also a Brentford player, was in the Great Britain team at the 1936 Olympics, won five amateur caps up to the eve of Word War Two, appeared as an amateur for the full England team in four unofficial wartime internationals while with Reading, and after his eventual retirement in 1952 became a leading television and radio commentator for football and tennis. W.W. Parr, of Blackpool, had nine amateur caps in the latter 1930s.

The most notable of this select group, though, was Bernard Joy, who captained the Great Britain team at the 1936 Olympics and earlier in the year had led the Casuals to success in the FA Amateur Cup Final and had become the last amateur ever to play for the full England side. He was also a Corinthian, appearing in 28 games during the mid-1930s, though his major commitment was to Arsenal, for whom he made 95 appearances at centre-half. He was a teacher in pre-war years but took up journalism after his retirement from playing in 1948 and became a respected football correspondent for *The Evening Standard* and *The Sunday Express*.

Howard Baker and his wife had now made their home in Beechwood Road, in Aigburth, and living opposite was one of Liverpool's other most prominent businessmen, Charles Scott Hannay, who had also been born in West Derby and was a past president of the Liverpool Cotton Association, with whom Howard Baker no doubt exchanged business confidences and also shared a sporting interest. Hannay had some experience of first-class cricket, if only briefly in one match for Oxford University against the MCC in 1901 when he had batted No.9, scoring 20 and four, and did not bowl.

It was lawn tennis, though, which was the game which continued to occupy Howard Baker's boundless energies for the remainder of the 1930s. Still good enough for the Lancashire team in 1938 at the age of 46, he would regularly play eight sets of doubles in a day at the annual Inter-Counties' Championships at Eastbourne. He continued his very agreeable association with the Welsh covered courts' tournament; in 1934 he and C.M. Jones, later to become a noted tennis writer, got to the semi-finals of the doubles and narrowly lost 7–5, 6–4. The next year Howard Baker even advanced to the singles semi-final, and in 1936 he and his wife were in the semi-finals of the mixed doubles. In 1937 he and F.H.D. Wilde were doubles finalists, losing to Henry Billington and E.J. Filby 6–4, 4–6, 6–3. Wilde, discerning in his choice of partners, was a Wimbledon men's doubles finalist both that year and in 1939. Billington would be a future Davis Cup player and was the maternal grandfather of Tim Henman. All these achievements at local level were maybe the sum total of Howard Baker's ambitions, but it could be that this was the one sport in which he did not fulfil his own expectations.

One of the most observant of tennis writers, E.J. Sampson, of the *Manchester Guardian*, who had himself been a very capable player at the turn of the century, had clearly discussed the very same matter with Howard Baker back in 1928 and had written then: 'There would appear to be few Worlds left for him to conquer, and yet he reckons there is. For, although he has played in county lawn tennis, Howard Baker is not satisfied with the considerable progress he has made but is impatient to attain a similar eminence in his last game to that which he enjoyed in others'. Sampson himself had reservations, and hardly surprisingly so as his subject was now 36 years old and could be thought of as too old a dog to learn new tricks. 'He is very conscious of his limitations, for his standard is a high one', Sampson continued. 'It is the ground shot that eludes this great jumper. As a volleyer, his powers are really considerable, but he is inclined to be cramped with the forehand, to get too near to the ball, and he thinks that the reason lies in his football instinct to get his hands to the ball'.

The next year, when Howard Baker and Billy Radcliffe had won the Welsh covered courts' doubles, Sampson had commented at length, implying that Howard Baker had corrected a serious earlier flaw in his game: 'Baker has improved and is now a daring volleyer. He was able to smash the most amazing lobs, thanks to his leaping powers, and also showed that he can serve well and not make double faults'. It would have needed a great deal more progress in his game than that for Howard Baker to have attained that 'similar eminence' that Sampson had commented upon because British tennis was about to enter a golden era that has never been remotely approached since. The Davis Cup, with Fred Perry and Bunny Austin as mainstays of the team, was to be won in three successive years, 1933, 1934, 1935, and Perry was three times singles champion at Wimbledon and in the US Open.

By 1934 it was too late for Howard Baker, at 42 years of age, to modify the somewhat impulsive nature of his game, as Sampson politely indicated in his report of a 6–4, 6–1 singles defeat in the Northern quarter-finals: 'Baker would leap from his service to the net on anything and everything, but his service was not sufficiently severe, and Pratt, the scarred veteran of a hundred Cheshire county matches, was passing Baker with nice shots which skimmed the net and found the lines'. G.A. Pratt, incidentally, regularly played at Wimbledon and had suffered the further 'scarring' experience of once having been beaten by the great Bill Tilden himself. Nice shots skimming the tennis-court net and leaving Howard Baker stranded must have seemed to him rather too similar for comfort to 'nice shots' from the opposition finding the back of his goalkeeper's net.

'WHY DO YOU WANT TO RAKE ME UP? LEAVE ANCIENT HISTORY ALONE'. BUT HOWARD BAKER STILL HAS A TALE TO TELL

At the start of World War Two Howard Baker, now aged 47 and a highly successful businessman, had made the most telling contribution he could to Britain's hurried preparations to fight the Germans. The ex-volunteer naval Lieutenant gave £25,000 to the country's 'Build a Battleship' fund – perhaps the equivalent of £1 million in 2012 terms – and as the admiral in charge of the project had also been a footballer in his youth the cheque was accompanied by a note which read 'From one goalkeeper to another'.

Liverpool was the port through which 90 per cent of war materials were imported and was the subject of sustained attacks by the German Luftwaffe, causing more than 4,000 civilian fatalities, which was a death toll second only among British cities to London. One of the victims was the film and stage actress, Mary Lawson, who had been engaged for a time to Fred Perry, and was staying at a hotel at Sefton Park, near to Aigburth, where one wing of Howard Baker's own home, 'Beechwood', was damaged by bombs. He turned over his property for use by the US forces and acquired an Elizabethan mansion, Gayton Hall, set in 34 acres of grounds on the banks of the estuary of the River Dee, near Heswall, in Wirral, which he made the family home.

The hall had a fascinating history. Howard Baker had bought it from the Liverpool Underwriters' Association, and it had been used during World War Two to store Liverpool's city archives away from the threat of air-raid attack. The hall had belonged to the Glegg family, owners of the manor of Gayton, for almost 600 years from 1359 to 1919, and the present building dated from 1663. As it was close to the ancient ferry-crossing of the River Dee to North Wales it was associated with numerous racy tales of smuggling and naval press-gangs. King William III, known as William of Orange, had spent a night there in 1690 en route to nearby Hoylake, from where he set sail for Ireland to fight the Battle of the Boyne, and had bestowed a knighthood upon the then owner, William Glegg, which seems like a generous reward for a night's lodging. There is still a public house nearby named the Glegg Arms.

Howard Baker and his wife now had two sons – the elder of whom, Philip, served in the navy during the war, as his father had done – and even in the midst of the conflict Howard Baker kept in touch with old friends. Philip Noel-Baker, who was now joint parliamentary secretary to the Minister of War Transport in Winston Churchill's government, wrote a charming reply recalling past athletics and footballing achievements in a letter, the second and third paragraphs of which were hand-written, from the House of Commons on 10 February 1942.

My dear Howard,

Thank you so much for your letter. I cannot tell you what pleasure it gave me, and what happy memories it evoked. Nor can I say how proud I am to know that your younger son is named Philip. I hope he will be everything that you can hope for. I shall hope to see him some day on the track. And soon.

I was very glad to hear all your news. I still sometimes wear Alec Nelson's shorts – but only to run very gentle cross-country in the Cumberland hills, and I am much better downhill than up. With all good wishes and hoping to see you soon, and with all thanks for writing.

Yours ever,

Philip J.N.B.

P.S. When my wife read your letter she said, 'Is this the Howard Baker who kept goal for the Corinthians at Crystal Palace at that wonderful Cup tie in 1924?' I remember it, too, and as if it were yesterday. By far the best goalkeeping I ever saw, and that is saying something! And how I remember your jump at Queen's Club in the first Empire-USA match!'

Note: for those readers bemused by the thought of the Government minister jogging over the Lake District hills attired in someone else's shorts, Alec Nelson was the Cambridge University athletics coach of the 1920, and no doubt Noel-Baker was referring to the apparel which Nelson had issued to him!

Howard Baker retained a close interest in sport after the war. Most notably he was a member of the British Olympic Association from 1946, which meant that he had some input to the organisation of the 1948 Wembley Olympic Games. He would certainly have taken careful note that in the high jump at the Games his successor as British record-holder, the 20-year-old Scot, Alan Paterson, did not quite live up to expectations, placing equal seventh, while in football the Great Britain team reached the semi-finals where they were beaten 3–1 by Yugoslavia, but in water-polo there was an 11–2 defeat by the eventual silver-medallists, Hungary, and a first-round exit.

He continued his extensive involvement with the Lawn Tennis Association, honoured as a life member and vice-president, and was a member of the Lawn Tennis Council and the All-England Club and president of the Lancashire LTA. He resumed contacts with the

Liverpool Harriers club, and he went along to watch his former football teams, Everton and Liverpool, play from time to time for many years until the 1970s. He also had a wide network of other social contacts. One of his numerous friends in exalted places was Sir Stanley Rous, who had been an amateur goalkeeper himself and then an international referee before becoming secretary of the FA from 1934 to 1962 and president of FIFA from 1961 to 1974. He had been knighted in 1948 for his contribution to the organisation of that year's London Olympic Games, and it was said of him that his patient diplomacy had been responsible for the home countries rejoining FIFA in 1946. In 1960 Howard Baker was one of a small group of people specifically approached by Sir Stanley to make suggestions regarding improvement of the standards of play in England.

His business interests expanded after World War Two to include a number of companies – Howard Baker (Soap and Chemicals) Ltd, B.H. Baker & Company (for which the telegraph address was 'Hijumper'), J.R. Pearce & Company, The Liverpool Soap & Oil Company – and he was chairman of a number of others, including the Allanson's store across the Mersey in Birkenhead and the Melia's chain which had 600 outlets in Britain. He became an elder statesman of business and commerce in Liverpool, just as he was of sport in so many forms, and was chairman of the city's Soap Makers' Association. Yet he kept a low profile throughout this second half of his life. He disliked any form of ostentation, and he was at pains to tell the sports historian, John Bromhead, in their taped interview in 1982, 'I'm not entirely immodest, but I hated publicity, and I hated to have any presentation which was flamboyant or any talking which was a lot of self-glorification'.

Even so, he relished to the end of his life one tale of an official reception some time in the 1950s at which he and Sir Stanley Rous were present: 'We were chatting to each other and Sir Stanley suddenly turned and called Frank Swift over, saying, "Come here, Frank, let me introduce you to a real goalkeeper!"' Swift, who played 14 wartime and 19 peacetime matches for England up to 1949 and is widely regarded as the national team's best ever goalkeeper, was to lose his life at the age of 44 in the 1958 Munich aircraft disaster. A fellow international, Raich Carter, once said of Swift that his physique loomed so large in the goalmouth that trying to score a goal against him was like trying to put the ball into a match-box. At 6ft 2in (1.88m) tall, Swift was a shade shorter than Howard Baker, and there must have been many a centre-forward during the 1920s and early 1930s who could have applied the match-box analogy to the man in front of him defending the goal – be it for Corinthian, Everton, Chelsea or England.

Long after he had retired from active sport, Howard Baker continued to attract press attention from time to time, and when the 1972 Munich Olympics were about to take place, more than 50 years after his last appearance at the Games, one of the experienced sports correspondents for the *Liverpool Echo*, Alf Green, decided to seek the great man out…or, to be more precise, was strongly advised to do so. Green candidly admitted in the opening paragraph of his profile that 'it was a veteran colleague in the office who said, 'If you're writing anything about the Olympics and Liverpool it would be unforgivable not to mention Howard Baker'.

Green continued: 'To a lot of people under the age of 60, unless they have some direct link with the world of sport, the name is one which probably rings only vaguely familiar: a name they have heard others speak of at some time or other'. That was undoubtedly a fair assessment, though it still left an awful lot of people – those keen followers of football, athletics, lawn tennis, swimming and water polo, especially on Merseyside, and others with an interest in business and commerce – who would have readily recognised Howard Baker's name. So the eyes of numerous *Echo* readers that Saturday evening would certainly have been caught by the pithy headline, 'Sportsman Supreme'.

The interview came about in curious circumstances. When Green had telephoned Howard Baker at the office which he still attended each day and asked for a meeting, the response had been characteristically dismissive. 'Why do you want to rake me up?' the 80-year-old had retorted. 'Leave ancient history alone and write something about the Reverend Tom Farrell instead. He's a Liverpool Harrier, a former Olympic hurdler, and an inspiration to a lot of the local youngsters. He will be a great asset in Munich as padré to this year's team'. Then Howard Baker was diverted to an urgent long-distance call on another phone, but instead of ringing back later the intrepid Green went out unannounced to his prey's Gayton Hall home that evening, and, as he records of his door-step reception, 'Howard Baker, one of the last of the Great Corinthians, was too much of a gentleman to turn me away empty-handed'. Green was treated to a gin-and-tonic in the baronial dining-room of Howard Baker's mansion and the impromptu conversation got under way.

'His life story might have stepped straight out of the pages of a boys' adventure book, for he was a flesh-and-blood version of that fictional super-athlete who has thrilled a million youngsters by taking on everybody at anything – and winning most of the time. The personality cult, as we see it today in relation to people like David Bedford and George Best, had not yet arrived', Green wrote of Howard Baker's sporting era. 'One was tempted to wonder, as he reluctantly pieced together the threads of his earlier life, what the present headline writers would have made of his exploits. Certainly, the handsome dark-haired giant that emerged would have become every woman's secret heart-throb and every father's dream of a son'.

Warming to his visitor as the evening wore on, which was not surprising because Green had a naturally disarming manner, Howard Baker pondered, 'An athletic preparation in those days was nothing like as intensive or methodical as it is today. The use of drugs and other medical aids was largely unheard of. We just did the best we could with what talent and strength we had. The only aid I used to have was massage. I was a great believer in that. We were under less pressure in a way because the exposure to publicity was not as great. You grow up with the times in which you lived, and it's hard – perhaps impossible – to make comparisons'.

The *Boys' Own* hero theme figured very prominently in another profile of Howard Baker which appeared in the 'Super Pink' football section of an edition of the *Echo* 11 years after Alf Green's pilgrimage to Gayton Hall. Under an emblazoned banner headline, 'HB – LAST OF THE GREAT CORINTHIANS', the racy opening paragraph proclaimed, 'Roy of the Rovers – the great Wilson, all-round sporting sensation of the Wizard comic – they're the dream idols of every sports-mad schoolboy. Now meet the real-life original'. Into his 90s and still only slightly stooped, Howard Baker was as retiring as ever, imploring his interviewer, 'Don't make me sound vain. It was all so long ago. It's really just a whole lot of damned nonsense'. The reason for featuring Howard Baker in the newspaper on this occasion was that he had been invited to attend the Liverpool v Everton derby match – and would probably be one of the very few in the ground who was not too concerned which side won. As it happened, Liverpool did 2–0, with both goals scored by Emlyn Hughes.

'Howard Baker will be at Goodison on Saturday for the derby game', was the preview by *The Echo* reporter. 'And if that bald announcement means little to to-day's younger Evertonians, 47 years ago it was like a win on the Irish Sweep for their seniors. It was 1926, the year of the Great Strike, and to add to the depression Everton hit a crop of injuries that made Goodison Park look like a casualty clearing centre. Dixie Dean, Hardy, Troup, Kendall and Peacock were all injured in trial games. Hardy and Kendall were the club's only goalkeepers, and with only a few days to go before the opening of the season at Tottenham, and just a month before the first derby game, things were beginning to look desperate. Then, like something out of 'The Wizard', came the announcement that B. Howard Baker was coming to the rescue'.

Among slightly earlier reminders of his sporting career was the choice of him as the final subject for a series of feature articles entitled 'Great Goalkeepers' which appeared in the Saturday editions of *The Lancashire Evening Telegraph* towards the end of the 1961–62 football season. The newspaper's football writer, Basil Easterbook, compiled a detailed summary of Howard Baker's achievements, suggesting with good reason: 'If Baker had turned professional, he would probably have been England's automatic choice for a great many seasons, but the game could never be the most important thing in the life of a man so favoured by birth, nature and circumstance. Howard Baker loved football, but very properly he only sought from it a balance and contrast for his other life as a manufacturing chemist, which was to lead him to the status of industrialist and man of stature in the nation's commerce'. The writer neatly concluded, 'Baker played for fun outside the shadow of the pay envelope'.

That deft turn of phrase was typical of Easterbook, who was a highly regarded cricket and football correspondent for Kemsley Newspapers and Thomson Regional Newspapers from 1950 to 1983. Easterbrook was that rarity, a genuinely humorous writer about sport, and he had a fund of stories to tell. His full name was Basil Vivian Easterbrook, and he recalled that on one occasion when he was phoning over his match report to his office he was asked by the copy-taker to repeat his name more clearly. 'Basil V. Easterbrook', he announced. 'What League is that?' the copy-taker asked. Easterbrook, who had been chairman of the Cricket Writers' Club, contributed a delightfully amusing article to the Wisden edition of 1971 which argued the case for giving the same attention to prolific scorers of 'ducks' as to century-makers.

'Any mug with enough talent and concentration can make a hundred', Easterbook wrote, citing his own club-cricket career in Devon. 'It requires the soul and tenacity of a martyr to score nothing and continue to score nothing. Once in 1935 at Dartmouth I made 16 out of a total of 43 against the Royal Naval College, but in self-defence I would point out that even Homer nodded and that if you go to the crease often enough there comes a day when you will get some runs regardless of what you do. I have remembered the innings for 35 years for I believe that it is as far as I got from the circular cipher in one innings'.

Easterbrook's article naturally made reference to famous cricketers who had scored nothing on their first-class debuts and these included one of Howard Baker's boyhood heroes, C.B. Fry, and two others that he played football with or against, Errol Holmes and Walter Robins. Incidentally, Easterbrook shared the same birthday as Howard Baker, 15 February, being born in 1920 and dying in 1995. Another of his endless fund of anecdotes which was repeated in a fond obituary by a cricket-writing colleague concerned the note which a club captain sent to a low-scoring batsman he had dropped from the team because he believed the fault was that he stayed up late at night reading: 'I have decided to leave you out because it has come to my notice that midnight frequently finds you immersed in Jane Austen'.

In December 1959 another vivid analogy had been found to describe the impact which the goalkeeping Howard Baker had on his contemporaries. Writing in the London evening newspaper *The Star*, a seasoned journalist, Jim Gaughan fancifully claimed, 'Between 30 and 40 years ago Benjamin Howard Baker had much the same effect on people as a 1959 Boeing 707 air-liner zooming away from London Airport. He, too, made heads turn skyways in utter amazement – but not because of an ear-shattering noise produced by mighty engines. In his case it was the swift and silent passage of a football – propelled prodigious distances by the thrust of one foot – which made open-mouthed crowds stand and stare. Nowadays any goalkeeper who lands the ball well over the halfway line, say 80 yards, is regarded as a long kicker, but that was child's play to Baker. Often his target was the opposite goalline – at least 120 yards away on the biggest grounds'.

Gaughan then provided a personal perspective on sporting history when he continued his tale: 'Probably any goalkeeper attempting to emulate Baker in these days of theoretical and tactical considerations would be condemned as an exhibitionist. Certainly, his manager would tell him that such performances were not in the best interests of his side. In Baker's time, however, football followers loved their personalities and delighted in their individual achievements – however extravagant and unorthodox. As a lad I remember being taken to Goodison Park, Everton, just to see this amazing man who, in the words of my father, 'could boot a ball further than any man alive'. And I recall the buzz of excitement round the ground whenever the tall, powerfully-built man in the black-and-white hooped sweater prepared to take one of his famous place kicks.

'But these huge punts achieved with a few graceful strides and an easy swing of the leg were not the only Baker-isms which made the soccer crowds gasp. Stay on the line until danger came to close quarters? Not Baker. He would race out to the edge of the penalty area, and often beyond, to meet the invaders. Sometimes these breath-taking dashes got him into trouble, but generally they were as startlingly effective as those tremendous leaps which made him invincible in the air'.

The amalgamated Corinthian-Casuals FC had celebrated the 75th anniversary of Corinthian in 1957 and that of the Casuals the following year, and Geoffrey Green, the exalted football writer for *The Times*, penned an erudite tribute for a privately-circulated commemoration booklet which listed 166 past and present members who had won international caps. 'The Corinthians, in fact, far overstepped the original limited aim of authority on the football field', Green wrote in expansive mood. 'By performance and by their code of behaviour they became a symbol within the game, a monument to moral standards as first displayed by the small but powerful universe of ancient Hellas. The Olympic and Isthmian Games of old found a nineteenth century echo, and it was perhaps more than a touch of fate that that echo should ring from such a name as Corinth. But whatever the happy choice, it is a name that lives on to this day when even the changing values of a shifting, restless world cannot smudge its purity or change its meaning'.

Half-a-century later the name of Corinthian still survives. There can be very few around who in their childhood would have seen the Corinthians play in Howard Baker's day, and if there are such veteran enthusiasts they would now be aged 90-plus, but there are those who have cared enough over the last dozen or more years to revive ancient memories. Edward Grayson's club history of 1955 was re-issued in 1996 by an enterprising publisher specialising in football subjects, whose other contributions to the literature of the game include such titles as *Rejected FC*, comprising no less than three volumes about the destinies of former Football League clubs, and the 'slightly bizarre' (the publisher's own description) *Little Red Book of Chinese Football*. Gary Lineker thought highly enough of the enterprise of Edward Grayson, by then aged 74, that he contributed an informed foreword, commending the idea of recalling 'an era when they did things rather differently'.

More recently, in 2007, another history of the Corinthian club appeared under the authorship of Rob Cavallini, who is an avid enthusiast for the amateur game, and it contains numerous match reports and an encyclopaedic statistics section which, among many other facts, lists the names of the players in every one of 1,433 Corinthian matches, except for a very few for which the records have long since disappeared.

So Howard Baker's goalkeeping achievements have been recalled here and there within recent memory, but his high jumping seems to have been largely forgotten. As mentioned at the beginning of this book, he was not one of the 78 athletes selected by the most authoritative of British athletics writers, Mel Watman, for his list of 'all-time greats' of the sport, published in 2006, and maybe if Watman had decided to cast his net wider to take in, say, the top 100 – which, for very good reasons, he didn't – then Howard Baker would have qualified for inclusion. Even so, he would still, perhaps, rate behind another Liverpool high jumper of a much later generation, Steve Smith, who also did not come into Mel Watman's reckoning.

Howard Baker's involvement with athletics, as with other sports, naturally diminished with the passing years. His wife died in the late 1970s and he suffered a car accident which caused him considerable pain and required regular visits for the next two years to hospital. He sold Gayton Hall in 1978, and more than 30 years later the new owner was to recall, 'Despite his age he had a twinkle in his eye and amused us with his stories. The whole transaction was a remarkable experience'. Chelsea FC's historian, Rick Glanvill, has noted that he was still in touch with the club in the 1980s, though at the time of Howard Baker's taped interview with John Bromhead in 1982 he was living in a residential care home in Colwyn Bay, North Wales, and this inevitably restricted his social activities. Mike Holmes, coach to Steve Smith and elected president of Liverpool Harriers in 2009, recalled:

'His direct connections with the club in the 1970s and 1980s were necessarily rather remote, even tenuous, because of his age, increasing frailty, and geography. Of course, he remained our president but not in a particularly active capacity. He did make efforts to attend annual general meetings, where tradition has it that the president takes the chair. As he was a very kindly gentleman, it often struck me that he was ill-equipped to deal with all the unpleasantness that such occasions can generate. I say that as a tribute to him! Clearly, at that stage of his life conflict among those sharing a sport and club left him bemused, probably saddened'.

Howard Baker's perplexity is fully understandable. The nature of sport had changed out of all recognition in the 50 years and more since he had been a competitor. Could it possibly be imagined that any aspiring Olympic athlete in the 21st century would set out his diary for the year with the proviso that football would take precedence over winter training, and that a leisurely end-of-season foreign tour or a spring-time call-up for the England team might delay the summer's track or field debut? And even then, an occasional game of cricket on a Saturday afternoon or water-polo the previous evening would need to be fitted in; and all that quite apart from keeping the wheels turning in an extensive manufacturing company on which hundreds of employees depended for a living.

Benjamin Howard Baker died at the grand age of 95 on 10 September 1987. The World record in the high jump was now 2.42 metres, which was the equivalent to 7ft 11¼in, and therefore 46 centimetres higher than he had ever achieved. Even the women's World record had surpassed him in 1976, and just 12 days before his death had been taken up to 2.09 metres. Comparisons between the generations in athletics are inevitable because the measurements are preserved for all to see, but they are sometimes invidious. At the risk of repetition, any account of his multitude of achievements must end as it began – no sporting life such as his will ever be led again.

When Howard Baker, self-deprecating to a fault, had looked back at the age of 90 on his marvellous sporting career, he told his interviewer, John Bromhead, 'I was a bit of a freak, actually. I was a big man with a good body and one that had been cared for, and I think that I've worn very well!' But there was a tinge of sadness, too. 'I can't walk far now because of pain in the spine, and I've been to the front gate only once in the past two months. It's not a very good way to finish'.

SOME FACTS AND FIGURES ABOUT B. HOWARD BAKER'S CAREER AS AN ATHLETE AND A FOOTBALLER

World's all-time best high jump performers – as at the end of 1921
How B. Howard Baker stood in the World rankings on his retirement from competition

(2.03) 6ft 7⅞in	Clinton Larsen (USA)	(1)	Provo, Utah	1 June 1917
(2.01) 6ft 7⁵⁄₁₆in	Edward Beeson (USA)	(1)	Berkeley, Cal.	2 May 1914
(2.00) 6ft 7in	George Horine (USA)	(1)	Stanford, Cal.	18 May 1912
(1.97) 6ft 5⅝in	Mike Sweeney (USA)	(1)	New York	21 September 1895
(1.97) 6ft 5⅝in	R.P. Chamberlain (USA)	(1)	Charlottesville, Va.	30 March 1921
(1.96) 6ft 5½in	Wesley Oler (USA)	(1)	New York	5 June 1915
(1.96) 6ft 5⅛ in	Dewey Alberts (USA)	(1)	Urbana, Ill.	20 May 1921
(1.95) 6ft 5in	Jim Thorpe (USA)	(1)	New York	12 June 1912
(1.95) 6ft 5in	Tim Carroll (GB/Ireland)	(1)	Kinsale	4 August 1913
(1.95) 6ft 5in	Alma Richards (USA)	(1)	Philadelphia	24 April 1915
(1.95) 6ft 5in	Benjamin Howard Baker (GB)	(1)	Huddersfield	25 June 1921

Note: This list is based on a compilation by Vladimir Visek which appeared in the bulletin of the Czech Athletics Statisticians Association (SAS a VSŽ), issue No.2 of 1971. George Rowdon (GB) is credited with jumps of 6ft 5½in (1.96) at Chudleigh, in Devon, 20 August 1890, and 6ft 5½in (1.96) at Haytor army camp, in Devon, 6 August 1890 but these are regarded as 'exhibition' performances. His official best was 6ft 2in (1.88) at Paignton, 24 August 1887. Pat Leahy (GB/Ireland) had unconfirmed marks of 6ft 5½in (1.96) in the USA in 1898 and 6ft 5¼in (1.96) at Mallow 15 August 1899, and his brother, Tim, who was a member of Polytechnic Harriers, had an unconfirmed mark of 6ft 5in (1.95) at Limerick 31 August 1913. Their official best performances were (1.95) 6ft 4¾in (1) Millstreet 6 September 1898 for Pat Leahy and (1.92) 6ft 3¾in (1) Mitchelstown 8 August 1910 for Tim Leahy.

British all-time best high jump performers – as at the end of 1951
30 years after the retirement of B. Howard Baker; including Irish athletes from pre-1921

(2.02) 6ft 7½in	Alan Paterson (Victoria Park AAC)	(2)	Glasgow	2 August 1947
1.99) 6ft 6⅜ in	Peter Wells (London AC)	(1)	Bristol	20 August 1949

(1.98) 6ft 6in	Ron Pavitt (Polytechnic H/Royal Navy)	(1)	London (White C)	6 August 1949
(1.95) 6ft 5in	Tim Carroll (Royal Irish Constabulary/Ireland)	(1)	Kinsale	4 August 1913
(1.95) 6ft 5in	Benjamin Howard Baker (Liverpool H & AC)	(1)	Huddersfield	25 June 1921
(1.95) 6ft 5in	Geoffrey Turner (Earlestown Viaduct AC)	(1)	Widnes	20 July 1929
(1.95) 6ft 4¾in	Pat Leahy (Limerick/Ireland)	(1)	Millstreet	6 September 1898
(1.94) 6ft 4½in	James Ryan (Tipperary/Ireland)	(1)	Tipperary	19 August 1895
(1.94) 6ft 4½in	Con Leahy (Limerick/Ireland)	(1)	Limerick	18 September 1904
(1.93) 6ft 4in	John Newman (London AC)	(1)	St Eval, Cornwall	19 June 1943
(1.93) 6ft 4in	Don Atherton (Liverpool H & AC)	(1)	Harrogate	25 June 1949

Note: See the World List above regarding George Rowdon (Teignmouth FC) and the brothers, Pat and Tim Leahy.

B. Howard Baker's international football appearances

22 January 1921 v Wales (*Amateur*), Wolverhampton. Lost 0–2.

21 May 1921 v Belgium, Brussels. Won 2–0.

11 November 1922 v N. Ireland (*Amateur*), Crystal Palace. Won 3–0.

27 January 1923 v Wales (*Amateur*), Middlesbrough. Drew 4–4.

8 November 1924 v N. Ireland (*Amateur*), Belfast. Won 3–2.

26 November 1924 v South Africa (*Amateur*), White Hart Lane, Tottenham. Won 3–2.

21 March 1925 v Wales (*Amateur*), Plymouth. Won 2–1.

24 October 1925 v N. Ireland, Belfast. Drew 0–0.

15 November 1925 v N. Ireland (*Amateur*), Maidstone. Won 6–4.

6 November 1926 v N. Ireland (*Amateur*), Belfast. Won 3–0.

19 March 1927 v Wales (*Amateur*), Reading. Won 4–0.

16 March 1929 v Scotland (*Amateur*), Leeds. Won 3–2.

Thus in 12 international appearances he was only ever on the losing side once.

England's goalkeepers in international matches 1919–29

England played 49 full international matches between 25 October 1919 and 20 November 1929, and 23 different goalkeepers were selected. In chronological order they were as follows, with the number of matches they played (*amateurs):

Sam Hardy (Liverpool) 21, John Mew (Manchester United) 1, *Bert Coleman (Dulwich Hamlet) 1, Harold Gough (Sheffield United) 1, *Benjamin Howard Baker (Everton/Chelsea/Corinthian) 2, Jerry Dawson (Burnley) 2, Teddy Davison (The Wednesday) 1, Ted Taylor (Huddersfield Town) 1, John Alderson (Crystal Palace) 1, Ernest Williamson (Arsenal) 2, Ted Hufton (West Ham United) 6, Ronnie Sewell (Blackburn Rovers) 1, *Jim Mitchell (Manchester City) 1, Dick Pym (Bolton Wanderers) 3, Henry Hardy (Stockport County) 1, Fred Fox (Millwall) 1, George Ashmore (West Bromwich Albion) 1, Albert McInroy (Sunderland) 1, John Brown (The Wednesday/Sheffield Wednesday) 6, Dan Tremelling (Birmingham) 1, Ben Olney (Aston Villa) 2, Jack Hacking (Oldham Athletic) 3, Harry Hibbs (Birmingham) 25.

Note: The careers of some of those listed above exceeded the 1919–1929 time-frame. For example, Sam Hardy began his career before World War One and Harry Hibbs continued his into the 1930s. Of the 21 other goalkeepers used, 13 played only one match, four (including B. Howard Baker) played two matches, and two played three matches. Only Ted Hufton and John Brown played more, but Hufton's six matches were spread over five years. Howard Baker is one of only two England goalkeepers to have conceded no goals on the two occasions that he was capped; the other is Dave Beasant (Chelsea) in 1989.

Scotland chose only seven different goalkeepers for their 34 matches during the same years, including Jack Harkness, who made the first two of his 12 appearances through to 1933 as an amateur with Queen's Park and later played for Heart of Midlothian. His full name was John Diamond Harkness.

Wales also chose seven different goalkeepers for their 32 matches from 1919–1929, including Len Evans, whose only cap was as an amateur with Aberdare Athletic and who later played for Cardiff City and then Birmingham. His full name was Sidney John Vivian Leonard Evans.

England played 25 amateur international matches during the same years for which seven different goalkeepers were selected. Again in chronological order, with the number of matches played, they were as follows: Bert Coleman 3, Jim Mitchell 5, Benjamin Howard Baker 10, H.P. Bell (Cambridge University) 1, A.M. Russell (Cambridge University) 2, Norman Jones (Aldermere) 2, Alf Solly (Dulwich Hamlet) 2.

The selection committee was the same for the professional and amateur England teams.

Amateurs who played for England in full internationals 1919–29

Full names, clubs, birthdates and dates of death, matches played, number of caps (bold type).

Armitage, George Henry (Charlton Athletic) 17 January 1898–28 August 1936 v Northern Ireland 24 October 1925 **1.**

Ashton, Claude Thesiger (Corinthian) 19 February 1901–31 October 1942 v Northern Ireland (captain) 24 October 1925. **1.** *Note: captain on his only appearance.*

Barry, Leonard James (Leicester City) 27 October 1901–17 April 1970 v France 17 May 28, v Belgium 19 May 1928, v France 9 May 1929, v Belgium 11 May 1929, v Spain 15 May 1929. **5.**

Bower, Alfred.George (Corinthian/Chelsea) 10 November 1895–30 June 1970 v Northern Ireland 20 October 1923, v Belgium 1 November 1923, v Belgium 8 December 1924 (captain), v Wales 28 February 1925 (captain), v Wales 12 February 1927 (captain). **5.**

Bryant, William Ingram (Clapton) 1 March 1899–21 January 1986 v France 21 May 1925. **1.**

Coleman, Ernest Herbert (Dulwich Hamlet) 19 October 1889–15 June 1958 v Wales 14 March 21. **1.**

Creek, Francis Norman Smith (Cambridge University/Corinthian) 12 January 1898–26 July 1980 v France 10 May 1923. **1.** *Note: scored a goal on his only appearance.*

Doggart, Alexander Graham (Corinthian) 2 June 1897–7 June 1963 v Belgium 1 November 1923. **1.** *Note: captain on his only appearance.*

Earle, Stanley George James (Clapton/West Ham United) 6 September 1897–26 September 1971 v France 17 May 1924, v Northern Ireland 22 October 1927. **2.**

Ewer, Frederick Harold (Casuals/Corinthian) 30 September 1898–29 January 1971 v France 17 May 1924, v Belgium 8 December 1924. **2.**

Gibbins, William Vivian Talbot (Clapton/West Ham United) 10 August 1901–21 November 1979 v France 17 May 1924, v France 21 May 1925. **2.** *Note: scored two goals on his debut.*

Hartley, Frank (Oxford City) 20 July 1896–20 October 1965 v France 10 May 1923. **1.**

Hegan, Kenneth Edward (Army/Corinthian) 24 January 1901–3 March 1989 v Belgium 19 March 1923, v France 10 May 1923, v Northern Ireland 20 October 1923, v Belgium 1 November 1923. **4.** *Note: scored two goals on his debut, the first after only five minutes.*

Howard Baker, Benjamin (Corinthian/Chelsea) 15 February 1892–10 September 1987 v Belgium 21 May 1921, v Northern Ireland 24 October 1925. **2.**

Kail, Edgar Isaac Lewis (Dulwich Hamlet) 26 November 1900–1976 v France 9 May 1929, v Belgium 11 May 1929, v Spain 15 May 1929. **3.** *Note: scored a goal on his debut.*

Knight, Arthur Egerton (Corinthian/Portsmouth) 7 September 1897–10 March 1956 v Ireland 25 October 1919 (captain). **1.** *Note: captain on his only appearance at the age of 32.*

Mitchell, James Frederick (Manchester City) 18 November 1897–30 May 1975 v Northern Ireland 22 October 1924. **1.**

Patchitt, Basil Clement Alderson (Corinthian) 12 August 1900–2 July 1991 v Sweden 21 May 1923 (captain), v Sweden 24 May 1923. **2.** *Note: captain on both of his appearances at the age of 22.*

Reade, Albert (Tufnell Park) 1899– v Belgium 21 May 1921. **1.**

Woosnam, Maxwell (Manchester City) 6 September 1892–14 July 1965 v Wales 13 March 22 (captain). **1.** *Note: captain on his only appearance.*

After the 1920s only one more amateur played for the full England XI in an official international match. He was Bernard Joy (Casuals), who made his only appearance against Belgium, 9 May 1936. He also played for Corinthian and for Arsenal during the 1935–36 season.

Corinthian FC's appearances in the FA Cup, 1923–39

Note: From 1922–23 to 1936–37 Corinthian were exempt from the competition until the first round proper. From 1937–38 onwards the club was required to play in the fourth qualifying round.

1922–23
13 January 1923 v Brighton & Hove Albion (away) drew 1–1, 25,000
17 January 1923 v Brighton & Hove Albion (home) replay drew 1–1, 20,000
22 January 1923 v Brighton & Hove Albion (Stamford Bridge) second replay lost 1–0, 43,780
1923–24
12 January 1924 v Blackburn Rovers (home) won 1–0, 20,000
2 February 1924 v West Bromwich Albion (away) lost 5–0, 50,000
1924–25
10 January 1925 v Sheffield United (away) lost 5–0, 38,000
1925–26
9 January 1926 v Manchester City (home) drew 3–3, 30,000
13 January 1926 v Manchester City (away) replay lost 4–0, 42,303
1926–27
8 January 1927 v Walsall (away) won 4–0, 16,613
29 January 1927 v Newcastle United (home) lost 3–1, 56,338
1927–28
14 January 1928 v New Brighton (away) lost 2–1, 9,256

1928–29

12 January 1929 v Norwich City (away) won 5–0, 20,159

26 January 1929 v West Ham United (away) lost 3–0, 42,000

1929–30

11 January 1930 v Millwall (home) drew 2–2, 45,000

15 January 1930 v Millwall (away) replay drew 1–1, 33,000

20 January 1930 v Millwall (Stamford Bridge) second replay lost 5–1, 58,775

1930–31

10 January 1931 v Port Vale (home) lost 3–1, 12,832

1931–32

9 January 1932 v Sheffield United (away) lost 2–1, 29,449

Following B. Howard Baker's retirement, Corinthian played nine more FA Cup ties before World War Two, as follows:

1932–33: 14 January 1933 v West Ham United (home) lost 2–0, 16,421

1934–35: 24 November 1934 v Watford (away) lost 2–0, 11,981

1935–36: 30 November 1935 v Reading (away) lost 8–3, 15,996

1936–37: 28 November 1936 v Bristol Rovers (home) lost 2–0, 2,204

1937–38: 13 November 1937 v Ilford (away) won 2–1; 27 November 1937 v Southend United (home) lost 2–0, 2,000

1938–39: 12 November 1938 v Dartford (away) drew 3–3; 16 November 1938 v Dartford (home) replay won 2–1; 26 November 1938 v Southend United (away) lost 3–0

Played 27, won 5, lost 16, drawn 6, goals for 33, goals against 65.

Claude Ashton appeared in all of the first 18 Cup ties up to and including the 1931–32 season; Benjamin Howard Baker in 17 (all but the 18th); Alfred Bower and Kenneth Hegan in 16 each; Norman Creek in 14, Harvey Chadder in 13; and Graham Doggart and Frederick Ewer each in 12. Ashton, Creek and Chadder also appeared in subsequent Cup ties.

Corinthian FC's European tour matches 1921–31
France, 1921

4 September v Red Star (Paris) won 2–1

5 September v Olympique Lillois (Lille) won 4–0

Denmark and Holland, 1922

14 April v Kjobenhavns Boldklub (Copenhagen) won 5–0, 25,000

16 April v Kjobenhavns Boldklub (Copenhagen) won 3–1

20 April v Be Quick (Groningen) won 5–2

22 April v Universities (The Hague) won 5–3

23 April v Swallows (Amsterdam) lost 1–0

Belgium and Holland, 1923

1 April v Daring (Brussels) lost 1–0, 35,000

2 April v Union St Gilloise (Brussels) lost 5–2
4 April v Willem II (Tilburg) lost 5–1
7 April v Universities (The Hague) won 2–0, 6,000
8 April v Swallows (Amsterdam) won 2–0, 30,000
10 April v Rotterdam (Rotterdam) lost 2–1

Germany and Austria, 1925
10 April v Cologne won 4–2, 10,000
12 April v Hamburg won 4–1
13 April v Berlin drew 1–1
16 April v Vienna lost 2–0, 50,000

Denmark and Germany, 1928
6 April v Bold Klubben 1903 (Copenhagen) drew 1–1
8 April v Kjobenhavns Boldklub (Copenhagen) lost 6–3
9 April v Odense Boldklub won 2–1
13 April v Hanover won 2–1
15 April v Hamburg drew 0–0

France, 1929
29 March v Club Français (Paris) lost 2–1
1 April v ASC Cannes won 3–2
2 April v South of France (Cannes) lost 4–2

Switzerland, 1930
19 April v Young Boys Berne won 7–1
21 April v Grasshoppers Zurich won 3–2

Switzerland, 1931
4 April v Young Boys Berne won 3–0
6 April v Grasshoppers Zurich won 2–1

Howard Baker took part in all of these tours except the last two to Switzerland. Corinthian FC also toured Canada and USA in August and September 1924, playing 22 matches, winning 10, drawing eight and losing four, goals for 48, goals against 34. Howard Baker did not take part in this tour.

BIBLIOGRAPHY

The following are the books and other publications which have provided the main points of reference:

Abrahams, H.M. & Dr Adolphe *Training for Health and Athletics* (Hutchinson & Co., 1936)

Baker, W.J. *Sports in the Western World* (Rowman and Littlefields, 1982).

Barrett, John *Wimbledon: The Official History of the Championships* (Collins Willow, 2001).

Belchem, John *Merseypride: Essays in Liverpool Exceptionalism* (Liverpool University Press, 2000).

Bland, Ernest A. (ed.) *50 Years of Sport* (*Daily Mail*, 1948).

Booth, Keith *The Father of Modern Sport: The Life and Times of Charles W. Alcock* (The Parrs Wood Press, 2002).

Booth, Dick *Talking of Sport: The Story of Radio Commentary* (SportsBooks, 2008).

Buchanan, Ian *British Olympians: A Hundred Years of Gold Medallists* (Guinness Publishing, 1991).

—— *The AAA Championships 1880–1939* (National Union of Track Statisticians, 2003).

Burke's Who's Who in Sport and Sporting Records (The Burke Publishing Co., 1922).

Cavallini, Rob *Play Up Corinth: A History of the Corinthian Football Club* (Stadia Tempus Publishing, 2007).

Collins, Mick *All-Round Genius: The Unknown Story of Britain's Greatest Sportsman* (Aurum Press, 2007).

Cox, Richard, Russell, David & Vamplew, Wray, (eds.) *Encyclopaedia of British Football* (Routledge, 2002).

Downer, Alf *Running Recollections* (1902, reproduced by Blairgowrie Books, 1980).

Fabian, A.H. & Green, Geoffrey *Association Football* (Caxton, 1960).

Glanvill, Rick *Chelsea FC: The Official Biography* (Headline Publishing, 2005).

Grayson, Edward *Corinthians and Cricketers* (The Naldrett Press, 1955, republished by Yore Publications, 1996).

Henderson, Jon *The Last Champion: The Life of Fred Perry* (Yellow Jersey Press, 2000).

Holt, Richard *Sport and the British: A Modern History* (Oxford University Press, 1990).

Hymans, Richard *Progression of IAAF World records* (International Association of Athletics Federations, 2007).

Lane Jackson, N. *Sporting Days and Sporting Ways* (Hurst & Blackett, 1932).

Lowe, D.G.A. & Porritt, A.E. *Athletics* (Longman's Green & Co., 1932).

Matthews, Peter, & Buchanan, Ian *All Time Greats of British and Irish Sport* (Guinness Publishing, 1995).

Matthews, Tony *Who's Who of Everton* (Mainstream Publishing, 2004).

McWhirter, N.D., McWhirter A.R. & Buchanan, Ian *British Athletics Record Book* (published by the authors, 1958).

Nelson, Alec *Practical Athletics and How to Train* (C. Arthur Pearson, 1924).

Pellissard-Darrigrand, Nicole *La Galaxie Olympique* (J & D Editions, 1996).

Riedi, Eliza, & Mason, Tony *Leather and the Fighting Spirit: Sport in the British Army in World War I* (Canadian Journal of History, 2006).

Shearman, Montague *Athletics and Football* (Longman's Green & Co., 1887).

Tempest, Ian *High Jump: A Statistical Survey of British Jumping* (National Union of Track Statisticians, 2000).

Tomlin, Stan (ed.) *Olympic Odyssey*, (Modern Athlete Publications, 1956).

Webster, F.A.M. *Olympian Field Events* (George Newnes, 1913).

— *The Evolution of the Olympic Games* (Heath, Garton & Ouseley, 1914).

— *Athletics of Today: History, Development and Training* (Fredrick Warne & Co., 1929).

— *Our Great Public Schools: Their Traditions, Customs and Games* (Ward, Leek & Co., 1937).

— *Coaching and Care of Athletics* (George G. Harrap, 1938).

Willcox, Paul (ed.) *Oxford v Cambridge Athletic Sports* (Achilles Club, 1989).

Wilson, Stanley *A New Approach to Athletics* (George Allen & Unwin, 1939).

zur Megede, Ekkehard *The Modern Olympic Century 1896–1996* (Deutsche Gesellschaft für Leichtathletik Dokumentation, 1999).

The principal newspapers consulted were *Athletic News, Daily Telegraph, Liverpool Daily Post & Mercury, Liverpool Echo, Liverpool Express, Manchester Guardian, Observer, The Times, Sporting Chronicle*.

The following websites were of particular value:
www.aafla.
www.britishpathe.com
www.ema-tech.co.uk/chelsea
www.englandamateurs.com
www. englandfootballonline.com
www. LFChistory.net
www.tennisforum.com
www. timesonline.com
www.thefa.com